Public and Political Discourses of Migration

Discourse, Power and Society

Series editors: Martin J. Power, Amanda Haynes, Eoin Devereux
and Aileen Dillane

Discourse is understood as both an expression and a mechanism of power, by which means particular social realities are conceived, made manifest, legitimated, naturalized, challenged, resisted and reimagined. This series publishes edited collections, monographs and textbooks which problematize the relationship of discourse to inequality, exclusion, subjugation, dominance and privilege. In doing so, the linkages between discourse, modes of social organization, lived experience and strategies of resistance are addressed.

Public and Political Discourses of Migration: International Perspectives, edited by Amanda Haynes, Martin J. Power, Eoin Devereux, Aileen Dillane and James Carr

The Discourse of Neoliberalism: An Anatomy of a Powerful Idea, Simon Springer (Forthcoming)

Public and Political Discourses of Migration

International Perspectives

Edited by
Amanda Haynes, Martin J. Power,
Eoin Devereux, Aileen Dillane and James Carr

ROWMAN & LITTLEFIELD
INTERNATIONAL

London • New York

Published by Rowman & Littlefield International Ltd
Unit A, Whitacre Mews, 26-34 Stannary Street, London SE11 4AB
www.rowmaninternational.com

Rowman & Littlefield International Ltd.is an affiliate of Rowman & Littlefield
4501 Forbes Boulevard, Suite 200, Lanham, Maryland 20706, USA
With additional offices in Boulder, New York, Toronto (Canada), and Plymouth (UK)
www.rowman.com

British Library Cataloguing in Publication Data
A catalogue record for this book is available from the British Library

ISBN: HB 978-1-78348-327-3
         PB 978-1-78348-328-0

Library of Congress Cataloging-in-Publication Data
Names: Haynes, Amanda, editor.
Title: Public and political discourses of migration : international perspectives / edited by
    Amanda Haynes, Martin J. Power, Eoin Devereux, Aileen Dillane, and James Carr.
Description: Lanham, Maryland : Rowman & Littlefield, 2016. | Series: Discourse,
    power and society | Includes bibliographical references and index.
Identifiers: LCCN 2015042628 (print) | LCCN 2016002383 (ebook) |
    ISBN 9781783483273 (cloth : alk. paper) | ISBN 9781783483280 (pbk. : alk. paper) |
    ISBN 9781783483297 (electronic)
Subjects: LCSH: Emigration and immigration—Political aspects. | Emigration and
    immigration—Social aspects. | Emigration and immigration—Public opinon.
Classification: LCC JV6255 .P83 2016 (print) | LCC JV6255 (ebook) | DDC 325—dc23
LC record available at http://lccn.loc.gov/2015042628.

∞™ The paper used in this publication meets the minimum requirements of American
National Standard for Information Sciences—Permanence of Paper for Printed Library
Materials, ANSI/NISO Z39.48-1992.

Printed in the United States of America

This book is dedicated to the memories of Aylan, Galip and Rehan Kurdi, who together with thousands of others have lost their lives in desperate attempts to cross borders.

Contents

Contents

List of Figures

List of Tables

Acknowledgements

The editors wish to acknowledge the generous support and funding received from the University of Limerick for the initial conference which ultimately led to the production of this volume. We would like to thank Professor Don Barry, president of the University of Limerick, who officially launched the Power Discourse and Society Research Cluster in 2014, the Department of Sociology and the Faculty of Arts, Humanities and Social Sciences at the University of Limerick; all of the contributors to this volume, and the many others who have offered encouragement and assistance along the way.

Grateful thanks are given to those who gave their permission to reproduce original images in this collection.

Finally, we would like to thank Martina O'Sullivan and Sinéad Murphy at Rowman & Littlefield International for all their assistance in putting this volume together.

In the Frame? Discourses of Migration

An Introduction to the Volume

Aileen Dillane, Martin J. Power, Amanda Haynes,
Eoin Devereux and James Carr

Migration – the process of moving across symbolic or political borders (Scott and Marshall 2005, 410). Yet, such dictionary definitions belie the variety and scope of challenges faced by many migrants who, for whatever reason, have been compelled to begin a journey whose outcome cannot be easily predicted. In September 2015, as we finalised this book, migration was very starkly humanised by the circulation of pictures of the body of a young Syrian migrant/refugee, but above all, a child, washed up on the shore of a Turkish beach, having drowned whilst trying to make his way into Europe with his family. The pictures were shocking and were made all the more poignant by recast images of the young boy, which attempted to reframe his lifeless body by placing it on a warm and safe bed in a 'photo-shopped' picture of an idyllic child's bedroom. He looked asleep, not dead. But the original picture has proven very difficult to erase from peoples' minds and because of that, at least for a while, Aylan Kurdi humanised and individuated the 'swarms'[1] of migrants trying to make their way into Europe. Throughout history, countless migrants have traversed the globe, oftentimes in large collectives. The manner in which such efforts have been discursively framed in more recent times, and how that framing impacts on individual and collective lived experience, whether through formal policies or through more nebulous and often hostile public attitudes, is what concerns us in this volume.

Adopting a critical approach, this text seeks to explore and problematise the relationship of discourse to issues of representation, and as such, highlights inequality, exclusion, subjugation, dominance and privilege in the context of migration. Discourse here is understood as both an expression and a mechanism of power, by which particular social realities are conceived, made manifest, legitimated, naturalised, challenged, resisted and re-imagined.

Public and political discourses on the matter of outward and inward migration are of crucial importance, as they are responsible for framing the issue, and for how, when and where it arrives on the public/political spectrum (Schain 2008, 465). As a result, such discourses have substantial influence over the general public's attitudes towards migration (McLaren 2001; Hainmueller and Hopkins 2014) and over the policies and legislation, which frame and regulate both the act of migration itself, and migrant residents, while concomitantly feeding back into the prejudices that are evident in those public attitudes (Facchini et al. 2008).

The objectives of this collection are to give space to both established and new scholars whose work 'makes strange' and, in many cases, dismantles accepted 'truths' regarding migration in the twenty-first century. Fundamental to this process is the question of whose interests these discourses, and the structures they underpin, serve. The chapters in this volume are drawn from among key disciplines in the field of migration studies, including sociology, geography, cultural studies, ethnomusicology and linguistics. The cases interrogated here emerge, as do their authors, from a broad range of national, political and cultural contexts. Contributing authors originate from Europe, the Americas and the Middle East and bring to the text a broad geographical spread of perspectives and cases. In this manner, the collection appropriately reflects the interdisciplinary nature of the fields of both migration and discourse studies.

This book is not an exhaustive account of the phenomenon of migration. Far from claiming to be definitive, this volume is unapologetically selective. It is worth noting in terms of the politics of the contributions contained herein that they are all supportive of migration. Through the application of a variety of theoretical lenses drawn from the broad canon of discourse studies, each contribution unpicks the productive power of discourse in shaping the reality of migration, migration policy and migrant lives in the twenty-first century and critically explores ways to think, talk about and analyse the relationship between discourse and migration in its social, historical, political and cultural context.

Key theorists whose ideas have exerted influence across the arts, humanities and social sciences in particular, are harnessed throughout this volume: from sociologists Pierre Bourdieu, Michel Foucault and Zygmunt Bauman (Bruno, chapter 2; Poupazis, chapter 11; Porsché, chapter 13; Helfrich and Mancera Rueda, chapter 15) to philosopher Jacques Derrida (Hill, chapter 14); from economist Yann Moulier-Boutang (De Genova, chapter 1) to linguistics and critical discourse studies scholars Ruth Wodak and Teun Van Dijk (Bruno, chapter 2; Reed, chapter 4; Lähdesmäki and Saresma, chapter 5; Helfrich and Mancera Rueda, chapter 15); from cultural theorist Stuart Hall (Bruno, chapter 2; Hannafin, chapter 6) to literary theorist and

postcolonialist Edward Said (Carr, chapter 3); from immigration and settlement studies scholar Harald Bauder (Burroughs, chapter 7) to post-Marxist
political theorist Ernesto Laclau (Lähdesmäki and Saresma, chapter 5); and
from one of the most important figures in contemporary postcolonial studies,
Homi K. Bhabha (Hill, chapter 14), to a central figure in Irish Studies, Mary
Hickman (Hannafin, chapter 6).

The volume is organised along thematic lines, beginning initially with two
chapters on 'liminal beings'. Nicholas De Genova's chapter argues that the
material and practical techniques and technologies of contemporary regimes
of border policing and immigration law enforcement are only apprehensible
in relation to another 'concrete' reality: the embodied materiality of 'irregular' or 'illegal' migrants. These migrants represent the incorrigible subject
of virtually all contemporary border regimes, in response to which the multifarious objective infrastructures and practices of border control must be
understood as reaction formations. Arrivals by sea are emblematic and iconic
of the more general coverage of migrations and have a particular resonance,
given the events in Southern Europe over the summer of 2015, where more
than 2,600 refugees and migrants had drowned in the Mediterranean Sea by
the end of August (BBC 2015). In that context, chapter 2 sees Marco Bruno
investigate and deconstruct patterns of representation and media construction
of the so-called 'landing emergence', as a very significant issue within the
wider image of the migratory phenomena in Italy.

There then follow a couple of sections addressing particular racialised
groups. In chapter 3, James Carr looks at the reality of anti-Muslim racism
in Ireland. Carr argues that historically informed racialised ideas of Irishness
coalesce in the contemporary context with international expansionist neoliberal discourses to construct Muslim people as 'Other', with global and local
media actors playing a crucial role in constructing and communicating the
figure of the Muslim as a threat. Similarly, in chapter 4, Autumn Reed uses
discourse analysis to demonstrate how US news coverage of the 2009 'honour
killing' of Noor Faleh Almaleki should be seen as a discursive site for the
construction of boundaries that further exclude Muslim, Middle Eastern and
South Asian migrants from the US nation. In chapter 5, Tuuli Lähdesmäki
and Tuija Saresma investigate the debate on Muslim immigration by closely
examining 'Islam Night', a talk show broadcast by the Finnish TV station Yle
in October 2013. The case of Islam Night raises interesting questions on the
responsibility of public, state-owned media. In their chapter, Lähdesmäki and
Saresma grapple with whether this responsibility is to maintain the ideal of
equality and integrity of various groups in the contemporary intimate public,
or to be involved in the 'public exercise in othering' (Haynes et al. 2006).

In chapter 6, Sara Hannafin tackles Irish migration, which has been historically understood as an act of leaving. Her work presents the stories of

second-generation Irish migrants returning from Britain, and in the process challenging the hegemonic discourse of Irish migration, and contributing to a redefining of what it is to be Irish.

For a number of decades the Irish State has supported the 'undocumented' Irish in America. In chapter 7, through a Critical Discourse Analysis approach, Elaine Burroughs relays the ways that 'illegal' and 'undocumented' migration is discursively represented in the Irish parliament (2002–2009) through five key argumentations; 'control', 'danger', 'economy', 'humanitarian' and 'culture'. This chapter argues that parliamentary discourses have a significant impact upon other institutions (such as the media) and upon the publics' understanding of 'illegal immigration'. She highlights the ethnocentric self-interest which informs whom political actors characterise as undocumented and whom they construct as illegal.

International research indicates that recessionary periods may be accompanied by a decline in the quality of relations between the majority population and migrant groups, as the latter are at risk of being scapegoated for the economic downturn. In that context, chapter 8 by Martin Power et al. examines how Irish politicians constructed non-Irish EU immigrants to Ireland during the period in which the Irish economy turned from 'boom to bust'. Their analysis finds that at the commencement of Ireland's great recession, politicians on all sides of the spectrum were not averse to perpetuating framing of migrant workers as an economic threat. The chapter argues that these constructions 'inform' public debate, and may ultimately impact detrimentally on how immigrants and their needs are publicly perceived and treated. Moreover, this chapter exposes the possibilities of pro-migrant politicians becoming ensnared in a reactive approach whereby the course of the debate is set by the problematisation of the issue.

Set in the immediate aftermath of the 'Maria' case in Greece, Aileen Marron and her colleagues examine media depictions of Roma communities in Ireland in chapter 9, with a view to interrogating the evidence-base of such coverage. What this chapter demonstrates is how well-worn tropes concerning the Roma, which only rarely allow for a more critical and informed perspective on this minority, were circulated with ease, and very significantly, it shows a lack of reflexivity on behalf of the media.

The next section of the book expands the discussion to consider the significance of music, dance and art as discourse. Moshe Morad, in chapter 10, demonstrates how Salsa music and dance became a unique identity factor; which created and maintained an artificial 'pan-Latin' identity among Latin-American labour migrants in Israel, simultaneously creating a cultural interface for interaction with the hegemonic society, and a source of cultural pride and respect. In chapter 11, Michalis Poupazis deals with musical, social and (a)political discourses among Greek-Cypriot migrants in Birmingham.

He argues that music-related de-politicisation is a practice of migrant social discourse, which, in turn, enables the migrants to establish an imagined community distinct from those of both Greece and Cyprus.

Kolm (1971) views the establishment of organisations that are exclusive to one ethnic group as a crucial event in the process of integration. It is a 'metamorphosis from an immigrant group to an ethnic group', which affords members a degree of visibility that is conducive to interaction with the dominant society. In that context, Sheryl Lynch, in chapter 12, examines the agency of a Cameroonian diasporic group in the construction of its public representation(s). This chapter focuses on musical performance as a particularly powerful medium in such constructions, in the process outlining the power of musical action in unpacking the prescribed canon of exclusivity, identity and integration.

In chapter 13, Yannik Porsché deals with a bi-national museum exhibition on immigration which was produced by four institutions in France and Germany. His study asks how the public is portrayed and enacted in museum exhibitions on migration, focussing on how images of the '*Self*' and the '*Other*' are produced on the micro level of interaction. The chapter demonstrates that not only does the content of the exhibition in question deal with public negotiations of immigrant representations, but that the museum work and reception itself constitutes an asymmetrical, cross-cultural stage for negotiation. The chapter, thus, investigates how the global and the local intertwine, as identities, knowledge and memory are attributed and negotiated in multicultural contexts.

The final section of the book contains a couple of chapters examining majority population discourse and online discourse. 'Traditions of hospitality' are readily invoked in order to contextualise, historicise and justify political standpoints and policy changes regarding immigration. In chapter 14, Emma Hill extends Gibson's (2003) analysis of such tropes to present an expanded model of the self-perpetuating systems of the British discourse of (in)hospitality, demonstrating how discourses of hospitality hinge on narratives of nationhood and how viewing immigration through a hospitality lens not only allows for a Derridean separation of absolute hospitality and hospitality by right, but also permits that gap to widen.

Young people are one of the groups that have suffered most from the current economic crisis. In 2011, a popular movement, Juventud Sin Futuro (JSF), became a major actor in the discursive media construction of the phenomenon of youth unemployment and (e)migration in/from Spain. In chapter 15, Uta Helfrich and Ana Mancera Rueda focus on the (multimodal) discourse strategies employed by the JSF to frame this topic in public discourse.

The collection concludes with a reflection on the possibility and challenges of mobilising discourse as resistance. Unashamedly partisan, it addresses researchers and academics as civil society actors, and considers the efficacy of various means and modes of disrupting and replacing anti-immigrant discourse.

Detailing each chapter in the order of appearance here as we have just done does not, of course, illustrate the connectivity between various chapters in different sections of the book. This is but one of a myriad of ways we could have organised these materials. Thematically, there are a variety of connections. Chapter 3 and chapter 6, for example, place ethnicity to the fore in particular ways, raising issues around the capacity for a migrant to make that critical move from emigrant to ethnic citizen. The idea of borders and liminal spaces is important in a number of chapters, not just in chapters 1 and 2. National borders become loose and less 'placed' in the imaginary when the 'diaspora' is included as part of its territory. Such nebulous connective tissue links nationals to migrants or ethnic others elsewhere, offering potential to encode certain migrant collectives in more positive language, which, in turn, has ramifications for other groups (e.g. 'undocumented' versus illegal immigrants – chapters 3, 4 and 7).

The connection between migration and labour is most evident in chapters 1 and 8 where tensions around the imagining of migrants as draining the economic system (as opposed to contributing to the economy, often in lowly paid jobs) underpin much of the analysis. The role of governments and policy makers in configuring discourses around immigrants comes to the fore in chapters 8 and 14.

Methodologically, approaches differ too. Chapters 3 and 6 lean heavily into qualitative research, and in particular into 'giving voice' to their participants. In other chapters, particular models of discourse analysis are applied. Notably, music as discourse, as a system with its own semantic meanings, and which is often experienced in a deeply affective way, is explored in chapters 10–12, raising interesting questions of how music itself may operate as a form of cultural brokerage in migrant contexts. But even where the cultural contribution that a migrant group brings is recognised (chapter 10), the language continues to be populated with stereotypes which, at their extreme, can essentialise an entire group in negative terms (see chapter 3). Such stereotyping can have detrimental effects on real people, as outlined in chapter 9, where the blonde hair of children was taken as evidence enough to warrant their removal from their Roma families.

These are but some of the ideas and arguments presented in this volume. Our purpose is to point out the operations and manipulation of the public and political discourse that we might better understand the degree to which we all participate (inadvertently or not) in its promulgation, and how difficult it is to resist the relentless onslaught in fraught times. It is also to acknowledge that many of these discourses are older than we might think and that their reassertion in the public sphere today may speak to a collective, historical amnesia. To that end, we cannot let the image of a young Syrian boy, lifeless on the shore, that most liminal of spaces, recede from our minds. *To bear witness is the first step. To act in solidarity is the next.*

NOTE

1. In July 2015, the British prime minister, David Cameron, spoke of a 'swarm of people coming across the Mediterranean' (see http://www.bbc.com/news/uk-politics-33716501).

Chapter 1

The Incorrigible Subject of the Border Spectacle

Nicholas De Genova

To contemplate the *framing* of public discourse and political debate concerning migration is to confront 'the border'. Indeed, borders manifest themselves as the crystallisation of all the material and practical techniques and technologies that define the ostensible 'inside' from the putative 'outside' of nation-state space, the partition of which is what literally constitutes 'migration' as such. After all, *if there were no borders, there would be no migrants – only mobility* (De Genova 2013b). Or, taking a cue from the classic slogan of the Chicano liberation movement in the United States: *We didn't cross the border; the border crossed us* (Acuña 1996, 109). Indeed, it is across and through borders that the distinction between citizens and (non-citizen) migrants, 'natives' and 'foreigners', is produced. In short, the border *is* the frame that delivers up 'migration' as a reified and fetishised object. Indeed, 'the border' itself is similarly the fetishised, thing-like effect of socio-political relations and spatial practices of bordering. Thus, a Border Spectacle (De Genova 2002; 2005, 242–49; 2012; 2013a) generates a proliferation of discourses and images that seem to unrelentingly verify the objectivity of a real thing – the border – and likewise serve to lend a semblance of credibility to the notion that particular types of cross-border human mobility can be understood to be 'illegal'. But how might we begin to appreciate the *subjectivity* that animates this spectacular process of objectification?

This chapter approaches the politics of migration by first identifying the subjectivity and autonomy of migration as the catalyst against which various regimes of immigration law-making and border enforcement are inevitably apprehensible as reaction formations. Situating the tactics and techniques of bordering as intrinsically political, the chapter reflects upon the differences that such bordering produces and how these effects serve to mediate the antagonism of the capital-labour relation. Thus, the ostensibly 'national'

1

politics of migration is inextricable from the global (postcolonial) politics of
labour subordination. What constitutes the specificity of this configuration of
the political in 'political' economy, therefore, fundamentally corresponds to
the embodied (racialised) inscriptions of borders on migrants, and contributes
to the expansive ubiquity of immigration policing that transposes borders
onto the racialised bodies of migrants throughout the putative 'interior'
of nation-state space. Drawing upon examples from the United States, the
proliferation of the purview of a deportation regime can be understood to
manifest the continuous struggle to subordinate the incorrigible subjectivity
and autonomy of migrant labour that animates the spectacle of the border.

MIGRANT SUBJECTS

'*¡Aquí Estamos, y No Nos Vamos!* [Here we are, and we're not leaving!]' So
rings out the resounding affirmation of migrant presence in the contemporary
United States. Here indeed is a defiant and joyful affirmation of the irrepress-
ible and inextricable presence of migrants – in this instance, specifically,
Latin American migrants – within the space of the US nation state. These
migrants' bold proclamation of their presence stakes a claim to space, and
asserts a sense of entitlement to appropriate and inhabit the United States, to
make it a space of belonging. When migrants chanted this slogan during the
unprecedented mass mobilisations of 2006, as they marched in their millions
all across the United States to defeat what would have been the most punitive
immigration law in the country's history, they repudiated the notion that, as
migrants, they could be treated as 'foreigners', people 'out of place' – displaced, disposable, deportable.[1]

In the context of these mobilisations, the ubiquity and emotive power of
the *¡Aquí Estamos!* chant can be understood in terms of a *queer* politics of
migration (De Genova 2010b). For, the assertion 'Here we are, and we're not
leaving!' is quite consonant with the renowned chant of queer mobilisation:
'We're here, we're queer, get used to it!' Both are defiant affirmations of
presence that literally ask for nothing, petition for nothing, appeal for nothing,
demand nothing. This comparison is especially illuminating when considered
in light of the second half of the migrant struggle chant, which follows '*¡Aquí
estamos y no nos vamos!*' with the rejoinder '*¡Y si nos sacan, nos regresa-
mos!*' [Here we are, and we're not leaving! And if they throw us out, we'll
come right back!]. Here, we appreciate all the more clearly that what was
at stake in this chant was precisely the question of migrant 'illegality' and
undocumented migrants' susceptibility to deportation. By implication, they
proclaimed: 'We're here, we're "illegal", catch us if you can!' In this spirit,
migrants matched their affirmations of presence with the assurance that even

if they were to be deported, they could never, in fact, be truly expelled and their presence could never be truly eradicated: they would come right back. Thus, this politics of presence in the United States was also a transnational politics of *mobility*, articulated from 'here' ('Here we are!') but also, simultaneously, from *beyond* the border, from *outside* the space of the nation state, from the *other* side of the horizon of deportation ('We'll come right back!').

Anticipating another slogan of the ensuing struggles over US immigration politics, Latino migrants (in their millions) were boldly announcing that they were *Undocumented but Unafraid*, deportable but insurgent nonetheless. Both chants, therefore, can be understood to be radically counter-normative and anti-assimilationist affirmations of the already established fact of *presence*. But they are likewise affirmations of a kind of defiant *incorrigibility*. They proclaim, in effect: Not only are we 'here', but also we are different, we have no proper place within your normative or legal order, but there's nothing you can do about it – you can never get rid of us. This sort of identification with migrant 'illegality' is remarkable in many respects. Unlike the common slogan, 'No Human Being Is Illegal', very notably, here, you have people who have been *illegalised* boldly calling attention to exactly that fact, and politically grappling with the very consequential reality of that sociopolitical human condition of *being* 'illegal'. As demonstrated in previous work on 'the legal production of Mexican/migrant "illegality"' (De Genova 2002; 2004; 2005), migrant 'illegality' has been historically rendered to be effectively inseparable from the Mexican/migrant experience in particular (and from a much wider Latino migrant experience, more generally). Therefore, during my ethnographic research in Chicago in the 1990s, one could find bumper stickers, caps and t-shirts that proudly announced (in Spanish): '100% Wetback' ['*100% Mojado*'], or declared defiantly: 'Illegal – So What?' ['*Ilegal – ¿Y Qué?*'] (De Genova 2005, 239). The irresistible recurrence of the *¡Aquí Estamos!* chant during the mass mobilisations ten years later was, therefore, a mass expression of those sorts of audacious Latino/migrant affirmations of their 'illegal' identity. From the vantage point of the dominant anti-Latino racial nativism, this might be considered to be a kind of shamelessness. But this shameless and unapologetic subjectivity in the face of injustice has another name: dignity. Hence, it is productive to reflect further upon the particular sort of subjectivity that is at work here, which we might consider to be *the incorrigible subject* of this politics of incorrigibility.

CAPITALISING ON THE DIFFERENCE THAT BORDERS MAKE

For, indeed, not only is this the self-styled subject of the migrant protests against the Border Spectacle of the US immigration regime and the anti-terrorist pretensions of the Homeland Security State; this is also the incorrigible subject of political economy itself. Not only is this the audacious expression of specifically Latino *political* mobilisation, simultaneously, it is also the articulation of the constitutive and inextricable presence of *labour* (migrant labour) – *within*, but also *against*, capital. How else to explain the designation of May 1st, International Workers' Day, as the 2006 protests' focal point for nationwide mobilisation, summarily reinvented by the migrants' struggle as the 'Day without an Immigrant' boycott and general strike? The autonomous subjectivity of migration here reveals itself to always be the autonomy and subjectivity of migrant *labour* also, in effect, declaring (to capital): Here we are – there's nothing you can do about your fundamental dependency upon us; you owe your very existence to our energies and vitality, so you could never get rid of us. This is, after all, the defining contradiction of the capital–labour relation – that living (human) labour is the source of all economic value.

Labour has always and everywhere been the truly integral and indispensable motive force driving the processes of capitalist production – the real expression of human subjectivity, creative capacity and productive power – the conscious and wilful *subject* driving the *objective* processes of 'the economy', and hence, a volatile and always at least potentially insubordinate force. Labour within capitalist social relations is, in this sense, always simultaneously labour *for* capital and also *against* capital, leaving both labour and capital deeply ensnared in a contradictory, interdependent and fraught condition.

Thus, capital's subordination of labour is the premier *political* problem. Indeed, this problem derives, first and foremost, from the labour process itself: the urgent and crucial necessity of subordinating the conscious attention of the labourer to the task at hand. The subordination of labour is, above all, the subordination of precisely the *subjectivity* of the labourer. The capitalist labour process requires that labour be purposeful and consistently trained upon its object, that it be attentive, disciplined, dutiful and docile (Marx 1867/1976, 284; cf. De Genova 2010a). On the other hand, the less satisfying and interesting the work, the more that it provokes the virtually inevitable excesses and excursions of the labouring subject's subjective dispositions. In these ways, then, in the context of estranged labour, there is a permanent tension between the imperatives of the labour process and the needs and desires of labour's subjectivity. The subject of alienated labour tends to be a subject persistently thinking about the fact that s/he would rather be doing something else, a subject who feels, in fact, compelled *to do* something else, with every opportunity – an *incorrigible* subject.

In this light, it is possible to return more specifically to *migrant* labour, and the contested and thus mobile controls at the margins of the state's territorial space, which constitute key features of border regimes.

The defining drive of capital accumulation is that it must operate on an ever-expanding scale. This, of course, means that capital is periodically challenged, in the event of labour shortages or political crises of labour subordination, with the predictable need to occasionally recruit more workers (or different ones), to *mobilise* labour – to set large masses of workers in motion, often in the form of migrations. This periodic imperative to recruit new workers, however, operates intermittently with capital's more routine need to reliably stabilise and maintain a more or less captive and tractable workforce. Thus, more commonly, labour subordination requires labour's *im*mobilisation – the effective suppression of what has poignantly been depicted as working people's freedom to 'desert' or 'escape' their predicament and seek better prospects elsewhere (Mezzadra 2001; 2004; cf. Holloway 1994, 31; Mitropoulos 2006; Moulier-Boutang 1998; 2001; Moulier-Boutang and Grelet 2001). States have played an instrumental role historically in trying to orchestrate the international choreography of labour control. In effect, the various territorially defined ('national') states seek to marshal their respective differences in competition with one another as devoted participants in capital's universal drive to subdue all resistances and coerce labour's recalcitrant subjectivity into productive submission to the imperatives of accumulation. The unbounded (effectively global) mobility of capital, then, demands that labour's freedom of movement be more or less regulated, when not inhibited altogether. In either case, however, the mobility of labour tends to be subjected to coercive strategies, most frequently (albeit not exclusively) exercised today through the border enforcement techniques of state power.

Borders make migrants because borders produce differences in space, and capital precisely *capitalises* upon those differences. This is why capitalism, in fact, requires borders and could never promote a truly borderless world. Contrary to the notion that the interests of employers demand more 'cheap' migrant labour and therefore can be understood to be somehow in conflict with the interests of states intent on controlling their borders and restricting migration,[2] I am proposing that we discern the more fundamental *complementarity* between these apparently opposed mandates of the state and capital. It is precisely border policing and immigration law enforcement that generate the variegated spectrum of differences among distinct categories of migrants and thereby render some migrants 'illegal', vulnerable to the recriminations of the state, and thus, presumably tractable. In other words, it is the state that *produces* the crucial conditions of possibility for the 'cheap'-ness of their labour-power. Here again we recognise the *scene* of exclusion (associated with border policing) to be inseparable from its *obscene* underside, the fact of (illegalised) migrants' subordinate inclusion (De Genova 2012; 2013a).

BORDER AS SPECTACLE

There is no denying that we now live in a world of fortified, militarised and securitised borders, a world that perhaps more than ever before resembles what Hannah Arendt memorably called 'a barbed-wire labyrinth' (1951/1968, 292). The human freedom of movement is beleaguered if not besieged, as never before. This is true, even as we also witness unprecedented schemes for the managerial facilitation of selective cross-border mobilities.[3] However, we must guard against some pervasive fallacies. The first fallacy would be to see only what is most obvious, only what is flagrant and flamboyant, only that which makes an ostentatious spectacle of itself, and commands our attention. The first fallacy is to perceive only the political, juridical and military enactments of state projects upon territory, which so commonly manifest themselves as the patrol and enforcement of relatively exclusionary borders. These sorts of Border Spectacle make a robust and grandiose display of their technologies and techniques of ostensible exclusion, above all directed against the most humble of human border crossers. But they also conceal something. Border patrols and the diverse efforts of state powers aimed at border control have everywhere arisen as *reaction formations*. They are responses to a prior fact – the mass mobility of human beings on the move, the incorrigible subjectivity and autonomy of migration, the manifest expression of the freedom of movement of the human species. Even to designate this mobility as 'migration' is already to collude in the naturalisation of the borders that serve to produce the difference between one or another state's putative inside and outside, constructing the very profoundly consequential difference between the presumably proper subjects of a state's authority and those mobile human beings branded as aliens, foreigners, and indeed, 'migrants' (De Genova 2013b). But there is one fact that must not be lost in the shuffle: the movement of people around the world, and hence across these border zones, came first. The multifarious attempts to 'manage' or control this autonomous mobility have always come as a response. Confronting the statist perspective of a global regime of 'barbed-wire borders', the basic human freedom of movement could only ever seem to be perfectly incorrigible.

A second pitfall that we must avoid is perceiving these efforts at border control as purely exclusionary. Much of what these border controls actually do is a work of *filtering* human mobility, sorting and ranking the movement of people around the world into a differentiated hierarchy of more or less permissible and more or less prohibited varieties of mobility (Kearney 2004). Thus, the spectacles of border policing and immigration enforcement present themselves as essentially exclusionary, but conceal what is frequently a massive process of *inclusion*.[4] In this way, the border and immigration regimes that have proliferated – largely, over the last century or so, and often much more recently than that – are less about simply precluding or eliminating the freedom of movement and rather more about facilitating it according to various formulae for control and management.

Yet another diversionary effect of the Border Spectacle: while increasingly militarised and securitised borders around the world conceal various state projects for the selective importation of migrants, in spite of their ostensible premier task of exclusion, they also conceal the fact that even those migratory movements that are officially prohibited, branded as 'illegal' and supposed to be absolutely unwanted and rejected are, in fact, objectively speaking, actively encouraged and enthusiastically facilitated. So-called 'illegal' and officially unauthorised migrations are, to various extents, actively and deliberately imported, and welcomed by prospective employers as a highly prized variety of labour-power. In other words, the Border Spectacle and its grand performance of exclusion is accompanied almost everywhere by the ever-expanding fact of illegalised human mobility.

This is well illustrated by the increasing fortification of the US–Mexico border. Take, for example, the following description of the border fence that separates Nogales, Arizona from Nogales, Mexico:

> The border is sealed tighter than ever, the result of billions of dollars spent with the prospect of billions more if [new] immigration legislation passes Congress. The fence is new, the technology up-to-date, the military hardware – planes, drones, all-terrain vehicles – abundant. (Downes 2013)

This would seem to be a depiction of the Border Spectacle at its most spectacular. And yet, in the very same article, one encounters the following (rather frank) assessment:

> The fence ... is a see-through wall of vertical steel rods 15 to 18 feet high [about 5 and a half meters], set four inches apart [about 10 centimetres] in a deep bed of concrete. It is a rusty ribbon that runs up and down dusty hills and streets, cutting one city into two and jutting into the desert for a few miles east and west.
>
> An impenetrable barricade it is not. A climber with a rope can hop it in less than half a minute. Smugglers with jackhammers tunnel under it.
>
> As a monument to futility and legislative malpractice, however, it achieves perfection.
>
> There is unavoidable cruelty and death. The fence shunts migrant's miles out into the burning, freezing desert. There they die, trying to make their way. (Downes 2013)

Nevertheless, in spite of the dominant discourse that the US immigration system and border enforcement regime are 'broken' and in spite of the perennial appearance of the US–Mexico border's inadequacy or dysfunction, this perfect 'monument to futility' (in the author's words) is a border (like most other borders around the world) that has long served quite reliably, effectively and predictably as a filter for the unequal exchange of various forms of value (Kearney 2004; cf. Heyman 2004). The filtering character of borders is especially visible in those instances where the intensified enforcement at border crossings of easiest passage relegates illegalised migrant mobilities into zones of more severe hardship and potentially lethal passage. The escalation of migrant and refugee deaths along the US–Mexico border zone bears a striking resemblance to the parallel proliferation of migrant deaths instigated by the unprecedented extremities and severities of the European border regime – particularly through the Mediterranean Sea[5] and externalised across the entire expanse of the Sahara Desert (Andersson 2012; 2014a; 2014b; Bredeloup 2012; Dunn 2009; Lecadet 2013; Nevins 2002/2010; Stephen 2008). In a de facto process of artificial selection, these deadly obstacle courses serve to sort out the most able-bodied, disproportionately favouring the younger, stronger and healthier among prospective (labour) migrants. The militarisation and ostensible fortification of borders, furthermore, proves to be much more reliable for enacting a strategy of *capture* than for functioning as mere technologies of exclusion. Once migrants have successfully navigated their ways across such borders – and this has been abundantly verified by the reinforcement of the US–Mexico border – the onerous risks and costs of departing and later attempting to cross yet again become inordinately prohibitive (Durand and Massey 2004, 12; Massey 2005, 1, 9). Rather than keeping illegalised migrants out, the militarisation and securitisation of borders simply tends to *trap* the great majority of those who succeed to get across, now caught – indefinitely – *inside* the space of the migrant-'receiving' state(s) as a very prized kind of highly vulnerable, precarious labour.

Again, the cross-border mobility of migrants is deeply inflected by those migrants' own heterogeneous projects. The border regimes that work to variously manage these transnational flows are always fundamentally *reacting* to the impulses and motives of migrants whose subjective dispositions and mobility projects are basically autonomous. At the centre of every border regime, therefore, is a diverse array of incorrigible migrant subjects, whose very subjectivity and autonomy is the decisive and defining target – to be subordinated, disciplined and subjected. That is to say, the disciplinary effect of these regimes of border policing and immigration law enforcement is necessarily directed at 'correcting' the obstreperous and incorrigible (migrant) subjects whose aspirations, desires and elemental freedom always exceed and overflow the narrowly construed role to which migrant workers are routinely relegated, as effectively subordinated labour.

Nevertheless, we could rightly say that this is generically true of *all* labour, which after all is the more general incorrigible subject of political economy.

We, therefore, have to attend all the more deliberately to the question of what exactly is 'political' about the capital–labour relation, a relation that otherwise might appear to be strictly and purely 'economic'. I have already suggested that the beginning of an answer to this puzzle resides in the fundamental problem of subordinating the subjectivity of labour to the material and practical requirements of the job at hand. Labour subordination is the key site where we can examine the *politics* of the production process itself. I will now turn this incorrigible subject of labour inside-out, once more, in order to see the subjectivity of *labour* in a more concrete and historically specific way, which will bring the questions of *migration* and *race* more sharply into focus.

BORDER AS COLOUR LINE

As the veritable source of all value, it is not unreasonable to say that labour-power is the premier commodity in the global circuitry of capitalist exchange. But the global movement of homogenised, *abstract* labour is finally embodied in the restless life and death of labour in a rather more 'concrete' form – which is to say, actual migrant working men and women. Capital can never extract from labour the abstract (eminently social) substance that is 'value' except with recourse to the abstraction of labour-power, which, however, can only be derived from the palpable vital energies of living labour – real flesh-and-blood working people. The accelerated transnational mobility of labour-power, therefore, is inseparable from the *migration* of actual human beings. Their 'migrant' (or non-citizen) status is a decisive (bordered) site where state power intervenes to mediate the terms and conditions for their subordination.

It is precisely the *non-citizen* status of migrant labour, therefore, that compels a still more incisive analysis of what exactly constitutes *the political* in the 'political' economy of migration and borders. For, if it is true that were there no borders, there would be no migrants, then it is likewise important to note that transnational migrants exist as such only because the borders that they cross are fundamentally meant to produce and uphold the spatialised differences between *states*. Hence, migrants exist always in a precisely *political* relationship to the jurisdiction of a state power (De Genova 2002). However, once we begin to examine the historical specificity of actual nation states and the migrations that cross their borders, we similarly can only account for the global inequalities of wealth and power at stake by also referring to the precisely *postcolonial* – and thus profoundly racialised – particularities at work in the historical production of distinct ('national') 'populations' and the distinct 'group' identities of various categories of migrants.

The effectively global mobility of capital exudes a pronounced indifference towards the particular locations and forms of the labour process where it invests in favour of a maximisation of surplus value, and is in this sense exceedingly versatile. This willingness to seek a profit anywhere and everywhere, and likewise this capacity to accommodate virtually any form of exploitation within the larger process of capital accumulation, has sometimes misled some commentators to imagine, falsely, that capital is truly 'cosmopolitan' and thus 'colour-blind' or otherwise impervious to the various racial (or 'ethnic'), national, linguistic, cultural, religious or gendered differences among distinct categories of working people. But this is precisely where the *politics* of the labour process is to be located – in the social relations among the embodied, 'concrete' particularities of actual working people (living labour). The homogenised abstraction of labour-power, which is utterly necessary for the larger functioning of the capitalist production of (economic) value, can be generated in practice only under the aegis of the social production of real heterogeneity and inequality. In other words, the relations of *economic* production must always be understood in terms of the social and *political* production of *difference* (Roediger and Esch 2012; see also De Genova 2010a).

In Europe much like in the United States, the postcolonial condition is nowhere more forcefully manifest than in the *racial* subjugation of migrants. The border of the European Union has the character not merely of an international (or intercontinental) boundary line but of a new reconfiguration of the proverbial *colour line*. Indeed, recalling the escalation in migrant deaths in these border zones over recent years, we may be reminded here of Ruth Gilmore's poignant proposition that this indeed may be taken as the very definition of racism: 'Racism', she contends, 'is the state-sanctioned or extralegal production and exploitation of group-differentiated vulnerability to premature death' (2007, 28). Thus, borders that systematically expose particular populations to the risk of premature death, according to Gilmore's definition, may be understood to be precisely instrumentalities of *racism*. If it is possible to suggest this sort of analogy, however, it is not reducible to the mere (naturalised) fact of 'racial' difference between migrants and their so-called 'host societies'. Rather, the significance and consequentiality of race for these migrants could only be activated and acquire such intensity *as a result* of the enduring coloniality of the inequalities of wealth and power between the formerly colonised countries and the imperial metropolitan destinations of these migrations. The incorrigible subject of the autonomy of migrant labour, the premier target of this sort of border regime, thus crucially intersects and substantially coincides with the incorrigible subjectivities of the complex cross section of postcolonial racial formations, once the migrants have made their way across the borders and deep into the putative 'interior' of the destination country. The various racialisations of these migrant groups demarcate the differential inscriptions of the border on their bodies (Khosravi 2010, 97–120).

In effect, they are made to carry the border on their backs, wear the border on their faces, ever increasingly subjected to various degrees of border enforcement wherever they may go.

THE UBIQUITY OF BORDERS

This chapter started with a discussion of the politics of incorrigibility that I attribute to the migrant political mobilisations in the United States, and folded that into a consideration of the incorrigible subject of labour. The mass migrant mobilisations of 2006 completely and decisively derailed the proposed law that had already passed in the US House of Representatives and was still being debated by the Senate, and no comprehensive immigration legislation has been feasible since. In short, in the face of the incorrigible subjectivity of the migrant struggle in 2006 and its extended aftermath, the political establishment in the United States was profoundly crippled. The insurgency of migrants (disproportionately non-citizens with no voting rights, including literally millions who were, and largely remain, 'illegal') – and the politics of sheer incorrigibility so forcefully manifested in that mass movement – produced a political crisis around immigration policy, which has remained fundamentally irresolvable. It is important to note nonetheless that the insurgency of migrant labour in 2006 was immediately met with an aggressive escalation in immigration policing in the interior of the United States, particularly in the form of workplace raids and subsequent deportations (De Genova 2009). Although these large-scale raids were subsequently discontinued under Obama, the transformation of routine traffic stops by local police into occasions for immigration surveillance and apprehensions dramatically expanded. This sweeping deportation dragnet was initiated under the administration of George W. Bush, but it has since become a disgraceful hallmark of the Obama presidency.

As of December 2013, Obama had presided over more than 1.9 million deportations – radically more than any other president in US history (Preston 2013). In spite of Obama's duplicitous claims that immigration enforcement has become more targeted and selective, purportedly going after 'criminals, gang bangers, people who are hurting the community, not after students, not after folks who are here just because they're trying to figure out how to feed their families',[6] the detention and deportation dragnet actually broadened substantially, with only one-fifth of deportations involving convictions for serious criminal offenses, whereas roughly two-thirds have committed only minor infractions (usually nothing more significant than a traffic violation) or none whatsoever. Notably, a very significant proportion of those 'removed' would historically have never been formally charged with any (non-criminal) immigration infraction. This group accounted for as many as one-quarter of those deported during the final year of the Bush administration, for instance. However, under Obama, 90 per cent of those deported are now officially charged with an immigration violation, thereby prohibiting them from returning to the United States for at least five years, and exposing anyone who might subsequently be caught returning 'illegally' to a prison sentence (Thompson and Cohen 2014). Yet, remarkably, in a rather predictable reflex of the intransigent partisan politics in the United States, when the most recent figures for Obama's deportation record were made public (towards the end of 2013), showing a 10 per cent decrease in deportations from the previous year, many Republicans responded with the contention that Obama is actually deporting *too few* undocumented migrants. Robert Goodlatte, the chairman of the House Judiciary Committee, said that the recent deportation figures were 'just more evidence that the Obama administration refuses to enforce our immigration laws' (Preston 2013). When the most vigorous enforcement of the deportation regime in US history can be castigated as nothing less than a 'refusal' to enforce immigration law, it ought to be made plain that immigration law making and legislative and policy debate have arrived at a veritable stalemate.

The US immigration stalemate is evident, above all, in the utter incapacity of the US Congress to pass any multifaceted national-level legislation since 2006.[7] On 20 November 2014, Obama finally announced executive action to institute a reprieve from the immediate threat of deportation for select categories of undocumented migrants.[8] Indeed, on this occasion, he addressed himself emphatically to the legislative stalemate: 'To those members of Congress who question my authority to make our immigration system work better, or question the wisdom of me acting where Congress has failed, I have one answer: Pass a bill' (Shear 2014). Congratulating himself for heightened immigration enforcement yet simultaneously dissimulating about the fact of staggeringly unprecedented numbers of deportations during his presidency, moreover, Obama disingenuously asserted that deporting millions is 'not who we are': 'Mass deportation would be contrary to our character'.[9] Predictably, while de-emphasising immigration enforcement in the interior and proposing modest relief for some undocumented migrants already resident, the executive action prescribes yet another expansion of policing at the US–Mexico border aimed at the interdiction of new 'illegal' arrivals.[10]

INCORRIGIBILITY

In conclusion, the material and practical techniques and technologies of contemporary regimes of border policing and immigration law enforcement must be seen as political tactics, only finally apprehensible in relation to another 'objective' reality: the embodied subjectivity of 'irregular' or 'illegal' migrants. These humble border crossers represent the incorrigible subject of virtually all contemporary border regimes, in response to which the multifarious objective infrastructures and practices of border patrol must be understood to be reaction formations. The freedom of movement of human beings around the world – the autonomy of migration that is everywhere in evidence, on an ever more mass scale – indubitably confronts a truly horrifying panoply of material and practical impediments and obstructions. Nonetheless, as autonomous subjects, with their own aspirations, needs and desires, which necessarily exceed and overflow any regime of immigration and citizenship, migrants' mobility projects enact an elementary freedom of movement to which borders are intrinsically a response, however brutal. Yet in spite of it all, everywhere, on a global scale, human beings continue to prevail in their mobility projects, unceasingly and tirelessly establishing migration as a central and constitutive fact of our global postcolonial present. Thus, our freedom of movement as a species asserts itself anew, staking a claim to the space of the planet as a whole. The incorrigible subject of migration, which is inevitably also the incorrigible subject of labour, is finally revealed to be the incorrigible subject of human life itself. *¡Aquí Estamos, y No Nos Vamos!* Here we are, and we're not leaving. So ....

Where shall we go from here?

NOTES

1. The ultimately abortive Border Protection, Antiterrorism and Illegal Immigration Control Act (HR 4437, also known as the Sensenbrenner bill, passed 16 December 2005 in the House of Representatives) would have criminalised all of an estimated 11 million undocumented migrants residing in the United States by summarily converting their 'unlawful presence' into a felony and rendering them subject to mandatory detention upon apprehension, and likewise would have converted any and all immigration violations – however minor, technical or unintentional – into felonies punishable with imprisonment, such that 'legal' permanent residents would have been irreversibly rendered as 'illegal aliens' for any variety of innocuous incidental infractions. In addition to numerous other draconian provisions, the bill also sought to impose criminal sanctions, with imprisonment as a penalty, on anyone construed to knowingly 'assist' an 'unlawful' migrant (including those previously 'legal' and subsequently criminalised), with definitions so expansive that even immigration lawyers could have plausibly been subject to imprisonment (Mailman and Yale-Loehr 2005; see also De Genova 2007).

2. The notion of 'cheap labour' naturalises the pernicious insinuation that there is something intrinsic about those migrant workers that makes their labour 'cheap' (Burawoy 1976, 1056–57).

3. The European Schengen zone of relatively unrestricted mobility – albeit more or less exclusively for 'Europeans only' – is, of course, a much-celebrated example of this sort of selective and differential access to mobility.

4. Albeit a kind of inclusion that seeks to subordinate the autonomous human freedom of movement into sufficiently docile and tractable categories of purportedly desirable or undesirable, deserving or undeserving, welcome or unwanted human mobility.

5. See chapter 2 in this volume by Marco Bruno.

6. Video of speech available at: http://www.nytimes.com/2014/11/21/us/obama-immigration-speech.html.

7. The sole exception is the perfunctory Secure Fence Act of 2006 (Public Law 109-367), which was remarkably narrow in scope: this law was singularly dedicated to providing for the further presumed fortification of the US-Mexico border with hundreds of miles of new physical barriers to be added to the existing 125 miles of fence.

8. Notably, amounting to fewer than two-fifths of the total estimated population, and contingent upon numerous eligibility restrictions and compliance with penalties.

9. Video of speech available at: http://www.nytimes.com/2014/11/21/us/obama-immigration-speech.html.

10. This inevitably includes countless returning migrants who were previously expelled by Obama's prolonged deportation dragnet.

Chapter 2

Framing Lampedusa

Between Alarmism and Pietism – The Landing Issue in Italian Media Coverage of Migration

Marco Bruno

This chapter investigates and deconstructs the mechanisms of news representation and media construction of the so-called 'landing crisis', a frame with a high iconic value within the more general image of migration to Italy. In particular, the focus of this chapter is on the events directly or indirectly connected with the so-called 'Arab Spring' and, therefore, on the arrivals of migrants on the Italian coast between February and April 2011.

The identification and deconstruction of prevalent frames in these news representations allows us to highlight the central role of the media in the definition of the situation and in the construction of immigration in Italy as a social problem. The news-frame analysis approach allows us to point out how visual images, lexical and argumentative constructs, metaphors, etc. are 'framing devices' (Gamson 1992) that contribute to establishing, structuring and enhancing the discourse on the *Other*, not only as a set of messages, but as a dynamic and potentially conflictual (sometimes consensual) field of representations and forces that push a specific definition and construction of reality.

Thus, the news media are both the arena, and an agent, in the discursive field. Media discourse on migrants and the focus on the so-called 'landings emergency' serve to make more concrete and effective representations, that in political debate, are routinely shared as symbolic materials in the definition of intervention strategies.

Specifically, the emergency frame of landings (and, to a lesser extent, the pietistic one) primes and supports the adoption by the Italian government of a patrol intervention, both humanitarian and military, in Italian coastal areas.[1] Such a policy, in combination with others, is functional – in a circular way – to the restatement of a conception in which Italy appears a spatial area besieged by the entry of 'outsiders' and the 'dangerous'.

MEDIA AND IMMIGRATION: A CRIMINALISATION
AND SECURITARIAN PERSPECTIVE

Many studies show that crime news is the prevailing perspective through which immigrants are narrated by Italian media (Maneri 2011; Calvanese 2011; Musarò and Parmiggiani 2014; Binotto 2004 and 2012). The securitarian discourse dominates and paints a picture of rising insecurity, directly linked to migratory phenomena (Binotto 2015; Dal Lago 1998). In many countries, there is a clear tendency to objectify the equation immigration = crime and define it as *the* problem. By the criminalisation of migrants, Palidda means 'all the discourses, facts and practices made by the police, judicial authorities, but also local governments, media, and a part of the population that hold immigrants/aliens responsible for a large share of criminal offences' (Id. 2011, 23). As Palidda notes (*Ibid.*) in summarising a much broader debate, although the criminalisation of strangers seems to be common in many European and non-European countries, there is no statistical relationship between changes in crime rates and an increase in the number of immigrant residents.

The link between *media – security – immigration – collective anxiety* structures itself in a homogeneous way, in countries with different histories and cultures. The regularity with which the ethnicisation of crime, and therefore the criminalisation of the Other, emerges within debate seems to suggest that there is a sort of *unconditioned reflex*, a cultural reaction to otherness that tends to repeat itself in ways remarkably similar in different cultural contexts.

Several studies have shown a positive relationship between the media attention towards crimes imputed to immigrants and growing support for populist and xenophobic movements. For example, in Belgium, a time series analysis of news coverage of this kind showed a parallel growth of electoral support for the Vlaams Blok (Flemish Block) movement, a group particularly hostile to immigration (Walgrave and De Swert 2004; for other contexts, see Boomgaarden and Vliegenthart 2009; Erjavec 2003; O'Doherty and Lecouteur 2007), and although news reports on the success of the integration processes are increasingly present, and focused on the commitment and personal success of some immigrants (Vliegenthart and Roggeband 2007; Benson 2009; Navarro 2010), the criminalisation, and a securitarian vision of migrations continue to be in evidence.

This difficulty in narrating and managing sociocultural change clearly affects the media system: the central role of the news regarding crimes committed by immigrants, the theme of irregularity and the attention to a securitarian dimension appear both as a mechanism of anticipatory social control towards immigrants and as a form of symbolic shift, that is to say, an attempt to shift the focus of the discussion from the long and laborious dialectic of conflict-integration to that, more simplistic and in many ways more reassuring, of the Other-as-threat.

THE CONSTRUCTION OF AN ICONIC IMAGE: THE *ARRIVALS* ISSUE IN ITALIAN MEDIA

Together with crime news stories, the theme of landings on the Italian coast – and more generally of immigrants' entries – is one of the most characteristic elements of the entire media representation of the phenomenon of migration. As previously emphasised, the landing often becomes an iconic media image of the phenomenon of migration (Bruno 2004). The representation of migration given by the Italian media is strictly visual and the vocabulary used has a symbolic value both in lexical and in textual terms.[2] The issue of migrants' irregularity and of their so-called 'clandestinity' is very significant: this issue is particularly important in reference to the lexical aspects of the definition of foreigner(s) (see, among others, Maneri 1998; Binotto 2004; Faloppa 2011) and it is closely related to the great attention that media are focussing on the theme of *arrivals*, in particular through landings. Attention is focused towards the shipwrecks that have resulted in thousands of victims over the years. In the public's perception, the images shown represent many, if not all, of the problematic aspects of the phenomenon of migration: large numbers of people, the uncontrollability of the phenomenon, menace to security, irregularity, etc., in spite of the fact that only a small fraction of migrants entering Italian territory, legally or illegally, arrive by sea.[3]

The divergence between real data and the perception of immigration in Italy is shown by several resources (i.e. Osservatorio di Pavia 2014; TTI 2011 and 2014). For example, on average, Italians think that immigrants represent 23 per cent of the population, *versus* an actual 8.1 per cent: 4,922,085 'non-Italian' people out of a population of 60,782,668 (Idos-Unar 2014).[4] Moreover, Italians estimate that immigrants are in the majority 'illegal' (and 'Muslim'), yet undocumented immigrants are approx. 400,000 (and Muslims constitute 32.9 per cent of immigrants, i.e. 1,651,000 people).[5]

The dimension of the arrival is essential if we wish to semantically trace the boundaries of the field of media focussing on migration and to define the limits and coordinates of this discursive space around the following categories: undesirability versus hospitality, social alarm or pietism. The definition of the limits and borders of the discursive space is even more meaningful, because it concerns the same spatial concept as the public discourse on alterity.[6] This aspect, therefore, assumes the characteristics of a discursive and metaphorical device, which appears to be essential for the media to construct social alarm in respect to the phenomenon of migration (Binotto 2015).

METHODS AND APPROACH

The data and empirical evidence here derive from a research project carried out in recent years by the author and by a network of scholars[7] gathered around the activities for the 'Carta di Roma', the 'Journalist's professional code of conduct regarding asylum seekers, refugees, victims of trafficking and migrants'.[8] The research contains different investigations, all intertwined in an effort to grasp the multidimensional reach of the image of the migratory phenomenon in the media. I focus on a specific section related to the 'landing crisis' in Lampedusa, conducted in 2011–2012, which analysed, utilising a mix of quantitative and qualitative methods, representations of the phenomenon given by Italian media (in particular by television news broadcasts and current affairs programmes).[9]

The study was conducted by using a frame analysis approach (Entman 1993; D'Angelo and Kuypers 2010; Gamson 1992; Iyengar 1991) and critical discourse analysis (CDA) (Van Dijk 1988; Wodak 1996), as non-standard methods (Ricolfi 1997), with the aim of identifying and analysing (1) the modalities of representation of the arrivals issue in mainstream media, (2) the journalistic construction of the figure of migrants and refugees and (3) the definition, in terms of vocabulary and lexicon of migration as a social problem.

We will look at this process essentially as the way in which the media frame an issue or an event; defining interpretative coordinates through the selection, the emphasis or the omission of some aspects and not others. In this sense, the empirical effort benefits from combining the linguistic and iconic analysis of journalistic texts with the deconstruction of the historical and socio-political context in which the discourse takes place, through CDA. In CDA, the focus is not on the use of language *per se* but on the linguistic and argumentative dimension of social structures and cultural processes (Wodak 1996), and aims to enlighten how social problems are built and represented, also with reference to social and power relations.

LANDINGS IN ITALIAN MEDIA (AND POLITICS): FROM COVER-UP TO EMERGENCY

Traditionally, quantitative data on media coverage of the issue of landings show large fluctuations, which are affected by seasonal factors (Binotto and Martino 2004) and also very often are significantly influenced by political factors. For example, in the larger study, we documented a concealment of the issue between 2008 and 2010 (Binotto, Bruno and Lai 2012) probably as a result of the rejection policies adopted by the Berlusconi government, policies that were severely criticised and then formally prosecuted by the

European Court of Human Rights in Strasbourg in February 2012.[10] The rejection policy was presented at that time by the government majority as a way 'to save lives',[11] but it had only sent migrants back to the dangers they were trying to escape from: the abuses, tortures and deaths happening in Libya (in the desert or in detention centres) and served only to shift the problem to a more distant place where it could be removed from the spectrum of visibility of the media.[12] The impossibility of exercising the right to request asylum actualised the connection and merging (both conceptual and semantic) of two images: the refugee asking for protection and the economic immigrant.

From 2011 onwards, the theme of the exodus of refugees and of the possibility of mass migration to neighbouring countries and to Europe again became a relevant issue in the media coverage, particularly in relation to the season of uprisings in North Africa.[13] From the point of view of the Italian media – in continuity with the traditional lack of attention on international politics and a certain provincialism of the news media – the coverage of the crisis in North Africa focused mainly on the arrivals of refugees on the coast of Lampedusa and the consequences this could have for Italy. Interestingly, the theme of the possibility of a mass migration has been normalised, within the more general discussion on immigration. The focus on the consequences of the arrival of refugees on the coast of Lampedusa has practically dominated the entire spectrum of representations of the conflict in Libya, which – like any act of war – had many other possible aspects to analyse. According to different estimates (e.g. UNHCR or ISMU Foundation), the number of people arriving in Italy throughout 2011 was between 50,000 and 60,000, yet the alarm around the issue of landings was intense. <Immigrati: sbarco record (Immigrants: record of landings)>, <Un assalto che il nostro paese non può arrestare (An assault that our country cannot stop)>[14] are just some examples of the headlines recorded.

It must be remembered that the position of Italy with respect to both the civil war and the Western military intervention in Libya was particularly complicated by at least two aspects. First, the colonial history of Italians in Libya: on the one hand, the legacy of the legitimate claims by the Gaddafi regime for the recognition of injustices; on the other hand the fact that the recognition of these faults, if and when it occurred, was limited to political-economic compensation, decided and implemented only at the level of relations between States and not at the level of public opinion. This compensation was not experienced by the public as a real process of reconstruction and sharing of memories and faults. This is mainly because, even though the Italian colonisation was very brutal, it has always been filtered through the widespread myth of 'Italians good people' (*'Italiani brava gente'*). Secondly, the ambiguous relationships maintained until a

few months earlier by Prime Minister Silvio Berlusconi with Colonel Gaddafi, who was received in Italy with State Honours, attracted the attention
of the media. The image of Berlusconi kissing Gaddafi's hand became an
iconic television image in that period, and was used by opponents of the
former Italian premier.

LANGUAGE AND REPRESENTATION: LAMPEDUSA
AND THE DEFINITION OF THE FRAME OF ALARM

The messages conveyed by the media operate on a multitude of levels and
report both manifest and latent content, beyond the intentionality or non-
intentionality of media producers. Therefore, in the definition and construction of meanings, it is not only important to use proper terminology,[15] it is
also fundamental to pay attention to the ways in which the various terms
are combined, which aspects are emphasised and which remain unspoken,
and what are the interpretative frames built precisely from these dynamics
of selection and emphasis and used to define events (Gamson 1992, 2001;
Entman 1993; Reese 2001). It is important to pay attention to the processes
of framing, which in this chapter are considered in relation to lexical choices,
metaphors, processes of theming, and in terms of macro or structural interpretative frameworks. The level of visibility of the news on landings and the
use of specific terminological associations that evoke social alarm and lack
of control show the influence that frames of interpretation have in proposing
certain readings, from which they structure public opinion around an issue,
and define a phenomenon as a threat or social problem (we will return to this
shortly below).[16]

From a terminological point of view, numbers are used more frequently
than other components of the lexicon when talking about the events of
Lampedusa. These are used in relation to numbers of arrivals and the presence of migrants, or when referring to repatriations or numbers of migrants
sent to shelters. The numerical strength of those arriving has strong elements
of newsworthiness and triggers the fear of an 'invasion' of foreigners, or at
least of an excessive and cumbersome presence.[17] The frequent association
between the terms <Lampedusa> and <emergency> (46 times in 36 newspaper articles, see Bruno 2014b) can be placed in the same alarmist dimension.
The frequent link between Lampedusa and the terms and categories related to
an 'emergency' gives the island the character of a 'citadel' in the 'war against
illegal immigration', of a 'besieged border region'. The island seems to represent, in a small scale, what the entire Italian community (the *us* implied in
media discourse) should fear, the invasion and social tension caused by the
alien coming from North Africa.

In analysing how the island of Lampedusa is described and characterised, the term <accoglienza (hospitality)> is often present in the lexicon used. However, the concept is not utilised to signify an action aimed at welcoming people in need, but rather in the sense of physical and bureaucratic organisation used to manage and <sistemare (arrange)> subjects who <sbarcano (disembark)> in a <frontiera (frontier post)> (Lampedusa), creating a <situazione (situation)> defined from time to time as <fortemente critica (very critical)> or <di emergenza (an emergency situation)>. During talk shows, wherein guests are invited to confront each other on the issue, they frequently use terms and metaphors that evoke the concept of 'home', in order to emphasise the distinction of us/them and the image of a 'violated area'. Sometimes, the expressions used would appear favourable to migrants, in a paternalistic way: for example, <aiutarli a casa loro (helping them in their homes)> is one of the most frequent phrases, typical of a certain way of interpreting migration policies. This expression is associated with one of the slogans used by politicians, especially members of the Lega Nord party (Northern League), and taken up by the media: <padroni a casa nostra (masters in our own home)>. Other expressions used during these occasions are <le persone che ci ritroviamo qui in casa (people we find in our homes)>, <non venite tutti qua (you cannot all come here)> and <a casa loro (back to their homes)>.

During the weeks preceding international intervention in Libya, we found abundant references in Italian media to mass migration as an 'unconventional weapon' used by Gaddafi to destabilise European countries. One of the most significant expressions used to define this aspect is <bomba migratoria (immigration bomb)>. Another exemplar metaphor is that of <tsunami umano (human tsunami)>, used several times by politicians and the media when referring to the landings in Lampedusa in 2011. This expression dehumanises the immigrants, treating them as an indistinct mass, while building and strengthening the frame of social alarm and uncontrollability. The construction of this mental picture (a human tsunami) conveys a sense of fear and uncontrollability, of something that *we* (the people of Lampedusa, but by extension all Italians) can only passively endure. This image appears effective and appealing in terms of media logic because it semantically binds the threat to the arrival from the sea. This same reference to the sea (coupled with expressions such as <assedio alle coste (border siege)>) reiterates the fact that the threat to *our* space originates from outside, reflecting an exclusive concept of territory.[18] It is interesting to report other metaphors relating to the dimension of alarm (in terms of emphasis on the quantity of the phenomenon) and of uncontrollability: <esodo (exodus)> (sometimes <esodo biblico (biblical exodus)>), <chilometri di persone (kilometres of people)> and <maxi sbarchi (maxi landings)>.

LANDINGS AND THE FRAME OF PIETISM

In addition to the frame of social alarm, we can distinguish a parallel, and partially alternative, frame characterised by a pietistic and paternalistic attitude. It is essential to emphasise that this frame is not really competing with the dominant frame of social alarm. The frame of pietism contains a series of representations that are distinctly minor in terms of quantity and only partially provide possible alternatives to the common ways of representing the theme of landings. This frame does not challenge the prevalent ways of treating the subject, but it can highlight less conformist ways of presenting the issue of landings. The frame of pietism is reflected in the use of stereotypical labels and representations, which draw widely from a series of stereotypical images of otherness, deriving from paternalism and from an ethnocentric attitude of superiority rooted in colonialism. This frame is often activated in relation to news reporting of tragedies at sea (e.g. the sinking occurred on 3rd October 2013 off the island of Lampedusa causing more than 360 deaths) and, to a lesser extent, in the case of articles and reportages specifically aimed at criticising the management of migration policies (usually by left-wing newscast or newspapers). The linguistic references are related to the terms <strage (massacre)>, <tragedia (tragedy)>, and <disperazione (desperation)>; the prevailing metaphors refer to death (<cimitero Mediterraneo (Mediterranean cemetery)>) or to a 'bet' on the future (<barconi della speranza (barges of hope)>, <alla ricerca di un porto amico (searching for a friendly harbour)>). Some Italian newspaper articles, following the shipwreck in October 2013, contained poignant titles such as 'Another massacre of migrants' (*Il Messaggero*), 'The massacre of migrants: My little brother has disappeared in the waves' (*La Stampa*), 'Shipwrecked and sold: the dramas of migrants' (*Avvenire*). The protagonists are defined as 'refugees', and 'desperate'. There is also a confirmation of the tendency (see Van Gorp 2005) to present images of women or children (rather than the image of young men, which characterises news that conveys the frame of alarm).

Table 2.1 attempts to summarise the two frames identified with respect to the iconic and discursive representative elements that constitute and support them. It is important to emphasise that, even if presented next to each other, the two frames, unlike other similar empirical acquisitions (i.e. Van Gorp 2005), do not have the same weight and the same representative power. In the first column in Table 2.1, I refer to certain elements of the media discourse: the choice of these elements derives from my synthesis and elaboration of various conceptions of the process of news-framing and of its components as framing devices.

Framing devices are merely mentioned in this contribution. According to Gamson (1992; 2001; Gamson and Modigliani 1989), these devices should

Table 2.1   Table of News-frame Devices Used in the Representation of Landings in Lampedusa

Framing devices	Frame of alarm	Frame of pietism (minority)
Depiction/Labels	Clandestines. Illegal immigrants.	Desperate. Migrants.
Role of subjects	Active.	Passive. Victims.
Metaphors and catchphrases	Human tsunami. Maxi landing. Wave of migration.	Mediterranean Cemetery.
Exemplars	'Last year's landings and chaos'.	Italian emigration in the past. Previous incidents at sea.
Visual images	Young men. Law enforcement officers, military forces.	Women and children. Rescuers. Boats.
Definition of the issue	Invasion. Uncontrolled immigration. Emergency landings.	Humanitarian emergency. Flight of refugees from war and misery.
Attribution of responsibility	Laxity and few controls. Lack of action from Europe.	Western countries. Migrant smugglers.

not be considered only as singular elements; it is important to look at how they connect to each other, building and structuring a more general key to representation and interpretation.

LANDINGS AS A *SOCIAL PROBLEM*: FRAMING AND DEFINING THE FIELD OF REPRESENTATIONS

The concatenation of individual events (e.g. the various landings, singularly real and concrete) used in the media discourse presents these events as a single social process somehow configured as a theme. Together with the demand for political intervention ('governments must act', 'we need tougher laws'), this theme presents itself as a social problem with its characteristics and consequences (let's say for example, an increase in the arrivals of 'outsiders' in the Italian territory and, consequently, the supposed increase in insecurity directly and explicitly linked to immigration). This dynamic (Figure 2.1) inserts the media system and its action of framing into the process of social construction of insecurity, which appears characteristic of the contemporary period.

The process is summarised in the graphic representation, though in much more simplified terms compared to what is likely to happen in reality. For example, the interaction between the different actors, and specifically between media and politics, is definitely multidirectional and multidimensional (and it is expressed on various levels and at different times). We should probably expect a significant role also for other *actors*, here considered only implicitly:

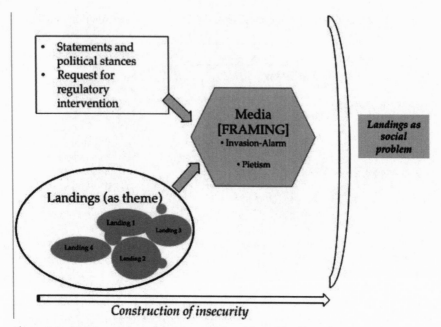

Figure 2.1   Construction model of the *social problem* of landings. *Source:* Author's Own.

the audiences and their opinions, or those 'real world indicators' (Norris et al. 2003) that during the process of construction and negotiation of the frame are connected to the different events and their characteristics. However, it is not possible to explore in depth all of these aspects in this contribution, where the focus is limited to a purely representative dimension.

The whole spectrum of media representations organised around a theme, intended as agenda setting (McCombs and Shaw 1972) or as agenda building, is certainly very important for the definition of the field on which public discourse is developed. The concept of 'field' proposed by Bourdieu (1980, 113–20; 1992) is referenced with a specific focus on the issues of media, social and collective representations, and on the conflict between different constructions and representations. The field of media representations, in this case relating to migration, is configured as a space in which the actors construct social problems and specify the possible solutions in terms of policies to be adopted.

TOWARDS A CONCLUSION: FRAMING, DISCOURSE AND POWER IN THE FIELD OF REPRESENTATIONS

What takes place in the sphere of media is a competition in which the 'social construction of reality' (Berger and Luckmann 1966) is shaped by relations of power, power that is semantising and undoubtedly political (Foucault 1971). In effect, this conflict is essentially a symbolic struggle that nourishes itself through the creation and reinforcement of definite frames. For example, between the various aspects there is surely a power of 'naming' (Bourdieu 1979), of labelling[19] subjects involved in news-stories, and of the definition of the situation (Gamson 1992). There is also the framing process as a set of limitations, as it were in reverse: that is to say, the matter of 'prohibition' (*l'interdit*), as 'procedures of exclusion' (Foucault 1971), the exercise of power in the definition of 'the bounds of acceptable discourse' (Entman 1993, 55). This process works through the a priori exclusion of some issues or positions that cannot find legitimacy in a discursive space, whose boundaries are in any case drawn by those who hold power (political, economic, editorial, and sometimes all these intertwined).

To explore the role of framing in the reconstruction of discursive and power connections, it may be useful to consider them in relation to the concept of *apparatus*, exactly as used by Foucault (*dispositif*), as 'a thoroughly heterogeneous ensemble consisting of discourses, institutions, architectural forms, regulatory decisions, laws, administrative measures, scientific statements, philosophical and moral propositions .... The apparatus itself is *the system of relations* that can be established between these elements' (*Id.* 1977, 299, *italic added*).[20] So, if it is possible to analyse media coverage as a set of 'framing devices' (Gamson and Modigliani 1989), connecting representation and political decisions, the whole framing process is a device in itself; an apparatus. Salience and selection (Entman 1993, 52) are also relevant to this 'system of relations', to connections and ties between the elements involved. A central element is, therefore, coherence in the set of representations, even if it is composed of distinct elements. When these elements become a set – not necessarily solid or stable, but at least with its own coherence – it is possible to talk about an apparatus, that, in analytical terms, can thus be considered (and named) in the singular: the 'emergency frame', the 'securitarian' one, that 'of hospitality' and so on.

The field of representation, as a system or configuration of objective relations between different positions, which for Bourdieu (1980) are often in conflict with each other, can instead show representations that are highly consensual (Maneri 1998) if they support widespread ideological positions on fear, exclusion and confinement of the Other. These stances are hegemonic, being perceived as obvious, natural and non-mediated. Media, thus, fulfil an ideological function (Hall et al. 1978), stating and restating the rules (real or hoped for) and defining as deviant behaviours or individuals who appear to disrupt a social order represented as desirable *per se*: the focus on images such as the 'illegal invader' (or the 'criminal immigrant' or 'dangerous immigrant') becomes crucial in order to build a consensus around exceptional and emergency measures for the symbolic defence of a space presented as *our* space under siege.

NOTES

1. For example, since 18 October 2013, various armed forces, the police and in particular the Italian Navy are involved in a 'humanitarian military mission' called 'Mare Nostrum' (see http://www.marina.difesa.it/EN/operations/Pagine/MareNostrum.aspx). The goal is 'to counter the landings' by patrolling the triangle between Malta, the coast of Libya and Sicily. Aircraft, amphibious ships, drones, as well as helicopters with infrared optical instruments, are being used (see www.ansa.it). For an analysis of the ambiguity of the mission, mainly relating to rules of engagement, objectives and costs, see http://www.ispionline.it/it/pubblicazione/mare-nostrum1-pro-e-contro-della-missione-militare-dellitalia-9254.

2. The Italian media system is characterised, at least in mainstream and *free to air* channels, by the so-called 'tv duopoly': on the one hand, the public broadcasting service (RAI), on the other hand, the Mediaset Group (owned by former prime minister Silvio Berlusconi). This ownership structure has clearly led to much controversy because of the fact that in the years of the Berlusconi centre-right government, almost the entire television system unconditionally supported his policies, with the exception of RAI-3, historically oriented to left parties (the Communist Party first and then the Democratic Party). Only in recent years have other broadcasters such as Sky (Murdoch Group) and LA7 gained in strength and influence; they are very focused on news and have a more neutral editorial policy. Overall, the Press system appears more differentiated, with newspapers and magazines representing in their editorial policies different political–cultural orientations (especially on the left-right axis); the two major editorial groups are RCS-Corriere della Sera (moderate-conservative) and Gruppo L'Espresso-La Repubblica (progressive). In general, on the theme of migration a consensus on a predominantly *securitarian* vision emerges, sometimes even in newspapers that could be described as 'progressive' (i.e. La Repubblica). There are some exceptions , particularly the news of RAI-3 and some small newspapers (historically linked to the left parties).

3. See Idos-Unar 2014; Caritas-Migrantes 2007–2011; Istat 2014. On the more general role of the figure of the migrant in contemporary society and on its criminalisation, see, among others, Palidda 2011a.

4. The same source estimates that the data is actually slightly higher (approx. 5,364,000 people) than the 8.8 per cent.

5. Estimates by different sources: Caritas-Migrantes 2007–2011; Idos-Unar 2014; Cesnur, www.cesnur.org. These are all evaluations based on data by the Italian Ministry of Internal Affairs.

6. On this spatial and territorial dimension in the discourse on the *Other*, see also Bruno 2014a. On the issue of arrivals and the so-called 'boat people', in relation to

the securitarian dimension in contexts other than the Italian one see Pickering 2001; Khosravinik 2009; Pugh 2004.

7. The network involves researchers from the 'Sapienza' University of Rome, the 'LUMSA' University of Rome, the universities of Verona, Turin, Bologna, Florence, Bergamo, Venice, Palermo and Milan 'Bicocca'. The network does not operate with a stable funding programme; only some sections of the surveys were funded by UNHCR, through the 'Associazione Carta di Roma'.

8. www.cartadiroma.org.

9. In this text, we will also show examples taken from newspapers and newscast. These surveys were conducted on different media formats, by the writer and, in parallel, by Francesca Ieracitano and Camilla Rumi ('LUMSA' University of Rome) and Maurizio Corte (University of Verona). See Ieracitano, Rumi 2014.

10. The court has recognised that Italy violated the European Convention on Human Rights and in particular the principle of *non-refoulement*, which prohibits the repatriation of migrants to countries where they may be persecuted or subjected to inhuman or degrading treatment. The court has upheld an appeal by a group of Somali and Eritrean citizens collected at sea by an Italian patrol boat in 2009 and handed over to Libya without having the possibility to submit an Asylum application. European Court of Human Rights – 23 February 2012 Judgment no. 27765/2009. For an analysis of the judgement, see Nascimbene 2012.

11. Statement given by the then Minister of the Interior on 17 March 2010: www1. adnkronos.com/Archivio/AdnAgenzia/2010/03/17/Politica/Immigrati-Maroni-la-Bossi-Fini-non-si-tocca_185518.php.

12. Italian media that have in the main gone along with this process.

13. See also Bertolucci 2013. The theme became very significant in 2013, both from a quantitative point of view and in relation to narrative models, especially concerning the nature of two key events that affected the way the theme of landings was treated: the visit of Pope Francis in Lampedusa (July 2013) and the shipwreck in early October that caused more than 360 deaths.

14. Terms and phrases here and later in the text appearing between the symbols <and> are reported verbatim as they appear within the media contents analysed.

15. On the categorisation of the various figures and in particular on international protection and asylum seekers, see O'Doherty, Lecouteur 2007; Gale 2004; Van Gorp 2005.

16. On media and the definition of *social problems*, it is essential to make a reference to Cohen, Young 1981; see also Gusfield 1967; Hall et al. 1978.

17. On the topic, see Bruno 2014a. Other examples of the use of numbers and *reification* of the alarm are the titles from various newscasts: 'landings in Lampedusa, over 285 Libyan people arrive on a boat', 'Lampedusa: 300 refugees landed', 'Emergency landings in Lampedusa, still 1000 refugees'. Also on the radio: 'Lampedusa, 231 rescued migrants', 'In Sardinia landing of 15 Tunisians', '1042 refugees arrived between last night and this morning in Lampedusa aboard of 4 boats set off from Libya'.

18. On the subject, see also Cvajner, Sciortino 2010.

19. See also Cesari 2004: in particular her notes about the 'metadiscourse' by the majority about the Islamic minority in Europe and the weight of some labels utilised.

20. See also Agamben 2006. I follow Agamben in the translation of *dispositif* to English as *apparatus*, while also being mindful of Bussolini's (2010) highlighting the problem of such a translation (and who instead proposes the term *dispositive*).

Chapter 3

'You Can't Have Muslim Irish Children' Media, Islamophobia and Ireland

Constructing Different Shades of Green

James Carr

Very little research exists on the role of the media in constructing Muslims and Islam as Other in the Irish context; less still on the perceptions of Muslim men and women towards various media outlets. This chapter bridges this gap.[1] A brief history of Muslim communities in Ireland is followed by a theoretical discussion of the role of racialising processes in constructing Muslims as outside of Irishness. This is followed by insights into the lived experiences of anti-Muslim racism in Ireland, focussing here in particular on the manner in which Muslimness and Irishness are constructed as incompatible. The latter half of this chapter critically looks at the role of the media in the propagation of anti-Muslim discourses internationally before turning to specifically investigate the role of the media in Ireland. Drawing on original research, this chapter provides heretofore absent perspectives of members of Muslim communities in Ireland towards the media and the manner in which they construct difference.

MUSLIM MIGRATION TO IRELAND

The presence of Muslims in Ireland can be traced as far back as the 1700s; however, it was not until the second half of the twentieth century that an established Muslim presence on the island emerged (Scharbrodt 2012, 226–27). In the late 1950s, numbering less than three-hundred, the first representative Muslim group became organised, and comprised predominantly of visiting medical students (Flynn 2006; Sakaranaho 2006; Scharbrodt 2012). Student-centric migration, albeit not exclusively, continued to form the basis of Muslim communities in Ireland through the 1970s and into the 1980s

(Sakaranaho 2006, 280–81; Scharbrodt 2012, 228–29). The 1990s witnessed a growth of Muslim communities in Ireland, and combined with generational growth, the numbers grew from under 4000 in 1991 to almost 50,000 in 2011 (Central Statistics Office 2012). In addition to economic migrants, these new arrivals included people fleeing conflict in Bosnia, Kosovo, Somalia and Iraq (Flynn 2006, 223; Sakaranaho 2006, 271; Scharbrodt 2012, 235–36). These new migrants added to established Irish Muslim communities, including Irish reverts to Islam (Scharbrodt and Sakaranaho 2011, 473).[2]

Muslim communities in Ireland are vibrant in their diversity and, in addition to Irish-born Muslims, include a broad range of ethnicities and nationalities as well as multifarious linguistic, cultural and ideological perspectives. A number of Islamic religious traditions are represented in Ireland, most notably the majority Sunni community, a large Shi'a community numbering approximately 4000, and a small Ahmadiyya community predominantly based in the west of Ireland (Sakaranaho 2006, 279; Scharbrodt 2012, 222; Scharbrodt and Sakaranaho 2011, 474–77). Despite their myriad diversity, Muslim communities are the subject of international processes of racialisation that set Muslims apart as Other, and they experience a specific racism that targets Muslimness.

RACIALISING MUSLIMS

According to Carr and Haynes (2013, 2),

> Racialisation is an ideological process utilized to justify or explain social stratification, inclusion or exclusion. Through this process, social groups are characterized (or self-identify) as embodying proclivities toward certain ascribed attributes and behaviours. Derived from fiction or fragmented 'fact', but always deemed innate, these operate on multifarious grounds including phenotype, ethnicity and/or religious identity. Different facets of the racialised being may be refracted through gender, class or sexuality; but there remains a core racialised identity.

Internationally, Muslim communities have been in the cross-hairs of racialised discourses at the interrelated levels of the political, institutional and public. The tropes that infuse these discourses share a striking similarity, replete with notions of atavism, terrorist threat, misogyny and of an alleged incompatibility with 'our Western values' (Allen 2010; Carr and Haynes 2013; Carr 2016). Historic imaginings of belonging frequently interact with more contemporary claims of Muslim Otherness. In the Spanish context, mosques have been vandalised with abusive terms that refer to historical notions of nation, including the term 'F****** Moors'. In Sweden, graffiti such as 'Keep Sweden Swedish' has been daubed on the walls of mosques. In Austria, Muslim women wearing the hijab are variously taunted as 'Turkish pig' or called 'barbarian culture ... terrorist' (European Monitoring Centre on Racism and Xenophobia 2006, 66–89). In addition to overt anti-Muslim hostility and criminal damage to Islamic sites, research in France also demonstrates the grating of Muslim religious practices and historical French secularist tendencies towards *laïcité* (Ameli et al. 2012; Open Society Foundations, 2011).[3] The aftermath of the attacks in early 2015 on the offices of *Charlie Hebdo* and on a kosher supermarket in Paris that resulted in the murder of seventeen people was replete with simplistic racialised discourses of an alleged incompatibility between Islam and the 'West' (Fekete 2015; Hassan 2015; Ramadan 2015; Younge 2015).

In Ireland, Muslim men and women are stereotyped and stigmatised in ways that reflect the interaction between historical, local and international discourses of Muslimness and belonging (Carr and Haynes 2013; Carr 2016). As I will demonstrate below, anti-Muslim racism in the Irish context manifests in a manner that evidences global racialised discourses of Muslim as Other which interweave with local, historically informed practices of autoracialisation (Miles and Brown 2003) that construct notions of 'acceptable Irishness'. As a result of these multiple processes of racialisation, Muslims are doubly racialised as a homogeneous threat to 'Western' society and as beyond the boundaries of Irishness (Carr and Haynes 2013).

METHODOLOGY

This chapter is based on original research that focused primarily on the lived experiences of anti-Muslim racism in the Irish context. Fieldwork commenced early in 2011, with contacts within Muslim communities in multiple locations across fourteen towns and cities in Ireland agreeing to take part in the study. Efforts were made to access as broad a constituency of participants as possible by acknowledging diversity in terms of Islamic tradition, religiosity, gender, age, nationality and ethnicity.

The quantitative findings of this study are derived from a survey, based on a non-representative sample of 323 Muslim men and women. While the sample might not be statistically representative, the gender distribution of the survey sample is remarkably comparable to the 2011 Irish Census; further, in terms of national origins, 51 different countries of birth are represented in the sample encompassing European, African, South Asian, American and Middle Eastern states. This initial quantitative phase was followed by seven in-depth interviews and three focus group discussions with Muslim participants purposively sampled to be inclusive of both males and females and representing a diverse range of ethnic and national backgrounds, including converts to Islam.

ANTI-MUSLIM RACISM IN IRELAND

There is a dearth of data on the rates and experiences of anti-Muslim racism in Ireland. Therefore, the findings related here break new ground in our understanding of this phenomenon in the Irish context. The first phase of this study comprised of a survey of Muslim men and women and commenced by asking all those who took part if they had experienced some form of hostility in the period from January 2010.[4, 5] Just over half of all participants indicated that they experienced some form of hostility in that timeframe. Over one-in-three (36 per cent of) survey participants felt they had been targeted on the basis of being identified as Muslim.

The manner in which this hostility manifested varied. The predominant form of hostility experienced was verbal assault (81 per cent). The verbal abuse meted out frequently made direct reference to the contemporary form of racialised Muslim identity, indicative of an internationalised prejudicial image of Muslims and Islam. Participants also reported experiencing physical assaults (22 per cent), which ranged from being struck, or having hijabs forcibly removed, to being pushed, and/or spat at. Others reported being threatened or harassed (20 per cent). A white Irish male convert to Islam recalls his experiences of physical forms of abuse: 'I have been pushed and have had people spit in my face, for being Muslim'. Fewer participants (14 per cent) indicated that they had property damaged. Those who detailed how this manifested referred to tyres being slashed, having eggs thrown at their home, inter alia. Unlike in other jurisdictions, attacks on Muslim property such as mosques did not feature in this study. Arguably, this may be the result of a paucity of recognisably Islamic structures in Ireland.

As with data on anti-Muslim hostility, there is also a dearth of official information on discrimination as experienced by Muslims in Ireland on the basis of their religious identity. Participants were asked about their experiences of discrimination in the period from January 2010.[6] One-third of all participants indicated that they had experienced anti-Muslim discrimination. As with anti-Muslim hostility, experiences of discrimination were heavily gendered, with Muslim women (40 per cent) almost twice as likely as Muslim men (22 per cent) to experience anti-Muslim discrimination. It is worth noting at this point that there are striking similarities between the experiences of participants here and the experience of anti-Muslim racism in international studies (see Poynting and Noble 2004). In what follows, I will briefly engage with the constructed incompatibility of Irishness and Muslimness before moving to the role of the media in the processes of racialisation.

DIFFERENT SHADES OF GREEN

Historical constructions of Irishness evince the shifting influence of power. During colonisation, and resonating long since, Irishness was constructed as atavistic, heathen and ape-like (Fanning 2002; Rattansi 2007). These discourses and associated imagery were utilised to legitimate colonisation by the British establishment and maintain the position of those with power over the Irish, who were constructed as the inept Other unable to govern themselves. As Garner (2009, 6) puts it, "'The legitimisation of English rule had always been based on the perceived civilizational discrepancy between the English and the Irish'", where the former is presented as civilised. In the period leading up to Irish independence, a counter-construction of Irishness that recalled a mythical halcyon Gaelic era was invoked, which also associated Catholicness and whiteness as inherent elements of Irish identity. In the decades since independence, this image of Gaelic Catholic Irishness came to occupy the institutions of state, structuring notions of belonging in Ireland along these autoracialised lines (Garner 2009; Miles and Brown 2003; Tracey 2000).

Muslims participating in this research elaborated on their experiences of differentiation, exclusion and eviction from the dominant imagining of Irishness. They were not Catholic; regardless of actual phenotypical characteristics, they were racialised as non-white; and those from an immigrant background were further marked out as Other regardless of the fact that Ireland was now their home. Labelled as 'different' from dominant constructions of Irishness in so many ways, participants recalled regular experiences wherein their national belonging was challenged. These included being told to 'go home' or to 'go back to where you come from':

'I participate in Dawah – calling others to Islam. I get called names, told to go home to my own country'. (Khalid, white Irish male)

The perceived 'natural' incompatibility of Muslimness with notions of Irishness was central to the experiences of participants who were regularly subjected to the vocalisation of the idea that Islamic faith and Irishness are mutually exclusive.

'"You're Irish and you're Muslim, wearing that thing on your head?" ... They do think that you have to be white and you have to be ... Catholic to be Irish'. (Ghadir, white Irish female Muslim)

'As an Irish girl ... I think basically you sometimes ... lose your identity. ... They forget that, you know, just because I put a scarf on my
head. ... I'm still Irish'. (Aalia, white Irish female Muslim)

In the context of the Irish 'decade of commemorations', it is worth noting that
Aalia recalled that members of her family participated in the 1916 Rising and
was keen to underscore her Irish identity.[7]

Like Aalia, Aatif is also a white Irish Muslim. He recalled one of his experiences upon returning to Ireland after living abroad:

'So [I am] a white guy, walking down the street with his wife who is
wearing niqab, wearing hijab and the veil, and I am pushing a pram with
our son. ... I was shocked to ... have an Irish person come up, look at
the child in the pram and turn around and say, "Yeah well definitely that
child can't be Irish you know" and I looked at the person and I said,
"What are you talking about?" and he said "No. You know, it can't be
an Irish child; you can't have Muslim Irish children"'. (Aatif, white Irish
male Muslim)

Racialised as non-Irish, these reverts to Islam – although the bearers of
some markers of belonging, namely being white, heterosexual, Irish born and
sedentary – are subjected to public challenges on the basis of their religion.
Neither whiteness nor other traditional symbols of Irishness are sufficient
proof of authenticity to protect them from the instantly exclusionary effect
of identification with racialised Islam. The pervasive perception of dichot-
omised Irishness and Muslimness is also evidenced in the experiences of
exclusion in institutional interactions:

'I knew straight away, he doesn't think I'm Irish, he doesn't know I'm
Irish, right? So, he asked, "Do you have residence? Do you have your
GNIB card?" Right? And I went, "Oh Garda, you're here to investigate
a car being hit, not whether we have residence or permit or whatever,
that's secondary". And that's ... when he asked me, "Where are you
from ... tell me where you're from, where do you live?" I said ...
"I'm from Ireland, I'm born in Ireland, I'm Irish"'. (Aatif, relating an
exchange with a member of the Irish police service)

Van Nieuwkerk's (2004) research in the Dutch context illuminates the
perceived incompatibility of Muslimness and national identity. The lived
experiences of participants in my study demonstrate the manner in which
embodying identities deemed other than the norm of Irishness result in the
visible policing of the boundaries of racialised belonging.

I suppose the worst case I had was when a man ... he came up and he said, 'Take that rag thing off your head. ... You're too good looking for that and ... you're betraying Ireland. ... You were born Christian, what did you have to change for?' (Jada, white Irish female)

When I said I was Irish, that's when he changed. He was like, 'How can you be Muslim and you're Irish? Why did you change your religion?' (Zaheen, white Irish female)

MEDIA, POWER AND REPRESENTATION

I now focus on the role of the media as a powerful location where racialised discourses arise. According to Frost (2008, 554), 'British and non-British Muslims have been criminalised and demonised not only in the press but also by the government through oppressive anti-terrorist measures'. Fekete (2009, 44–47) concurs stating that in the contemporary context 'the media has combined with the current political and security agenda to create a culture of suspicion against Muslims'. Likewise, I recognise the interrelationship of outlets of racialised discourses and I am keen to stress that I do not argue that media are the only sites where racialised tropes of otherness are (re)produced. Indeed, uncritical engagements with such discourses at the level of the individual frequently result in the 'you and me' recycling of racialised imagery. It is vital that we encourage critical engagement if we are to challenge the promulgation of discourses of otherness.

Edward Said (1997), writing prior to 9/11, noted the manner in which Muslims and Muslim majority societies were encapsulated under a homogenous, pejoratively framed catch-all descriptor of 'Islam'. While acknowledging the various conflicts and acts of terrorism engaged with by a minority in the name of Islam, Said (1997) underscores how analyses of these conflicts often elide their structural underpinnings. Instead, they are presented as core to the faith of Islam, definitional by association of the behaviour of all Muslim men and women regardless of the diversity in Muslim communities throughout the world. Said (1997, xvi) notes how in relation to 'analyses' of Islam:

Instead of scholarship, we often find only journalists making extravagant statements, which are instantly picked up and further dramatized by the media. ... Given the tendency to reduce Islam to a handful of rules, stereotypes, and generalisations about the faith, its founder, and all of its people, then the reinforcement of every negative fact associated with Islam – its violence, primitiveness, atavism, threatening qualities – is perpetuated.

This process has continued in the years since Said's (1997) analysis. In the immediate aftermath of the attacks in Norway in 2011, so-called media experts were quick to apportion blame for these atrocities on some, indeed any, 'Islamist' group. The *Sun* newspaper in the United Kingdom ran with the headline: '*Al-Qaeda Massacre: Norway's 9/11*', even though it was quickly established that this was the work of a right-wing extremist (Brooker 2011). Githens-Mazer and Lambert argue that if the manner in which Muslims are vilified was meted out to other vulnerable social groups, there would be public outrage (Githens-Mazer and Lambert 2010), raising the question: Why are Islamophobic sentiments, regardless of their source, allowed to persist? I argue that this lack of condemnation *vis-a-vis* anti-Muslim sentiment is a noted aspect in contemporary Islamophobic discourses. There is today an acceptability and normalisation of Islamophobia. The role of the media in this normalisation cannot be ignored (Allen and Nielsen 2002).

Allen (2010, 99) argues that the media play a pivotal role in 'communicating and disseminating ideas and meanings about Muslims and Islam', discourses that are replete with stereotypical images. Stereotypical characterisations communicated through the media associate Muslim identity with cultural deviance, terrorist activity and notions of threat (Frost 2008, 565). These stereotypical representations operate through generalisation wherein all members of the social group in question become associated with the stereotype, while all diversity within these communities is denied (Frost 2008). These 'stereotypes serve as mental short-hands' which both the producer and the audience can read and understand (Haynes 2007, 177). Media actors in a given social context (e.g. the so-called 'war on terror') can encourage racist prejudice through re-presentations of group identities that actively transmit 'stereotypes of one group to other groups' (Hall cited in Frost 2008, 570). The process of transmitting meaning through the recurrent use of stereotypical imagery in relation to Islam serves to normatively position Muslim communities as the Other in Western discourses, stigmatising Muslim identity, regularly conflating the faith of Islam with terms such as fundamentalist or terrorist, and constructing them as 'truth' (Allen 2010; Baker 2010). Moreover, the process of stigmatisation cultivates a hostile attitude towards Muslim communities legitimising hostility and discrimination (Frost 2008; Frost 2008a). Of course, this is not denying agency with regard to how individual people receive and interpret or 'decode' media messages (Allen and Nielsen 2002; Hussain 2000). Furthermore, it is also important to note that not all media actors are the same; there are differences to be found among media producers in relation to how they engage with Islamic issues and in terms of the images of Muslims they convey (Baker 2010). Thus while it can be argued that media actors play their part in directing how minority groups are perceived socially, which in the case of Muslims is an image of threat, it is not simply a case of dictating perspectives (Frost 2008a). Nonetheless, I concur with Lewis et al. that 'journalism specifically seeks to persuade its audience that a particular version of events is ... "true"' (Lewis et al. 2011, 42). While the media is only one of the cultural institutions through which racialising constructions are transmitted, these organisations play an important role in constructing Muslim identity in the public imaginary (Baker 2010; Lewis et al. 2011).

There has been an increased focus on Muslims in the British print media since the terrorist attacks in New York in 2001 (Lewis et al. 2011). In 2006, the Greater London Authority commissioned research into the manner in which the press represented Muslims and their faith in a 'normal week', that is, a week devoid of anything that may unduly influence the level of coverage afforded to Muslim issues. The findings of this analysis demonstrated that stories involving Muslims had increased by two-hundred and seventy per cent when compared with a 1996 study. Further, over 90 per cent of coverage negatively represented Muslims/Islam, while half referred to Muslims/Islam as threatening (Allen 2010). Between the years 2000 and 2008, Lewis et al. (2011) conducted an analysis of images and discourse of the manner in which the British print media represent Muslims and their faith, encompassing nine-hundred and seventy-four articles, focussing on 'everyday' news coverage of Muslims. They identify what is described as the three most 'common "news hooks"' in Muslim-related reports in the British print media. These include 'terrorism, or the war on terror', 'religious or cultural issues' and 'Muslim extremism'. When combined, these categories totalled almost 70 per cent of all stories related to Muslims (Lewis et al. 2011, 45–48). Such repeated exposure to pathologising depictions of Muslims and Islam increases the likelihood that these representations will be internalised as 'truths', leaving an indelible mark on those reading such constructions (Allen 2010, 99).

According to Frost (2008a), knowledge of Islam amongst the non-Muslim population is for the most part limited to that which is communicated through the media. Hussain (2000, 100) also contends that where access to other sources of information is limited, our 'cognitive frames of interpretation and understanding in that area of knowledge and information are provided for the most part by media discourses', discourses that for Muslims are mainly negative. Indeed, a 2010 *YouGov* (see Inspired by Muhammed 2015) opinion poll of UK adults illustrated that almost 60 per cent of respondents cited television news as their primary source of information about Islam, while 41 per cent obtain their information about Islam from the print media. Nearly two-thirds of these respondents stated that they did not know very much about Islam, with 17 per cent knowing nothing at all. Moreover, almost 70 per cent claimed they believed Islam was repressive of women;

almost 60 per cent associated Islam with 'extremism', while half associated the faith with terrorism (see Inspired by Muhammed 2015). Moreover, Lewis et al. (2011) found that the focus on the supposed Muslim/non-Muslim cultural schism rose from under 10 per cent in 2002 to almost two-thirds of all print media reports by 2008, actually surpassing terrorism in prominence *vis-a-vis* British Muslims. Indeed, 80 per cent of the British national press 'associate Islam/Muslims with threats ... or opposition to dominant British values' (Lewis et al. 2011, 47–48). Issues involving cultural difference and/or incompatibility focussed on veiling by Muslim women, questions of Sharia law and the relationship between Britain and the Islamic faith (Lewis et al. 2011).

Contrary to the speed at which negative news images related to Muslims and Islam circulate, reports of the rights of Muslims or judgements of innocence in cases involving assumptions of terrorist activity fail to attract the same level of attention. Research conducted by the Institute of Race Relations in the United Kingdom has demonstrated that while media actors have in the past given high levels of coverage to arrests made under the anti-terrorism legislation, subsequent findings of innocence and admissions that individuals were wrongly arrested have not attracted the same level of attention (Frost 2008). Lewis et al. (2011) discovered that media discourse in respect to the rights of Muslims and the defence of these rights had actually decreased during the period of 2000–2008, with UK media interest in Islamophobia accounting for only 5 per cent of coverage.

Irish Media Representations

In the Irish context, media actors have played their part in the discursive chorus that stereotypically characterises all Muslims as terrorist fundamentalists through sensationalist reportage depicting Muslim communities as the 'enemy within', fuelling what Cole (2011, 128) refers to as the perception of Muslims as the 'green menace'. In the past decade, press headlines on Muslim communities in Ireland have included 'Fascist fundamentalism is rife among young Irish Muslims' or 'The green jihadis' published in 2006 (see National Consultative Committee on Racism and Interculturalism 2007, 1–2) and more recently 'Al Qaeda's Irish Terror Cell: Jihad fanatics hiding out amongst us' (McElgunn 2011). Exposure to repeated pathologising depictions of Muslims and Islam increases the likelihood that these representations will be internalised as 'truths', leaving an indelible mark on those reading such constructions (Allen 2010, 99). Calls have, thus, been made for greater press accountability in relation to reportage of Muslim communities. It is argued that more responsible, accountable media reporting could help dispel the 'truth' that currently circulates about Muslim identity (Frost 2008a).

The role of the media in constructing Muslims as Other was not lost on participants. Repeatedly during this study casual conversations with key stakeholders and potential research participants evinced an unexpected readiness to lay blame at the feet of media actors. Problematically, this focus on the media diverted attention from the role of state actors and securitisation policies that are negatively biased towards Muslims as a suspect community (Fekete 2009). Curious of perceptions of the role of the media, the first, quantitative phase of this included a question which asked participants if they had witnessed or encountered anti-Muslim sentiment in Irish-based print, web or broadcast media. Over one in four (26 per cent) participants stated that they had indeed witnessed anti-Muslim sentiment on/by Irish media outlets. On appearance, this number is arguably small. However, this study focused specifically on *Irish* media outlets, given the lack of research in this area. Thus, if taken to include *all* experiences of media representations of Muslim communities, this percentage may have been much higher. In terms of locations, the quotes below, derived from responses to open questions in the questionnaire, demonstrate a perception of the fluency of anti-Muslim discourses in moving across various, different, but often interrelated media forums.

Radio:

'On Monday evenings [national radio show presenter] speaks to [contributor] from Boston, Massachusetts who always has (anti)Muslim rhetoric!!'

'Radio … the speaker demonise Islam and Muslims, and says bad things which are not even true, he is attacking us almost every morning' (Local Cork station)

Online:

'Very harsh and extremely provocative language used in comments by users in on-line version of The Independent about a news item related to a [Muslim] family living in Canada; very bad language used'

'boards.ie had a thread about the islamisation of Ireland'

'The Irish Independent/Politics.ie and a host of other outlets constantly help fuel Islamophobia'

Television:

> 'Newspaper journalist and blogger for "Irish ... ." (Can't remember name or newspaper but was on a documentary on RTE1 following his time staying and chatting to Muslims across Ireland)'

Print:

> 'I can't remember which Irish newspaper it was, but it had an article about how Libya is better off with its leader [Muammar Gaddafi] because otherwise terrorists would be running the country'

Participants also noted their interactions with some media representatives and the manner in which these 'journalists' sought out sensationalist stories about Muslim communities and Islam in Ireland, endeavouring to further construct the image of the risky, suspect Islamic Other:

> 'When Osama bin Laden was murdered ... reporters were interviewing the Muslim students in University. They manipulate the students' words and wrote in a way [that presented] the students [as] supporting war on terrorism, if we refused they accused us of supporting the militants'.

The research presented here illuminates the role of the media in Ireland in constructing Muslims as Other. The original insights on the perceptions of Muslim communities in Ireland towards media representations of those who practise their faith offers the heretofore un-researched perspectives of those in the cross-hairs of racialising processes in the Irish context. These are valuable contributions that can be usefully deployed as a foundation from which further detailed analyses of media representations of Muslim communities in Ireland can be based. This future research is vital if the racialising discourses of Muslim Otherness in the Irish context are to be challenged.

CONCLUSION

The evidence presented in this chapter demonstrates the reality of anti-Muslim racism in Ireland. Chiming with the experiences of Muslim communities in various international contexts, Muslims in Ireland are in the cross hairs of racialising processes that construct Muslimness as a threatening, risky Other. As has been argued, the media, while not alone, play a central role in (re)producing racialised tropes that inform public perceptions of Islam and Muslim identities. Stereotypical media representations, generalised and extended to all Muslims, construct these communities as a homogenous

group who are then racialised as innately anathema to an equally erroneously homogenised 'West'. Ireland is no exception. The evidence presented
above clearly demonstrates the problematic manner in which media represent
Muslim communities in Ireland. These representations are not lost on participants, who are acutely aware of the role of the media in presenting Muslims
as suspect and un-belonging to Ireland. The media are not the only source of
racialising discourses, neither are all media actors equally culpable in (re)pro-
ducing these discursive constructions. Nonetheless, the evidence presented
in this chapter clearly places the role of the media in sharp relief and raises
even more questions in terms of the extent of, and the dominant actors in,
anti-Muslim reportage. In conclusion, I would argue that it is only through
informed, critical and detailed analysis that the role of the media in Othering
Muslims can be challenged.

NOTES

1. The research conducted for this chapter was funded by the Irish Research Council Postgraduate Scholarship 2010–2013.

2. Some, not all, Muslims for theological reasons which I will not engage with further here refer to those who choose to become Muslim or convert in Christian terms
as reverts to Islam. I use the term 'revert' to reflect what I feel is a term closer to the
Islamic understanding of conversion.

3. In principle, *laïcité* refers to the practice of separation between church and state
in France (Akan 2009). According to Tariq Modood, 'French laicite ... seeks to create
a public space in which religion is virtually banished in the name of reason and eman-
cipation, and religious organisations are monitored by the state through consultative
national mechanisms' (2012, 136).

4. Participants were first asked if they had experienced hostility, anytime from
January 2010, in the following forms: physical assault, theft, graffiti (home or work),
damage to property, verbal assault, threats or harassment. I placed an emphasis
on ascertaining the extent to which people felt that they were or were not selected
because they were Muslim. If participants answered 'yes' to any of the aforementioned options, subsequent questions enquired whether or not they felt that this happened because they were identified as Muslim.

5. The survey was distributed in September 2011 and closed in June 2012.

6. Participants were asked if they had experienced discrimination in the following
spheres: at work, looking for work, in/accessing education, accessing health services,
restaurants, public transport, obtaining accommodation and accessing financial services. If participants answered 'yes' to any of these options, subsequent questions
enquired whether or not they felt that this happened because they were identified as
Muslim.

7. A range of significant centenaries occur between 2010 and 2020, marking key
events in Irish history. See http://www.decadeofcentenaries.com/about/.

Chapter 4

Drawing Discursive Boundaries in US News Coverage of the 'Honour Killing' of Noor Almaleki

Autumn M. Reed

THE MURDER OF NOOR ALMALEKI

On 20 October 2009, in a parking lot in Phoenix, Arizona, 49-year-old Faleh Hassan Almaleki climbed behind the wheel of his Jeep Grand Cherokee and ran over two women – his 20-year-old daughter, Noor Almaleki, and her boyfriend's mother, 43-year-old Amal Khalaf. A seriously injured Amal survived, but Noor died two weeks later. From the day of the hit-and-run in 2009, to Faleh's conviction for second-degree murder and aggravated assault in February 2011, the national US and local Arizona news have covered the murder as an example of yet another 'honour killing' of a young 'Westernised' woman by her Muslim, Middle Eastern and/or South Asian father.[1]

This chapter uses a critical discourse analysis (CDA) to uncover how US news narratives of the 'honour killing' of Noor Almaleki are a discursive site for the construction of 'bright' boundaries between members of the Muslim, Middle Eastern and South Asian (M/ME/SA) minority communities and majority members of the US nation. Illuminating these bright boundaries shows how 'honour-killing' news coverage speaks to debates about the disruption of US cultural identity, in which conversations about mitigating violence against women are secondary. A CDA of headlines, lexical choices, voice and metaphors substantiates how gendered, ethnic, national and religious differences intimately link the murder of a single woman to metadiscourses of immigration regarding questions of national belonging and the societal and national security of the US nation.

DISCOURSE AND BOUNDARY CONSTRUCTION

Discourse(s) are 'a group of statements which provide a language for talking about – a way of representing knowledge – ... a particular topic at a particular historical moment. ... Discourse is about the production of knowledge through language' (Hall 1997, 44). Korteweg and Yurdakul (2009, 219) note, as discourses produce knowledge, they also 'provid[e] shared meaning through which to articulate belonging [and non-belonging] to social groups[,]' in particular, to national majority social groups. Membership in the national community is often determined by conformity to the dominant cultural values as expressed in the intersecting social constructs of gender, sexuality, race/ethnicity, culture, religion and class.

Korteweg and Yurdakul (2009) identify two types of discursive boundaries; *bright* and *blurred*, which also correspond with *absorptive* and *blurred* material patterns of national belonging. Bright boundaries 'imply that society is structured around a sharp distinction between "insiders and outsiders" so that individual members of minority groups (but not groups in their entirety) can cross into majority society only if they give up part of their group identity and adopt some of the practices of majority society' (Korteweg and Yurdakul 2009, 219). These bright boundaries signal a climate of absorptive assimilation, in which minority groups must shed their cultural practices in favour of those of the national majority. Conversely, Korteweg and Yurdakul (2009) argue that blurred boundaries 'imply tolerance for various forms of difference and for multiple memberships in different groups so that, for example, an immigrant group can be considered Muslim and Dutch' (219). These blurred boundaries signal a climate of assimilation in which minority groups are able to integrate into majority society, without giving up all of their cultural practices. As discursive constructions, bright and blurred boundaries co-exist and overlap with one another; however, one boundary type is hegemonic.

BOUNDARY DRAWING IN WESTERN EUROPEAN 'HONOUR-KILLING' NEWS COVERAGE

Korteweg and Yurdakul (2009; 2010) examine news coverage of 'honour killings' in Western Europe and Canada in order to demonstrate the discursive formation of bright and blurred boundaries between the M/ME/ SA minority community and majority national groups. Additionally, they identify three prevailing forms of 'honour-killing' discourses in the news: *stigmatising*, which draw on ethno-national or religious explanations for the practice; *culture-blind*, which draw on domestic violence and isolate gender and patriarchy as the culprits; and *context-specific*, which view 'honour killings' as a form of violence within certain minority communities but do not stigmatise these communities. Their findings show how bright and blurred boundaries, the type of 'honour-killing' discourses and the differences emphasised depend on each nation's politics of location with the M/ME/SA minority community.

Research on 'honour-killing' news stories in Western European nations such as the United Kingdom (Gill 2006; Meetoo and Mizra 2007), Germany (Ehrkamp 2010) and Sweden (Reimers 2007) substantiate Korteweg's and Yurdakul's (2009) claim that this coverage serves as a boundary-drawing arena. The research also demonstrates how 'honour-killing' news coverage is a venue for expressing fears surrounding societal and national security in Western European nations. Discourses about the on-going immigration crisis and threats of terrorism are frequently injected into 'honour-killing' news stories. Dicle Koğacıoğlu (2004, 138) contends that the news, particularly the international (read: Western) news' coverage of 'honour crimes', promotes 'anxiety over the transplantation of honour crimes into areas of the world that are not its "native habitat"'. Werbner (2005, 26) adds that the current Global War on Terror climate has 'raised tensions regarding the loyalty of Muslim citizens to the European states in which they have settled'. Overall, this research suggests that bright boundaries tend to prevail in 'honour-killing' news narratives, which limits the opportunities for M/ME/SA national inclusion. Often, the news portrays M/ME/SA men as violent national outsiders, while depicting M/ME/SA women as victims of oppressive gendered, ethnonational and religious practices, who must be saved and incorporated into the national community. These discursive formations illustrate the Orientalist rescue narrative of 'white men saving brown women from brown men' (Spivak 1994, 93). This connection situates 'honour-killing' news coverage within a larger paradigm of Western nations' tendency to focus on violence committed against 'other' women as means to legitimise their superiority. Consequently, the findings of this research illustrate that addressing violence against women is not the primary aim of 'honour-killing' news coverage; instead, the work of this coverage is complex, drawing on alarmist discourses of national and societal security to erect boundaries between majority members of Western European nations and M/ME/SA minority communities.

EMERGENT LITERATURE ON US 'HONOUR-KILLING' NEWS DISCOURSE

In the United States, there is a paucity of scholarship that considers the role of 'honour-killing' news narratives in the formation of boundaries between majority national members and the M/ME/SA minority community. Work by

Terman (2010) and Grewal (2013) are two notable exceptions. Both problematise the use of the terms 'honour' and 'honour killing' and point to how the Western media uses ethno-national, racial and religious distinctions to mark those involved with 'honour killings'; however, neither work focuses exclusively on the United States. Given the documented role of 'honour-killing' news coverage in forming boundaries in Western Europe, understanding how and what types of boundaries form in the US context requires immediate attention. The United States's politics of location with the Middle East and South Asia is distinct from that of Western Europe. For example, it was not until after World War II that the United States expressed direct interest in this region, and M/ME/SA minority communities did not begin to settle in the United States until the relaxation of immigration restrictions in 1965. One must also consider 9/11 and the United States's leading role in the Global War on Terror. Unquestionably, this unique history influences the discourses within US 'honour-killing' news coverage.

CRITICAL DISCOURSE ANALYSIS (CDA) OF NEWS TEXTS

The analysis presented here uses the 2009 'honour killing' of Noor Almaleki as a case study of the US news' representations of 'honour killings'. The dataset includes 147 news texts from 17 different US national (12 outlets, 72 texts) and local Arizona (5 outlets, 75 texts) news outlets from across the political spectrum. Spanning from the day of the hit-and-run to 31 August 2012, well over a year after the conviction of Faleh, the dataset demonstrates the national impact of the case. This study employs CDA to examine the texts. CDA is 'fundamentally interested in analyzing opaque as well as transparent structural relationships of dominance, discrimination, power and control as manifested in language' (Wodak and Meyer 2009, 10). CDA is most suitable for the study at hand, which is concerned with exposing the taken-for-granted power dynamics of national belonging expressed in the coverage of Noor's murder. This study employs Teun A. van Dijk's (1991, 2003) CDA approach, which investigates the discursive structures of headlines, lexical choices, voice and metaphors as powerful mechanisms that aid in the construction of boundaries of difference.

'HONOUR' IN THE HEADLINES

Headlines not only serve as titles for news texts, but also structure and foreshadow the content within a news story (van Dijk 1991). The headlines from the dataset brightly delineate boundaries through ethno-religious and cultural lexical markers that frame 'honour killings' as an M/ME/SA practice. The lexical term 'honour killing' appears in 52 per cent of the headlines (n = 76/147), while a second term, 'honour violence', appears in only two news texts. Examples include 'Muslim Man Guilty of "Honor-Killing" in Daughter's Death' (Schabner and Netter 2011) and 'Iraqi Father Guilty in "Honor Killing"' (Tang 2011). Even those headlines that use other such terms like 'ran over', 'ran down', 'killing', 'death', 'murder' or 'hit and run' instead of 'honour' signal this form of violence is un-American by using the ethnic marker, 'Iraqi', the religious marker, 'Islam' and the cultural marker 'Westernised'. Thus, whether identified as an 'honour killing' or murder, US news coverage of Noor's death is a fault line between majority members of the American nation and the M/ME/SA communities.

The frequency and contrasting lexical marking of Faleh and Noor, in such headlines as 'Police Charge Iraqi Father Who Allegedly Ran Over "Westernised" Daughter' (Saltzman 2009), exposes the gendered dimensions of bright boundary drawing. The headlines disproportionately focus on Faleh, who appears in 64 per cent (n = 94/147) of the headlines, as opposed to Noor, who appears in 42 per cent (n = 61/147) of the headlines. This disparity demonstrates how 'honour-killing' news texts, which apparently focus on the murdered woman, in reality emphasise the male perpetrator. If the coverage was truly concerned with violence against women, why do the headlines practically omit Amal, who was also seriously injured by Faleh?[2] This tendency demonstrates Liddle and Rai's (1998) contention that 'other' women are not the subject of the discourse, or in some cases, not even the objects, but merely grounds for other agendas in Western discourses about violence against their bodies. Moreover, such headlines explain that the 'honour killing' of a daughter for her 'Western' lifestyle choice indicates the refusal of M/ME/SA minority communities to adopt US national norms. Additionally, the 97 headlines that include Faleh ethno-nationally mark him as 'Iraqi' 33 per cent (n = 32/97) and religiously mark him as 'Muslim' 4 per cent (n = 4/97). Conversely, the 61 headlines that include Noor employ the cultural marker 'Westernised' 38 per cent (n = 23). Unlike her father, this cultural lexical marking signals Noor's inclusion in the US nation. Furthermore, the headline choices of 'daughter' and 'woman' to describe Noor and 'father', 'man', 'dad' and 'immigrant' to describe Faleh, rather than their first names, configures Noor as a symbol for all M/ME/SA women and Faleh as a symbol for all M/ME/SA men. This lack of specificity represents 'honour killing' as a collective M/ME/SA crime and demonstrates the operation of bright boundaries in which only a few, specifically 'Westernised' M/ME/SA women, like Noor, belong to the US nation, while M/ME/SA men, like Faleh, are excluded. This ethno-religious and cultural lexical marking foreshadows the voices included and the types of definitions for 'honour killings' present in the coverage.

DEFINING HONOUR KILLING: VOICE AND AUTHORITY

An analysis of voice, or who is authorised to speak within news stories, aids in the formation of discursive boundaries. In news coverage of minorities, van Dijk (2000, 39) relays that

> minorities are quoted less, and less prominently than (white) elites. If sources are quoted, we may also expect that those are selected that confirm the general attitudes about the group in question. Minority representatives will seldom be allowed to speak alone: a white person is necessary to confirm and convey his or her opinion, possibly against that of the minority spokesperson.

Likewise, Hall (2006) describes the news as a 'white-eye' institution whose discourses overwhelmingly correspond to the dominant ideologies and interests of majority groups. A review of the dataset indicates that US news coverage of Noor's murder limits minority voices in favour of those from majority institutions and individuals that support hegemonic stigmatising 'honour-killing' discourses.

MAJORITY VOICES

Hegemonic Stigmatising Discourses

The voices that dominate the coverage of Noor's murder are from such influential NGOs as the United Nations (UN), the World Health Organization (WHO), Amnesty International and Human Rights Watch. Additionally, the voices of other prominent individuals, including academics, journalists and members of law enforcement, are frequently incorporated within the coverage. Often, these voices reproduce bright boundaries and stigmatising discourses by defining 'honour killing' as a decidedly un-American, ethno-national practice with origins in Middle Eastern and Asian nations and/or Islam. Moreover, these bright boundaries predominate because of the symbolic, social, economic and cultural capital that many of these majority voices wield.

USA Today, for example, shares data from the WHO, which explains how 'thousands of such killings have occurred in Muslim countries such as Egypt, Jordan, Pakistan, and the Palestinian territories' (Dorell 2009). Likewise, *Fox News* reports that 'the United Nations has found that honor killings are all too common in Islamic countries' (Cangelosi 2011). The *Arizona Republic* quotes Joshua Rubenstein, from Amnesty International, who explains:

There is a lot of discussion within the Islamic world about honor killings and other things. Yes it's disorienting for immigrants. ... Americans come from lots of different backgrounds and hold onto certain traditions and identities from our ethnicity and we celebrate that. ... But certain things are out of bounds. We don't allow murder in the name of disrespect of religion or anything. (Montini 2009)

Regarding voices from law enforcement, the *Peoria Times* relays how 'Prosecutor Laura Reckart told the jury that Almaleki grew increasingly angry at his daughter's Westernised behavior and failure to obey her parents' traditional Iraqi and Muslim ways' (Stafford 2011). *CBS News* cites Chris Boughey, lead detective in Noor's murder investigation, who argues that 'in certain traditions and certain cultures ... if a father believes that ... a female has acted in a dishonorable or disrespectful way ... the only way to restore that honor is to kill them' (Feed and Leach 2012). Phyllis Chesler (2011), Emerita Professor of Psychology, contends that 'in the West, honour killings are mainly Muslim-on-Muslim crimes'. Pulitzer-prize-winning author Leonard Pitts Jr. (2009) describes 'honour killings' as 'an act of appalling cowardice suggestive of not simply religious extremism but of a people in fear of the sexuality and independence of women'. Robert Spencer, co-founder of Stop the Islamisation of America, who the Southern Poverty Law Center (2015) describes as 'one of America's most prolific and vociferous anti-Muslim propagandists', asserts that, regarding Noor's murder, 'there is a broad support and acceptance of this idea in Islam, and we're going to see it more and more in the United States' (Dorell 2009). The manner in which these majority voices ethno-nationally or religiously mark 'honour killings' reproduces the same bright boundaries found in the headlines and leverages this gendered violence to explicitly justify the exclusion of the M/ME/SA minority communities from the United States.

Counterhegemonic Culture-Blind Voices

Voices from majority groups infrequently challenge the prevailing ethno-national and religious marking of 'honour killings' through culture-blind discourses that (re)situate this practice within the global paradigm of violence against women. One example is a *Huffington Post* editorial by John Esposito, professor of religion and international affairs at Georgetown University, and Sheila B. Lalwani, research fellow at Georgetown (2010), who described 'honour killings' as 'symptomatic of highly patriarchal systems, where women are held responsible for maintaining personal family and community honour'. Their counterhegemonic emphasis on gender breaks down bright barriers by illuminating how gender violence is endemic across cultures, ethnicities and religions; yet this is also problematic because it ignores some of the unique cultural aspects of 'honour killing'.

MINORITY VOICES

The Almaleki Family and the Local Community

Unlike majority voices, the news curtails voices from the M/ME/SA communities, including from members of Noor's family. When the news includes these voices, they typically arrange them in such a way that they validate stigmatising 'honour-killing' discourses. The *Phoenix New Times* offers a quote in which Ali Almaleki, Noor's brother, explains that 'Noor had been "most disrespectful" to their parents (to him too) since her return and continued to reject "traditional" Iraqi values' (Rubin 2010). *Time Magazine* includes the voice of Saher Alyarsy, a Muslim woman, who attends the al-Rasool mosque in Phoenix, Arizona. When asked about Noor's murder, Alyarsy responds, 'I think what [Faleh] did was right. It's his daughter, and our religion doesn't allow us to do what she did' (Labi 2011). In both examples, the news selects and arranges each voice so that Ali and Alyarsy appear to support Faleh's actions, which paints the M/ME/SA communities as minority groups that reject US national norms.

Minority Stigmatising Voices

Other M/ME/SA minority voices include individuals, many of whom lead non-profits that address violence in their communities. Their position on 'honour killing', however, tends to mirror the stigmatising discourses of majority voices. One such example is Ayaan Hirsi Ali, the Somali-Dutch-American founder of the AHA Foundation, whose mission is to 'protect and defend the rights of women and girls in the West from oppression justified by religion and culture' (AHA Foundation 2015). Ali underwent female genital mutilation as a child in Somalia and was later granted political asylum in the Netherlands to escape a forced marriage before settling in the United States. *CBS News* features Ali's remarks at a conference on 'honour violence' and forced marriage organised by the AHA/John Jay College, in which she asserts:

> The women in these cultures don't own their own bodies. ... Their sexuality is a commodity and it's of high value which is owned by their families. If a young woman refuses to comply with her father's choice of a husband for her (as Noor Almaleki did) this strips the father of his honor. ... Fathers will kill their daughters over this. (Dahl 2012)

Likewise, M. Zuhdi Jasser, president of the American Islamic Forum for Democracy, remarks, 'I hope that [Faleh] becomes an example that Muslims in this country will not get special treatment, that they get the full force of Western law. ... This honor killing is a sign of a deeper issue' (Holland 2011). Or Riffat Hassan, a former professor at the University of Louisville, who states, 'Muslim culture has reduced many, if not most women to the position of puppet on a string, to slave-like creatures whose only purpose in life is to cater to the needs and pleasures of men' (cited by Rubin 2010). The voices in each example clearly single out culture, 'Muslim' culture in particular, as the rationale for 'honour killing'. This, and their 'insider' position within the M/ME/SA communities, may explain their inclusion in the coverage. Their inclusion in the news coverage, by virtue of their stigmatising 'honour-killing' discourse, however, is detrimental to the M/ME/SA minority communities. Indeed, Ali, Jasser and Hassan, as model minorities, limit opportunities for blurred national belonging and context-specific discourse.

Minority Counterhegemonic Voices

Asra Q. Nomani and Rana Husseini are examples of minority voices who, like Esposito and Lalwani (2010), offer a counterhegemonic violence understanding of 'honour killing', but whose discourses are more context-specific. Nomani (2009), in a *Daily Beast* editorial, writes, 'So-called honour killings are universal crimes of violence carried out by people of all faiths, from Sikhs and Hindus to Christians. Noor is a victim in the culture wars between a puritanical interpretation of Islam and the West'. Here, Nomani universalises 'honour killings', a move that allows the association of this practice with violence against women but at the same time acknowledges the operation of an extremist religious element in her death. Husseini, a Jordanian journalist and activist, describes how 'some families think that women of the family represent their reputation. ... If a woman has committed a violation in their point of view, they believe if they kill her, they have ended the shame. Blood cleanses honor' (Labi 2011). Because these discursive moves cloud the boundaries between violence against women, 'honour killings' no longer carry the same bright rhetorical force, thereby permitting the blurring of boundaries between majority members of the US nation and M/ME/SA communities. Moreover, although such context-specific minority voices are limited in the coverage, the fact that neither Nomani nor Husseini have abandoned their identity means that their presence offers hope for alternative discourses on 'honour killing'. These alternative, context-specific, discourses focus on stopping the violence, as opposed to leveraging 'honour killing' to justifying the exclusion of the M/ME/SA minority communities.

'HONOUR KILLING' METAPHORS
AND BOUNDARY DRAWING

Metaphors are common rhetorical devices that appear in the news. In news narratives concerning minorities, however, van Dijk (1991) explains that these 'non-obligatory additional structures in texts ... may draw attention and may therefore emphasise specific meanings' (217) that are often negative. Cisneros (2008) identifies 'disease, infection, crime, infestation, invasion, burden, and flood' as metaphors that are typically affixed to immigrant minority groups (572). Metaphors, like those Cisneros (2008) identifies, appear throughout the US news coverage of Noor's murder; however, the news stories affix metaphors, which are not essential to the narration of Noor's murder, to the practice of 'honour killing' rather than the M/ME/SA communities. The metaphors found in this news coverage foster a discursive climate of moral panic about US national and societal security, thus intensifying bright boundaries between majority and minority national members.

Invasion

Invasion metaphors are most commonly featured throughout the news texts. Examples include 'honor killings have washed up on our shores' (Pesta 2011), 'the practice has followed immigrants from countries like Yemen and Iraq to the West' (Labi 2011), 'honor killing on main street' (Nomani 2009), 'something as foreign as an honor killing could happen in their backyard' (Feed and Leach 2012) and finally, 'Noor's ["honour-killing"] shocked a lot of people. ... This stuff's real; we've watched it on the news and heard about it in Florida, New York, and other places in the U.S. It really is in our front yard' (Myers 2011). These metaphors draw bright boundaries by framing the cause of Noor's death, an 'honour killing', as a harbinger for a much larger threat to the US nation, namely the growing M/ME/SA minority communities, who it associates with this violence. These metaphors distinguish Noor's murder from killings of majority women because unlike these 'everyday' instances of violence against women, Noor's murder serves as a public service announcement about the imminent threat that the M/ME/SA culprits of these crimes pose to the public space of the nation (front yard) and potentially to the private spaces of majority homes (back yard). As a result, these metaphors call for the bolstering of US national borders and the increased scrutiny, if not exclusion, of the M/ME/SA minority communities.

Disease

Disease metaphors also appear within the coverage of Noor's murder. Examples include 'honor killing is a silent epidemic' (Leach 2012) and 'law enforcement worried the practice may be spreading to America' (Cangelosi 2011). Like the invasion metaphors, those associated with disease also target the practice of 'honour killing', rather than the M/ME/SA minority communities. These disease metaphors are comparably alarmist and suggest that the US national body is not immune from the onslaught of the 'honour killing' contagion associated with minority communities. In sum, disease metaphors suggest that the US nation is sick and in dire need of an 'honour killing' health check to treat and prevent further infection of the national body by the M/ME/SA communities.

Roots

Roots metaphors are another type of metaphor prevalent in the coverage. *Marie Claire* describes 'honour killings' as 'a practice with deep tenacious roots in the tribal traditions of the Middle East and Asia' (Pesta 2011), while *TIME Magazine* refers to 'honour killings' as 'deeply rooted', and even Asra Q. Nomani (2009) states that this practice is 'rooted'. This metaphor of rooting represents 'honour killings' as an entrenched, immutable practice from the Middle East and Asia. This rhetorical move works in tandem with discourses that mark the culture of the M/ME/SA communities as regressive, as opposed to the 'modern' cultures of Western nations (Mani 1988; Mohanty 1991; McClintock 1995). Consequently, the 'rootedness' of 'honour killing' in M/ME/SA communities solidifies bright boundaries by presenting these communities as so bound to their ethno-national and religious cultures that they are inassimilable to the US nation.

Crime and Terror

Metaphors of crime and terror also facilitate the formation of bright boundaries. Regarding crime, *CBS News* shares how Detective Chris Boughey likens 'honour killing' police investigations to gang cases (Dahl 2012). This rhetoric stigmatises M/ME/SA families and communities as criminal organisations. Unlike American families, this metaphor portrays M/ME/SA families as having a gang mentality that emphasises the well-being of the group over that of the individual. In the case of 'honour killing', this gang metaphor suggests that the rights of women are secondary to the collective 'honour' of M/ME/SA families and communities. Metaphors of terror work similarly to crime metaphors, but situate 'honour killing' as symptomatic of the larger Global War on Terror that threatens the US nation. Phyllis Chesler (2010), for example, calls 'honour killings' 'the other side of jihad' and exhorts, 'not all honor killers actually hijack airplanes – but they probably support those who do'. This metaphor elevates 'honour killing' as a small-scale terrorist attack and strengthens the erroneous interpretations of jihad as an Islamic battle against Western culture, rather than an internal spiritual struggle. Terrorism metaphors exhort the US public to take notice of 'honour killings' on US soil, in particular the M/ME/SA men committing these crimes, because this violence merely foreshadows their participation in and/or support of future terrorist assaults upon the US nation.

Drawing Boundaries with Metaphors

These 'honour-killing' metaphors of invasion, disease, roots, crime and terror are powerful, pathos-laden and stigmatising rhetorical devices that draw bright boundaries between majority members of the US nation and the M/ME/SA minority communities. These boundaries are covertly formed, as they target the practice of 'honour killing' and, in most cases, do not directly reference M/ME/SA communities. The ethno-national and religious marking of the crime within the headlines and by various voices throughout the body of the news texts makes these overt associations unnecessary. Moreover, because metaphors are non-essential to the narration of the facts of Noor's murder, they also demonstrate how the presence of 'honour killings' in the United States becomes a barometer for measuring the M/ME/SA minority communities' purported disruption of US national and societal security. Finally, these metaphors discursively elicit moral panic, so that the murder of one woman, Noor, portends an assault upon the national body of the United States.

BLURRING THE BOUNDARIES IN 'HONOUR KILLING' NEWS DISCOURSE

The CDA of the headlines, lexical style, voice and metaphors circulating throughout the US news coverage of the murder of Noor Almaleki reveals the presence of bright boundaries supported by stigmatising 'honour-killing' discourses that underscore gendered, ethnic, national, cultural and religious differences to marginalise M/ME/SA minority communities from the US nation. Likewise, this analysis exposes how in instances of 'honour killing', the violence against such women's bodies as Noor's serves other agendas related to US national and societal security. Ultimately, these hegemonic stigmatising discourses are counterproductive and divisive. They fail to constructively address this form of violence beyond demonising M/ME/SA minority communities, especially men therein, situating all M/ME/SA women as potential victims of their families and communities. Consequently, these discourses prescribe the adoption of US majority cultural norms as the only antidote. Noor's dead body serves as a foundation for arguments about all that is right with the norms of US majority cultural norms and all that is wrong with those of M/ME/SA minority communities. These discourses are dangerous not only to M/ME/SA minority communities but also to majority members of the US nation because they conceal the endemic nature of violence within their own communities.

Uncovering these bright boundaries and stigmatising discourses is the first step in shifting towards context-specific discourses in US 'honour-killing' news coverage. Although this analysis identifies some instances of context-specific discourse in the coverage, more work is required in order to raise awareness about the intricate relationship between 'honour-killing' discourse in the US news and its ability to delineate belonging to such social groups as the US nation, and the material results of such distinctions for M/ME/SA minority communities. This chapter offers an initial effort; however, its focus on the single murder of Noor Almaleki is limiting. There is a pressing need for an expanded body of research and critique of discourses in US 'honour-killing' news coverage so that a meaningful, discursive change that blurs boundaries and allows for multiple forms of membership for individuals and groups within the US nation can be brought about. Most importantly, such changes must occur in order to end such violence.

NOTES

1. The term 'honour killing' is commonly used to describe the murder of a woman (and occasionally of a man) by family members for purportedly bringing dishonour through a perceived impropriety that is almost always sexual. Scholars and activists (Terman 2010; Abu-Lughod 2011; Grewal 2013) continue to debate the use of the term 'honour killing', arguing that such terminology often stigmatises the Muslim, Middle Eastern and South Asian communities, who are erroneously associated with this form of violence against women.

2. Amal appears in only two headlines, neither of which mention her by name.

Chapter 5

Emotive Strategies and Affective Tactics in 'Islam Night'

Tuuli Lähdesmäki and Tuija Saresma

During the past decade, populist and nationalist movements have gained prominence side by side with anti-immigrant or 'culturally racist' (Mulinari and Neergaard 2012) political parties. Both have objected to current cultural and societal changes by criticising what they perceive as (over)liberal immigration policies, the development of multi- and intercultural societies and weakening traditional values. Their agendas have often centred on creating or maintaining borders and rejecting threats that are considered to result from the increasing 'borderlessness' of societies and cultures (Lähdesmäki and Saresma 2014a; 2014b). Extremist and populist movements commonly circulate rhetoric in which diverse discriminative discourses are brought out and conjoined. In this rhetoric, anti-immigration-minded, xenophobic, Islamophobic, heteronormative, homophobic, chauvinist and misogynic notions and opinions mingle (Lähdesmäki and Saresma 2014a; 2014b). These notions are commonly explicitly expressed in extreme right-wing activity, while in populist discourses, explicit expressions are often avoided, censored or 'cleaned up'. These discriminatory views can be rhetorically hidden under seemingly neutral utterances, such as 'immigration criticism' instead of anti-immigration (Mäkinen 2013), 'culture' instead of ethnicity and 'immigration' instead of race (Balibar 1991), veiling prejudiced or racist connotations.

The widespread use of the Internet and social media has had a major effect on contemporary civic activism: blogs and online discussion fora are central sites for debate today (Lähdesmäki 2013; Saresma 2012; 2014a; 2014b). They have also played a crucial role in the rise of populist and extremist movements in Europe. The potentially democratising and equalising effects of social media have been celebrated, but the blogosphere offers the possibility to promote *both* progressive and reactionary ideologies (Pole 2010). Public discussion on the topics of multiculturalism and immigration takes place particularly in social media. Although online discussions do not represent the opinions of society as a whole, they are, however, influential in shaping public opinion by allowing those with the 'loudest' voice to promote their views (Nikunen and Horsti 2013). While in traditional media, journalistic material is filtered through a professional editing process, social media enables the publication of largely unfiltered material, which may encourage the polarisation of views and increase aggressive and discriminative rhetoric (Saresma 2014b). The practices and content of edited and unfiltered media are, however, closely intertwined: traditional media is influential in shaping opinion and encouraging discussion on the Internet by providing topics and launching debates, and the unfiltered online debates and views published in the blogosphere are often reacted to in traditional media.

In this chapter,[1] we investigate the debate on Muslim immigration by closely examining 'Islam Night', a talk show broadcast by the Finnish TV station Yle in October 2013. Islam Night combined the traditional format of a talk show – with hosts and prestigious guests – with the velocity of social media, engaging the audience to participate by suggesting studio guests and sending tweets and SMS texts to be published and discussed during the live broadcast.

DEFINING POPULISM

According to Laclau (2005), populism is a social logic that is mobilised by rhetoric. Populist rhetoric constructs and justifies populist movements through its functional performativity. In studies on populism, populist rhetoric is often described as relying on affective, emotive and metaphoric language as well as on polarisation, simplification, stereotypes and vague expressions. Populist rhetoric perceives threats, faults and enemies and appeals to 'cultural commonplaces', that is, 'shared physical places or more abstract sentimental areas of cultural meanings which need no justification and cannot be rationalized' (Thévenot 2011). The 'discourse of people' and appealing to 'the people' is in the core of the rhetorical strategies of populism (Westlind 1996).

The rise of the populist climate in Europe is closely related to the crumbling of the traditional socio-political order, characterised, for example, by the blurring of the right/left-dualism (Mouffe 1995, 498; 2005). In place of the traditional dualistic socio-political order, the antagonist logic of populism is usually articulated through the distinction between 'right' and 'wrong', or in the moral register through the categories of 'good' and 'evil' (Mouffe 2005). These categories include a strong emotive dimension.

The rise of populist and right-wing extremist movements in Europe has to do with the meanings and functions of the emotions that draw people to them

(Salmela 2014). Emotions are, according to Illouz (2007, 2), not action *per se*, but 'the inner energy that propels us toward an act', giving it 'a particular mode or coloration'. If emotions are 'cultural meanings and social relationships that are very compressed together' (Illouz 2007, 3), it is important to look at both individual psychological mechanisms and socio-economic changes in explaining the emotionally affected attraction of these movements (Flecker 2007). Several studies (e.g. Haynes et al. 2006; Hoggett et al. 2013) have emphasised that feelings of injustice, resentment, powerlessness, vulnerability, defeat and lack of self-esteem are associated with xenophobic, nationalist, ethnocentric, authoritarian and neoliberal or welfare chauvinist political responses and attitudes. In addition, scholars have emphasised the feeling of shame as a catalyst for anger in populist and extremist movements. As Turner (2007, 517) notes, when individuals cannot meet expectations in encounters lodged in key institutional domains, such as family, education, economy, polity or religion, or are negatively sanctioned in these encounters, they are likely to experience shame. Shame experienced in different personal and social identities accumulates and intensifies anger at 'wrongs' committed by others who are perceived to have attacked one's social identity (Salmela 2014; Saresma, forthcoming).

Pupcenoks and McCabe (2013) have noted that extremist fringe groups (both Islamist and right-wing anti-Islamist groups) have managed to gain a notable influence on national public discourse in Britain, although their direct electoral impact had been minor until 2014.[2] Populist groups are given extensive media coverage because their simplistic arguments make for punchy headlines and sell articles – a prerequisite to media organisations' survival in the global contest for publicity. The emotive nature of extremist activities and protests has had a broad influence on the dynamics of public discussion on migration and especially on Islam in today's Europe. The affective anti-Islamic and anti-immigrant protests and debates about racialisation (see Meer 2013) have also produced public emotive counter-reactions, therefore turning the public discussion on Islam and immigration into an exchange of affective arguments using emotive rhetoric, in which appeals to rationality and reason are common (Alsultany 2012). The emotive and affective rhetoric of extremists and populist parties has also impacted the rhetoric of their political opponents: traditional political parties have either distanced themselves from this rhetorical style or have adopted hardened vocabulary in their own political discourse (Bos and Brants 2014). The rise of populist movements and the spread of their emotive and affective rhetoric have caused political agents to reposition across European societies. Similarly, the development of social media as a key forum for public debate has affected the position of national media companies. What is the role of publicly owned media companies in the public debate on Muslim immigration and the pluralisation of European societies? To whom do they give voice, and are they also influenced by the increase in populist discourses?

EMOTIVE DISCUSSION ON ISLAM IN
FINNISH MEDIA PUBLICITY

In Finland, the rise of populism coincides with the success of Perussuomalai-set (The Finns Party), established in 1995. The party has increased its popu-larity in each parliamentary election, gaining 19 per cent of the vote in the 2011 election. Since then, its support has varied between 23 and 15 per cent in the opinion polls (Luukka and Roppola 2014).[3] The Finns Party could be classified as nationalist–populist, and both these terms are indeed used in a positive sense in both the party programmes and the writings of the party leader Timo Soini (Mickelsson 2011). Its agenda is a mixture of traditionally left-wing social and income distribution politics, right-wing conservative values, Euroscepticism and nationalist interests. Emphasising the role of the party as that of an alternative which challenges the 'old' political parties and their consensus-seeking politics has blurred the divisions of the Finnish political sphere. This emphasis has enabled the party to draw together pro-tests against a variety of faults found in society and thereby bring together politicians with diverse interests and views (Pernaa et al. 2012).

The concept of the nation had become increasingly central to the rhetoric of The Finns Party by the end of the past decade. The establishment of The Finns Party Youth in 2006 and the launch of the anonymous online discussion forum Homma in 2008 increased interest in questions of culture and identity. The party's youth organisation and debaters in Homma have been particularly concerned with the effects of immigration on Finland and Europe.

The number of Finnish residents who were born outside the country is one of the lowest in Europe (Embassy of Finland 2014). There has, however, been an annual increase in the figures and anti-immigration views have simultane-ously gained ground and prominence in Finnish public and political debates.[4]

The Finnish national, publicly funded broadcasting company Yle[5] partici-pated in the lively discussion on immigration and the increased plurality of the Finnish society by hosting and broadcasting a live prime time talk show entitled 'Islam Night' on 28 October 2013. The show can be interpreted as reflecting Yle's operational principles which emphasise democratisation, by making topical issues widely accessible (Yle 2014a), and the education of citizens. In addition to these noble motives, Yle's operations are guided by the need to compete for viewers in the mediatising and digitalising culture (Hellman 1999). Islam Night was a part of a series of similarly organised thematic talk shows which Yle has broadcast since 1969.[6]

Within Islam Night, the topics ranged from the warlike politics of the Islamist groups to the everyday religious practices of the Muslims; from the history of Muslim immigration to the position of women and gay and lesbian people in Islam; and from human to animal rights. Twenty guests representing various groups and communities involved in the public discussion on Islam in Finland were invited to the studio. They included religious figures such as representatives of Christian communities and imams; politicians with both Finnish and immigrant backgrounds representing the Finns Party, the Greens, the Social Democratic Party, the National Coalition Party and the Center Party; a researcher of Islam; a Muslim school teacher of Islam; a foreign correspondent; young Muslim women who had decided to stop wearing a veil; and young Muslim women who were defending their right to wear the hijab. The show had 628,000 viewers (13 per cent of the national population, Finnpanel 2013).

Yle's aim was to involve the public in the preparation of Islam Night: audience members were involved in the process by letting them nominate guests and suggest themes and questions for the hosts via Facebook, Twitter and a live chat on the Yle website. The show itself was interactive, emphasising the active role of the audience. They were asked to send SMS texts and tweets that scrolled on the screen throughout the show. In addition, the viewers were able to participate in the show in two chat rooms – moderated and unmoderated – which were open on the Yle website on the evening. Some of the talk-show guests participated in the moderated chat and some of the questions posed in this chat were discussed in the talk show. The moderated chat contained 221 messages and the unmoderated chat 3,588. The unmoderated chat attracted various trolls and aggressive comments directed at different groups of people, and the messages shown on the TV screen also contained discriminatory expressions.

The public discussion regarding the talk show started on various online forums before it was actually broadcast and continued weeks after it, bringing to the fore polarised views in which certain stereotypes of Muslims were reinforced. In the discussion preceding the broadcast, the debaters assumed, for example, that the hosts would favour the views of Muslims and liberal guests; that the discussion would be aggressive and polarised; that the guests would not listen to other speakers; and that there would be no attempts from the different parties to understand each other. The hosts posed open questions and interaction between the guests in the show mostly consisted of a calm, good-humoured and well-structured dialogue, despite the fact that the structure of the talk show was organised under highly polemic headings and some extreme opinions were brought out in relation to, for example, jihad and sharia. However, we argue that the externally calm interaction included emotionally charged argumentative strategies and that the tactics used for justifying opinions were affective.[7]

ISLAM AS FRAMED BY FINLAND'S NATIONAL
PUBLIC BROADCASTING COMPANY

The talk show lasted for approximately two hours.[8] The show consisted of several polemic themes that will be presented shortly. The themes are familiar from the widely repeated Western orientalist narrative, in which Islam is represented through negatively charged stereotypes and extreme imagery (Alsultany 2012; Meer 2013).

The talk show started with an insert, with one of the hosts asking, 'How to do as the Finns do, when Islam is already part of Finnishness and Finnishness is part of Islam. Today, as many as 60,000 Muslims live in Finland. Does Islam constitute a possibility or a threat for Finland?' After the insert, video clips from the Middle East and East African countries were shown, framing the topic of 'Islam' through aggressive and menacing connotations (1.06–1.53). The clips displayed a large number of Muslims praying; minarets; a massive crowd of pilgrims circling the Black Stone in Kaaba; women wearing niqabs; a crowd of men in an aggressive demonstration burning US, Israeli and UK flags; a bomb exploding; the training of armed jihadists; shooting; panic in a mall in Nairobi after the October 2013 terrorist attack; burning buildings; and at the end of the montage, another bomb explosion. The soundscape of the clips included Arabic praying, traditional Arabic music, shouting crowds, clacking of firearms and explosions, followed by the exclamation 'God is Great' in Arabic. The images bound together religion, aggression, war, terrorism and the idea of a huge mass of supporters of a bellicose ideology.

The talk show was divided into six sections, all of them containing polemic headings. The first heading, displayed immediately after the video clips, asked, 'Religion of Peace or of War?' (1.53–4.25). The themes through which the hosts led the discussion in the first section were the nature of Islam in relation to war and peace, jihad and the meaning of Islam to Finland – whether it is a threat or a possibility. The second section, entitled 'To the Holy War from Finland?' (4.26–35.05), focused on jihad and on the feeling of rootlessness, together with other reasons that might explain why several young Muslim men have left their home countries in Europe in order to join the wars in conflict areas in the Middle East and in Somalia. Besides rootlessness and the impact of the Internet, the male host also took up the contents of Quran as a possible cause for the interest in war: 'Nevertheless, isn't it so that this kind of old media, such as Quran, is an extremely good source, like, if someone is in this spiral, is frustrated and searching for something, well in Quran there really are a lot of verses which urge one to join an armed battle, right?'

The themes of war and conflict continued in the third section of the show, focusing on differences between Sunnis and Shias (beginning at 35.06).

The section was entitled 'The Wrong Kind of Islam?' The female host started the section by asking, 'What is this feud about? Does it reach Finland?' She laid the ground for the discussion by foregrounding sectarian/political conflict between Muslim communities in certain geographic locations. A young Finnish imam was interviewed about the differences between Sunnis and Shias. After the imam had described the history of the two communities and explained some practical differences between them, for example, how Sunnis and Shias hold theirs arms differently when praying, the male host noted: 'These sound like quite minor issues, and of course for a Finn, this hundreds of years old ... 1400-year-old explanation too sounds a bit far-fetched, but of course it is true to you'. The hosts took up the number of mosques and prayer rooms in Finland, and indicating the locations of mosques and prayer rooms on the map, asked, 'Why it is so that you do not fit in the same mosque? Why must there be such a large number of prayer rooms?' (41.39). The factional disputes of Muslims were also discussed in the context of teaching Islam in schools and the problematic of selecting a representative spokesman for the Islamic community for official societal events in Finland.

The second hour of Islam Night started with the question of whether a Muslim can marry a Christian (0.49). The discussion functioned as an introduction to the fourth section of the talk show entitled 'The Oppressed Woman?' (4.07–43.20). The section was preceded by a collage (3.26–4.06) displaying photos from the art project *Finlandia – National landscape* by the Finnish artist Rosa Liksom. In her photos, Liksom has depicted people wearing burqas in typical Finnish landscapes. In the images, the blue burqas and snow-white natural environment highlight the colours of the Finnish flag, creating, however, a strong symbolic tension. In the talk show, the photos were accompanied by a famous sentimental, national-romantic Finnish tango entitled 'Blue and White' by Jukka Kuoppamäki. In the show, the recontextualisation of burqas in Liksom's photo series was itself re-recontextualised, when the image collage was followed by a serious discussion regarding the clothing of Muslim women. The discussion dealt with the gender and family roles in Islam, views on homosexuality, sharia law and its contradictions with human rights, for example, its view on the death penalty for homosexuality (28.01–36.31) – the latter being the most discussed topic in both traditional and digital media after the broadcast. During this section, two manikins wearing a burqa and a niqab stood in the studio. The image of a veiled woman has a strong symbolic dimension in populist and right-wing extremist imagery, manifesting the various threats associated with Islam (Wodak 2014; Alsultany 2012; Meer 2013). By showing the photos of women wearing burqas in a characteristically Finnish landscape and by bringing in the veiled manikins, the symbolic and threatening Other was made present in the studio.

Figure 5.1 Studio set during the section 'The Oppressed Woman?' displaying photos from Rosa Liksom's art project *Finlandia – National landscape* and traditional Muslim dress: burqa, hijab, niqab and kufi. *Source:* 'Islam Ilta' Yle Finnish Broadcasting Company.

The short fifth section was entitled according to the Finnish version of the proverb 'When in Rome, do as the Romans do' (45.40–51.45). The section started with a Muslim butcher and a Halal food merchant explaining how animals are slaughtered according to the Halal rules. The female host emphasised that a section concerning Halal meat was especially requested by the public during the preparation of the show (51.30). The interview was framed in an affective way: the butcher was asked to sharpen his knife and cut raw meat in the studio. The hosts of the show framed the discussion on Halal food by asking whether it can be considered as animal cruelty and whether it adheres to the Finnish animal rights legislation. The theme of killing, earlier visualised and discussed with references to bombs, jihad and violence and later manifesting in a debate on the death penalty for homosexuals, was returned to in a concrete way in discussing Halal food.

The show ended with a short section entitled 'The Tatar formula for success' (51.50–1.07.50) which brought to the fore the Finnish Tatar minority, the roots of which go back to the nineteenth century. In the show, the Tatars[9] were represented as 'good Muslims' – an example of a group of Muslim immigrants who have totally integrated into the Finnish society through work and entrepreneurship (1.00.12). After an interview with a Finnish Tatar, the Muslim guests in the show started to talk about how they might integrate into their new homeland and that all Muslims are not immigrants but have their roots deep in the Finnish soil. The last shown tweet suggested that the hosts and the guests should end the show with a group hug (1.07.59). Although the hosts stated that the discussion on social media had been fiery and was continuing as such, the talk show ended with a peaceful image of diverse people hugging one another.

The staging of the studio utilised visual references to Islam, such as the manikins wearing the traditional outfits of Muslim women, yet the visual elements used in the staging originated from ancient Greece and Rome. The guests were sitting on benches forming a quarter segment of a circle, which was reminiscent of the auditorium of an ancient Greek theatre. Behind the benches were white columns surrounded by a border displaying more white columns on a blue background, strongly referencing European cultural heritage and Western civilisation. As for the graphics, the introduction shots of the talk show and the graphics in the background of the section headings repeated the image of a circle of white columns on a blue background. In addition to the reference to the colours of the Finnish flag, the national sentiments were emphasised by ending the show with the song 'Blue and White' in which the narrator ponders what to tell the listeners about Finland, the home country he has left behind.

EMOTIONALLY CHARGED ARGUMENTATIVE STRATEGIES AND THEIR AFFECTIVE TACTICS IN ISLAM NIGHT

The inserts of the show as well as the questions posed by the two hosts were aimed at provoking the guests and the audiences to join the debate. The mode of discussion of the hosts of Islam Night was, in principle, very objective, but in practice their tone was repeatedly highly outspoken, even provocative, using emotionally charged expressions and vocabulary. This is in line with other 'Yle nights' dealing with controversial subjects.

The guests and the audience sending SMSs and tweets to Islam Night also used emotionally charged argumentative strategies and concrete affective tactics in their attempts to promote or resist either anti-immigration or anti-Islamic views. One of the most common strategies was to bring to the discussion alleged threats posed by Islam that were claimed not only to endanger the Finnish societal order, Western values and 'our' profound understanding of equality and justice, but also to oppress Muslim women and to expose young Muslim men to fundamentalist recruiters. The affective tactics that were used varied: threats could be emphasised by, for example, expressing a variety of concerns and worries regarding Muslims; naming various dangers allegedly connected to Islam; discussing Muslims and their religion in the context of morally and ethically reprehensible incidents and ideologies such as suicide bombings and terrorist attacks; and inciting fear by bringing in highly affective topics such as Nazism, the terror of Anders Behring Breivik and pedophilia.[10]

The guests' discussion, led by the hosts, was often at least implicitly polarised between right and wrong, good and evil. Moral standpoints were addressed particularly when the discussion focused on jihad and sharia law. In addition, discussion of gender and sexual norms elicited opinions as to their moral righteousness, and the argumentative strategy of assuming a position of moral superiority was employed. The tactics used in this strategy had different registers. The subtlest tactic was to indicate that the speaker 'knows better' or has 'true information' on the topic. Moral superiority could, however, be asserted in a more straightforward way by reference to the Quran and by appealing to it as a source of immutable truth. These views were commonly refuted through criticism of Islam and its religious values and by asserting the moral superiority of one's own position by appealing to Western values, human rights and national legislation.

Besides taking a moralistic and a more or less normative stand on questions of right and wrong, the debaters commonly appealed to a subjective understanding of the topics. In this argumentative strategy, the debaters emphasised ethics as the source of justification for their views and the various subjective choices they had made in their life. This strategy was particularly common among female Muslim guests when explaining their relation to the teachings of the Quran, clothing and religious practices in everyday life. However, politicians also used the strategy in their argumentation. The concrete tactics deployed in this strategy focused on legitimating one's knowledge of right and wrong through reference to one's feelings, subjective understanding and 'following one's heart', an utterance used by both Muslim and anti-Islam/anti-immigration-minded guests.

Whereas the strategies described above were often used to produce or support the existence of adversarial groups of 'us' and 'them', the topics of the discussion could also be approached by emphasising the connections between the groups and the consolidation of people living in Finland. The need for consensus, mutual understanding and co-operation was repeatedly brought to the fore by both the guests – Muslims, a representative of the Christian community, a researcher of Islam and a politician of the Green Party – and the audience in their SMSs and tweets. The somewhat orientalist narrative of the show that described Muslims as the Others and the more or less provocative approach of the hosts particularly urged many of the guests to criticise the polarisation between Muslims and non-Muslims and to foster the idea of consensus. The affective tactics used in fostering consensus varied from describing the concrete examples of the similarities between Muslims and non-Muslims to reminders of the faults and excesses of every religion, not just Islam. However, the hosts of the show incited friction between the representatives of Muslim migrants and the 'natives' in subtle ways. When, for example, the radio personality and member of the city council Abdurahim Hussein said, 'Let's not talk out of turn, I would like to prove that even though there are so many people here today, they are just common peaceful people, and ... I hope we could continue [the discussion] in a [peaceful] way' (37.50), the male host responded, 'C'mon, surely you can [talk out of turn] a bit so that the critics will have something to criticize' (38.01).

What is of interest to one's understanding of affective publics (Berlant 2008) is that despite the controversial topic and affective contents, the talk show itself mainly embraced an unemotional discussion on the themes introduced by the hosts. The SMSs and tweets scrolling on the screen, however, were frequently ironic and sarcastic in tone and were simultaneously often explicitly hostile and Islamophobic – comments in which the audience criticised the discussion in the studio as well as Islam and immigration more generally. This kind of emotive strategy is common in online debates in general (Saresma 2012; 2014a; 2014b).

SOCIAL RESPONSIBILITY OF NATIONAL, PUBLICLY OWNED MEDIA COMPANIES?

Illouz (2007, 4) considers emotions to be 'the principal characters in the story of capitalism and modernity', leading to the dissolving of 'the conventional division between an a-emotional public sphere and the private sphere saturated with emotions'. It is, thus, no wonder that the emotive and affective logic of the debate on immigration and Islam influences the dynamics of discussion on both public media and semi-public Internet forums. This logic works by polarising opinions, producing emotive discourses and counter-discourses and involving emotions and affects as a means of political argumentation. In Islam Night, the emotive strategies used by the guests and the audience included (1) taking a normative stand in relation to moral questions, (2) appealing to subjective understanding, ethics and 'following one's heart', (3) emphasising commonalities between various religious (or secular) groups and (4) presenting discriminative, even explicitly hostile views of 'the Other' in the guise of humour, irony or sarcasm. The strategies utilise various rhetorical tactics that are based on affective argumentation and populist black-and-white reasoning with wide appeal.

The effects of the emotionalisation of public discussion are present in Islam Night. Albeit produced by the publicly funded Finnish broadcasting company, the mission of which is to educate citizens, the talk show sought to gain a big audience and provoke ardent opinions. Its aims were fulfilled as it started a lively discussion both in print media, particularly in columns and editorials, and in social media, where it was referred to in Facebook and Twitter and commented on in various discussion forums and blogs by both anti-immigration- and pro-immigration-minded writers. The opinions of the writers were divided: some applauded the show for its courageous way of dealing with the controversial issue of Islam, whereas others criticised it for cementing either the prejudices of the anti-immigration-minded or the presuppositions of the pro-immigration-minded. Obtaining visibility in the media follows the logic of virality. Studies on social media (e.g. Berger and Milkman 2009) have indicated that news and topics of discussion invoking high-arousal positive (awe) or negative (anger or anxiety) emotions are much more viral in social media than other news. In addition, messages arousing anger are spread more quickly and broadly in online networks than other emotions (Fan et al. 2013). Virality of emotive, negatively charged messages generates polemical public debates and polarisation of views. Bringing to the fore volatile subjects may function as a tool to improve the position of media companies in the tightening media competition. By participating in the flammable debate on immigration and Islam, Yle not only encouraged a civil dialogue but also gained a position in the 'loud debate' on immigration.

Yle as the national, state-owned broadcasting company aims at extending, in the name of democracy, its services to the public which includes 'special and minority groups' (Yle 2014b). By including Muslim immigrants as a minority group in a prime-time television show, Yle is accomplishing its mission. In addressing a timely topic, Islam Night also engaged the audience in the making of the show, following the logic of 'from users to producers' popular in social media. The preparation process was based on enabling the participation of the audience in its production. On the one hand, the preparation process and possibility of sending chat messages, SMSs and tweets to the show increased the interactivity of the show and thus reflected the idea of serving the public. On the other hand, these aims and possibilities created a populist frame for the discussion of Islam. Thus, Yle's aims to enable the 'public' to participate in the discussion, to give the audience a voice and to let it be heard, also had negative effects, which is a common downside of the 'democratizing effects' of social media (Keren 2006). The efforts of Yle to tackle the controversial subject turned the talk show into a forum well known from the Internet: the programme brought to the fore and helped to maintain, perhaps even promoted, discriminative rhetoric. In this sense, the programme represented the national broadcasting company as an authoritative institution, accepting othering, discriminatory ideologies by approving the rhetoric of hatred disguised as sarcasm and irony (see Haynes et al. 2006).

Islam Night evidences Yle's attempt to be socially responsible by covering a timely societal issue, but it is simultaneously an example of the dangers of public broadcasting companies entering the competition of media houses by utilising affective representations on controversial issues at the cost of analytical distance. Yle, like many other public broadcasting companies, has lost the monopoly on broadcasting that the state once had and operates now in an economically difficult situation, competing with commercial media companies. This has led them to adapt to the modes of commercial media. In this development, critical societal topics are easily transformed into entertainment. Today, public broadcasting companies have to seek acceptance for their actions on the same criteria as those of commercial media: success is commonly measured by the volume of audience. In the case of Yle, the volume has not developed in an expected way (Blåfelt 2014) and therefore Yle's managing director has aimed to increase the attractiveness of its programmes. The managing director Lauri Kivinen recently stated in a newspaper interview: 'We have been too careful. More effervescency should be expected from us, shall it then be the black Mannerheim or the effervescent talk-show "Russian Night"' (Luukka 2014). Kivinen referred to two Yle programmes that aroused heavy debates in Finland: an autobiographical movie about the Finnish war hero Marshal Carl Gustaf Mannerheim filmed in Kenya and played by local black actors and a live talk show on Russia which was a part of the same series as that of Islam Night.

The display of Islam Night places the talk show within the frame of Yle's recent attempts to gain broader audiences and arouse affective feedback with sensational topics and emotive formats. The black-and-white narrative constructed through the intervening shots between separate sections of the programme, and the themes of Islam Night, represented Islam as an extremist, bellicose religious movement that oppresses women, or at least as an exotic orientalist culture with different, unfamiliar and foreign music, aesthetics and values. If the sensationalism of the show aimed to attract more audiences, it also revealed implicit negative attitudes towards Islam.

The stated intention of Islam Night – to promote more constructive dialogue in society – is in line with the operational principles of Yle to also serve minority groups in Finland. Despite its ambitious aim, Islam Night brought to the fore the polarisation of opinions, offered an arena to express discriminatory views on other people and repeated certain stereotypical themes commonly attached to Islam. In this sense, the Yle policy to tackle timely, affective and controversial topics is part of a populist programme policy that seeks to compete with the commercial broadcasting companies instead of implementing the strategy and aims of 'supporting democracy'; 'taking educational and equality aspects into consideration in the programmes'; 'supporting tolerance and multiculturalism and providing programming for minority and special groups'; and 'promoting cultural interaction', as is declared in the Act on Yleisradio, Section 7. The case of Islam Night raises the question of the responsibility of the public, state-owned media: Is it to maintain the ideal of equality and integrity of various groups in the contemporary intimate public or to be involved in the 'public exercise in othering' (Haynes et al. 2006) Muslims?

NOTES

1. This work was supported by the Academy of Finland under Grant SA21000019101 (Populism as movement and rhetoric).

2. In the European election in 2014, UKIP won the majority of the votes, making it the largest UK party in the European Parliament (BBC News 2014).

3. In the parliamentary election in 2015, the vote dropped to 18 per cent, but the party was chosen for the first time to join government.

4. In 2013, there were 207511 (3.8 per cent) persons with a foreign nationality, 289068 (5.3 per cent) persons with a foreign first language (other than Finnish, Swedish or Sami) and 301524 (5.5 per cent) persons with foreign background (persons both of whose parents, or only known parent, have been born abroad) permanently residing in Finland. The largest groups of foreign nationals were Estonians (44,652), Russians (30,878), Swedes (8,468) and Somalis (7,590); the most spoken foreign first languages were Russian (66,379), Estonian (42,936), English (15,570) and Somali (15,789); and the largest groups with foreign backgrounds had their origin in the Soviet Union (68,669), Estonia (40,990), Somalia (15,723) and Iraq (11,942) (Official Statistics of Finland, 2014).

5. Yle is Finland's national public service broadcasting company that operates four national television channels and six nation-wide radio channels as well as 25 regional radio programmes. Yle TV1 was the most popular television channel in Finland in 2013: its share of Finns' daily television viewing was 41.9 per cent. Yle was the dominant market leader in radio broadcasting also, reaching 51 per cent of the radio listeners. Yearly, Yle's TV and Radio programmes reach 100 per cent of the Finnish people. In Finland, Yle is commonly considered as a reliable source of news and current affairs. Its operations are financed by a public broadcasting tax; it is 99.9 per cent state-owned; it operates under the Act on Yleisradio OY and it is supervised by an administrative council appointed by the Parliament (Yle 2014b).

6. The topics of these talk shows have tackled topical and controversial societal issues such as nuclear power, taxation, unemployment, Internet, sex work, sex crimes, alcohol, obesity, hate speech, homosexuality, drugs, begging and Russia – all of them arousing polemical debates and emotive responses.

7. Scholarly interest in the emotional and affective qualities of culture and social interaction has increased remarkably during the recent decade. In what is called the 'affective turn in human sciences', affects have become foregrounded (Liljeström and Paasonen 2010). They are perceived as complex powers that include both mental and bodily dimensions (Hardt 2007) and are something that cannot be precisely and unequivocally defined or measured (Helle 2013). The concept of affect, like the concept of emotion (Illouz 2007), refers to the understanding of feelings and sensations as social, shared and circulated (Ahmed 2004). Lauren Berlant (2008) describes

the contemporary *affective public* as the intimatisation of the media and the public domain. Focusing on the affectivity of public discussion enables us to analyse the emotive reactions of the discussants not as those of individuals but as those of members of an audience shaped by the affective public. In our investigation, the affective public forms the theoretical frame through which we look at the emotive elements of the rhetoric in the discussion on Islam. The investigation was conducted in two phases. First, the editorial narrative and visual and auditory elements were subjected to a qualitative thematic analysis. The chat comments were excluded from closer investigation, since they form a vast text corpus that merits its own analysis. In the thematic analysis, distinct themes are defined as units derived from patterns such as 'conversation topics, vocabulary, recurring activities, meanings, feelings, or folk sayings and proverbs' (Taylor and Bogdan 1984, 131). Themes can be expressed in 'a single word, a phrase, a sentence, a paragraph or an entire document' (Zhang and Wildemuth 2009, 310). Similarly, themes may appear in images and sounds, which function as semiotic signs transcending their iconic meaning. The fundamental point of departure for the qualitative thematic analysis is in the researcher's hermeneutic interpretation process. Utilising the idea of interpretation as a process with many layers, both researchers watched the talk show carefully, taking notes on the visual, verbal and aural aspects of the show, the comments of the talk-show guests and the tweets and SMSs scrolling at the bottom of the screen. We completed the first round of the interpretation process by discussing our preliminary findings and constructing a model of the focal themes of the show. Then, the interaction in the talk show was investigated by identifying different emotive modes of argumentation, sense-making and justification of opinions used in appealing to and convincing other people, again done first individually by both researchers and then taking them to a more abstract level by discussing our observations theoretically.

8. Islam Night is available on YouTube in two parts: the first part, 49.42 minutes, at https://www.youtube.com/watch?v=AkgYx-Jfdik, and the second part, 1.09.47 minutes, at https://www.youtube.com/watch?v=1oqDOHNDA88.

9. The last tactic was not used by the hosts or guests of the show and only appeared in the SMSs and tweets.

10. The Tatars are originally Turkic people who espouse the Muslim faith. They are the oldest Muslim minority in Finland and in the Nordic countries. At the moment, there are less than one thousand Tatars living in Finland. They are well integrated into Finnish society, but simultaneously they have preserved their own cultural and religious characteristics (Embassy of Finland 2014).

Chapter 6

Being Part of the Irish 'We'

The Experience of Return Migration for the Second-Generation Irish From Britain

Sara Hannafin

This chapter[1] explores the experience of return migration to Ireland of second-generation Irish from Britain. It considers the extent to which this group is included in understandings of Irish identity, what this tells us about Irishness and explores how return migrants articulate dual national identities. The chapter begins with a brief consideration of the relationship between Ireland and its diaspora in Britain. Using the outcomes of qualitative research with a small group of returnees, the chapter illustrates how growing up in Britain with Irish parents created a sense of connection to Ireland, exploring what the experience of return has been like with specific reference to feelings of inclusion or exclusion. This is followed by a discussion of the recent historical attitudes to emigration from Ireland and the need for a greater recognition of mixed Irish-English/British identities.

There is a paucity of research into the experiences of immigrants to Ireland from Britain resulting in their absence from much of the discussion of the 'new Irish' (Gilmartin 2013). This research with second-generation Irish from Britain fills a significant gap in the academic literature on migration to Ireland and contributes to one's understanding of the relationship between Ireland and diaspora. This chapter shows that second-generation returnees are an important measure of the relationship between a country of emigration and its global community through the extent to which they are allowed to experience their parental home country as insiders. If 'identity is produced and reproduced in the course of social interaction' (Jenkins 1994, 209), then the encounters between second-generation returnees and Irish people highlight how and why people are excluded from or included in the Irish national 'family' and how the position of immigrants to Ireland from Britain, especially for people with Irish parents, is not straightforward.

In the 1990s, Ireland became a receiving country for immigrants due to its rapid economic growth. Initially this change was mainly due to the return of Irish-born emigrants (Ní Laoire 2008b) and was followed by, for the first time on a large scale, new immigrants from multifarious countries. The British born were Ireland's largest foreign-born group with 230,157 people recorded in 2011 as born in England, Wales and Scotland (CSO 2011); importantly, this includes people born in Britain who returned to Ireland as children with their Irish-born parents (Ní Laoire 2008b).

Research with second-generation Irish return migrants illustrates how their presence problematises what Ní Laoire describes as 'hegemonic and mono-cultural constructions of Irishness' (2008a). Ní Laoire argues that 'popular discourses of Irish society are often structured on the basis of dualisms which oppose a perceived native/Irish/white/settled/host community to a ... foreign/ non-white/non-Irish/nomadic/immigrant/newcomer community'. She further illustrates how Irish-born returning migrants blur the boundaries between these dualisms, arguing that the return migrant shifts constantly between the positions of 'host' and 'newcomer' (Ní Laoire 2008a, 35–36). Second-generation returnees further blur this dualism through their experience of choosing to return to a perceived 'home' in which they are often received as English and 'foreign'. They move instead between the shifting positions of 'cultural insiders' who are frequently assumed to be 'outsiders' while also learning that they are not as 'inside' as they had perhaps assumed. Lentin refers to this native/Irish/white/settled/host community as the Irish 'we' and writing, in 2001, on Ireland's responses to its (apparently) newly evolving ethnic diversity, proposes an interrogation of what this means. She states that 'interrogating the Irish "we" cannot evade interrogating the painful past of emigration, a wound still festering because it was never tended and which, I would suggest, is returning to haunt Irish people through the presence of the immigrant "other"' (Lentin 2002, 228). The aim of this chapter is, therefore, to explore the experience of second-generation return migrants as a further contribution to the process of interrogating this Irish 'we' both in terms of Ireland's relationship with its diaspora and in terms of its response to its immigrant newcomers.

THE IRISH: HOME AND ABROAD

Despite generations of emigration, the idea of the Irish abroad, and their descendants, as connected to the modern nation state is a new one. Scully notes that the concept of an Irish diaspora evolved in the 1990s and was invoked as evidence for the diverse nature of Irish identity and a way of 'articulating a more progressive Irishness' as well as an economic resource to be tapped in to (2012, 193–94). The children of the Irish in Britain are but one strand of this diaspora; removed by one generation and a short distance from the territory of the Ireland, they occupy a unique position in the relations between the Irish at home and the Irish abroad as well as between what are described as the binary oppositions of Irishness and Britishness (Hickman 2000).

The diaspora was a central theme of Mary Robinson's Presidency (1990–1997) who, in 1995, argued that the diaspora 'highlighted the diverse nature of Irish identity both within and beyond the island of Ireland' (Scully 2012, 193). However, as Scully states, 'In acknowledging the Irish diaspora, contemporary Ireland had entered into a somewhat contradictory and troubled relationship' since the reality of the '"lived" diaspora often "failed" to live up to the idealised version of the theorised diaspora' (2012, 193). In terms of the Irish in Britain, this 'failure' has often included accusations of clinging to memories of an Ireland now gone. It has also meant that for the second generation their identity claims are deemed inauthentic resulting, at times, in the derogatory label 'Plastic Paddy' (Scully 2010).

The return of the diaspora to Ireland in the form of the second generation from Britain is a meeting of this 'lived' diaspora and the modern nation state. The diaspora as a way of invoking Ireland's 'pluralism, hybridity and new-ness' (Scully 2012, 193) becomes the everyday reality of immigrants from Britain with family connections in Ireland. To complicate things further, for this second-generation group, the identities of the children of the Irish in Britain exist in the gap between nationalisms, historically been defined in opposition to one another (Ní Laoire 2002). In this context, there is no place to claim a hybrid Irish-British identity since the idea of Britishness or Irishness exists in binary opposition (Hickman 2000) with the possibility of a multi-placed identity unrecognised. In addition, this opposition is one in which Britishness is conceived as superior to Irishness (Scully 2012). As a result, the Irish in Britain have been incorporated into the white, yet con-comitantly, many experience anti-Irish sentiment (Hickman 1998; Hickman 2000). Despite these assumptions of shared whiteness, as the children of the 1950s' migrants became adults and increasingly voiced their mixed and multiple identifications, the homogeneity of the British white majority has come under question. Research with the second-generation Irish in Britain identified a range of 'positionings' resultant of lives at the intersection of the binary oppositions of Irish and Britishness (Hickman et al. 2005). Thus, in an English/British context, the identity claims of this group 'reveal the limita-tions of whiteness and the boundaries of Englishness' (Hickman et al. 2005, 178) and the reality of this (at times difficult to articulate) hybrid identity.

METHODOLOGY

This chapter draws from a larger research project on second-generation return migration from Britain to Ireland. The focus was on the children of those who emigrated to Britain in the 1950s, a decade in which over 400,000 people emigrated (Delaney 2007) and who, as adults, chose to 'return'. The majority of the participants were born in the 1960s and all grew up in cities and towns in Britain at a time when claiming an Irish identity could be problematic due mainly to the colonial histories and the political conflict in the north of Ireland. Information was collected from thirty second-generation Irish returnees using a qualitative methodology utilising written commentary and in-depth interviews. Participants were recruited through local print and radio media and notices in small shops. Participants were asked to 'write ... something about how you have come to be living in Ireland'. This was followed up with in-depth interviews where the general themes of growing up in Britain and the decision to move to Ireland could be explored. Participants recalled events which shaped their sense of themselves as connected to Ireland through everyday activities in Britain, combined with holiday visits 'home' to Ireland. They also gave examples of how this claim of connectedness is often not understood by an Irish population who know of the diaspora as 'out there somewhere' but seem unable to comprehend the reality of meeting an individual with an English accent who is living in Ireland, who claims to be Irish and is knowledgeable about this place.

The work was, in part, motivated by my own experience as a second-generation Irish-returned migrant. My positioning as an 'insider' to this research enabled a freedom in which 'we' could discuss 'them' the Irish or 'them' the English/British; a freedom that was particularly useful when considering issues surrounding our Irish/British identities including the extent to which we feel we are, or are not, a part of the Irish 'we'.

GROWING UP 'IRISH' IN BRITAIN

Many of the participants described how growing up in Irish families and communities in Britain shaped their awareness of themselves as connected to Ireland and a sense of being 'different' from English people. In terms of the taken-for-grantedness of Irish childhoods, Catherine[2] described the world in which she grew up, in north Manchester, as 'our own little Irish bubble', explaining that 'most of the people we knew were Irish, all of our neighbours, all of my parents' friends, all of my parents' colleagues. I went to a Catholic school where a lot of the children were either born in Ireland or second generation Irish'. Michael, who grew up in Southampton, also referred to being immersed in an 'Irish' way of being: 'The priests were all Irish, from Cork, Murphy, O'Connor. Most of Mum's friends seemed to be Irish. It wasn't massively Irish dancing, Irish music it just seemed to be more ... *"craic"* and we just thought this was normal'. Participants referred to typical Irish dinners of 'meat and two veg' and the Catholicism of their families, which meant regular mass attendance and attending Catholic schools. For some, there were visits to Irish shops for everyday goods such as sausages and cheese which took on an exotic quality when bought in Willesden or Tooting, and/or the local paper arriving by post from 'home' and of parents trying to listen in to *Céilí House*[3] or matches of the Gaelic Athletic Association[4] despite crackly radio signals.

As well as this immersion into the Irish worlds shaped mainly by their parents, the short distance home to Ireland meant that the children of the 1950s' migrants could and did return to Ireland regularly. This usually took place during school summer holidays where, as Buckley (1997, 111–12) notes, 'an unshakeable sense of continued belonging to their native neighbourhoods in Ireland' emerged 'anchoring' their identities there. Recollections of visits included great anticipation and excitement about the journey, usually by train and ferry, the welcome from family and neighbours and the freedom of the countryside, as Tony explains: 'We'd just land there and really feel that we were at home and all of the clichés are absolutely true about the freedom, just being able to wander around, the friendliness of neighbours'. There were also sensory memories of the place in terms of the different smells (such as turf smoke), different tastes and a different pace to life. These children were returned to 'home', demonstrating the way that these visits 'reinforced a sense of ethnic and national identity' for the individual, while for families they 'inserted new generations into strong social networks of grandparents, uncles, aunts and cousins' (Walter 2013, 18).

Despite descriptions of what seemed to be idyllic, rural summers, outside of the family, there was occasional hostility to these 'English' children during their visits in the 1960s and 1970s. Chris described that where his father was from in Sligo, everyone assumed that the person with the English accent was somebody's cousin and therefore accepted locally. His experience in his mother's home area in Limerick was different; there his accent defined a more negative experience, and he was told not to speak lest he be 'accused' of being English:

'Where my Mum's from there wasn't really a history of emigration. We used to be out with my cousins in the rural areas, they'd be like "if anyone asks where you're from – don't talk" and people used to hear your accent, other kids and they'd be like "oh English scumbags" what they'd hear from their parents, no experience, they just assumed "oh he's English", you might as well be carrying the Union Jack'.

Brian described a similar experience between Kildare and his father's home place in a village on the borders of Counties Limerick and Clare: 'relishing our departure from my mother's home in Kildare where we were often called English b******s by the kids in the nearby estate as we walked by to get to our grandparents farm'. These experiences indicate the lack of understanding for the identity claims of this group who have grown up with a sense that Ireland is home, yet find it is not always welcoming.

THE REALITIES OF RETURN MIGRATION – BEING PART OF THE IRISH 'WE'

Most participants described their migration as coming back, coming home or at least returning to a familiar place. Kate explains: 'It was that sense that it was always, "are you going home for summer?" Ireland was always called home'. The fact that Ireland was 'home' was not necessarily understood by others in England. Frank recalls conversations about his summer holidays: 'We're going home. Are you going home in August or whatever? And a lot of my English friends couldn't get that but the Irish ones would understand it'. For many the decision, as adults, to settle in Ireland was, therefore, a decision to 'go home'. Steve stated that 'really for the first time in my life I do know I am at "home", a feeling that I never really felt in England, despite a relatively happy childhood there, a good education, and subsequent early career in the UK'. Tom recalled confusing his boss at work with his reference to home: 'People said to me what are you doing? It was coming home. When I told the charity [employer] I said I'm going home, I remember the boss saying "you're going home?"' Despite the sense that this is a form of return migration, the narratives of the group evidence that this return 'home' is not always straightforward. They provide an insight into the 'identity rules' and 'identity markers' (Kiely et al. 2001, 36) of Irishness in Ireland in terms of the circumstances in which a migrant is allowed to be inside the Irish 'we' and what it feels like to challenge the boundaries of Irishness.

The audibility of the Irish in Britain acts as the key marker of difference between them and the host British population (Walter 2008), and for the second generation, it is the absence of this audible difference that has often led to assumptions of assimilation into Englishness. Inevitably, it is these English accents by which the next generation are judged here in Ireland, supporting Ní Laoire's findings that 'belonging and being accepted as fully Irish is to a large extent a question of voice' (2008a, 44). This was summed up by Paula: 'After living here for the past twenty years as I said, no matter what, your accent makes you English'. For some, this consciousness of sounding different made them feel that they had to justify being in Ireland, as Caroline explains:

'You always feel like you have to prove it to people. I may sound English but actually I'm the same as you and now I've been here for twelve years you don't feel like you need to make that point so much and you'd also think people were a bit suspicious of you in the beginning. I mean they weren't but that's how I felt. They were trying to explain things to you because you might not understand and I do, I know, I have an Irish Granny and I've been to Ireland on holidays'.

For some, comments about the accent go one step further. Steve recalled, 'Someone said to me once "you've got a fine Tan[5] accent"', and Sean stated, 'On my good friend's phone I'm "Tan B*****d"', and added, 'but that was *just a joke*'.

The importance of accent in signifying what a 'real' Irish person is was illustrated by Chris, growing up in Manchester and now living in Sligo. He felt that it was a 'dirty secret for some people too that they were born in England. I know guys born in England who came here before they started school' and therefore could hide their 'foreignness' with their Irish accents. For Daniel, who moved from London to Galway with his pre-school age children, their Irish accents were essential to fitting in. He stated: 'Two of them were born in London but no one's ever going to know as they've got Irish accents'. Their British birth can be 'disguised' by their Irish accents, a family secret to be concealed. It also indicates that he has internalised the fact that his London accent positions him as 'not quite Irish', something that he has experienced directly. In November 2009, Daniel went to his local pub to watch the Republic of Ireland play a football match against France. As a result of an incident of handball during the game, France qualified for the 2010 World Cup at Ireland's expense. Daniel recalled his experience:

'We were all in there watching it, all Irish lads, one or two of them actually born in London but came back here, got Irish accents, one of them said "Dan, oh it doesn't matter to you, Dan, you're English" and I said "you know my surname why am I sitting here watching an Ireland game? Don't be talking to me", "oh I'm *only joking*", so I was raging anyway'.

Daniel clarified: 'But no they wouldn't be malicious now, it would *just be craic*', emphasising that these comments are often made as a joke which in itself can be disempowering, taking away one's right to be angry or insulted.

Although not confronted with regular anti-Englishness, Daniel's experience evidences the boundary of the Irish 'we' at a crucial moment of emotion for the nation, in the form of the national football team. A similar experience of exclusion was described by Brian, also in the sporting context, in a Limerick pub:

'I remember being in the pub one time watching the Irish team play and [rugby player/landlord] was behind the bar and I remember saying to him, "oh we played really well there" and he said to me "what do you mean, *we*?" and I said, "well Ireland" and he said, "what do you mean *we*?" I never went there again'.

It is significant that the boundaries of the Irish 'we' are contested in specific spatial and social settings. None of the participants felt that their Englishness limited them in terms of, for example, employment. However, in the social environment of the pub, at times of heightened national feeling, such as a sporting event, who is 'inside' or 'outside' the group takes on a new significance. In a similar social setting, Geraldine reported, 'I was in a pub and the group I was with was singing Irish songs that I knew and I joined in singing. Someone made a comment about me singing that I was a Brit or something like that, I made some comment and stood up for myself'. Rob also illustrates the significance of specific places (outside of the pub) to affirming his outsiderness: 'I was a steward at Pearse Stadium[6] for two years. That was an odd experience, being crowd control at a completely Irish dominated thing, I got some real hassle, if I'd say "you can't come through that gate" I'd get "who the f*** are you telling me"', indicating that his English accent has no authority in such an Irish environment.

In terms of religion, the following comment was made to Joe, who lives in Galway: 'One particular person, she said, "you don't come to Mass, you're a Protestant". Am I? "Cause you're English". Am I?' In this case, Joe's English accent resulted in local people making assumptions about other aspects of his identity. A similar comment was made to Tom by his mother-in-law. Tom lives in Sligo and his mother-in-law is from Dublin, suggesting that these misunderstandings and denials may also have a spatial variation across the country.

'I met my mother-in-law for the first time and she's like "you're Protestant". I said "why would I be a Protestant?" She said "all English people are Protestant". I said "well my mother and father are Irish", "well are they Irish Protestants?" I said, "no, people from the country had to go to England because there was no work" and I thought everyone would know that, to me that was strange. I thought everyone knew people emigrated, there was no work'.

Even in families, therefore, there is difficulty recognising these 'foreign born Irish' and to include them in the 'we' as Amy illustrates with this comment from her mother-in-law in which she is assumed to be English and therefore responsible for the loss of the native language: 'I said one day, "it's a shame that people don't speak Irish" and my mother-in-law said "well that was your lot that came and stamped it out"'.

The above comments illustrate the power of an accent to act as an 'identity marker' (Kiely et al. 2001, 36) of Irishness and from which other assumptions are frequently made about behaviour and identifications; as Daniel put it, 'You could be dressed in green and your first and second name could be in Gaelic and people still only hear your accent'.

DISCUSSION

Responses to Emigration from 1950s' Ireland

It is difficult to explain fully this lack of recognition for the second-generation Irish from Britain and their exclusion from the Irish 'we'. One participant felt his return with a young family was a way of confronting a silence: 'We're coming back, confronting Ireland with the history it would like to forget, which is migration, "I'm here to remind you that you couldn't keep my mother, you couldn't create conditions that would keep her, you couldn't keep my father"'. His 'foreign' presence was a living reminder of migration as an important aspect of local and national history.

The political response to the mass emigrations of the 1950s of which the parents of this group were part was, at best, ambivalent. The 'blame' for emigration often focused on the individual and the need to change a mindset that sought the excitement of abroad rather than question economic policies which consistently failed to provide employment (Lee 1989). Lee describes a 'political and professional elite' who were 'spiritual collaborators in the mass eviction process that drove more than half a million out between 1945 and 1960' (1989, 384), detached observers of a phenomena about which they believed they could do nothing. Lee adds that this political and professional elite were so effective in 'the techniques of indoctrination that many of the victims would continue to cherish the values responsible for their own plight' (1989, 385). Thus, these emigrants sent remittances, returned regularly and instilled in the next generation a love for the nation which had promoted their own departures. Smyth argues that emigration at the time simply did not 'fit' the Ireland that was imagined by the cultural nationalists in the early years of independence (Smyth 1997) and going to Britain was seen as crossing into the 'other camp' (Ryan 2004). Emigration was also perceived as a useful release for social tensions that might otherwise lead to radical change (Lee 1989), an attitude that persisted into the 1990s (O'Leary and Burke 1998). Emigration, therefore, allowed Ireland to continue to imagine itself in a particular way – rural, traditional and Catholic – and this was often in opposition to the imagining of the old enemy – urban, industrial and secular Britain.

The Possibility of Hybrid Identifications

Although movement to and from Britain has been ongoing, the mass emigration of the 1950s slowed in the following decades, with Ireland recording positive net migration between 1971 and 1981, composed mainly of Irish-born returning migrants and their families. In 2006, an ethnicity question was included on the census for the first time due to the increasingly ethnically diverse population and pressure from Irish Traveller representatives (King-O'Riain 2007, 519). Cadogan posits that 'censuses, in seeking to quantify ethnic identity, do not simply collect data, but also simultaneously help shape the emerging identities they seek to objectively record and document' (Cadogan 2008, 50). In the case of the Census of Ireland, this 'implicitly consolidates a large "white Irish" ethnic grouping as culturally homogenous' (2008, 52) and suggests that this is how it has always been. In the white category where the options are 'Irish', 'Irish Traveller' or 'Any other White background', there is no possibility for hybrid identification on the lines of Irish-English or Irish-British. There is a long history of entanglement between these two nations, yet it is as if this entanglement happens without touching individual lives. If census categories help create social reality (Cadogan 2008), then there is a denial of the social reality of living a hybrid Irish-English identity as lived daily by people in both Ireland and Britain.

For participants in this study, this is not necessarily an issue, for many of them would describe themselves as ethnically Irish. Most, not all, have Irish passports and most would support the Irish national team. Some maintain many links with Britain, others less so; however, none would deny their links to Britain and many describe very successful educational and career experiences and happy upbringings in Britain. Having recognised their 'not fully Irish' status and the way that they have tested the boundaries of Irishness, it is also worth exploring the agency of the individual migrant. Rather than being left abandoned by their home nation and outside the Irish 'we', many choose to claim a space in which their Britishness can be included. Again, accent was an important feature of this, as Amy explained:

'I'm conscious of wanting to keep my own [accent] because I think it is important to know who you are. It's important to be comfortable. ... I mean I don't think I can ever call myself Irish and I don't think I could ever call myself English because I'm just not either, I don't feel I'm Irish, I feel like I'm London-Irish and that's a unique experience and I think it's unique to the economics of the time, I don't know if people will be that again, it's a very specific time'.

On a general level, the presence of an Irish-English label allows the possibility that such an identity could and does exist, opening up the idea of a hybrid identity as an option. This enables recognition of the social reality for all resulting from the long history of movement between the two countries. In the British context, Campbell (2011) has recently explored the contribution of the 'Irish-English' to British popular music, arguing that being brought up in England by Irish parents shaped a particular sensibility identifiable in the music of second-generation musicians such as the members of *The Smiths* and *The Pogues*, among others. In the literature on migration, there is increasing recognition of the hybrid nature of migrant identities which incorporate multiple places, lived and remembered. For Lavie and Swedenburg, this hybridity is signified by the hyphen in an identity label such as in Irish-American where, they argue, that the hyphen is the 'third time-space' or 'imaginary homeland' in which diasporas exist or borders are represented (1996, 16). However, for the Irish-English/British community, there is no such label as John, who described himself as Leeds-Irish, explained, 'There's something to do with the whole concept of somebody being "Irish British", it just doesn't quite sound right. It's normal enough for people to refer to themselves as African-American, Irish-American, West Indian-British, or whatever, but Irish-English, well which is it? It can't be both!!'

CONCLUSION

Diaspora has become increasingly visible in current discourses around migration. This 'catch all' term for the multifarious versions of the Irish abroad masks a diversity of diasporic experience. It also results in a perception of the diaspora as fixed in the 'elsewhere' and not a position from which an individual might return. Returning to Ireland is rarely a straightforward homecoming, as much of the literature on return has found (Ní Laoire 2008a inter alia), and it is further complicated for the second-generation Irish from Britain. Despite the changed and improved relations between Britain and Ireland, the everyday reality remains one in which audible difference matters and the point at which Irishness is defined is in its 'not Englishness'.

Concomitantly, for the individuals involved, there is a reassessment of self in the context of their changed relationship with place through migration. If identity is about what we might become rather than 'who we are' or 'where we came from' (Hall 1996, 4), then for many of the participants their return led to a reassessment of their identity in the place in which they have chosen to make their future. For some, their lifelong belief in their Irish identity did not change, although they learnt to adjust to the fact that Irish people may not always acknowledge their claims. For others, their experience in Ireland led them to a greater realisation of their Englishness and their dual belongings. This, however, leads to additional complications for this group of migrants for whom a hybrid identity label is not an option resulting in the need to repeatedly justify or explain who they are.

The second-generation Irish from Britain are one strand of the Irish 'we' who are barely acknowledged. Their accents announce them as English while at the same time their family connections and Irish names mean that to a certain extent they can assimilate, and their children with Irish accents and Irish names are likely to disappear back into the majority 'we'. The returning second-generation Irish from Britain, therefore, blur the dualisms between 'Irish host' and 'immigrant newcomer' and they blur the dualisms between the Irish in Ireland and the Irish abroad, in a sense, through their status as insiders from 'outside'.

NOTES

1. The author wishes to thank the Irish Research Council for funding this research into second-generation return migration from Britain.

2. All names have been changed in order to provide anonymity to the research participants.

3. *Céilí House* was (and continues to be) a radio programme of Irish céilí music which has been broadcast on Saturday night at least since the 1950s. In its early days, before television, it is thought to have attracted over one million listeners every Saturday, made up of the Irish both at home and in Britain (Browne 2004).

4. The Gaelic Athletic Association (GAA) supports Irish culture through organising and promoting traditional Irish games including hurling and Gaelic football. Every year, inter-county matches take place with a championship competition in the summer months. In the past, the major games were broadcast by the state broadcaster *Radio Éireann* (now RTE) with the Irish abroad going to great lengths to listen in (see Ó hEithir 2005 for examples).

5. Being called a 'Tan' is a reference to the Black and Tans, an auxiliary unit of the Royal Irish Constabulary who were brought in to Ireland in 1919 and are remembered for their brutality.

6. Pearse Stadium is the ground of the GAA in Galway City.

Chapter 7

Irregular Migrants in Ireland and the United States

Discursive Representations by Irish Parliamentary Members

Elaine Burroughs

IRREGULAR MIGRATION AND THE IRISH PARLIAMENT

The European Commission (2004) defines an irregular migrant as 'any person who does not, or no longer, fulfils the conditions for entry to, presence in, or residence on the territories of the Member States of the European Union'. The terminology used to refer to irregular migrants in public and political discourse is multiple, contested and implicitly loaded with meaning and significance.[1] Furthermore, different types of migration are conflated as one, particularly in relation to those seeking asylum and refugees, who are referred to as irregular/illegal and vice versa (see Burroughs and O'Reilly 2013).[2] Many of these terms criminalise migrants, and in an attempt to remain independent, academics and migrant support groups tend to use terminology that focuses on the immigration system (e.g. sans papiers). A variety of terms are employed by Irish parliamentarians, but the general trend is to refer to those with an irregular immigration status in Ireland as *illegal immigrants*, while Irish emigrants in the United States are referred to as the *undocumented Irish*. By using language in this way, Irish parliamentarians are able to make distinctions between these migrant groups. In an attempt to step away from the various discursive devices that are at play here, this chapter utilises the term irregular migration/migrant when discussing this type of migration.

Irish people have emigrated to the United States for many decades and an established Irish community resides there. A substantial proportion of these Irish migrants have an irregular immigration status, and local community groups and Irish politicians continually lobby authorities in the United States in order to establish a regularisation scheme. During the 2000s, members of the Irish government and the opposition continually stated their support for the undocumented Irish and noted how they are contributing financially to their cause and lobbying for a change in their status (e.g. Ahern 2004, 593; Kenny 2008, 666; McGinley 2004, 593). In contrast, irregular migration in Ireland is a very recent phenomenon and it is only since the 1990s that significant numbers of immigrants began to arrive due to the Celtic Tiger boom economy and the accession of EU member states (Mac Éinrí and White, 2008). However, this migration occurred in a legislative vacuum. Very little immigration legislation existed in Ireland prior to the Immigration Act 1999, other than the Aliens Act 1935 and the Aliens Orders (1946 and 1975) (Quinn and Kingston 2012, 9). A range of immigration legislation was introduced in the 2000s, but it was implemented in a piecemeal and reactive manner, with no clear long-term plan (Collett and Lacko 2006, 3). No one piece of legislation deals solely with irregular migration in Ireland and different components of numerous bills, acts and policies govern it.[3] The eight-year period between 2002 and 2009 is highly important, as Ireland experienced an increase in the levels of migration and an increase in the governance of migration. Therefore, references to migration were also heightened during this time.

Various societal institutions (e.g. media outlets) are important places of power and frequently disseminate political discourses. Yet, the Parliament remains highly important, as it represents a tangible site for the functioning of power and democracy, and it is a place from which official political discussions are disseminated (Van Der Valk 2003; van Dijk 2000a). This chapter subscribes to a Foucauldian understanding of power formation (Foucault 1991) and contends that parliamentary discourses can operate as subtle and obscure instruments of power. Parliamentary discourses hold great authority and the legitimised information that parliamentarians (re)produce is disseminated into society, where it can lead to the establishment and/or reinforcement of a variety of 'mentalities' or 'dominant' discourses (van Dijk 2000a). Furthermore, immigration policy and legislation is formulated, debated and defended in this place (Bauder and Semmelroggen 2009). The various representations that parliamentary members distribute about irregular migration can form legitimised 'truths', which frame how it is conceptualised and understood at both the institutional and individual level (van Dijk 2000b).

It is important to deconstruct discourses that refer to irregular migration in order to uncover materialisations of governmental ideologies and 'dominant' ways of thinking about it (van Dijk 1997; van Dijk 2009; Wodak et al. 2009). The nature of parliamentary discourses are also notable, as they tend to be strategic, argumentative, persuasive and formal in tone (Pujante and Morales-Lopez 2008; Van Der Valk 2003). Parliamentary speeches are usually prepared in advance, approved at the political party level and placed on the official record. One liberating mechanism for Irish parliamentarians is the provision of 'parliamentary privilege' (Article 18 1922)[4]; thus some parliamentary discourses may not be 'sayable' in other societal contexts. Nevertheless, given the Irish laws that prohibit explicit expressions of discrimination or racism, most parliamentary members will refrain from making overt prejudicial remarks. If parliamentarians do express such sentiments, they will usually be undertaken through subtle or indirect means (van Dijk 1997), as implicit discrimination does not attract major attention from parliamentary colleagues, the media or the public.

A substantial body of work has examined parliamentary texts that refer to migration (e.g. Bauder and Semmelroggen 2009; Rojo and van Dijk 1997; Triandafyllidou 2000; Van der Valk 2003; Wodak and van Dijk 2000). In the Irish context, research that explores political discourses of migration is minimal (Burroughs 2015; Haynes et al. 2010). This chapter aims to address this gap by presenting a critical discourse analysis (CDA) of discourses produced about irregular migration in the Irish parliament. This chapter begins by outlining the CDA methodology undertaken – Topoi Analysis. It then relays how the parliamentary data was gathered and organised and explains the rationale behind interviewing political elites. The main body of this chapter conveys the findings from the parliamentary data, discussing each topos (argumentation) individually. In order to further unravel the ideological underpinnings of discourses that surround irregular migration, these findings are supplemented with the discourses from interviews with political elites.

TOPOI ANALYSIS

This research employs a Topoi Analysis to analyse Irish parliamentary texts in order to uncover how irregular migration is ideologically conceived and discursively produced during a noteworthy period in Ireland's recent history. This method was developed by Utz Maas (1984) and is based on a Foucauldian understanding of the operation and function of discourses. Through this framework, the aim is to identify argumentation schemes that are implicitly embedded within a given text. These argumentations or topoi represent 'common-sense' rationalities relating to a body of collective knowledge that is shared among groups and communities (Bauder 2008a, 2008c; van Dijk 2000a). Thus, what one seeks to identify in texts are taken-for-granted arguments that are tied to concepts rather than specific words. These 'common-sense' rationalities function to strengthen 'dominant' ideologies, through their various formations and repetitive use over time. By identifying differing topoi within a given text, multiple perspectives, thought schemes and hidden premises of argumentation can be uncovered (Grue 2009).

SOURCING PARLIAMENTARY AND INTERVIEW DATA

Data was sourced from the lower house of parliament (the Dáil), the upper house (the Seanad) and two executive committees that debated migration (the Committee on European Affairs and the Committee on Justice, Equality, Defence, and Women's Rights).[5] An array of relevant keywords (i.e. illegal immigrant[s], illegal, migrant[s], migration, undocumented and irregular) were used to identify over 1,000 texts in the form of transcripts of parliamentary debates (including bills and motions), written answers, priority questions and statements.[6] This research found that five distinct argumentations (topoi) framed discussions about irregular migration. This included the following categories: control, economy, humanitarian, danger and culture.

Interviews were undertaken with politicians who were members of Parliament during the period under analysis. As parliamentary texts often refer to irregular migration as a side issue, or discuss it in relation to other topics, the aim of the interviews was to allow a space for irregular migration to be discussed as a sole issue of concern, for expansion upon parliamentary data, and to assess if similar argumentations arose. Potential interviewees were selected as a target population on the basis of having referred to irregular migration in Parliament. Over twenty politicians (from all political parties) were contacted and a total of six interviews were conducted. Interviewees were asked a series of in-depth questions about irregular migration in Ireland and the United States, focusing particularly on the 2000s. Of course, the opinions expressed by these interviewees are not representative of all political views. Nonetheless, they offer an insight into how key individuals, who were involved in the debate on irregular migration, conceptualised the issue.

Table 7.1   List of Interviewees

Interviewee	Status Between 2002 and 2009	Name	Code
1. Fianna Fáil Minister	Member of Government	Identity is confidential	(Fianna Fáil 2011)
2. Fine Gael TD	Member of the Opposition	Bernard Durkan	(Durkan 2011)
3. Fine Gael TD	Member of the Opposition	Denis Naughten	(Naughten 2011)
4. Green Party TD	Member of Government	Ciaran Cuffe	(Cuffe 2011)
5. Sinn Féin TD	Member of the Opposition	Caoimhghín O'Caoláin	(O'Caoláin 2011)
6. Independent TD	Member of the Opposition	Finian McGrath	(McGrath 2011)

PARLIAMENTARY DISCOURSES OF IRREGULAR MIGRATION

The sample of parliamentary texts discussed in this chapter mainly refers to irregular migration in Ireland; however, irregular migration in a number of other countries is also discussed (34 per cent of all texts). This discrepancy in the geographical focus of the texts is important, especially in relation to the deconstruction of the topoi, as a migrant's country of origin can determine how they are represented. While parliamentarians conceptualise irregular migration through five topoi, the most distinctive dimension of this taxonomy is the domination of one topos – control. It is the most prevalent of all the topoi and constitutes 61 per cent (786) of texts. The topoi with the next highest frequency are the economy and humanitarian topoi, with each accounting for 8 per cent of texts. This is closely followed by the danger topos with 7 per cent. Culture is the least utilised topos at 4 per cent. Not only do these five topoi stand alone as distinctive argumentations, but they also intertwine on multiple levels to form 'dominant' discourses about irregular migration. These topoi are consistently and repeatedly used, resulting in them becoming 'natural' ways to think about irregular migration. This chapter argues that governmental power operates through the (re)production of particular ideologically laden discourses over time. Therefore, these topoi provide evidence of the manner in which broader power formations can operate (Gordon 1991).

THE CONTROL DISCOURSE

Parliamentary texts that discussed irregular migration mainly referred to issues relating to control and prevention (61 per cent of texts). Three key discourses construct irregular migration through the lens of control. The first discourse argues that irregular migration in Ireland must be prevented and controlled. This discourse is formed through a variety of narratives that centre on portraying immigration enforcement at both an Irish and a European level as strong and inflexible:

> 'All foreign nationals have a responsibility to ensure that they have permission from the immigration authorities to be in the State and the fact that they have entered into a relationship with an Irish national in no way dilutes this obligation. Any person who is unlawfully present in the State would be expected to leave'. (Ahern 2009, 696)

As many references to irregular immigration in Ireland are part of broader discussions of other 'types' of migration (e.g. asylum or trafficking), this strict control attitude is applied to various types of unauthorised or unwanted non-EU migration. In this context, the phrase *bogus refugee* is employed on a number of occasions (e.g. O'Flynn 2003, 565), which implicitly legitimises the notion that claims for asylum are mostly unsubstantiated (Mountz 2010). Justifications for enforcement measures were made by representing irregular migrants in Ireland as deviant characters, as unknown entities and ultimately as those that embody the 'other'. For instance, the implementation of the Citizenship Referendum in 2004 (see Quinn 2005) was legitimised by portraying immigrants[7] as deceitful people who intentionally target Ireland as a place to have their children, with the aim of gaining residency rights:

'It was never intended that people coming in from abroad, mostly illegal immigrants, would seek to take advantage of that in respect of children born here. Ireland is the only EU Member State to grant an automatic citizenship right and we cannot ignore the fact that non-nationals are coming here so that they can have children born as Irish citizens'. (O'Donoghue 2004, 583)

On occasion, arguments in favour of control measures were expressed in conjunction with denials of racism (e.g. O'Flynn 2003, 565; Power 2008, 648), which aimed to buffer explicitly racist attitudes (van Dijk 1993, 180). Although this control discourse has several layers and is complex in its production and formation, it expresses a core message: irregular migration in Ireland must be prevented, managed, controlled and expelled.

The second key control discourse maintains that the Irish government's controlling of irregular migration in Ireland is too restrictive. These texts call for tolerance in relation to migrants' rights, for protection measures to be implemented and for amnesties to be established (e.g. Naughten 2008). Similarly, the third control discourse contends that US immigration policies are too restrictive and seeks regularisation for the undocumented Irish in the United States. The prevalence of this discourse is intriguing, as it is a clear indication of how certain migrant groups are conceptualised differently depending upon their country of origin. Place-based identity formation plays a significant role in how particular migrants are discursively represented. Indeed, the undocumented Irish are seen to be part of the Irish diaspora:

'Does the Minister agree that, at a conservative estimate, 50,000 young Irish men and women, our kith and kin, have not been regularised for various reasons?' (McGinley 2004, 593)

Irish parliamentarians proudly express how they have prioritised the issue of the undocumented Irish and are tirelessly working to address this situation (Ahern 2004, 593). In contrast, irregular immigrants in Ireland are not seen to be part of the broader imagined Irish community. Thus, it is argued that they should obey Irish immigration procedures and should not enter or remain in the country illegally. Accordingly their exclusion is legitimised. These discourses provide evidence of how identities are constructed and are linked to broader conceptualisations of national identity.

THE ECONOMY DISCOURSE

Immigrants are frequently perceived purely in economic terms (Bauder 2008b; Bauder and Semmelroggen 2009). Parliamentary texts that refer to irregular migration in an economic sense account for 8 per cent of the cohort of data. There are four distinct discourses that exist within the economy topos. The first of these discourses focuses upon the cost of border control. The expenses incurred in defending Irish borders and the Common Travel Area are portrayed as necessary (Ahern 2009, 693). Additionally, a range of control measures are justifiably implemented, as they are said to prevent illegal entry and the associated expenditures that stem from this. In particular, the policy of Carriers' Liability – where transportation carriers are fined for allowing those who do not have correct documentation to travel (see Quinn 2003) – was legitimised with claims that it would save on government funds in the long term by preventing illegal entry and subsequent deportations (e.g. Hoctor 2004, 579; O'Flynn 2003, 565).

The second economy discourse expresses concern over the range of perceived costs associated with irregular migrants when they are in Ireland, such as the expenses incurred in providing housing, legal aid or interpreters. Although irregular migrants are not permitted to claim any welfare payments in Ireland, the language that promotes this misgiving includes 'remain on social welfare payments', 'rely on the State for a long period', 'sponge off the State' (Kehoe 2004, 591) and 'costing us €85,000 a day' (Naughten 2009).[8]

A notable linguistic aspect of Irish parliamentary texts is the justification of a racist attitude in Irish society due to the perceived economic costs of irregular migrants: 'This is a perfect opportunity for ordinary citizens to become racists' (Kehoe 2004, 591). This type of statement is typical of elite racism (van Dijk 1993, 189–90), as the politician deflects racism from himself and his own elite group (politicians), yet projects this attitude onto the Irish people. Furthermore, irregular migration is directly associated with criminal activities: 'Detect illegal immigration and associated criminality' (Ahern 2009, 693). Irregular migration is frequently mentioned in conjunction with a range of unlawful behaviour, such as (social welfare) fraud, prostitution and human trafficking. These practices are said to cost the State a 'significant amount of money' (Naughten 2009, 682).

Similarly, the third economy discourse concentrates on the expenses associated with removing irregular migrants from Ireland (e.g. McDowell 2003, 569; O'Flynn 2003, 565). The deportation of irregular migrants is said to be costly, 'particularly in the case of removals to distant countries such as Nigeria, China, etc.' (Ahern 2009, 679).

The final economy discourse relays how irregular migrants can benefit the economy. A proportion of these discourses actually referred to Eastern European migrants in Ireland (e.g. Allen 2006) and once again a conflation of migrant groups occurs. This positivity was due to the buoyant Irish economy of that time and the requirement for immigrant workers. In contrast, a substantial number of these economy discourses discussed the way in which the undocumented Irish 'contribute greatly to the US economy' (Ahern 2005, 609), 'own businesses and are employing people there', and contribute to the United States both 'socially and economically' (English 2007, 641). The differences in how irregular migration in Ireland and the United States are conceptualised in relation to the economy are noteworthy. The inclusion and acceptance of irregular migrants in society clearly depends upon their country of origin.

THE HUMANITARIAN DISCOURSE

The humanitarian topos represents 8 per cent of texts and mainly argues that irregular migrants must be afforded rights and protection: 'We must give them support, legal rights and a helping hand while making sure they are treated humanely' (Crawford 2003, 565). A number of parliamentarians request 'compassion' and 'sensibility' in dealing with 'vulnerable' migrants (White 2009, 675) and calls are made for the safety of those smuggled or trafficked into Ireland. This concern is heightened in reference to minors (e.g. Ahern 2009, 698). Parliamentarians also offer considerable sympathy towards irregular Irish in the United States and relay the various consequences of living with an irregular status. An inability to attend family events and a lack of access to healthcare (e.g. Kitt 2009, 686) are described as 'a basic human right' (Connaughton 2007, 641) that 'our people' (Ó Murchú 2009, 194) should be assigned. Although Irish parliamentarians express much sympathy towards irregular migrants in Ireland, on the whole, parliamentarians represent them as victims in need of assistance from the state. In contrast, irregular Irish migrants are portrayed as good citizens, who are being treated unfairly by US authorities.

THE DANGER DISCOURSE

The danger topos accounts for 7 per cent of texts and expresses concern over the apparent threat that irregular migration poses. Irregular migrants are portrayed as a threat to border control[9] and are represented as criminal elements[10] who could invade or who could be operating as terrorists (e.g. Ahern 2005, 609). In conjunction with this, irregular migrants are mentioned in relation to several criminal acts, including (welfare and passport) fraud and sexual offences (e.g. rape, prostitution, trafficking). These portrayals function to create a sense of fear, which justify the requirement to implement increased border controls and to exclude unwanted immigration. Discourses that take an alternative view[11] are also evident and argue that irregular migrants are not dangerous or 'sinister' individuals; they merely want to reside in Ireland (Durkan 2008, 647). In relation to irregular Irish migrants in the United States, the primary argument is that they are not a danger to the economy or to the national security of the United States (Kenny 2006, 621).

THE CULTURE DISCOURSE

The culture discourse accounts for 4 per cent of texts and describes irregular migrants as possessing desirable or undesirable cultural attributes. While irregular migrants in Ireland are sometimes portrayed as 'decent, hard-working' people, who want to actively partake in Irish society (McGrath 2005), the majority of these discourses refer to the undocumented Irish in the United States. They are said to contribute to 'the economic, cultural and social life' of the United States (O'Mahoney 2007, 641) and are portrayed as hard-working, family and community orientated and law abiding (Cowen 2009, 679; Kenny 2008, 666). These representations feed into the broader agenda of parliamentarians to regularise the status of the undocumented Irish in the United States. In contrast, another discourse argues that irregular migrants in Ireland are undesirable due to their different cultural practices, perceived criminality and potential negative financial implications they may have on the Irish State: '... to meet the challenges of the marked increase in international travel with the increased threat of illegal immigration, serious and organised crime and terrorism' (Cowen 2007, 640). This discourse functions in the legitimate exclusion of irregular migrants from Irish society.

INTERVIEW DISCOURSES OF IRREGULAR MIGRATION

One of the key findings from the interviews with political elites reveals that irregular migration was discussed through the same five argumentations as the parliamentary texts. However, there are also differences between these sources. First, although irregular migration in both Ireland and the United States was mentioned during the interviews, the interviewees concentrated upon the Irish context. Second, the discourses that stemmed from these interviews were quite positive with regard to irregular migration in both Ireland and the United States.

THE CONTROL DISCOURSE

The Irish immigration system is heavily criticised by the interviewees. They describe it as 'chaotic' (Naughten 2011), that it 'showed a lack of compassion and understanding' (McGrath 2011) and that it is 'appalling, circuitous, laborious, not open to change' (Durkan 2011). Naughten (2011) argues that the Irish immigration process was so disjointed that it caused delays and forced people into an irregular immigration status. Even though some interviewees maintained that regularisations can act as an incentive for further irregular migration (Fianna Fáil 2011; Naughten 2011), it was generally thought that regularisations should have been available to migrants (Cuffe 2011; McGrath 2011; Naughten 2011). It is noteworthy that although sympathy is expressed towards the restrictions placed upon irregular migrants in the United States, interviewees also acknowledged the hypocritical attitude of the Irish government in its support for these people and its quite controlled approach towards irregular migrants in Ireland (Durkan 2011; Naughten 2011; O'Caoláin 2011).

Some discourses of control that emerged from the interview data reflect similar sentiments expressed in the parliamentary data and argue that irregular migration in Ireland must not be tolerated (Durkan 2011; Fianna Fáil 2011). Another similarity involves one interviewee distancing his elite group from racist sentiments and projecting it onto the Irish public. This individual describes the government as a judicious, rational decision maker, while the Irish people are said to be 'anti-illegal migration' and want to 'throw people back' (Fianna Fáil 2011). This interviewee discloses his thoughts on deporting children: 'It's hard to justify throwing little children back on a plane, back to their country. ... These are not easy things to do' (Fianna Fáil 2011). It is evident that the interviewee (a former minister) struggled with this particular issue. Yet, the phrase 'back to their country' points to a broader ideology that views these migrants as not belonging, and the concept of the 'other' functions to justify their deportation.[12]

THE ECONOMY DISCOURSE

Only a small number of interviewees state that irregular migrants have a positive impact on the economy. O'Caoláin (2011) refers to how a negative impression of irregular migrants in Ireland is constructed through misinformation about welfare payments. Overall, irregular migrants in Ireland were said to have a negative impact on the economy by 'undermining legitimate employment and legitimate employers' (Naughten 2011). Furthermore, some of the interviewees conceptualise asylum seekers and irregular migrants as the same entity. Indeed, Fianna Fáil (2011) describes them as 'not-genuine' people, and both Fianna Fáil (2011) and Naughten (2011) refer to the huge expenses incurred by the state on account of the asylum system and associated legal costs.

THE HUMANITARIAN DISCOURSE

Similar to the parliamentary data, the interviewees were overall positive about providing humanitarian assistance, asserting that the state should offer protection to those that require it. Yet, one interviewee constructed asylum seekers as disingenuous characters: 'The vast majority of people that came into the country were illegal immigrants, they weren't running from persecution, they were economic migrants' (Fianna Fáil 2011). By blurring the boundaries between asylum and irregularity, this statement functions to dismiss genuine claims for protection and justifies the high percentage of migrants who were denied humanitarian protection in Ireland. Additionally, the manner in which the term 'economic migrant' is used constructs the act of immigrating for employment as an unlawful and deceitful practice.

THE DANGER DISCOURSE

Interviewees stated that the act of migrating 'illegally' is a crime, and a number of interviewees linked irregular migration with criminal activities (Durkan 2011; Naughten 2011). As Naughten (2011) asserted, those with 'serious convictions' or those that have a 'record in other jurisdictions' should be deported (Naughten 2011). Irregular migrants were also viewed as a potential security threat, and it was stated that it is important to 'know exactly who those illegal immigrants are' (Naughten 2011). Alternative argumentations mainly took the form of countering argumentations that constructed irregular migrants as a threat to society (Cuffe 2011; Durkan 2011).

THE CULTURE DISCOURSE

Interviewees primarily represented irregular migrants as desirable individuals, who hold many positive elements that Irish people should embrace in order to enhance Ireland's culture and society in general (Cuffe 2011; O'Caoláin 2011). They were described as good characters, hard workers, people who are seeking a better life and as people who contribute to society:

> 'The vast majority of illegal immigrants that I know, they are here, they want to work, they want to make a contribution, they don't want to go home or to the country they came from due to the negative situation they came from and they want to better themselves'. (McGrath 2011)

Notably, O'Caoláin (2011) stated that portrayals of irregular migrants as culturally undesirable can encourage racist attitudes.

CONCLUSION

Utilising a CDA approach, this chapter has deconstructed discursive representations of irregular migration in Ireland and the United States by Irish politicians and drawn attention to how ideological discourses, which are based on the nation-state rationale of governance, can lead to legitimised practices of exclusion. Overall, the argumentations inherent within the parliamentary discourses are place-based – irregular migrants in Ireland are mainly portrayed through a number of negative discourses, while irregular Irish migrants in the United States are usually represented through positive discourses. The interview discourses were mostly positive about irregular migration in Ireland. Some negative discourses were evident, especially in relation to the economy and danger topoi, but these were minimal. Furthermore, even though questions relating to irregular migration in both the Irish and US contexts were posed to interviewees, the focus remained on the Irish context. Therefore, although some similarities exist between the parliamentary discourses and the interview discourses, there were differences between these sources.[13] Nonetheless, it is notable that the five core argumentations still frame discussions of irregular migration by Irish politicians during the 2000s.[14]

Dominant discourses can influence how elites, members of other institutions and the general public conceive of irregular migration. This chapter has shown that five topoi intersect and overlap in order to ensure that an overall negative message about irregular migration in Ireland is disseminated into Irish society, while a general positive image of the undocumented Irish in the United States is maintained.[15] Nevertheless, these discursive normalisations link to broad ideological 'knowledges', which serve to (1) justify the implementation of immigration legislation that 'legitimately' exclude non-EU immigrants from Irish society and (2) resolve the immigration status of Irish undocumented migrants in the United States.

NOTES

1. Some of these terms include clandestine, unauthorised, non-compliant, unlawful, sans papiers, undocumented migrant, illegal immigrant and illegal alien. Often, this terminology is used interchangeably, which is perhaps inappropriate, as each term relates to different entities in different contexts; for example, identity documents, national histories and institutional discourses.

2. For a fuller discussion on the political milieu that surrounds the term 'illegal', see Bauder (2013) and De Genova (2002; 2013).

3. Namely, the Immigration Act 2003, the Employment Permits Act 2003, the Immigration Act 2004, and the Twenty Seventh Amendment of the Constitution Act 2004 [the Citizenship Referendum]. These acts permit a number of policies, including 'leave to land', Carriers' liability, Dublin II transfer, 'safe country of origin', repatriations, voluntary returns and readmission agreements (Quinn and Hughes 2004).

4. This ensures that statements expressed in Parliament are free from legal proceedings.

5. On a point of clarity it is to be noted that the main political party holds the most speaking time in Parliament and therefore a significant proportion of discourses identified here stem from the Fianna Fáil Party (a centre-right party).

6. Drawing on Bauder (2008c), a pilot analysis was undertaken in order to ensure that this approach was suitable. This involved reading a substantial cohort of material and identifying specific themes. With the aim of ensuring a consistent application of the coding scheme, the analysis was rechecked at numerous points in the research process. Information relating to each text was recorded, including the topoi, the date, the keyword(s), the geographical location the text referred to and the name and political affiliation of the parliamentary member.

7. Most especially in relation to female immigrants from outside the European Union.

8. It must be noted that some of the above statements may not relate directly to irregular migration, as asylum seekers/refugees are often referred to as irregular migrants (e.g. Lenihan 2008, 648). Nevertheless, these statements feed into a discourse that irregular migrants have a negative impact on the state's finances.

9. This was also evident within the control topos.

10. This was also conveyed through the economy topos.

11. However, even counters of misinformation can strengthen 'dominant' discourses, as the argumentation is repeated in the course of discrediting it. Therefore, even denials of danger can amplify the danger discourse. Indeed, this can be said for all of the topoi identified in this research.

12. This quotation highlights the advantages of conducting in-depth interviews, as it shows how those tasked with implementing deportation orders may have compassion for these people. Even so, the rationale of appropriate law enforcement outweighs any sympathy and legitimises the process.

13. This may be due to a number of factors: (1) the nature of the interview setting and the assumption of the researchers' position on irregular migration, (2) parliamentary debates mainly follow party lines and the interviews represent the

views of individual politicians and (3) the timing of the interviews may be important. The interviews took place in 2011, and those who were in power between 2002 and 2009 were no longer in government and could perhaps speak more freely and those who were members of the then opposition could easily criticise the politics of the governing parties of that time.

14. It must be noted that these five argumentations do not occur in isolation. Indeed, the international literature reveals that irregular migration is constructed through similar discursive devices in political discourse in a range of other countries. This includes the construction of irregular immigration as a threat in the United States (Salter and Piché 2011) and Europe (Vollmer 2011); the criminalisation of irregular migration in France (Van der Valk 2003) and Europe more broadly (Vollmer 2011); the concentration on border control against irregular migration in the United States (Salter and Piché 2011), Greece (Karyotis 2012), Spain (Rojo and van Dijk 1997) and Italy (Quassoli 2013); and the construction of migration through the argumentations of economy, humanitarianism and culture in Germany (Bauder 2008c).

15. It is acknowledged here that some positive references to irregular migration in Ireland are evident. Furthermore, individuals who produce these various discourses may not be consciously taking part in this process.

Chapter 8

Explaining EU Migrant Workers

Irish Political Interventions in Public Discourse

Martin J. Power, Amanda Haynes and Eoin Devereux

Since the expansion of the European Union (EU), Ireland has experienced a significant increase in the proportion of immigrants from EU states (Quinn 2010). Between 2002 and 2006, the fastest growing category apart from Irish or UK nationals, were EU nationals (6.6 per cent of the population). Polish nationals numbered 63,300, while the number of Lithuanian nationals was 24,600 (CSO Census 2006). This trend continued in the period to 2009: 'Between 2005 and 2009 an average of 44 per cent of the immigration flow and 54 per cent of the non-Irish immigration flow has been made up of nationals of EU States that acceded in 2004 together with Romania and Bulgaria which acceded in 2006' (Quinn 2010, 3). The 2006 census showed that Dublin South City had the highest concentration of foreign nationals anywhere in the state, with the figure standing at 18.7 per cent of the total population. Of this figure, 9.3 per cent were EU citizens.

Immigrants to Ireland, including EU nationals, often find themselves concentrated in the lowest paid and lowest grades of employment. In some cases, they are subject to exploitation on the part of employers who deny them access to the full rights to which they are entitled, both as EU nationals and as Irish residents. Despite these circumstances, migrant workers have nonetheless faced pockets of popular resistance to their presence; they have in some cases been characterised as undercutting and displacing Irish workers for example. In this chapter, we discuss the manner in which Irish politicians have framed EU migrant workers for the Irish public, focusing in particular on their experiences of their position in, and contribution to the economy, and their social welfare entitlements. We deconstruct politicians' contributions to public discourse by analysing the content of their statements in the print media, rather than through government or party press releases. This decision was informed by a desire to analyse those political statements that are most accessible to the public and therefore most likely to influence public opinion.

The data and conclusions discussed in this chapter are drawn from a larger research study of Irish politicians' statements regarding EU migrants living in Ireland, which was funded by Doras Luimní, a migrant support service based in Limerick City in the mid-west of Ireland. The methodology employed adopted a content analysis approach. Specifically, we undertook a qualitative content analysis of statements published over a two-year period. Print media content was sampled[1] from three newspapers – a national Broadsheet (*Irish Independent*) and two local imprints (The *Limerick Leader* and The *Limerick Post*). The *Irish Independent* was chosen as the national newspaper with the highest circulation figures within the period of the study. The time period within which we selected articles was 01/01/08–31/12/09. We selected this timeframe in order to enable us to examine the possibility of change in the nature of political statements in a period of transition from prosperity to recession.

Articles that met the sampling criteria were subjected to qualitative content analysis. Content analysis can be defined as 'a research technique for making valid and replicable inferences from texts ... to the contexts of their use' (Krippendorf 2004, 18). Content analysis involves identifying themes, concepts and patterns thereof within the data. We infer meaning through interpreting these patterns. Themes and concepts may emerge from the data as a result of close reading and constant comparison, a process facilitated by sensitivity to

- the relationship between the research question and the text and
- the relationship between the texts and the context to which meaning will be inferred.

We have endeavoured to identify the constructions which politicians contribute to public discourse regarding EU migrants and any misinformation in the content of their statements. We have restricted our analysis to the statements attributed to politicians and excluded the journalists' interpretations of these statements from our analysis. As a consequence of this process of data analysis, we identified nine key themes[2] (see Haynes, Power and Devereux 2010 for a full overview). In this chapter, we present the results of this analysis relating to discourse on the positioning of transnational EU migrant workers in the economy, and their social welfare entitlements.

IRELAND'S MIGRANT POPULATION

Prior to the start of the global economic crisis in 2008, migration became an increasingly important political issue in the wider context of social and economic change, with policy debate focused on a number of propositions. First, that replacement migration was needed to meet demographic shortfalls and provide for an ageing population, and secondly, that immigration was an engine of economic growth in what had become a competitive global skills market. In this regard, immigration was seen as a 'brain gain' and a way to avoid labour and skill shortages, contributing to economic growth and slowing wage inflation in the process.

Ireland experienced strong economic growth from the later part of the 1990s up to the middle of the 2000s, with the number in employment almost doubling to 2.1 million in 2007. Furthermore, the rate of unemployment dropped to approximately 4.5 per cent in 2007. The openness of Ireland's economy in 2007 was reflected in strong migratory flows and high levels of foreign direct investment. In fact, in that year, net inward migration stood at over 67,000 people (Economic and Social Research Institute 2010). In 2007, labour force participation rates were up to 80 per cent for migrants, compared to a national participation rate of 64.5 per cent, and in 2008, foreign nationals comprised 16 per cent of the labour force (FÁS 2009). Migrant workers tended to be concentrated in the areas of hotels and restaurants, wholesale/retail, manufacturing, financial services and health (Awad 2009). By the end of 2006, displacement of indigenous workers was still not a major or widespread phenomenon; however, Foras Áiseanna Saothair (FÁS), the Irish National Training and Employment Authority of that time (2007, 7), warned that 'displacement could become an issue for low-skill workers should there be an economic slowdown. Much would depend, in such circumstances, on the extent to which immigration to Ireland fell rapidly and existing foreign nationals returned home'.

Economic growth slowed in the second half of 2007, with Ireland eventually moving into a recession, which deepened in 2009. This economic collapse manifested itself in the labour market, with the numbers on the Live Register increasing by 70 per cent in 2008, while the average rate of unemployment for 2009 is estimated to have reached almost 12 per cent (Economic and Social Research Institute 2010). The construction, retail, hotel and restaurant sectors, which had particularly high concentrations of migrant labour, experienced a significant decline. Accordingly, there was acceleration in the rate of unemployment among immigrants for much of 2008, especially among accession state nationals, exceeding the rate of decline among natives (Barrett 2009).

The economic downturn would also appear to have had a major impact on the migration patterns of EU nationals to and from Ireland in 2008/2009. Of the 65,100 emigrating from the state between April 2008 and April 2009, EU12 nationals were by far the largest group. Additionally, immigration to Ireland from the EU12 countries manifested the largest fall of any group (from 33,700 to 13,500) between April 2008 and April 2009 (CSO 2009, 1). Yet, a significant proportion of immigrants appeared to remain in Ireland despite the decline in economic fortunes (Barrett 2009).

The economic downturn saw the public finances rapidly move into deficit. The situation worsened throughout 2008 and the general government deficit reached 14 per cent of GDP in 2009. It was estimated that the level of national debt may have exceeded 41 per cent of GDP in 2009, up from 12 per cent in 2007 (Economic and Social Research Institute 2010). Experts expressed concern that this vastly changed situation in the economy might negatively impact attitudes towards immigrants (Barrett 2009).

THE IMPORTANCE OF POLITICAL LEADERSHIP

In this economic and social context, political leadership on the matter of immigration is of crucial importance. This is because political elites, political parties – or processes implemented or controlled by political parties – are responsible for framing the issue of immigration, and for how, when and where these issues arrive on the political spectrum (Schain 2008, 465). Political elites also have substantial influence over the general publics' attitudes towards immigration. If all political parties and political elites are supportive of a particular policy, it may well result in 'politically aware individuals ... incorporating these preferences into their own belief systems' (McLaren 2001, 87). With a more differentiated spectrum of political positions, individuals have a choice to align with the party advocating policies most in agreement with their own ideological convictions (McLaren 2001, 87).

Some commentators would argue that political parties are often merely 'conduits of public opinion'. But political parties are substantially more than conduits; they structure as well as reflect voter opinion (see Lens 2002). Political parties are ultimately composed of a hierarchy of ideological individuals (Bale 2008, 453). Thus, if political elites and political parties play a key role in creating public attitudes, it is important to investigate the discourses constructed in relation to migration (McLaren 2001, 88).

International literature suggests that immigration poses a more severe challenge for the centre-right than for the left. In general, parties of the left have tended to be supportive of immigration and immigrants as they are viewed as additional working-class electoral support. However, left-wing parties have also supported restrictive immigration policies. Such instances usually occur when employers are seen to be using immigrant labour to deflate wages or because reaction to immigrants by displaced native working-class voters has made them electorally susceptible. Parties of the centre-right experience similar tensions regarding issues of immigration. For these parties, immigration is of substantial benefit to their 'business wing', but they face a challenge to please those business interests without disaffecting their 'identity wing' who are concerned about national identity (Tichenor 2002, 169–75 cited in Schain 2008, 467–68).

POLITICIANS EXPLAINING MIGRANT WORKERS

In an article entitled 'Shortage of work leads to drop in immigrants' (8 October 2008), Conor Lenihan, Junior Minister[3] for Integration, warned against projecting 'phobias, worries or concerns' about the economic recession onto migrant workers in Ireland. He further stated that research indicated far higher rates of unemployment among migrants than among Irish citizens. The minister continued to highlight this issue in an article entitled 'Ethnic tensions alert as immigrants fight for jobs' (29 December 2008). He warned of 'tensions' which could develop in the competition for jobs between Irish and immigrant workers as unemployment rose and Irish people returned to sectors of the economy that they had largely abandoned (and that were subsequently filled by migrant labour) during the economic boom. The minister stated that 'there is potential for tension because people project their anger on to ethnic groups when they see their friends, uncles and aunts losing their jobs. You tend to have that pattern, by international evidence. It's not defined that it's going to happen in Ireland, but we have to guard against it'. Lenihan went on to say that 'we still have a need for immigrant labour, and it is here to stay' (29 December 2008). In the preceding months, Lenihan was also on record as insisting that it was 'not correct' that transnational migrants were displacing Irish workers (19 July 2008).

Concerns about the displacement of Irish workers were apparent in public discourse as far back as 2005 and 2006 (Quinn 2010, 6; also see Smith 2008, 426). Minister Lenihan's statements sought to undermine the politicisation of fear by presenting contradictory evidence. However, Hajer and Versteeg (2009) assert that to effectively oppose divisive and conflict-generating statements, politicians need to reframe the issue by presenting the public with alternative understandings of the situation at hand, rather than simply countering the opposing argument. Rebuttals, they argue, often serve to reinforce the original framing in the public mind. Although the content of Lenihan's statements is to be welcomed, there is a danger that the stylistic focus on denial may be counterproductive. A reframing of the issue as one of a requirement for solidarity in recessionary times might be more effective.

As an example of how the economic aspect of citizenship is emphasised within neoliberal political discourse, Fine Gael immigration spokesman Denis Naughten, in commenting on the rate of unemployment among migrants, said, 'The figures showed a need to provide extra language support for foreign nationals' and that 'by equipping migrants with the required English language skills, it will allow them move up the value chain which will in turn benefit our economy' (4 October 2008). An alternative proposal, drawing upon a resource competition frame (van Dalen and Henkens 2005; Espenshade and Hempstead 1996) was introduced by Fine Gael's Leo Varadkar, who suggested that as unemployed foreign workers cost the state €400m every year in dole payments, it might be prudent to pay six months of social welfare benefits to foreign national workers prepared to return to their country of origin (see 5 September 2008 and 29 September 2008). Varadkar argued that his proposed repatriation scheme would be strictly voluntary. However, Fianna Fáil backbencher Thomas Byrne said it was 'a very dangerous proposal and sets a new low in Irish politics' (5 September 2008). Furthermore, Social and Family Affairs Minister Mary Hanafin said:

> All European nationals have free movement. The only people [Mr Varadkar] could be talking about are non-EU nationals, which must mean he was talking about the Africans, which means it's a racist comment. ... He would want to think where he's putting his foot before he puts it in his mouth. It is undoubtedly racist to do it. ... We are delighted to have these people; they are making a contribution to our economy. The Irish were never rejected anywhere when things got difficult for them. (10 September 2008)

Varadkar responded to these accusations of racism by stating that 'if Fianna Fáil is accusing me of racist comments, then they are guilty of racist acts and ... hypocrisy' (10 September 2008). However, the accusations would appear to have stifled any further debate on this issue. By late September, Varadkar said he did not want to comment further on the issue, but did add that 'despite the over-reaction from Conor Lenihan and Mary Hanafin, it is already being done on a small scale basis so I don't see why it can't be extended. ... The government doesn't want to talk about immigration. Anyone who says anything is accused of playing the race card. If official Ireland ignores it, it will come back to bite us' (29 September 2008). It is interesting that after Varadkar made this argument, a member of his own party, Senator John Paul Phelan, accused a Libertas[4] candidate for the European Parliament elections of 'playing the race card' when that person suggested that given Ireland's economic difficulties and the rising unemployment rates, no additional foreign nationals should be given residency, but those already resident in Ireland should be allowed to remain. Senator Phelan stated: 'I was shocked at his outrageous statement. ... To try and blame foreign nationals for our economic problems is completely missing the point' (15 May 2009).

Statements relating to assisting foreign citizens to return 'home' suggest an understanding of immigration as a temporary phenomenon (see Greenwood and Adshead 2010, 6; Canoy et al. 2006, for a discussion of the limitations of this understanding of migration). However, many immigrants chose to remain in Ireland as the recession deepened. Even where employment is the initial impetus for inward migration, other factors such as intimate relationships and Irish children's affiliation to the nation may result in the decision to remain despite an economic downturn. Loyal (2010, 88) also asserts that the 'global nature of the recession has meant that even many of the EU nationals who can leave and re-enter without restrictions are unwilling to do so'.

FRAMING MIGRANT LABOUR EXPLOITATION IN IRELAND

It is crucial that strong regulations are in place to ensure that employers comply with labour legislation so as to avoid the exploitation of workers (FÁS 2007, 7). In an Irish context, the key pieces of equality legislation are the Employment Equality Acts, 1998 and 2004, and the Equal Status Acts, 2000 and 2004. These acts proscribe discrimination in employment, vocational training, advertising, collective agreements, the provision of goods and services etc. on nine distinct grounds: gender; marital status; family status; age; disability; race; sexual orientation; religious belief and membership of the Traveller Community. Yet, research indicates that public perception of resource competition promotes negative attitudes towards immigrants (Semyonov et al. 2008; Coenders et al. 2005),[5] particularly in times of recession. J. J. Lee (1989) asserts that the Irish have historically tended precisely towards such perceptions, viewing economic prosperity in particular as a 'zero sum' game, in which others' betterment necessarily equates to the worsening of one's own fortunes and vice versa. In such contexts, the role played by our political leaders (and the media) is of paramount importance, particularly in the context that these groups have the power to define our social world and subsequently 'impose a framework within which migrants are perceived' (O'Donoghue 2010).

In examining the sample of articles, only three contained relevant statements highlighting discrimination against EU nationals with regard to pay, all published in the *Irish Independent*. Statements concerning EU migrants on this theme were made by individuals from across the political spectrum, including Fine Gael's Denis Naughten, Fianna Fáil's Dara Calleary and Councillor Jimmy Mulroy, Sinn Fein's Kevin Meenan, Joe Higgins and Clare Daly (then) of the Socialist Party and Labour's Joe Costello.

In August 2009, Fine Gael's immigration spokesperson Denis Naughten was named in an article criticising a shortfall in the number of National

Employment Rights Authority (NERA) inspectors. Deputy Naughten is cited as highlighting the exploitation of transnational migrant workers and is quoted publicly critiquing the government's enforcement of labour law in this regard:

> Fine Gael immigration spokesman Denis Naughten said, 'Cowboy companies were breaking the law by paying less than the agreed minimum wage rates to migrant workers in particular. The Government is refusing to enforce the law and both Irish workers and migrant workers are paying the price', he said. Mr Naughten pointed to examples in the construction industry where Irish workers were let go and replaced by migrant workers at much lower rates. 'Some have hit national prominence such as the treatment of Gama construction workers from Turkey and the Polish workers at the ESB station in Moneypoint, Co Clare', he said. ... Mr Naughten said it was time for companies who exploited workers to be 'weeded out'. 'The only way that this can be effectively eradicated is by putting in place a stringent inspection system', he said. (*Irish Independent*, 24 August 2009)

In the same article, then Junior Minister for Labour Affairs Dara Calleary is cited as defending the adequacy of the government's response to the exploitation of workers and placing the responsibility on individuals to report cases of exploitation:

> Junior Minister for Labour Affairs Dara Calleary called on people to complain to NERA if they were aware of cases where migrant workers were being exploited. 'I'm happy there is enough protection in place. We have inspectors who have a key knowledge of the migrant sector, so we are responding to the challenge'. (*Irish Independent*, 24 August 2009)

The statements of both representatives highlight the need to address exploitation of migrant workers, although they evaluate the efficacy of the government's record in this regard very differently. The comments attributed to Junior Minister Calleary reflect a process of individuating responsibility which Gilbert (2002) associates with a broader rolling back of the state. It is important to recognise that provisions to protect the vulnerable, which depend on individuals reporting discrimination, are limited by the power differentials between the individual and the person or organisation against whom they wish to make a complaint. Particularly in the case of exploited migrant workers, it may be very difficult for them to submit a complaint, given fears of the loss of employment (see Primetime Investigates, RTE Television 2008). The Migrant Integration Policy Index (MIPEX) acknowledges the importance of Ireland's Equality Authority's remit with regard to instigating investigations of discriminatory practices and providing legal advice to victims but criticises the state's policy of denying aid to individuals taking equality-related cases (Niessen, Huddleston and Citron 2007, 96).

In 2007, MIPEX criticised the Irish state for off-loading its responsibilities in leading public discourse regarding anti-discrimination onto the then (increasingly poorly resourced) Equality Authority (Niessen, Huddleston and Citron 2007, 96). The comments attributed to Deputy Naughten highlight the significant role that opposition politicians can (but in this sample infrequently do) play in stimulating public awareness of issues impacting immigrant workers and, perhaps more significantly, in providing a critical voice regarding the state's response to the needs of immigrants, although the content of the comments are also reflective of Smith's (2008, 415) assertion that 'Fine Gael has primarily criticised the way the government implements its policies rather than showing any fundamental difference over substance'.

An article dating from 19 February 2008 provides a starkly contrasting illustration of the use to which politicians may put their public platform. In an article entitled 'FF councillor is branded absurd over call to pay foreigners less', then chairman of Louth County Council (2007–2008), Councillor Jimmy Mulroy, is cited as advocating differential pay for migrant workers in response to a motion by Sinn Fein Councillor Jim Loughran that the government should include the principle of equal treatment in any legislation relating to agency workers:[6]

> In a debate on the abuse of workers by some employment agencies, he said that while Irish people, 'need 12.50 an hour, people from Lithuania are doing very well on 8.50 an hour'. … Speaking after the council meeting, Cllr Mulroy defended his remarks, arguing that many migrant workers were 'very happy with 10 an hour', which could be equivalent to a month's wages in their home country. While acknowledging that his remarks would probably 'hit the headlines', the councillor – who runs an electrical contracting business – stood by the remarks. (*Irish Independent*, 19 February 2008)

The article records that the councillor's political party disassociated itself from his remarks. As well as referring to Councillor Loughran's proposal, which highlights both the exploitation of agency workers and the government's responsibility with regard to the same, the article also records that during the debate Cllr Kevin Meenan (Sinn Fein) challenged the framework of understanding proffered by Councillor Mulroy stating that immigrant workers 'do not fly home at night. If they live and work here they should get the same money (as Irish workers)' (*Irish Independent*, 19 February 2008).

The minutes of the council meeting, which do not record Councillor Meenan's remarks, do note that Councillor Loughran's motion was seconded by Councillor D. Breathnach and agreed by the members (Minute No. 31/08,

Minutes of Council Meeting of Louth County Council held in County Hall, Dundalk on Monday, 18 February 2008).

A third article, dating from 8 September 2009 and relating to the Lisbon Treaty Referendum (2) debate, further illustrates that divergent frameworks of understanding regarding migrant workers may be deployed in service of a wider ideological arguments. In an article entitled 'Punish State with "No" vote, Higgins urges', Socialist Party MEP for Dublin Joe Higgins is quoted as stating that

> to ratify Lisbon would copperfasten the right of business to exploit migrant workers and enforce wages and conditions a way inferior to accepted norms in particular member states of the European Union. 'This happens because the Lisbon Treaty institutionalises the rulings of the European Court of Justice, which endorsed the actions of foreign contractors in importing workers from one member state to another and seriously breaching the agreed rates of pay and various protections for such workers', Mr Higgins added. (*Irish Independent*, 8 September 2009)

In the same article, Socialist Party Councillor Clare Daly is quoted as stating that

> voting 'No' on October 2 would not 'move things forward' but would 'strongly refute the argument of the "Yes" side that claims workers' rights would be protected'. (*Irish Independent*, 8 September 2009)

Deputy Joe Costello (Labour, then Spokesperson for European Affairs and Human rights) is cited as having

> rebutted minimum wage claims last night. He said the minimum wage in Ireland 'is our own business' and a 'Yes' result would strengthen workers' rights and protect jobs. (*Irish Independent*, 8 September 2009)

The Socialist Party representatives and Deputy Costello demonstrate that vigorous debates regarding appropriate frameworks of understanding do not require either side in the debate to adopt an anti-immigrant stance. However, this was not always the case in relation to the Lisbon Treaty debate, and some stakeholders did seek to frame immigration as a threat to the Irish citizenry (Migrant Rights Centre 2010).

POLITICAL CONSTRUCTIONS OF MIGRANTS' RELATIONSHIP TO THE WELFARE STATE

The economic crash saw 65,793 EU (non-Irish) citizens on the Live Register by August 2009 (Central Statistics Office 2010, 7). We argue that it is in this context that we see greatest evidence of discourses concerning resource competition. The state training agency, FÁS, responded to the increase in Live Register figures by arguing that there was a 'need to ensure that sanctions and eligibility conditions are sufficiently tight to ensure that the Irish social welfare system does not become a pull factor for migration at a time when unemployment is rising in many EU countries' (FÁS 2009, 17). The year 2009 subsequently saw the practice of the electronic transfer of funds being replaced with the requirement to physically sign on for one's payment at a post office/social welfare office (FÁS 2009, 17). However, it is crucial to note that on 1 May 2004, in the context of an enlarging EU and processes implemented in other existing EU member states, a habitual residence condition (HRC) was introduced into Irish social welfare legislation, which affected all applicants regardless of nationality. This was an extremely important development in the context of politicians' utterances about welfare entitlements.

Our analysis identified eight articles with a focus on welfare. Articles containing relevant commentaries on this theme included statements from Labour and Fine Gael politicians only. If the general public is to support high levels of welfare spending, particularly in times of economic crisis, then citizens must be kept informed of the needs of those requiring the assistance of the welfare state, the costs of addressing those needs and the return that the state is getting for that investment (Lens 2002). Consequently, what is omitted from public discourse is just as important as what is included. Given that the HRC is a key component of the Irish social welfare system and given the controversy surrounding the application of the rules governing the HRC, we expected some statements on this issue. However, we instead found that all bar one of the politicians' statements concerned 'welfare fraud' specifically.

Under regulations in existence since 1971, migrant employees from any EU member state can claim child benefit from the EU country in which they work, even if their children are living in their home country. It was interesting that on 23 July 2008 the then Labour Party spokesperson on Social and Family Affairs, Róisín Shortall, said there was a need for greater vigilance against child benefit fraud. 'They need to keep on top of that because the situation is changing so quickly. There will be huge numbers of people returning to Eastern European countries'. She also called for the state to stop such payments abroad, while maintaining them for EU workers who were living here with their children (5 May 2008). Given that these reciprocal provisions are enshrined in legislation, it was surprising that Ms Shortall would make such a call in the public arena. Indeed, she later accepted that the proposal may have been 'aspirational', given that the current payment arrangement is provided for under EU law (O'Brien 2009).

Prior to the period covered by this research, a new system was introduced, which saw non-Irish EU nationals in receipt of child benefit required to prove that they were still resident or working in Ireland. Between November 2007 and April 2008, the Department of Social and Family Affairs wrote to 27,840 non-Irish EU child benefit recipients, giving them up to 21 days to return proof of residency or employment.

In an *Irish Independent* article of 12 May 2008, a department spokesperson said that 'in the case of non-Irish national recipients who are resident in Ireland with their children, certification is requested that the children continue to reside here, while in the case of non-Irish recipients who are working in Ireland but who have qualified children living in another EU state, certification by their employer of continuing employment is requested'. Totally, 4,960 recipients did not return with proof of residency or employment and payment was suspended. Fine Gael front bench member, Olwyn Enright, subsequently claimed that

> the percentage of foreign nationals who are claiming fraudulently is higher than Irish nationals. There needs to be communication with other countries to find out if these children exist and then we need proof of where they are living. ... Fraud is fraud. If you're talking about 5,000 out of about 27,000 – that is almost a fifth and that's a high proportion. It may seem small but I still see it as significant. ... That's money that could be going to people who need it more. (12 May 2008)

In addition, Fine Gael immigration spokesman Denis Naughten said the social welfare system encouraged those who were living elsewhere to claim benefits in Ireland. Mr Naughten said: 'It is clear that this is not working, or we would not have the scale of fraud exposed today. ... The disclosure that up to 11pc of non-nationals claiming social welfare were not resident in the State again highlights the need to strengthen co-operation between the immigration service and the Department of Social and Family Affairs' (3 July 2009). Finally, in the same article, Olwyn Enright insisted that an 'incalculable number' were still getting away with open fraud against the taxpayer.

The picture painted by both Enright and Naughten is that of a worst-case scenario. The 4,960 cases which saw claims 'suspended' were all defined as fraudulent in their discourses on this matter. However, there is no information on whether the actions that led to the initial inclusion of these individuals in this category were later rectified (e.g., as a result of submitting documentation which was not acceptable as 'proof of residency or employment', and later resubmitting documentation which was acceptable). In fact, there are a myriad of scenarios whereby individuals could have had their claim suspended and reinstated at a later date. The claim that all 4,960 cases were fraudulent on the basis that the individuals had not returned 'proof of residence or employment within the specified 21 days' requires further support. Indeed, it is worth highlighting that in late 2008, Minister for Social and Family Affairs

Minister, Mary Hanafin, had asserted that 95 per cent of foreign workers with PPS numbers were not claiming benefits at all (10 September 2008). It was interesting that only one statement relating to this theme was not about welfare fraud. In an article entitled '"United Nations" of claimants costing State €150m' (5 August 2008), Labour deputy leader Joan Burton said it was particularly troubling that young immigrants from Eastern European states were reliant on the rent supplement scheme due to unemployment, when that scheme could potentially become a poverty trap: 'The critical thing is that you need to encourage people back to work because if they are bringing up children in rented accommodation and are barred from the workforce, it's not great for the kids'. Deputy Burton's statement demonstrates an understanding of the structural barriers that many individuals experience on a day-to-day basis. However, in this instance, the statement also reflects a neoliberal view of the welfare state, in that the rent supplement scheme is portrayed as assisting in the creation of 'poverty traps' and therefore possibly developing a culture of welfare dependency. Burton's assertion that the 'critical thing is that you need to encourage people back to work' reflects a variant of the 'Social Integration Discourse' (Levitas 2003), which sees paid labour as the only way for individuals of working age to be fully included in contemporary society. However, this perspective ignores the fact that entry to the labour market at (or sometimes below) minimum wage can no more address social exclusion than welfare payments can.

Barrett and McCarthy (2008, 3) note that the comparatively small amount of research literature on immigration and welfare is in conflict with the concerns that are expressed over the supposedly excessive welfare claims by immigrants in public discourse. Yet, growing hostility towards migrants is something that occurs during a recession, and politicians should be cognizant that constructing immigrants as disproportionally involved in defrauding the social welfare system may have serious implications for the treatment of migrants in this country (O'Donoghue 2010).

DISCUSSION

Research on attitudes to minorities in the United States and Europe has identified self-interest and competition for resources as key explanations for hostility to migrants (Bobo 1988; van Dalen and Henkens 2005; Espenshade and Hempstead 1996). 'Members of the ingroup' – in our case, Irish citizens – 'enjoy privileged access to resources such as jobs, power, money, welfare benefits, and housing. If this relationship is challenged by competition from outgroups' such as migrants, 'then prejudice is manifested, as a tool to retain a grip on the good life' (Gibson 2002, 72, cited in McLaren and Johnson 2004, 713).

Although it is often alleged that social and political attitudes are fundamentally driven by individual self-interest, research indicates (see Sears and Funk 1990; McLaren and Johnson 2004) that people's perceptions of the effect of various policies on society, the economy or the nation as a whole are also key factors. Indeed, findings from US research show that 'sociotropic concerns about the economy are far more powerful than personal economic circumstances in explaining anti-immigration hostility' (Citrin et al. 1997; Espenshade and Hempstead 1996, cited in McLaren and Johnson 2004, 714). Interestingly, such findings suggest that attitudes to immigration 'may be driven by group interest', with opposition to immigration 'linked to concerns about the loss of resources of one's ingroup' (McLaren and Johnson 2004, 714).

This group conflict theoretical framework (Blumer 1958) holds that how members of outgroups are portrayed/perceived is dependent on whether they pose a potential threat to the advantages enjoyed by the ingroup; in effect, those in the outgroup may be 'perceived as taking resources that "belong to" one's own group' (McLaren and Johnson 2004, 714–15). Group conflict theory is extremely relevant to understanding the representation of migrants (Quillian 1995) as they are often seen as 'newcomers who threaten the jobs and benefits of established native-born citizens' (McLaren and Johnson 2004, 715).

Considine and Dukelow (2010, 412) assert that Irish immigration policy 'is primarily concerned with border control and law and order, including the regulation of migrants' movement in and out of the state, and their residence within the state'. While there may be little support for groups who could be classified as being on the far right of the political spectrum in Ireland, Lentin and McVeigh (2006) demonstrate that the Immigration Control Platform (ICP),[7] for example, made distinctions between immigration from different places, which, when combined with portrayals of 'immigration as invasion', served to construct mainstream discourse on immigration in terms of its problematisation. In such a context, the ICP played a prominent role in creating a discourse where 'Irishness [was] ... politically racialized' through a language calling for the defence of Irish 'heritage, citizenship and resources against claims of un-assimilable Others' (Garner 2007, 117). Smith (2008, 528) argues that nonetheless immigration was not really a highly politicised issue in Ireland prior to 2007 and that centre-right parties saw little electoral advantage to be had in contravening what she perceives as a 'liberal consensus' on immigration, a consensus that arose in part because the possible 'negative' social effects of immigration had been minimised by a sustained period of economic growth. But, the first signs of economic contraction saw concerns being expressed by trade unions in particular that migrant workers would displace Irish workers (Smith 2008, 427).

Despite widespread avoidance of participation in an ideological debate on immigration, we do, however, find moments in which particular issues are politicised in temporally and sometimes geographically localised ways. Statements regarding exploitation of migrant workers and the social welfare entitlements of immigrants evidence this phenomenon. While, at a national level, the positions adopted in such debates are more likely to be expressed by party spokespersons on immigration (although rarely party leaders themselves in the statements in our sample), contributions on such issues by individuals without a party brief are prevalent in national (and also local) debates. In the absence of the guidance provided by a clear party line, members may disseminate statements that are ill-informed, anti-immigrant or that their parties would not support. Where parties fail to publicly and effectively censure such claims or proposals, we argue that they effectively give them credence. In our sample, there are examples of such failures; equally there are instances of political parties actively disassociating themselves from the comments of candidates who adopt positions that their parties choose not to support. However, to be fully effective, we argue that such acts of disassociation should include, not merely the rejection of one position, but also a clear statement of the alternative position that the party does support. Research indicates extensive misinformation and confusion among the public regarding immigration (Haynes, Devereux and Breen 2009). Political leadership, therefore, requires that parties counter misinformation with accurate data *and* provide their membership and the public with the alternative frameworks of understanding to interpret the meaning and significance of the same.

CONCLUSION

This analysis finds that at the commencement of Ireland's great recession, politicians on all sides of the spectrum were not averse to perpetuating framing of migrant workers as an economic threat. Although politicians of the left are more likely to support migrant rights, representatives of all mainstream parties contributed directly to a discourse whereby migrants are constructed as a burden on the economy and/or as fraudulent. While comments from politicians in relation to the economy primarily focussed on the possibility of tensions developing between Irish and immigrant workers in the competition for jobs as unemployment grew, and the cost of social welfare payments to unemployed foreign workers, there were a number of important omissions from this debate. First, we found an absence of statements from politicians explaining unemployed foreign workers' social welfare entitlements to the media audience. Second, there was little discussion of the fact that between April 2008 and April 2009, EU12 nationals were by far the largest group emigrating from the state, and immigration to Ireland from the EU12 countries evidenced the largest decline of any group, dropping from 33,700 to 13,500 (CSO 2009, 1). Almost all of the politicians' statements on the issue of welfare were concerned with welfare fraud. Yet, our analysis does not suggest that politicians used their media platform to explain to the public either the HRC or the manner in which Irish emigrants in other EU countries benefit from entitlements similar to those enjoyed by EU citizens here. Our sample indicates that neither did the existence of evidence that rules governing the HRC were being applied inconsistently (Smith 2010) attain a high profile as the result of political statements. The low profile of these issues in political commentary contributes to their low visibility in public debate, impacting on citizens' awareness of these issues and may ultimately impact detrimentally on how immigrants and their needs are publicly perceived and treated.

It is important to note this negative space in Irish public discourse regarding migration. While many of the statements made by politicians in this recessionary period were not overtly negative, neither did many explicitly champion migrant workers' rights or communicate their experiences and perspectives. Indeed, the majority of 'pro-migrant' statements were framed as rebuttals of anti-immigrant claims and positions rather than as agenda-setting frameworks of understanding in their own right. A defensive rebuttal of negative framings may, in fact, serve to reinforce, rather than undermine, their perceived salience and is arguably a weak substitute for providing alternative frameworks of understanding (Hajer and Versteeg 2009).

There is a danger that in pursuing this course, pro-migrant politicians will at best become ensnared in a reactive approach whereby the course of the debate is set by the problematisation of the issue and at worst will leave the field for alternative frameworks of understanding open to anti-immigration actors.

NOTES

1. We began by searching both Nexis Lexis and the proprietary archive of the Limerick Leader for the following terms: 'immigration', 'immigrant', 'migrant', 'foreigner', 'foreign national', 'non-national', 'non-citizen', 'newcomer' and 'nomad'. Our sampling strategy returned a final total of 71 articles (*Irish Independent* – 53; *Limerick Leader* – 15; *Limerick Post* – 3) which were then analysed. While we do not claim that our sampling strategy has produced a complete sample of relevant political statements attaining media coverage in 2008–2009, we do assert that, by focusing on two Limerick imprints and the most widely circulated national newspaper,

our strategy has identified the highest profile statements and those that reached the widest audience in that period, in our geographical areas of interest (Limerick and nationally).

2. The Irish economy, social welfare fraud (see Power et al. 2012), marriages of convenience, education, road safety, crime (including trafficking), racism and discrimination, the exploitation of migrant workers and political, social and cultural integration.

3. Since 1977, the parliamentary system in the Republic of Ireland has allowed for the creation of junior ministers (also referred to as ministers for state). Junior ministers assist the minister but do not attend cabinet meetings.

4. Libertas Ireland was a short-lived centre-right political grouping led in Ireland by Declan Ganley.

5. Although Esses et al. (2001, 394) clarify that the resources in question need not be exclusively economic and that the perceived competition for social, cultural and political privilege are also factors in negative attitudes towards immigrants.

6. The complete text of the motion: 'This Council notes the increase in agency employment throughout the economy; we are aware that many workers from home and abroad are offered agency employment when they are seeking direct and permanent employment. We understand trade unions have raised concerns that many of these workers are retained on minimum conditions and in some instances are not receiving all their entitlements. Agency employment should not be used as an unnecessary substitute for direct employment or as a mechanism for avoidance of, or undermining of fair pay and conditions. Noting that legislation will come before the Oireachtas on the issue of Agency Employment, this Council believes and will recommend to the Minister, that the principle of equal treatment should be included in any such legislation on this issue' (Minute No. 31/08, Minutes of Council Meeting of Louth County Council held in County Hall, Dundalk on Monday 18th February 2008. http://www.louthcoco.ie/en/Louth_County_Council/Minutes_of_Statutory_Meetings/2008/Council-Meeting-Minutes-February-2008.doc).

7. The ICP first emerged prior to the 2002 general election in Ireland.

Chapter 9

Print Media Framings of Those Blonde Roma Children

Aileen Marron, Ann Marie Joyce, James Carr,
Eoin Devereux, Michael Breen, Martin J. Power
and Amanda Haynes

On 16 October 2013, police carried out a raid on a Roma camp in Farsala in Central Greece. They rescued 'Maria', a four-year-old child, who was presumed to be the victim of child abduction (Okely 2014). Blonde, with fair skin and green-blue eyes, it was believed that she could not be related to the Roma gypsies claiming to be her family. DNA tests revealed that the child was not a blood relative of her Roma parents, who were arrested on suspicion of child abduction. The child was subsequently removed from the camp and placed in the care of a local charity. Greek Police appealed to the international community to help identify Maria. Old myths of child abduction were quickly resurrected within media discourse. Children, it was said, were bought and sold for begging or for claiming social welfare payments. Media commentators asked how many other children might be hidden in such camps, and references were made to high-profile missing children such as Madeleine McCann and Ben Needham (Richardson 2014).

While the Maria case was still dominating the global news cycle, the Gardaí (the Irish Police Force) invoked Section 12 of *The Child Care Act*[1] (1991) to forcibly remove a seven-year-old blonde child from a Roma family living in Tallaght (Logan 2014, 22–63). Within 24 hours, Gardaí in Athlone used the same legislation to remove a two-year-old blonde child from another Roma family (Logan 2014, 64–100). Both instances arose out of emails sent to the Gardaí by members of the public, alerting them to the existence of blonde children living with Roma families. Both emails referred to the Maria case. The children were returned to their parents within forty-eight hours, once DNA tests revealed that they were, in fact, the biological children of the Roma couples in question. Before the children's return, however, details of both cases were leaked to the media, resulting in headline news stories across the world as well as being the most tweeted about topic in Ireland in 2013.

The decision to take two children into care and the public controversy which followed resulted in a decision by the Ombudsman for Children to launch an official inquiry (Logan 2014). Her report acknowledges the influential role of the media's reporting of the Maria case. It also points to the leaking of confidential information to journalists concerning the Roma children (Logan 2014, 37–38).

Recognising the media's power in determining public discourse and beliefs, we take a closer look, in this chapter, at how the decision to take two Roma children into care was explained by the Irish print media. Our analysis finds that five distinct media frames dominated in the coverage. The first frame justifies the actions of the Gardaí and the Health Services Executive (HSE) by portraying the case as an issue of child protection rather than one of racial profiling. The second frame suggests that the removal of the Roma children was a case of racial profiling. The third frame focuses on the actions of the HSE and Gardai, portraying these state agencies as heavy-handed and unaccountable. The fourth frame serves to question the media's involvement and reporting of both cases, depicting their role as irresponsible. Finally, the fifth frame examines the trauma experienced by the Roma families involved in both cases. We begin our examination of media framings of the Roma in Ireland by discussing the ways in which the Roma are routinely racialised and excluded in Ireland and beyond. We also plot a timeline of events as they unfolded and note the media's pivotal role in the unfolding moral panic (Cohen 2002).

RACIALISING THE ROMA

It is estimated that there are between three and six thousand Roma people living in Ireland (European Union Fundamental Rights Agency 2012; NASC 2013). Roma communities have been part of European societies for centuries. They have been treated as outsiders and subjected to policies and practices that have resulted in repeated evictions and forced migration in search of refuge (ENAR 2014; Guy et al. 2010; Tosi Cambini 2011; Miskovic 2009).[2] Roma communities 'form a group that is disadvantaged in several respects and is particularly vulnerable to social exclusion, poverty and discrimination' (General Affairs Committee of the Council of the EU cited in Guy et al. 2010, 8). Manifesting as lives lived on the periphery of European societies, Roma communities experience structural discrimination in education, health, housing and employment, as well as in hate crime and police harassment (European Union Agency for Fundamental Rights 2009; Guy et al. 2010;

Human Rights First 2009; Sein 2014). Migration offers a potential means to escape such experiences. Fuelled by socio-political discourses and practices that stigmatise Roma communities as 'less than citizens' (Human Rights First 2009, 1), and despite *being* EU citizens, European Roma communities have been subjected to mass deportations from EU States on the basis that they are a threatening *Other* interested only in 'taking advantage of the system' (Cahn 2004; Clough and Sigona 2011; Tosi Cambini 2011; Miskovic 2009; Woodcock 2007).

EU wide studies demonstrate that the aforementioned practices of exclusion are not the preserve of any one state (European Union Agency for Fundamental Rights 2009). Irish research similarly demonstrates discrimination experienced amongst the Roma communities when accessing goods and services, employment, healthcare, social protection and housing. Roma are treated as a security risk by the police, subject to practices of ethnic profiling and related incidents of harassment. Instead of being offered protection by the police, Roma in Ireland are faced with a 'crime control model of justice' (NASC 2013, 61). A fact made all the more alarming, given the exposure to hate crime that the Roma experience. Reports on hate crime in Ireland published by the European Network Against Racism (ENAR Ireland 2015) evidence racially aggravated assaults, verbal abuse and damage to property directed towards the Roma, fuelled by discourses propagated on conventional and social media platforms.[3] It is evident that, whether in experiences of discrimination or in hate crime, Roma communities continue to be stigmatised. They are constructed as a racial underclass, the labelling of which further embeds and legitimises the social exclusion of Roma communities in Ireland and elsewhere.

ROMA AS DIVERSE COMMUNITIES

Roma communities are diverse communities. The European Union uses the term 'Roma' as a collective term which includes a diverse range of communities or 'sub-groups' (NASC 2013, 9) such as the 'Roma, Sinti, Travellers, Ashkali, Manush, Jenische, Kaldaresh and Kalé' (ENAR 2014, 1; see also Guy et al. 2010). Despite this diversity, Roma have been constructed homogenously as the 'ultimate "outsider European"' (Miskovic 2009, 209), 'a mysterious wandering folk with no links or loyalties other than to kin and clan ... with a propensity to crime and fraud' (Cahn 2004, 482). Processes of racialisation lie at the core of these constructions of Roma as Other and it is these processes that inform anti-Roma racism.

According to Miles and Brown (2003, 103), 'racism is ... a representational form which, by designating human collectivities ... functions as an ideology of inclusion and exclusion'. As an ideological formation, racism results in disadvantage or 'exclusionary practices' for those constructed as Other (Miles and Brown 2003, 103). Racism is premised upon processes of racialisation, that is, processes of signification where meaning is attached to 'markers' of the 'self' or the Other, defining those who belong and those who do not (Dunn et al. 2007, 569; Miles and Brown 2003, 85, 103). Racialisation is not contingent on phenotypical difference but can also operate on what are constructed as cultural or religious markers of difference. Carr (2016) demonstrates the manner in which Irish Muslims have been categorised as outside of Irishness, not on the basis of phenotypical difference but for not bearing other constructed aspects of belonging, in this case, Catholicness. Carr and Haynes (2013) argue that for those constructed as the 'outgroup', processes of racialisation present the Other as innately and negatively different, categorising who belongs to the in-group while contemporaneously legitimating exclusionary practices toward the Other. Thus, the process of racialisation underscores the manner in which 'races' are socially constructed as opposed to 'biological realities' (Miles and Brown 2003, 89). Further, racialisation is not just about defining the Other, it also involves defining the 'self' and idealised notions of who belongs and who does not (Miles and Brown 2003). Racism infuses an 'explicitly negative evaluative component' to constructions of the un-belonging Other (Miles and Brown 2003, 104). Representations of the Other, infused with the negative evaluative component, affirm the place of those with the power to define who belongs, informing racist practices and beliefs, resulting in lived experiences of hostility and discrimination among the outgroup (Miles and Brown 2003, 103).

STATE ABDUCTION OR STATE CARE?
A TIMELINE OF EVENTS: OCTOBER 2013

On October 20, TV journalist Paul Connolly[4] received a message on his professional Facebook page which stated:

> Hi Paul, Today was on the news the blonde child found in Roma camp in Greece. There is also little girl living in Roma house in Tallaght and she is blonde and blue eyes. Her name is [names her] and her address is [address is given]. I am from [Eastern European country] myself and it's a big problem there missing kids. The Romas robing [*sic*] them to get child benefit in Europe.

Connolly forwarded the information in this Facebook post to the Gardaí on the morning of 21 October.

The Children's Ombudsman's report (Logan 2014) details the key events surrounding the decision to take the children into state care. Connolly's email received the attention of a Garda sergeant at 2 pm, and the sergeant spent the next hour and a half carrying out preliminary enquiries. These included checking child protection records, speaking with a Garda colleague who knew the family, contacting the principal of the local school, contacting the Department of Social Protection and contacting the HSE Social Work team. It emerged that the child was commonly known by a name that differed from official records, but there were no recorded concerns relating to the child, and the school principal had no concerns relating to the child or her family.

Although the sergeant attempted to make contact with the author of the post on Connolly's Facebook page, this had not happened prior to the decision being taken to progress the investigation further by calling directly to the child's house without the aid of an interpreter. Upon doing so, the Gardaí decided to invoke legislation designed for the protection of children in urgent, compelling (and thus rare) circumstances in order to remove the child from her family and place her in the care of social workers without the prior agreement of a district court judge. In the subsequent inquiry, the sergeant cited the following key reasons for his making this decision:

- The child did not resemble her family (Logan 2014, 70).
- The hospital at which she was born was unable to immediately find a record of her birth (Logan 2014, 70).
- Whilst her mother produced a PPS number (social security number) for her, she did not have a birth cert or recent passport available (Logan 2014, 70).
- A consultant doctor, contacted by phone, advised that it was highly unusual for a blonde and blue-eyed child to have two parents of dark hair and eyes (Logan 2014, 70).
- The child went by a name that was different from her official name (Logan 2014, 70).
- Extended family members had criminal records and resided outside the state, and the family was, thus, deemed a flight risk (Logan 2014, 71).

The following morning, news of the story broke and a large number of journalists began to arrive at the home of the Roma family. Citing Garda sources, minute details of the events as they unfolded at the child's house were revealed. These included who was in the house at the time Gardaí arrived, the child's appearance, her place and date of birth and the opinion of the consultant doctor previously contacted by phone.

Having spent two nights with a foster family, the child was returned to her parents when DNA testing revealed she was, in fact, their biological daughter.

The Special Inquiry Report (Logan 2014) also evidences the key events leading up to the removal of the second Roma child. On the morning of 21 October, Gardaí in Athlone received an email, which had been sent to the Missing Persons Bureau from a member of the public with the subject heading of 'Suspected Child Abduction'. The author of the email had been at a festival that summer where her daughters had their hair braided at a stall run by a Roma family with a baby boy:

> While my children were getting their braids in I preoccupied myself with the little baby. He had very blonde hair and the bluest eyes and his complexion was also fair. ... Apart from the baby, all the others were completely dark in complexion, eyes and hair. ... The recent news about the little Maria who was found made me realise that I should have reported it.

Because of the subject heading of the email, the Gardaí deemed it necessary to treat the case as potentially high-risk and requiring urgent action. Having checked Garda records for any concern relating to the child and having found none, the decision was made to visit the child's home address. Once there, the child was found to indeed be blonde, with blue eyes and a pale complexion. The child's birth certificate did not include the father's name. A local Garda who knew of the family had not known of the child, and so the family was asked to attend the Garda Station. An interpreter was not sought at any time. Although the local hospital confirmed the birth of the child, it was finally decided that evening to invoke Section 12 of *The Child Care Act* (1991) in order to remove the child from his family and place him in the care of a foster family. The reasons cited by Gardaí in this instance included the following:

- The child matched the description given in the email.
- A local Garda had knowledge of the family, but had never seen the child before.
- The family was deemed to be transient and was, thus, a flight risk (Logan 2014, 29).

The following morning it was ascertained from medical records that the child had albinism, and this accounted for his fair hair, eyes and complexion. He was returned to his parents, but crucially, not before the story was leaked to the media, and there was a media presence outside the family's home when the members returned after having collected him from the social worker.

eyes seven birth health point social little haired old hair away justice removed questions two blonde take ireland greece house authorities independent living

father care girl families cases dublin tallaght hse roma risk

parents taken children boy act child one family

couple protection community ombudsman garda minister gardaí blond welfare case investigation daughter returned shatter nightsister blue dna serious people home concerns hospital mother profiling racial born son state pavee irish court reports report young

Figure 9.1 Word cloud featuring dominant media discourses concerning 'Those Blonde Roma Children'. *Source:* Author's Own

PRINT MEDIA FRAMINGS[5]

Frame One: An Issue of Child Protection

The first frame identified from our sample of articles[6] contained twenty nine articles and constructed the incidents in Tallaght and Athlone as issues of 'child protection'. The frame was evident in nine articles published in the *Irish Independent*, eight in the *Irish Examiner*, seven in the *Irish Times*, four in the *Irish Daily Mail* and one in the *Irish Daily Mirror*. Twenty-two of the articles were news reports, six were opinion pieces and one was an editorial.

The frame functions mainly through the voice of government sources (seventeen articles in this frame) and also to a lesser extent through the voice of journalists (five articles) and columnists (four articles). According to both Entman (1993) and Reese (2001), media frames are 'organising principles' which serve to structure information through the processes of selection and salience. This frame is structured on the basis of a 'moral panic' (see Cohen 2002) that is anchored mainly on the 'Greek case' but also on previous high-profile child abductions and cases of Irish child abuse. These 'reasoning devices' combined to produce a clear and consistent 'interpretive package' that invoked a heightened sense of risk and focused attention onto the idea that it is always 'better to be safe than sorry' when dealing with matters concerning children.

[Headline] 'Family vows child belongs to them in case similar to Greece'. News Report – *Irish Daily Mirror* 23/10/2013)

'Emphasis Framing'

This frame functions like an 'emphasis frame' by focusing attention onto a particular 'subset of potentially relevant considerations' (Iyengar 2005, 5). For example, on October 23, seven of the thirteen articles published on that day highlighted the supposed similarities between the circumstances surrounding 'Maria' and the events concerning a Roma family in Tallaght, Co. Dublin. The articles 'othered' the Roma families in question on the basis that the 'blonde-haired' and 'blue-eyed' children looked physically different from their 'dark' parents and siblings. In addition, eight of the thirteen articles questioned their legitimacy by expressing doubts over the authenticity of their birth certificates, medical records and passports, thus increasing suspicion and placing the burden of proof onto the Roma families in question. This, in turn, justified and normalised the actions of the Gardaí and the HSE.

[Headline] 'DNA to test if girl is Roma couple's daughter'. (News Report – Irish Examiner 23/10/2013)

Comparisons were also made with the high-profile abduction of Madeleine McCann in four of the articles. One of these articles, an editorial/opinion piece written by a columnist from the *Irish Independent*, suggested that the Greek case and the Tallaght case would cause people to re-evaluate what happened to Madeleine McCann, noting towards the end of the article that there had in the past been reported 'sightings of Madeleine' with a 'tall swarthy man' (Editorial/Opinion Piece – *Irish Independent* 23/10/2013).

In eighteen articles, an attempt was made to move the focus away from the idea of racial profiling, and a more sympathetic view of the state institutions involved in both cases was made salient. For example, in a news report published by the *Irish Independent* on October 25 entitled 'Damned if they did and damned if they didn't', a comparison was made to a widely reported incest case, in which (in a subsequent inquiry report – see Gibbons 2010) the HSE was criticised for failing to intervene on behalf of the children involved. The suggestion here in relation to the cases in Tallaght and Athlone was that the Gardaí and the HSE were in a Catch-22 situation, given that they had been criticised in the past for not acting swiftly to protect children.

Similarly, one news report published by the *Irish Independent* entitled 'Gardaí have powers to take a child from family into care' (*Irish Independent* 23/10/2013) saw this argument emphasised through the voice of child law expert, Geoffrey Shannon. He stated that *Section 12* is only used in circumstances that are deemed by the Gardaí to be 'absolutely urgent' and that 'there had long been criticism of state agencies for being too slow to act in protecting children' and said 'the State had a duty to do so'. This sentiment was also expressed in two statements issued by the Irish Association of Social Workers and was also adopted by government sources.

Use of Sources

The majority of direct and indirect sources quoted in articles in this frame originated from government officials. In particular, they articulate the voices of the Taoiseach, Enda Kenny; the then Minister for Justice, Alan Shatter; and the then Minister for Children, Frances Fitzgerald. These voices were apparent in both the main body and in the headlines of articles.

> [Headline] 'Always a balance to be struck on child safety says Taoiseach'. (News Report – The *Irish Times* 25/10/2013)

Eighteen statements made by Justice Minister Alan Shatter sought to sympathise with and minimise the actions of the HSE and the Gardaí by stating that they were 'acting in good faith' *in* response to public concerns. A further nineteen statements issued by government representatives and five statements issued separately by the Gardaí contextualised these cases as being about child protection and deflected attention away from questions of institutional racism. What is noteworthy here is that the Special Inquiry Report conducted by the Ombudsman for Children into the incidents in Tallaght and Athlone found no evidence that the children at the centre of these cases were in any immediate danger and that there were no child protection concerns on record relating to these children (Logan 2014, 34, 66). In this respect, it appears that it was primarily the government that constructed these two cases as issues of child protection.

Frame Two: A Case of Racial Profiling

The second frame identified constructs the incidents in both Tallaght and Athlone as cases of racial profiling. Characteristics of this frame featured in twenty nine articles. Of these, eight appeared in the *Irish Independent*, six in the *Irish Times*, seven in the *Irish Examiner*, five in the *Irish Daily Mail* and three in the *Irish Daily Mirror*. Twenty-three articles were news reports and six were opinion pieces. Again, this frame operates mainly through the voice of sources (twenty two of the articles) from groups such as Pavee Point,[7] the Roma Support Group, the Immigrant Council and members of the political opposition. Five articles written by columnists and one by a journalist expressed, to varying degrees, the view that the actions of the Gardaí and the HSE amounted to racial profiling.

Use of Sources

There were thirty-eight direct and indirect statements made by Pavee Point which compared the events in both Tallaght and Athlone to a 'witch-hunt' and argued that the state's actions were based on appearances rather than evidence. On that basis they called for an independent inquiry into the actions of the HSE and the Gardaí.

> [Headline] 'Pavee Point says taking children into care shows racial profiling in the extreme'. (News Report – *Irish Times* 24/10/2013)

Six statements came from members of the political opposition, five came from the Roma Support Group, four came from NASC Irish Immigrant Support Centre and one statement came from a government official, Doras Luimni, the European Roma Rights Centre, Amnesty International and the Integration Centre. All of these statements expressed similar views.

> [Labour TD Aodhán Riordain] 'What is really at the core of this whole episode, this whole circus, has been a pure raw, naked, poisonous, racism that lies at the heart of Irish society', he said. (News Report – *Irish Examiner* 25/10/2013)

Twelve statements from the Immigrant Council condemned racial profiling and called on the government to provide assurances that there were safeguards in place against it citing the 'Incitement to Hatred Law' as being ineffective in dealing with racism.

'Thematic Framing'

This frame is somewhat comparable to Iyengar's (1990) conceptualisation of a 'thematic frame' in that it places the incidents in Tallaght and Athlone into a wider contextual perspective. In contrast, 'episodic frames' examine issues in terms of 'single instances'. The degree to which content is framed either thematically or episodically can impact on how the reader attributes responsibility to an issue. With thematic frames, this responsibility is likely to be attributed to systemic causes, whereas episodic frames will focus on the individual. This frame contained four articles which took an historical look at the Roma community and highlighted the racism and poverty experienced by both the international Roma community and those living in Ireland. Attempts were also made in three articles to deconstruct some of the common myths and stereotypes commonly attributed to the Roma, such as being labelled as 'child snatchers'.

> The myth of a particular ethnic group being behind child kidnapping has been perpetuated in Europe before. The myth of the blood libel, which has ebbed and

flowed for the best part of a millennium across Europe, led hysterical Christians to believe that Jewish people were kidnapping young children and using them in ritual sacrifice during Passover. Even after the Holocaust, such ridiculous accusations continued. In 1946, in Kielce in Poland, 40 Jews were killed by a mob following a false tale of child kidnapping and blood libel. (Opinion Piece – *Irish Times* 24/10/2013)

A news report entitled 'Many of them come here to escape persecution' (*Irish Times* 25/10/2013) explains that many of the Roma came to Ireland in the 1990s to seek asylum with many gaining refugee status. Another opinion piece written by the *Irish Times* columnist Una Mullally highlights that the Roma are commonly the victims of crime and quite often live in poverty. Similarly, a separate opinion piece written by representatives from Pavee Point called 'Cases highlight the plight of vulnerable Roma children' stressed the racism and hostility experienced by the Roma (*Irish Examiner* 24/10/2013).

Although the idea that racial profiling took place was a strong theme in the reportage, the argument tended to be framed in the context of, or in reaction to, the problem of child protection. This pattern was evident in news reports and to a lesser extent in opinion pieces, where structurally the racial profiling frame and the child protection frame appeared in relation to one another as either the first or second half of the article. One possible explanation for this pattern is that the approach being employed here by the print media professional is to fulfil the journalistic principles of 'objectivity' and 'balance' by being seen to present two sides of the story. This practice is not uncommon. Tuchman's (1972) analysis of media professional's conceptualisation of objectivity revealed that the notion of objectivity is best understood as a 'performance strategy' whose function is to protect journalists from criticisms of bias and libel accusations. By using statements from both sides of a debate, the journalists in question believed that by introducing someone else's opinion they were removing themselves from the story and allowing the 'facts' to speak for themselves.

Frame Three: Heavy-Handed, Incompetent and Unaccountable

This frame portrayed the Gardaí and HSE as being heavy-handed in their approach, incompetent and unaccountable. Words and phrases such as 'shambolic', 'monstrous invasion' and 'omnishambles' were used to describe the actions of both the HSE and the Gardaí in both cases.

[Headline] 'Shambolic episode as HSE is forced to return two children'. (News Report – *Irish Independent* 24/10/2013)

The frame featured in twenty-four articles: fifteen news reports, seven opinion pieces and two editorials. Unlike the previous two frames discussed, this frame operated mainly through the voice of the media professional (with seven articles being written by newspaper columnists and journalists respectively) and from a combination of the political opposition and Pavee Point (who were a source in eight articles). The bylines of three articles could not be identified. Focusing on the voices of media professionals, one opinion piece written by the *Irish Times* columnist John Waters, entitled 'Racism isn't the most ominous aspect of these child snatchings', stated:

> Racism is arguably among the least ominous aspects of what happened this week. Far worse was the denial of due process, the misuse of the law, the trampling on constitutional rights and the cruelty to the children and families involved – all perpetrated by people charged with upholding the Constitution and protecting citizens. (Opinion Piece – *Irish Times* 25/10/2013)

A separate opinion piece written by the *Irish Daily Mail* columnist, Brenda Power, entitled 'Go into the mind of this poor child and ask yourself: who are the kidnappers and who are the rescuers?' outlined:

> An essential element of our social contract with powerful State agencies is an understanding that they will not abuse their power, but that they will use it without fear or favour when it is required. And another element of that contract is that we can trust them to tell the difference. (Opinion Piece – *Irish Daily Mail* 24/10/2013).

Another news report published by the *Irish Times* on October 24 questioned the decision-making practices of the Gardaí and whether the public could have faith in the country's child protection policies:

> Gardaí as well as the HSE have failed children who were at risk. Now, this heartrending episode which left a little girl traumatised and her family distraught, raises new concerns about the decision-making at the highest level of the Gardaí in particular. ... Would this stand up to an independent test by experts on child protection? What kind of discussion took place with paediatricians? The veil of secrecy surrounding so many cases means we don't know how many other families may be, on the face of it, targeted in this way. Cases are argued behind closed doors in courts not open to the public. (News Report – *Irish Times* 24/10/2013)

A further seven articles in this frame questioned the nature of the investigations into the removals of the Roma children, suggesting that by carrying out their own internal reviews, the HSE and the Gardaí were essentially investigating themselves. This, they argued, lacked transparency and account-ability. This view was mainly expressed through the voice of sources such as Pavee Point and members of the political opposition:

> [Martin Collins – Pavee Point] 'In relation to the format of the inquiry Pavee Point is not happy at all', he said. 'It is not a full, independent, transparent inves-tigation'. 'It is a case of the HSE and the Gardaí carrying out internal reviews and passing them to the ministers who will forward it on to the Ombudsman for Children'. (News Report – *Irish Examiner* 25/10/2013)

Frame Four: Irresponsible Media Reporting

Sixteen articles in this sample, to varying degrees, referenced the role of the media in these cases. Of these, six were published by the *Irish Times* and the *Irish Independent*, respectively, and two were published by the *Irish Examiner* and the *Irish Daily Mail*, respectively. Of these articles, eleven were news reports and five were opinion pieces. In nine of these articles, criticisms of the media's reporting of the cases and the close relationship between Gardaí and the media featured only through the voice of a source. Of these sources, five statements were made by politicians, two were made by Pavee Point and one was made by representatives of the European Rights Group, the Roma Support Group and the Integration Centre.

> [Independent TD Clare Daly] 'Elements in the Gardaí are feeding their pet poodles in the media' as she hit out at 'a media frenzy and irresponsible journal-ism'. (News Report – *The Irish Times* 25/10/2013)

Separately, an opinion piece written by the leader of the Socialist Party, Joe Higgins, entitled 'Demonised: Blonde Roma children and the jobless' (*Irish Daily Mail* 25/10/2013), pointed to the stereotypical assumptions made by journalists and to the role of the social media platform Facebook in the initial breaking of the story. In contrast, there was one news report published by the *Irish Independent* on October 23 entitled 'How anonymous Facebook tip led to drama', which detailed the role Facebook played in tipping off the *Paul Connolly Investigates* TV programme on TV3, and subsequently the Gardaí, to the fact that the child in Tallaght looked different from its parents. These events and the actions of the journalist, however, were normalised in the story and presented as being unproblematic.

There were three opinion pieces all of which were published on October 25 written by columnists, which criticised media reporting of these cases. Two appeared in the *Irish Times* and one in the *Irish Independent*. For example, an opinion piece written by *Irish Times* columnist, Una Mullally, entitled

'Questions to ask now the Roma hysteria is over' criticised the Irish media's role in perpetuating anti-Roma discourses in an effort to get 'the good story'.

> Truth, nuance, shades of grey and patience are often seen as irritants that journalism just doesn't have the time to deal with when there's a scoop to be pursued. ... The story spread rapidly both here and internationally. At a loss for a photograph, newspapers republished the one of the Greek girl 'Maria'. Conversations online and off were in many cases coloured with prejudice against Roma people. Then the unfortunate truth reared its head to disrupt this 'good story'. (Opinion Piece – *The Irish Times* 24/10/2013)

Overall, it would seem that although there were some print media professionals who engaged critically and reflexively with the media's role in these cases, in the main, the reportage across the time period examined as part of this analysis was firmly focused to a much greater extent on the actions of the state. This pattern subsequently moved the attention away from the role of the media in reporting both in the incidents in Tallaght and Athlone, and in general, in constructing Roma as the racialised Other. It is important to note here in relation to the statement made by the Independent TD Clare Daly in the previous section that the Ombudsman's report into these cases also criticised the close relationship between the Gardaí and the media and the leaking of confidential information concerning the families involved (Logan 2014, 101).[8] The report also noted the influence of the Greek case on Irish reporting of the incidents in Tallaght and Athlone, 'namely the mistaken view that the Roma community does not include individuals with fair hair and features, combined with an immediately heightened suspicion that the presence of such children with Roma families would be readily explained by abduction' (Logan 2014, 99).

Frame Five: 'Episodic Framing' – The Ordeal of the Roma Families

Twelve articles in this sample were categorised on the basis that they fitted the characteristics of an 'episodic frame'. Episodic frames construct issues in terms of 'single instances' and unlike 'thematic frames' they typically lack in contextualisation. This type of framing was a strong feature of the tabloid publications accounting for nine of the twelve articles in this frame (six published by the *Irish Daily Mail* and three published by the *Irish Daily Mirror*). Two articles were published by the *Irish Independent* and one by the *Irish Examiner*. All twelve articles were news reports and provided a human-interest angle to the issue. Unlike the previous frames, the voice of the Roma families was dominant in this frame and was used to explain the ordeal they had experienced as a result of the actions of the Gardaí and the HSE.

[Headline] 'I cried and cried' – Roma child tells of trauma after being taken from family for three days. (News Report – *Irish Daily Mail* 25/10/2013)

Although these stories humanised and sympathised with the Roma families involved in these specific cases, their lack of depth and consideration of wider systemic problems, such as poverty or racism, which have historically impacted on the Roma community in general, would suggest that these sympathetic accounts may not be enough to counter stereotypical constructions of the Roma. It should also be noted that these humanising accounts only emerged on October 24, after it was revealed that DNA tests proved these children had not been abducted. Up until that point these very same publications had played a role in heightening suspicion of child kidnapping by the families involved.

CONCLUSION

In October 2013, sensationalist and racist media discourses concerning the plight of the 'Blonde Angel' Maria gave rise to yet another moral panic concerning the Roma. Media coverage of the Greek case rehearsed previously circulated tropes and myths about alleged child stealing and Roma criminality more generally (Tosi Cambini 2009, 653). The media-generated moral panic, which ensued after the discovery of Maria, was clearly influential in the actions of those who reported the sightings of blonde Roma children to an Irish journalist and to the Gardaí.

We hold that the media's reporting of the Greek case, replete as it was with ethnic stereotypes, racism and suspicion, served as a trigger for the subsequent actions of the Irish authorities. Our chapter raises some important questions concerning the ways in which the Irish print media reported on the events in Tallaght and Athlone. The first concerns reporting practices. The Children's Ombudsman's report into these events notes how personal confidential information was leaked to and used by some of the media. Similarly, respect for the right to privacy in what was obviously a very sensitive matter was also ignored. The case demonstrates not only source bias but also a relationship between sections of the media and state authorities, which appears to be too close.

The framing of the Greek and Irish Roma cases took place in a media setting. Media frames are never neutral. They represent the social world in ways that are partial, biased, ideological and particular. This chapter points to the ways in which the media manage to create the illusion that they are objectively reporting on things as they happen.

Our critical analysis of the media frames employed shows how a moral panic was generated through an initial emphasis on child protection and by the repeated suggestion of there being parallels between the Irish and Greek cases. While the media discourses examined here do allow for some consideration of whether or not racial profiling had taken place, the focus in the coverage moved quickly to blame the state for being too hasty to act. In that context, and with some notable exceptions, the lack of reflexivity on the media's own part as to their role is quite striking.

NOTES

1. Section 12 of the Child Care Act, 1991 relates to the power of An Garda Síochána to take a child to safety and is available at: http://www.irishstatutebook. ie/eli/1991/act/17/section/12/enacted/en/html. The provision requires that a member of An Garda Síochána have reasonable belief that '(a) there is an immediate and serious risk to the health or welfare of a child and (b) that it would not be sufficient for the protection of the child from such immediate and serious risk to await the making of an application for an emergency care order by a health board'.
2. See Miskovic (2009) for a brief introduction to the history of Roma communities in Europe.
3. In relation to conventional media, an article published, for example, in a national broadsheet described Roma communities as a 'parasitic, ethnic underclass' and 'criminal Roma' (O'Doherty 2013, cited in ENAR Ireland 2015a, 14). Various racisms also persist on social media platforms (ENAR Ireland 2015). In October 2014, an anti-Roma mob-demonstration, numbering up to 200 individuals, gathered and attacked the home of three Roma families in Waterford City (Holland 2014; Hosford 2014). This 'demonstration', organised via a Facebook page entitled 'Get Roma Criminal Gypsies Out' (Holland 2014), resulted with windows being broken and terrified men, women and children being evacuated for their safety by police (Hosford 2014).
4. Paul Connolly is well known in Ireland for his tabloid-style investigative programmes that have in the past focused on Roma in the context of begging and alleged gang criminality. He has also presented programmes focused on the alleged criminal activities of the Irish Traveller Community.
5. A framing analysis approach was adopted as the main methodological framework of this study and draws on both qualitative and quantitative analysis techniques. In essence, framing is concerned with the ways in which culture and the gamut of interests involved in the communication process converge to produce clear and consistent ways of understanding the social world. With its emphasis on 'how' media texts are structured and organised, this approach is a particularly useful way of capturing meaning and the ways in which media texts are both discursively and ideologically constructed (for an elaboration, see Reese 2001).
6. The analysis of print media articles was conducted by capturing data from the 23rd to the 25th of October 2013. Using the Lexis-Nexis database, data was sampled from three broadsheet newspapers (*Irish Times*, *Irish Independent* and the *Irish Examiner*) and two tabloid newspapers (*Irish Daily Mail* and the *Irish Daily Mirror*).

This data was drawn from this database using the search terms, 'Roma', 'Gardaí', 'HSE', 'Tallaght' and 'Athlone'. The final sample contained 57 newspaper articles for analysis. These articles included a mixture of news reports, editorials and opinion pieces. Letters to the editor were not included in the study. These stories were then systematically examined for the use of framing and reasoning devices (see Gamson and Modigliani 1989; Entman 1993) with the aid of *NVivo*. Both the headlines and the main body of the articles were considered during this analysis.

7. Pavee Point is the Irish Traveller and Roma Rights Group.

8. On 28 May 2015, a Senior Garda officer was arrested over his alleged dealings with journalists when the two Roma children were removed from their families. On May 29, the Garda Press Office confirmed that the officer had been released without charge and a file was being prepared for the director of Public Prosecutions. This case is still live as of 16 September 2015.

Chapter 10

The 'Salsa Factor'

Music and Dance as Identity among Undocumented Latino Labour Migrants in Israel

Moshe Morad

The old central bus station in Tel Aviv, known as 'the backyard' of Israel, is nowadays mostly populated by refugees and labour migrants from Sudan and Eritrea, and by aid workers from the Philippines and India.[1] In the late 1990s and early 2000s, it was the transient home of labour migrants from many different places around the globe, including Latin America. Walking along Neve Sha'anan street in the old bus station area in 2003, my ears caught the sounds of *salsa* and Colombian *cumbia* coming from a small bar nearby; 'Cantina Andina',[2] said the improvised sign. Colombians, Bolivians, Ecuadorians and other Latinos, mostly young males, were sitting, drinking, singing and sometimes dancing. This discovery precipitated my fieldwork among undocumented Latino labour migrants in Israel. Today, there is no salsa to be heard on Neve Sha'anan street and Cantina Andina has been turned into an Eritrean Bar (see its exact location in Figure 10.1). A big wave of deportations wiped out the Latino enclave in the central bus station area, and undocumented labour migrants and asylum seekers from Africa now dominate.

In this chapter, I look at a community of undocumented Latino labour migrants in Israel in the early 2000s, pinpointing the unique role of salsa music and dance in consolidating group identity and in creating an interface for interaction with the Israeli host society. In his 2005 paper examining the role of music amongst two Afghan settlements in Pakistan and California, John Baily notes that 'many things can happen *to, with and through* music in the migration situation' (2005, 215–16). This chapter concentrates on the 'with' and the 'through', rather than on the 'to', in relation to the Latin American labour migrants in Israel. Unlike Baily's article, my objective was not to investigate 'what happens to music culture and its performance in the migration situation' (2005, 216) but rather to uncover what happens to migrants *via* music and dance.

Figure 10.1   Neve Sh'anan Street in the old central bus station area in Tel Aviv. This part of the street where 'Cantina Andina' was located is where I conducted much of my fieldwork and had conversations with the Latino undocumented labour migrants. Photograph © Moshe Morad 2015.

My fieldwork, carried out in Tel Aviv in 2002–2003 among undocumented Latino labour migrants and Israelis, and its analysis as framed by theories on migration and identity, lead me to the conclusion that salsa music and dance have played a key role in migrant and Israeli configuring of pan-Latino identity, in a narrative that revolves around aspects of belonging, escapism, sensuality, musicality and stereotyping. Written through the lens of ethnomusicology, the first half of the chapter describes and explains the context of undocumented labour migration in Israel in general and the Latino labour migrants in particular, and the second deals with the role of salsa music in their lives.

FIELDWORK AND INFORMALITY

My fieldwork methodology consisted of 'deep hanging out' (Geertz 1998, 69) in Cantina Andina and other bars frequented by Latino labour migrants on Neve Sha'anan street, in numerous rented rooms they occupied in South Tel

Aviv and in mixed Israeli/Latino salsa dance parties. At that time, I became involved in many informal conversations with migrants, some initiated by me and some that the migrants themselves began. These informal conversations were central to the fieldwork. One of the main challenges I experienced was suspicion provoked by the fear of Israeli police. Although most of these informants were friendly and talkative, some were hesitant about interacting with an Israeli who was trying to obtain information from them. My previous experiences in prodding people to talk – as a journalist, broadcaster, and airport security officer – stood to me in this process, but I had to remain aware of unequal power relations.

In terms of interpreting information collected from the field, my sources' tendencies towards affective subjectivity were frequently an advantage rather than a disadvantage, since in most cases I was more concerned with my informants' viewpoints, feelings and interpretations rather than in obtaining objective data with regard to their experiences of migration. To this end, I have included their voices throughout this chapter; that which is marked in quotation marks represents snippets remembered and extracted from these informal, though deeply informative, conversations.[3]

I find that the process of Latino migrants' identification with salsa music and dance forms is subjective, inter-subjective and objectifying; the first where the Latino migrants, many of whom never really engaged with salsa music in their adult lives 'at home', turn to it in the diasporic experience; the second and third occurring where Israelis embrace Latinos as authentic bearers of an embodied pan-Latin cultural tradition which they value and enjoy. I examine these processes by framing them in the unique circumstances of labour immigration in Israel and in the context of 'absorption' and migrant interactions with Israelis.

For a general overview of the Latino labour migrants' scene in Israel during the early 2000s, I conducted additional formal interviews with social workers and volunteers in the Tel Aviv municipality. My main source was Adi Azov, a social worker at Mesilah, The Centre for Aid and Consultation to the Foreign Community in Tel Aviv, whose insight and experience inform my broader research. To summarise, I used four main methods for fieldwork and data collection:

1. observation ('deep hanging out');
2. informal interviews and conversations with undocumented Latino labour migrants;
3. informal interviews and conversations with Israelis (interacting with the Latinos) and
4. formal interviews with social workers, municipality officials and volunteers.

BACKGROUND: IMMIGRATION AND
LABOUR MIGRATION TO ISRAEL

Immigration is the major strategy of nation building in the state of Israel. Modern Israel is a nation of immigrants and their offspring. To be an immigrant in Israel is, therefore, normative.[4] There are two distinct categories of mass immigration into Israel, the main one being Jewish immigration, referred to as *aliyah* or ascending in Hebrew, terminology that demonstrates a positive ideological attitude towards Jewish 'home-coming' migration into Israel.[5] The second category is non-Jewish labour migration, something that has a completely different meaning and value in Israeli society. The term used in this case is *ovdim zarim*, foreign workers.[6] In contrast to the *klita* or 'absorption' ideology applied to the new *olim* or Jewish immigrants and the efforts made by the authorities to quickly absorb and integrate them into the society, labour migrants remain outsiders in the cultural, social and political sense, a fate shared by labour migrants in many Western countries.

The Israeli–Palestinian conflict plays an important role in the history of labour migration in Israel. Following the first *intifada*, the Palestinian uprising against the Israeli occupation which lasted from December 1987 until the signing of the Oslo Accords in 1993, Israel imposed closures on the Palestinian borders and territories. Palestinians who used to come and work in Israel were replaced by foreign workers legally imported by manpower companies, mostly from Eastern Europe and the Far East. The government approved quotas of visas to workers in sections experiencing labour shortages, such as agriculture and construction (Levush 2013). In addition to this 'legal import' system, a parallel process of illegal labour migration from various parts of the world began.

The major wave of foreign labour migrants to Israel started in the early 1990s. The number of permits for legal foreign labour jumped from 4,200 in 1990 to 103,000 in 1996 (Willen 2003, 4, based on Israeli Ministry of Labour and Social Welfare, cited in Bartram 1998), and at the same time there were influxes of undocumented migrants. The rapid and dramatic increase in the number of both documented and undocumented migrants paralleled a marked decrease in the number of Palestinians working in Israel (Willen 2003, 4). By 2003, the number of migrant workers was estimated at around 189,000, of which 109,000 were undocumented, according to the Central Bureau of Statistics.[7] In the previous years the total number of migrant workers had reached 250,000 according to the same source. The sharp decrease reflects the strategy of mass deportations, which overshadowed the well-being and social life of undocumented labour migrants during my fieldwork.

Undocumented migrants used two main methods to get into Israel: entering the country on a tourist visa (usually limited to three months) and staying in the country after its expiry; or entering under a work visa (which is usually limited in time and restricted to a specific employer) and then, upon expiration of the visa, seeking other employment and remaining in the country illegally.

But why did Latino labour choose to come to work in Israel? According to the many conversations I held in the bus station area in 2002–2003, the main 'push' factor for this wave of migration was the ongoing unstable socio-economic and political conditions in the migrants' own countries. The main 'pull' factor was the relatively high salary one could earn in Israel at that time. While in their country of origin, workers earned around 300 US dollars per month, in Israel they could expect to earn between 1000 and 1500 US dollars per month. Coupled with this, entry into Israel in the late 1990s and early 2000s was still considered easier than entry into most Western European countries. This has drastically changed in the intervening years, with the Israeli government implementing tough and strongly contested immigration policies in relation to non-Jewish labour migrants. It is a policy that has involved intimidation, operations of mass imprisonment and deportation.[8]

Other more psychological and social 'pull' factors drawing Latino labour migrants to Israel were mentioned. The attraction of 'feeling welcome' was cited by informants; reflecting the perception of a positive Israeli attitude towards Latinos in comparison with their attitude towards other labour migrant groups, and, interestingly, in comparison with the Latino labour migrants' experience in other destinations. Israelis living in the Southern Tel Aviv neighbourhoods, where many labour migrants chose to live, described the Latinos to me as 'friendly, unlike the other foreign workers' (personal communication 2002, 2003). Latino migrants also regularly mentioned 'Feeling at home'. Many of them pointed to the similarity between the warm weather in Israel and that of their countries of origin, in contrast to other potential labour destinations in Central and Western Europe. Many also pointed to what they perceived as a similarity in mentality with the Israelis, something I discuss at greater length in the next section. Finally, many of my interviewees mentioned that, as Catholics, they felt particularly privileged and 'blessed' to live in 'the Holy Land'. Even the deadly terror attacks in the old bus station area during these years (January 2002, July 2002, January 2003), in which some foreign workers were killed and many injured (Singh 2003), did not seem to intimidate or deter the Latino labour migrants living in Israel.

INTERACTION WITH ISRAELIS

Latinos were arguably unique among the labour migrant communities when it came to interacting, 'mixing' and socialising with Israelis. In a field research project conducted in 1997, Dr Isaac Schnell asked Israeli residents in the central bus station area in South Tel Aviv to describe the foreign workers living in their neighbourhood per group of origin (each group consisting of approximately 15–19 per cent of the total number of foreign workers in the neighbourhood, according to Schnell). The results show that, in general, 60 per cent of the interviewees described foreign workers in negative terms. The worst image was attributed to Romanians who were described in negative terms by 90 per cent of the interviewees – 50 per cent described them as 'drunk' and 20 per cent said they 'pollute' the neighbourhood (Schnell 1999, 53–55). 'Africans' (as they were collectively described in the survey) and Filipinos received mixed views. Africans were described as 'quiet' by about a third of the interviewees, but 'violent', 'smelly' and 'noisy' by others, and Filipinos were presented as 'weird' and 'strange'. Only Latin Americans were described using mostly positive terms such as 'nice' and 'quiet' (Schnell 1999, 54). A common descriptor used by Israeli residents in South Tel Aviv in reference to the Latin American foreign workers during my research period was 'friendly'.

Following the results obtained by Schnell, I asked both Israelis and Latino labour migrants, what they believe facilitated their perceived positive interaction. The main factors mentioned were related to the idea of 'similarity'. Unlike Filipinos, Thai and Africans, Latinos were perceived to have physical features and outer appearances similar to those of many Israelis, being configured by many of my Israeli and Latino interviewees as 'white (Caucasian) with a dark complexion'.[9] Given Latinos could, therefore, be mistaken for Israelis, many were able to avoid being victims of immigration police harassment and xenophobia. In relation to public behaviour, many Israelis made the point that Latinos 'behave like Israelis', being warm and friendly, but also 'hot tempered', and having similar physical gestures and gesticulations (i.e. hugging each other, using hands a lot when talking, etc.). My own observations, supported by those of Adi Azov, a social worker at Mesilah whose work informs much of my research, also identify a similar business mentality, which was perceived to make it easier for the Latinos to 'do business' or discuss financial issues with Israelis. For example, informal arrangements *de palabra*, that is, 'by word', and 'handshake contracts' or *mutua confianza*, that is, 'mutual trust', were common to both (Azov 2002).[10]

Language was another factor that seemed to help bring Latinos closer to Israelis. Most Israeli residents speak basic English, so labour migrants (including those from the Philippines, Ghana, Thailand and India) who can already converse in that language do not need to learn Hebrew to communicate with locals. According to Azov, most Latinos arriving to work in Israel did not speak English at all and only spoke Spanish. Latinos, therefore, had to learn Hebrew to get along and to be able to communicate with Israelis.

They picked up some Hebrew 'on the street' and in Hebrew classes given in the volunteer aid organisations. Azov indicated that in the Mesilah centre, the Latinos preferred to attend lectures in Hebrew rather than in English.[11] The result was that most Latino migrants spoke better Hebrew than other labour migrant groups.

Latinos were also advantaged, in comparison with other migrant groups, by the presence of a sympathetic Latin American Jewish community. According to Azov, Israelis of Latin American origin (mostly Argentinian) created social contacts and extended help to the Latino foreign workers. Some of the volunteers in Mesilah were Israelis of Latin American origin, working in close contact with the Latino migrant community. One unique example of such collaboration between both Latino communities is La Escuelita, a non-profit organisation founded in the year 2000. A cultural enterprise, La Escuelita aimed at preserving the customs and culture from 'home', as well as offering assistance in the integration into Israeli society of newly arrived migrants. La Escuelita became a community centre for Latin American labour migrants, being run and supported by volunteers from Latin American origin and 'serving as the link between the Latin community, the Israeli society and migrant workers rights organizations', according to Ofer Chama, a volunteer at La Escuelita (email correspondence 2014).

Coming from Catholic countries and having an associated high educational standard (Kemp et al. 2000, 9–14), most of the Latinos, unlike many other migrant groups, came to Israel with some knowledge of the country's history, its biblical heritage and the Jewish people's history. Finally, with many Latinos coming from coastal areas in their countries, a shared 'beach culture' meant Latinos easily adapted to the Mediterranean scene in Tel Aviv, hanging out on the beach, playing beach games, etc. However, one of the main factors in facilitating and promoting interaction and socialising between Latin labour migrants and Israelis was found in the performance and reception of salsa.

SALSA IN THE LATINO LABOUR MIGRANTS COMMUNITY

According to Azov, in the early 2000s, each labour migrant community evidenced a typical social activity. Filipino aid workers (mostly female) organised karaoke evenings and beauty contests, while some Filipino male aid workers performed in drag shows.[12] In the case of the Latinos (mostly young male migrants), the main social activity was football and salsa dancing.

Salsa was born in the *barrios*, the Latino neighbourhoods of New York City in the 1960s and 1970s among Latino immigrants, mainly from Puerto Rico and Cuba (Waxer 2002, 4). In the United States, the collective identity of 'Latinos' was attributed to and adopted by immigrants from different Latin American countries, and salsa has become the musical expression of this new pan-Latin identity. It then spread to Puerto Rico, where it became 'a potent emblem of Puerto Rican identity', and to the rest of Latin America, especially Venezuela, Panama and Colombia (Waxer 2002, 4). In Israel, I argue that salsa became the catalyst for a bond between labour migrants from different Latin countries (mainly Colombia, but also Bolivia, Ecuador and Argentina), backgrounds, cultures and music traditions, and crucially provided the main point of interaction with the host society. According to Javier, a twenty-five-year-old construction worker from Colombia (2003), 'It was what made me feel closer to other Latinos here (Ecuadorians, Bolivians, etc.) and socialise with them, and also [was] what Israelis expected from me'. Salsa is, as Kapchan (2006) finds, a meaningful and permeable site for the performance of ethnic identity.

Interestingly, many of my interviewees, comprising male Latinos in their twenties, as was typical of the labour migrant population then, told me that back at home they hardly listened to or danced salsa. Most were, in fact, into rock and pop music. They told me they had only started listening and dancing to salsa in the context of their diasporic status in Tel Aviv. Many rediscovered the pleasure of salsa as migrants in Israel, the music and dance taking them back to their youth after many years of relative disinterest. Andrés, a twenty-eight-year-old construction worker from Colombia, told me:

> At home I was never into salsa, or tropical music. I was more a rock person, Jimi Hendrix, you know, and me and my friends really did not like salsa or tropical music at all and used to look down at it as very provincial and inferior. Only when I was a child I used to hear a lot of cumbia and mambo at home because my parents liked it. Now, here in Israel I started dancing Latino dances and enjoy it very much. (Personal interview, 2003)

Salsa also met socio-psychological needs in that the music helped migrants to overcome fear, loneliness and homesickness. Over the course of my fieldwork, I noticed that one of the first instinctive reactions to news about an imminent police raid or a friend who had been deported was simply to resort to the cassette player to listen to salsa music. Forty-two out of forty-five Latino migrants with whom I spoke said that listening to and dancing salsa helped them overcome the fear of deportation, strengthened them and helped them to feel more secure. Such views resonate with Alan Lomax's study of the psychological role of music where he asserts:

> The primary effect of music is to give the listener a feeling of security, for it symbolizes the place where he was born, his earliest childhood satisfactions, his

religious experience, his pleasure in community doings, his courtship and his work – any or all of these personality shaping experiences. (Lomax 1959, 929)

Whereas this section has discussed the social and psychological role of salsa *within* the Latino labour migrants community, the next section discusses its role in mediating relations between Latino migrants and members of the host society.

'THE SALSA FACTOR' IN ISRAELI–LATINO INTERACTION

Latin music was and remains very popular in Israel. There are dedicated radio programmes and dance clubs throughout the country and Latin rhythms and melodies shape local pop music to this day.[13] The reasons for this are varied, from the influence of the traditional sources of Ladino (Judeo-Spanish)-speaking Sephardic Jews, and Jewish migration from Argentina and Brazil, to its impact upon the wave of young Israeli *mochileros* (backpackers) travelling to South America after their army service, and to the popularity of Latin American *telenovelas* (TV soap operas) in Israel. The influx of young Latin American males to Tel Aviv in the late 1990s and the early 2000s was, therefore, a welcome addition to the already popular and receptive salsa-dancing scene in Israel. Furthermore, this embedded love and appreciation of salsa music and dance had primed a sense of Latino identity as musically constructed via salsa, an identity that the labour migrants embodied in a dynamic and recursive way.

Mixed Israeli/Latino salsa clubs and parties became a popular phenomenon in Tel Aviv from the late 1990s until the wave of deportations beginning in 2002. During the course of my fieldwork, many Latinos were afraid to visit the clubs they used to frequent together with Israelis in 'quieter times', such as the popular Bailatino in Tel Aviv. But many also expressed that they could not 'live without music'. Young Latino males 'took risks' and attended private parties organised by Israeli salsa aficionados. I attended such a 'mixed' salsa party at a private home in Jaffa in 2003 where there were approximately a hundred people in attendance, thirty of whom were Latinos. These men turned out to be 'the stars' of the party as the Israelis watched their dancing with admiration, talked to them in broken Spanish and asked to dance with them. This was the first time during my fieldwork that I encountered a group of Israelis and a group of undocumented immigrants interacting on what the participants perceived as 'equal terms'; having fun and valuing one another and each other's culture. Migrants' experiences of the Israeli 'gaze' were, in this situationally specific context, positive. Through the 'bodily communication' of their sensuality and 'virtuosity' (Borland 2009, 481) they momentarily acquired a status which, in their perception, elevated them above their everyday objectification as cheap labour power and above other similarly constructed migrants.

Leo Chavez makes an interesting observation about the manner in which host societies regard undocumented immigrants: 'The larger society endows the identity, character and behaviour of the illegal alien with mythic qualities' (Chavez 1998, 22). I would add 'mystic' to 'mythic'. This mythification/ mystification of 'the alien' bears mostly negative overtones. Certainly, in the course of my fieldwork, I heard some Israelis of a lower socio-economic background residing in the bus station area saying that foreign workers had 'mystic' and even 'demonic' qualities. I recall hearing comments that African labour migrants practise 'witchcraft and voodoo', while labour migrants from Thailand were labelled as 'dog eaters'.[14] Latinos were also endowed with mystic qualities, but in their case it was in relation to their 'sexual charm', and more especially, though not unrelatedly, to the way they danced. '*Hem sexi'im*' ('they are sexy') and '*hem rokdim be'hushaniut*' ('they dance in a sensual way') were the main responses from most young Israeli salsa aficionados (male and female) when I asked them about Latino labour migrants attending salsa clubs and parties (Personal communication 2002, 2003).[15] Dalit, an eighteen-year-old Israeli woman from Bat Yam (a suburb of Tel Aviv), told me:

> When you go to a salsa club, you see the way these guys move. It is like witch-craft. They move their torso and look into your eyes and I just melt. It's not just being sexy. It's witchcraft, I tell you. I know too many cases of broken hearts because of these guys. (Personal interview, 2003)

The Latinos I interviewed were aware of the effect their music and dancing had on many Israelis. José, a twenty-four-year-old construction worker from Colombia, told me:

> During the week days I work on a building site, my Israeli boss usually shouts at me, but on weekends I am 'king'. ... When these Israeli girls come to my room and I play my salsa cassettes and dance with them, or when I go to the parties, I know they want me. We don't dance for them. We dance for ourselves but they admire the way we move our bodies. ... When I dance I feel proud that I am a Latino. But when I notice them watching me, my pride goes higher. Maybe the police think I am inferior, but thanks to the salsa, the Israeli girls don't think so. (Personal interview, 2003)

Through the medium of Salsa, the technical capacity to awe the audience (Borland 2009), the gendered allocation of leader roles and the position of the more experienced partner (McClure 2014, 131) all served, at least momentarily, to shift power relations between the migrant worker and his hosts. As Kalchan (2006, 373) argues, 'Dancing affords mastery and compensates for lack of control in other aspects of life'.

Another interesting musical point of interaction I discovered was that the Latino migrants' favourite Israeli musical genre was *muzika mizrahit* (oriental music), which emerged from, and is identified with, Sephardic Jews who migrated to Israel from Arab countries in the 1950s and who were subject to discrimination by European Jews. The emergence of *muzika mizrahit* in the 1970s was associated with the protest movement of Sephardic Jews against the Ashkenazi/European 'elite'. *Muzika mizrahit* was the Israeli genre mostly played and sold in the counterfeit CD and cassette stalls in the central bus station, but out of all groups of labour migrants, it was among the Latino community that I found the greatest appreciation and interest in the genre as a whole. This appropriation of the music associated with the previous wave of the discriminated by the current 'underdog' is intriguing. Looking into this cultural phenomenon, I found many historical, social and musical similarities between *musika mizrahit* and salsa (Morad 2011). For example, both are hybrid musical genres emerging and gaining social significance in the 1970s, spreading, evolving and achieving mainstream status since the 1990s. They are both connected with the formation of ethnic identities, and furthermore, with the formation of new, pan-ethnic identities, affected by migration, discrimination and marginalisation. Musically speaking, both genres originate from, and are fed and influenced by, protogenres from the countries of origin and rich musical heritages of the migrant groups among which they developed. Yet, they are also 'Western' in nature, strongly influenced by the host society's music, and as such, sometimes dismissed by 'purists'. Just as American-born salsa differs from the traditional genres from which it is imbibed, such as Cuban *son*, so does *muzika mizrahit* 'depart' from the traditional music of the Jews from Islamic countries that, in modern Israel, was either 'museumized', 'ethnicized' or, in the early years, 'plainly rejected' (Seroussi 2003). I also found similarities in the lyrics and topics used in both genres, in their dance routines, in their use of typical rhythm patterns, in the 'royal' status and terminology associated with their respective heroes ('king', 'queen', etc.), in the tragic life stories of some of their heroes, and even in the nasal vocal expression typical of both styles (Morad 2011).

CONCLUSION

This chapter looked at salsa as a unique identity factor in the life of Latino labour migrants in south Tel Aviv during the early years of the 2000s, when a rather large community of undocumented labour migrants (mostly young males) arrived from various Latin American countries. Through engaging with salsa music and dance, these migrants created an emotional connection with 'home' and consolidated their diasporic identity in Israel. Furthermore, 'their' music helped them create positive social interactions with the host society, helping them feel welcomed, appreciated and even admired for their music and the way they danced to it. Salsa's pan-Latino identity reflects and complements the pan-identity given to the Latino migrants by the host society that, in general, favourably constructs them collectively as 'the Latinos' or 'the South Americans', in spite of their different countries of origin and cultural backgrounds.[16]

Closer observation within the Latino labour migrant community helped me identify salsa's three main 'identity maintenance' roles; maintaining a minority group identity, 'uniting' and creating a unifying social environment among the labour migrants coming from different Latin American countries with different national identities and cultural backgrounds, and having a socio-psychological function in helping to overcome fear, loneliness and homesickness. However, the more intriguing and unique role discussed in the chapter was the manner in which the music and dance creates an inter-face with the host society, providing a means to earn a sense of respect and express self-esteem, in spite of all the problematic issues this raises in terms of stereotyping and exoticism, or to avoid euphemisms – racism.

While the Latino migrants' own subjectivities are foregrounded in this interpretation, the embracing of salsa music as a marker of identity and as an interface for interaction with the host society raises many questions of authenticity and exoticism, which is both inflicted by Israelis, but also self-imposed by the Latinos. For the latter grouping, it offers a means to elevate their status in the interaction process, being a temporary solution to hide and 'dance away' inequality. Therefore, in spite of their apparently positive aspects, the scenes described and investigated in this chapter are as problem-atic, unstable, delusionary and transient as the status of the undocumented labour migrants in Israel.

I have shown in this chapter how salsa has become the discursive trope, the idea, the embodiment and the practice, into which the labour migrants' national identities are poured and distilled into a diasporic Latino pan-identity. This identity is remade in the Israeli context by both Israeli expecta-tions of Latin-ness and by Latinos embracing this globalised pan-Latin form as an expression of the self. To frame this in a more cross-cultural context, this chapter illustrates the unique role of music (and dance) in mediating transient and illegal exile conditions and in providing a medium and a site of interaction between a predominantly marginalised community and the host society.

NOTES

1. In January 2003, a few months after the summer that I spent in Tel Aviv for my first fieldwork period, two suicide bombers blew themselves up in the Old Central Bus Station, on the street frequented by many undocumented labour migrants, right where I used to sit, drink beer and listen to salsa with my Latino friends and informants. Twenty-four people were killed and 111 wounded, many of them undocumented labour migrants, including one of my informants. I dedicate this chapter to them and to the victims of conflict everywhere.

2. This translates as 'Andean Tavern'.

3. Owing to the nature of this research among illegal immigrants trying to avoid the attention of the immigration police, most informal conversations were not recorded, and the quotes appearing in this paper are re-created from memory or from short notes taken during or following the conversation, unless stated otherwise. I incorporate these quotes to retain the nature of the discourses used by my informants, both Latino and Israeli. Subjective, stereotypical, stigmatising, and in certain cases, offensive and politically incorrect, the discourse is an integral part of the scene described and is, therefore, necessary to the understanding and analysis of the relationships and identity processes discussed in this chapter. Crucially, these discourses are also present in the media, being used by 'right wing' politicians and anti-undocumented immigration activists, which are then countered by contrary discourses used by 'left wing' politicians and human rights activists. An example of such contradictory discourses commonly used is as follows: Likkud (right wing) Party MK (member of the Knesset, the Israeli parliament) Miri Regev, in a 2012 demonstration against asylum seekers and illegal labour migrants in South Tel Aviv, using the 'disease' discourse referenced later in this chapter stated: 'They are cancer in our body. We will do everything we can to send them back to where they came from, and we will not allow foreigners to come and look for work in Israel' (http://www.haaretz.co.il/news/education/1.1715061). The 'cancer' metaphor is one that was frequently used following Regev's speech by anti-immigration activists and members of the public. A typical counter-discourse was used by Hadash (left wing) party MK Dov Hanin, in his speech in 2012, in which he opposes anti-immigration law by stating, 'This thing is opposed to all the values of the Jewish and the human tradition'. Source: http://www.dovblog.org/dov/tag/%D7%9E%D7%A1%D7%AA%D7%A0%D7%A0%D7%99%D7%9D. The reference to the 'Jewish values' of accepting the immigrant and treating him equally is frequently used in pro-immigration discourse though quoting the Biblical order: 'And if a stranger sojourn with thee in your land, ye shall not do him wrong. The stranger that sojourneth with you shall be unto you as the home-born among you, and thou shalt love him as thyself; for ye were strangers in the land of Egypt' (Leviticus 19:33, 34).

4. Source: http://www.focus-migration.de/Israel.5246.0.html?&L=1.

5. See The Jewish Agency website: http://www.jewishagency.org/.

6. In recent years an even harsher term, *mistenenei avoda* (labour infiltrators), has been introduced by the government for the Sudanese and Eritrean asylum seekers, a term that was quickly adopted by the media and the population in reference

to all illegal labour migrants. The term was used by the minister of interior and the prime minister during numerous interviews and parliament debates since the influx of African asylum seekers started increasing significantly in 2005, reaching a peak in the public debate in 2011. In November 2011, the government initiated an 'infiltration prevention' plan (http://www.ynetnews.com/articles/0,7340,L-4160014,00.html). The media uses, and at the same time often challenges, the term. Whereas politicians and journalists with a liberal, 'human rights oriented' agenda insist on using a different term: 'asylum seekers', right-wing politicians insist on 'labour infiltrators'. The term has entered the general public discourse and is now being used to reference undocumented labour migrants. An article in Ynet news portal, entitled 'Who are the Sinai infiltrators?' (12.12.11), reflects the agenda-laden discourse and asks, '"Infiltrators", "asylum seekers", refugees or maybe "migrant workers"? Who are the people crossing the southern border in thousands and what is the problem?' (Efraim, Omri, Ynet 12.12.11 – http://www.ynetnews.com/articles/0,7340,L-4160678,00.htm).

7. Central Bureau of Statistics, The Statistical Abstract of Israel Annual Report 2003, Jerusalem: The Government of Israel [in Hebrew].

8. In 2002, Israeli prime minister Ariel Sharon announced a policy of deportations and a target of 50,000 undocumented labour migrants to be deported by the end of 2003. To implement this policy, Rashut Ha'hagira (The Immigration Authority) was established, consisting of 400 policemen. Since the establishment of the immigration authority in 2003, the number of undocumented labour migrants substantially decreased, due to deportation or intimidation, and by the end of 2005, 145,000 undocumented labour migrants have left the country by deportation or of their own will, according to Moked Siyua Le'ovdim Zarim, the centre for aid for foreign workers, 2000.

9. This, of course, is a generalisation, which not only essentialises a non-homogeneous group but also speaks to ideas of archetypes of ethnicity. Yet at the same time, such ideas hold sway within the imagination of people, something I address at greater length shortly.

10. It is important to take into consideration that not only the descriptions by the neighbourhood's residents and the labour migrants are subjective, as discussed in the introduction, but also most of the observations made by social workers are not based on official surveys or statistics, are subjective and can be influenced by stereotypical ideas. The issue of how discourses of migration are influenced and informed by stereotypes is widely discussed and theorised upon, especially in disciplines such as social psychology and migration studies (see, e.g., Stangor and Crandall 2013; on stereotyping and migration in Israel, see Leshem and Shuval 1998).

11. Other sources I used to learn about the behaviour and circumstances of Latino Labour migrants approaching Mesilah aid centre were Nezer 2001 and Nezer and Alter 2002.

12. The 2006 documentary 'Bubot Neyar' ('Paper Dolls') directed by Tomer Heymann describes Filipino men who work as health care aids for elderly Orthodox Jews in Israel and who, in their free time, perform as drag queens. In 2013, the story was adapted for the stage and performed as a musical at the Tricycle Theatre in London.

13. A few examples: Shlomo Yidov and Pablo Rosenberg are two well-known Israeli singers born in Argentina, who combine songs in Spanish and Latin rhythms in their music. Yidov even released a successful album entirely in Spanish in 2014. The album, entitled 'El Primer Amor' ('First Love'), includes Latin American classics such as 'Duerme Negrito' and 'Volver'. A group from Jerusalem called 'Atraf' (an Israeli colloquial expression, of Arab origin, meaning 'excitement') had an Argentinian-born leader and performed original Israeli songs with a salsa rhythm and feel. Dozens of Brazilian songs were translated into Hebrew and performed by top Israeli artists, songs such as *Bo Lerio* ('Come to Rio') sung by Yehudith Ravitz (1983), which is a Hebrew version of *Boiadeiro* by Jorge Ben Jor.

14. Again, it is important to note that these negatives stereotypes were mostly expressed by a minority of Israelis from a low socio-economic background, living in the area around the central bus station.

15. Sexuality is not discussed in this article, as it is not directly relevant to the discussion and the argument presented here. I stated that both male and female Israelis found the Latino dancers 'sexy'; however, this does not necessarily indicate a sexual attraction, but rather an expression of appreciation and admiration.

16. Unlike most Israelis, the Jewish Argentinean volunteers at Mesilah clearly made a distinction between the different Latinos, as per their countries of origin.

[*This chapter is based on my MMus dissertation at SOAS and my essay in the SOAS Journal of Graduate Research, Vol. I, 2005.]

Chapter 11

'An Affirmation of Key Postmodernist Tendencies'

Musics, Apolitics and Placebo Nostalgias Within the Greek-Speaking Diaspora of Birmingham (UK)

Michalis Poupazis

We got along great before politics got the best of us. My late husband worked with and had lots of Turkish[-speaking Cypriot] friends, who all loved him! (Androniki Myrmidoni – Greek-speaking Cypriot from Larnaca [age: 82], interviewed 8 May 2013)

I remember before the war, we used to have lots of Greek[-speaking Cypriot] friends. I still do and also made new ones since I ... moved to Birmingham. (Zübeyde Arif Mehmet – Birmingham-based Turkish-speaking Cypriot [age: 70], interviewed 9 October 2014)

During my 2012–2014 ethnographic work in Larnaca (Cyprus) and Birmingham (UK) and four decades after the 1974 Turkish 'invasion' or 'military offensive' (depending on perspective) in Cyprus, Androniki and Zübeyde reminisce like many other native and migrant elders about an island where politics did not define life. Yet, modern native and diasporic Cypriot identity takes in past conflict and largely opposes such fluid romanticisms, portraying political discourses as determinative of everyday life. This politicising phenomenon has, since its mid-twentieth-century beginnings, been termed by the Cyprus popular media the 'Cyprus problem' (Christophorou et al. 2010, 5). As such, the antecedents and aftermath of 1974 still influence contemporary social (and musical) choices for natives and migrants alike.

The war, and the division of the island that followed, caused Cypriot society and its indigenous culture to be lost and subsequently re-found within a post-1974 fragmented reality. As geo-ethnic separation of the island has inevitably generated different sociocultural representations on each side of

Table 11.1 Definition and Abbreviations Used to Describe a Series of Cypriot Complex Identities

Abbreviations	Definitions
TsSM	Turkish-speaking Sunni Muslims
GsOCC	Greek-speaking Orthodox Christian Cypriots
BbGsC	Birmingham-based Greek-speaking Cypriots
LbGsCC	London-based Greek-speaking Cypriot Community

the border, narratives like Zübeyde's and Androniki's have become derelict, leaving the younger generations warming towards their motherlands' (Greece's and Turkey's) resources instead of revisiting and reviving their indigenous ones. There is no such thing as *new* traditional (folk) Cypriot music these days, and some people now adopt a multitude of labels for themselves and others, including Turkish, Turkish-Cypriot or Turkish-speaking Cypriot (there is a similar set of Greek-labelled equivalents), thereby shaping Cypriot diasporas around the world. Table 11.1 provides descriptors for these complex identity groupings.

This chapter focuses on Birmingham-based, Greek-speaking Cypriots (BbGsCs) and follows the intersections between politics, religion, memory (nostalgia), music and the diasporic imagination. In diaspora, music interplays (and competes) with religious and political praxes[1] in actualising memories from homeland Cyprus. My aim is to explain how a diasporic ethnos detaches itself politically and how political discourse can evolve into apoliticality and, finally, into depoliticalisation. This evolution is narrated in stages: from mainland macropolitics to London-based mimetic politics and then, through acculturation, into institutionalised micropolitics manifesting as emotional and memory discourses and musical practices. My study of an intracommunal cluster – the Greek Orthodox churches and the Greek schools in Birmingham – reveals a series of migrant, emotionally expressive, discursive and musical narratives, where 'nostalgia' operates as a placebo amongst BbGsCs.

The chapter begins with an explanation of the 'Cyprus problem' before and after the pivotal moment of 1974. This is followed by a closer look at the diasporic life of Birmingham Cypriots as the second largest diasporic community outside London, which is more concerned with Greek-speaking Cypriot cultural activities than with political praxes, a theme that is developed in subsequent sections on communal apolitical construction and the churches' and Sunday schools' micropolitics. I then define and theorise the concept of 'placebo-nostalgia' to describe these institutionalised and migrant micropolitics, which are evidenced in the musical listening and performance practices of BbGsCs. Drawing on the musical genres *laika* and *xenitia* and their intracommunal utterances, I track the placebo-nostalgias of these migrant musical expressions, as evidenced in the case study of a school celebration featuring music and dance. Focussing on the creation of experience in the migrant moment, the ethnographic vignette shows how memories, feelings, settings, habits, desires and actions combine to add new layers onto human experience and/or imagination, elements which build incrementally into a musical diasporic life. Here, people move into contemporary cultural expressions and create a new reality where politics does not determine life, something that speaks to the contemporary significance of discourses of culture relative to other classic social science themes (politics, civil rights, etc.).

THE 'CYPRUS PROBLEM': PRE-1974 CONTEXTUALISATION

A cultural element of 'Greekness' has persisted in Cyprus since the 1st millennia BC when cities began to be built, including Phoenician Kition on the site of modern Larnaca. From 1185, Catholic culture under the invading Franks (and, later, the Venetians) failed to prevail over Greek Orthodoxy (which traced its roots to the mid-first century ad foundation of the Cypriot church). A further invasion ushered in Ottoman rule from 1571 to 1878, punctuated in 1765 by a revolt by Greek and Turkish speakers, who at that time coexisted and functioned as compatriots. Cyprus came under British political control from 1878, ultimately gaining independence in 1960.

Although the trauma of 1974 partitioned the island into northern Turkish and southern Greek-speaking areas, the 'Cyprus problem' has, in reality, developed over time. Rebecca Bryant and Yiannis Papadakis (2012, 4) list these phases as 'anti-colonial [British] struggle, interethnic and intra-ethnic violence [amongst and between Turkish- and Greek-speaking Cypriots], postcolonial instability, war [1974] and external interventions [East and West]'. Early twentieth-century conflicts among Greek-speaking Orthodox Christian Cypriots (GsOCCs) and Turkish-speaking Sunni Muslims (TsSMs) traced both nationalistic and religious discourses, taking place first in Nicosia before expanding throughout the island by mid-century. Colonial-era interplay between Greek and Turkish speakers and the desire of the GsOCCs to unite the island with mainland Greek (*enosis*), and the TsSMs' firm stand for *taksimi*[2] (meaning division into two states), led to the formation of the National Organisation of Cypriot Fighters (EOKA) in 1955 among Greeks, and the Turkish Resistance Organisation (TMT) three years later, among Turks.

Under the presidency of Archbishop Makarios, the island became an independent Republic in 1960. This did not hold back the antagonistic relationship of the GsOCCs and the TsSMs, who were still in full pursuit of *enosis* and *taksimi*. These ambitious drives erupted in a series of violent incidents, with TsSMs counting most casualties at the hands of the GsOCC majority. Play on the Cold War chessboard brought the United Nations (UN) to Cyprus in 1964 as an anti-violent answer to the interethnic conflicts. After a success-ful three-year campaign, and in contrast to developments in mainland Greece (where a military junta took power), the UN eased tensions and contained the GsOCCs' enotic ambitions.

By the late 1960s and early 1970s, many people were caught up in the intraethnic violence of an extremist nationalist GsOCC minority still commit-ted to *enosis* (calling themselves EOKA B) who terrorised fellow GsOCCs loyal to the Republic of Cyprus. The leadership of the Republic was also tar-geted; EOKA B launched a coup d'état against Archbishop Makarios in 1974, encouraging the military intervention that divided the island into the Turkish Republic of Northern Cyprus (TRNC, still internationally unrecognised except by Turkey) and the remainder of the Republic of Cyprus in the south.

THE 'CYPRUS PROBLEM': POST-1974

Race in the contemporary Cypriot context still underpins politics, which, in turn, can lead to natives' involvements in violent racism (Anthias 1992, 11–19).[3] Cyprus' twenty-first-century socio-politics are expressed as iden-tity contradistinctions (West/East, modern/traditional), endorsed and tacitly proffered by political parties. AKEL on the left promotes Cypriotism based on distinctive Cypriot customs, detached from Greek or other influences, while DISI on the right promotes Greek nationalism among Cypriots who usually consider themselves purely Greek and who are strongly attached to cultural roots shared with mainland Greece. This political dichotomy has been consistent throughout Cyprus' modern history, mapping onto a series of sociocultural binary divisions (rural/urban, working class/elite). Dealing with Greek-speaking elementary school children in urban and rural areas of the island, Avra Pieridou-Skoutella's (2007) work reveals how these dichotomies extend into the musical praxis of the modern Cypriot adult. Skoutella shows the development of fragmented national musical identities as the outcome of 'ideological messages children receive from their musical enculturation contexts' (251). This music-infused reality in the island follows children up to their adulthood, where ideological messages mature into adherent expres-sions of musical enculturation contexts and narratives, connecting traditional Cypriot music to the left and Greek (and Western) popular music to the right. This stratification is a theme which runs throughout this chapter.

'Modernised' Greek-speaking Cypriots have been keen to portray to outsiders their 'Westernised', 'highbrow' side. The island's educated elite has always encouraged Greek nationalism. Desiring to portray themselves domestically and internationally as an educated, European elite, Cypriot natives also generate a blurred Greek/Cypriot identity that runs through their culture (including music).[4] Such discourses have migrated with Cypriot expatriates to all corners of the world, including Britain, Cypriots' preferred destination; and of course, people take their musics with them into their new locales.

THE 'CYPRUS PROBLEM': IN DIASPORA

While the BbGsC diaspora is linked to other geo-dispersals within and outside the United Kingdom, the Birmingham community configures itself in particular in relation to the London migrant community. The London GsOCCs and their socio-politico-cultural discourses are mimetic of native ones and more agile than those of BbGsCs. This idea of mimesis is central to my discussion. The conventional meaning of mimesis is imitation, but I adopt Paul Ricoeur's (1984) understanding of it as a more multidimensional praxis, where *three-fold mimesis* becomes an 'active sense of organizing the events into a system' (33). The structure is complete only when the reader reads the whole text, that is, reading and understanding the full spectrum of GsOCC migration to the United Kingdom,[5] offering an explanation of the contemporary interplay that I observed between London-based and Birmingham-based migrants.[6]

Although no other scholarship on the London-based Greek-speaking Cypriot Community (LbGsCC) uses the term mimesis, it is always a quiet agent in their narratives. As early as 1967, Vic George and Geoffrey Miller-son pointed out that the 'two factors that influenced the character of Cypriot associations in London [were] the immigrants' need to spend their leisure time as they used to do in Cyprus ... [and] politics' (287). Robin Oakley (1979) stressed how the LbGsCC family model followed the patriarchal native prototype, while in 1992, Floya Anthias explained how the racialised boundaries of the LbGsCC both followed and extended Cyprus' sociopolitical landscape. More recently, Gilles Bertrand (2004, 93) has talked about 'two Cypriot diasporas', explaining how native sociopolitical patterns are also mirrored among Turkish-speaking émigrés. In one of the most recent Cypriot diasporic works, Janine Teerling and Russell King (2012, 19) reverse direction to examine the different 'diasporic hubs and hinterlands' in Cyprus.

Andreas Papapavlou and Pavlos Pavlou (2002, 92) estimated that there are 300,000 LbGsCs, and official sources (Cyprus Statistical Service, 2011 Census) suggest a current UK-wide GsOC population of 4,00,000–5,00,000. LbGsCs' stronger political involvement reflects both their much larger numbers than the 12,000 found today in the UK Midlands, and the London community's founding during a period when political activity concerning Cyprus was taking place on its doorstep: 'the pre-invasion arrival in Britain of [Turkish Prime Minister] Ecevit ... [and] President Makarios for top-level talks, and [Makarios'] personal appeal to thousands of British Cypriots from the pulpit of the Orthodox Church in Camden Town' (Constandinides 1977, 269). London expatriates' stronger political praxes endear them to the major native political parties, and both AKEL and DISI nurture in their ideologies amongst them, garnering votes at home.

In contrast, my ethnography shows that BbGsCs feel overshadowed and neglected. BbGsC political praxes also echo these discourses, but without replicating or imitating native modes; instead, they draw on reconstructions of the past – myths, stories and an imagined reality – rather than on mimesis, as LbGsCs do. BbGsCs have developed throughout their migrational narrative a competitive relationship with the LbGsCC. The testimony of Birmingham's Greek-Cypriot Consul reveals that this perception leads to intensive local involvement, as community members work hard to create an identity as the United Kingdom's *second*-biggest Greek-Cypriot migrant group. This accords with their observed close involvement with Greek-speaking Cypriot cultural activities, rather than with political praxes, a theme developed below. However, their conspicuous ways of preserving their heritage foster a stronger sense of ethnic identity than the London migrants', an almost undefined nationalism mirroring the comparisons drawn by George and Millerson (1967), Oakley (1970) and Constandinides (1993) between London migrants and the even less ethnically aware mainland Cypriots.

BbGsCs: AN APOLITICAL CONSTRUCTION

Micropolitics refers to small-scale interventions that are used for governing the behaviour of large populations of people … a political regulation involved in shaping the preferences, attitudes, and perceptions of individual subjects. Micropolitics contributes to the formation of desire, belief, inclination, and judgment in political subjects. Its regulations take place at local and individual levels in locations such as prisons, hospitals, and schools … but also in arts. (Scherer 2007, 563)

In place of the Marxist binary model of struggle between antagonistic classes and the modernity of the major macropolitical forces contesting social power and economic control, Michel Foucault (1980) introduces the postmodern concept of micropolitics. He notes: 'We had to wait until the nineteenth century before we began to understand the nature of exploitation, and to this day, we have yet to fully comprehend the nature of power' (Foucault 1977, 213). Five years previous, Foucault (1972) prognostically framed the above as a rejection of all meta-theories, thereby harmonising with key postmodernist tendencies. Similar postmodern tendencies are observed within the migrant community in question, something that I expand upon later. For BbGsCs, 'doing politics' traditionally (macropolitics or micropolitics) does not apply as praxis. In a sense, their *politically conscious* behaviour may be understood as a postmodern rejection of all meta-theories. In contrast to LbGsCs' emphasis on the micropolitics of local liberation struggles, the Birmingham community rejects speaking for others in a unified movement, offering prolific examples of fragmented identity and meaning.

I have observed a dichotomy between BbGsCs' *political consciousness*, by which I mean what they *believe* they are doing, and their *politically unconscious* praxis, which is what they are tacitly *encouraged* to do under the rubric of being a *model migrant* (guilt) and emotional attachment to homeland (nostalgia). Both praxes, conscious and unconscious, are, I suggest, products or by-products of the grand pan-Orthodox schema in the United Kingdom. Instead of using the binaries of conscious and unconscious, I use the term 'apolitical' and its cognates.[7] The BbGsCs do apolitics in two ways: first through expressing a fragmented identity serving the need for a more pronounced identity than the London migrants and second by an intracommunal interplay of social and religious practice and involvement. Both homogenise into unique and idiosyncratic apolitical expressions, and one way in which this is done is through churches.

BbGsCs AND THEIR CHURCHES' (MICRO)POLITICS

Foucault (1982) argues that pastoral power in Christian institutions is unique, appearing 'more reciprocal' than governmental power, as it 'respond[s] to the community and the individual for their salvation' (Godfrey 2012).[8] This kind of pastoral power is perceived as a sign of modernity within the relationship of the Orthodox Church and BbGsCs. The approximately 12,000 BbGsCs form two parishes: Apostle Andrew, and Apostle Luke and Holy Trinity.[9] Most BbGsCs are pledged to their parish churches, practising religious beliefs. Older members, trying to live out a migrant model based on concepts of heritage taught by the church during their upbringing, appear to have the strongest religious affiliations. Constandinides (1977) suggests that LbGsC heritage concepts stem from political ideologies, while in Birmingham, fieldwork reveals that what might be termed 'guilt' is the root, not politics. Either way, there are high levels of intracommunal cultural involvement from migrants. Younger migrants tend to discover Greek-Cypriot traditions through Westernised lenses, hybridising their national heritage with British popular culture and exploiting British philhellenism linked to Greece's ancient culture, alongside the European orientalism that modern Greece projects. The Birmingham churches' pastoral power is also mirrored in the BbGsC's social adoptions of the institution's hierarchy. Families transparently structure themselves on patriarchal models, with the eldest male exercising appreciable power. Hierarchical structures are also found in parish committees and groups open to any migrant willing to become involved. This might be understood as the church's effort to draw migrants closer (perhaps in part through satisfying personal vanity, which involves the use of a title, for example).

With Orthodox beliefs promoting Greekness, BbGsC religious praxes are acute and fervent; *everything* is Greek to them. My observations initially suggested that the church's early nurturing (through its Sunday Greek schools) and sponsoring of Greekness was an effort of the DISI where '[experiences or] events become depoliticized, redefined, disembedded from traditional political concerns, and even re-territorialised ... as a new way of imagining communities' (Sant Cassia 2000, 297, 299). The Orthodox schema is very strong among BbGsCs, allowing institutionalised (church) micropolitics founded on political naivety to overpower mainland macropolitics; Greekness in this instance does not link to the DISI, as in the native parallel or in London. Identity, religion and cultural discourses are proposed here as the apolitical praxes of the BbGsCs, with the observed naivety understood as a 'depoliticised' manifestation of distinctness and fragmented identity declarations, leading to emotional discourses which construct an imagined communal reality. Central to this imagined communality are the operations of nostalgia, and specifically, what I term 'placebo-nostalgia'.

MICROPOLITICS OF MEMORY: *PLACEBO-NOSTALGIA*

> Except that it is stressed and imagined through listening in new ways nostalgia can be seen as a new way of imagining communities, harnessed in and by the post nation-state, an attempt at a connivance of a recovery of a lost childhood, a return to the m(other)land. Nostalgia, often the erosion of memory into (and as) history, helps create frameworks of interpretation (and narration) for sites of memory. (Sant Cassia 2000, 299)

Hylland Eriksen (1995, 157–75) explains how the church institutionalises and drives its members' praxes to prevent the potential social degeneration that being in a foreign country might prompt. This relationship also derives, according to BbGsC testimony, from memories leading to an emotional longing (nostalgia) for social continuity with the homeland. In Birmingham, the churches are institutionalised assembly points, *ekklesiai* in the classical sense, or in Ritivoi's (2002) terms, 'the familiar'. According to Ritivoi, the familiar generates nostalgia, and Boym (2001) underlines nostalgia's function of generating a need for social continuity. Malpas (2001, 88–89) argues that in time, nostalgia refocuses from the spatial to a temporal, painless homesickness and a 'memorandum home' composed of intimate smells, symbols and sounds. Daynes' (2005) observations on the Rastafarian diaspora show the considerable efforts that migrants invest in maintaining symbols such as food and music to preserve social continuity; and this is how BbGsCs act around their two *ekklesiai*. She further argues that social continuity is sustained through social groups' historical narratives and division of memory into *before* and *after*. In contrast, Matsuoka and Sorenson (2001) argue that migrants care for outdated traditions in their diaspora, with their *after* consisting of 'ghosts and shadows' of the *before*.

BbGsCs subsidise their two already rich churches with personal, financial and other resources to resist social dissolution (as they understand it) and to satisfy their memory-emotional-nostalgic expressions of social continuity with Cyprus. I have observed churches in Birmingham tacitly using fears of social dissolution to do a kind of micropolitics that contrives migrants' apolitics; this is placebo-nostalgia in action.[10]

Boym's work (2001, xvii) reveals a darker side to late twentieth/early twenty-first-century nostalgia, warning of its hazardous misemployment in exploiting political feasibilities through memory. Appadurai's (1996) work on Filipinos' homesickness talks of a 'world they never lost' (29–30), warning of nostalgia as a 'fashioned', commodifying 'instrument of [the] merchandiser's toolbox', an 'ersatz nostalgia' ('nostalgia without a memory', 75–85) that appropriates the past merely to sell fashion (Markas 2011). From my perspective, as I have stated elsewhere:

> Placebo-nostalgia comprises the tactics and calculations imposed by an institution on its subjects to subordinate them unconsciously *via* emotions and memory, and covertly guide them into apolitical praxes. It is another form of micropolitics, with an agenda including memory, emotions and cultural resources. (Poupazis 2014, 94)

Even if it manifests as an ersatz and painless nostalgia, a genuine longing for home still remains within BbGsCs, who usually draw on cultural resources such as food and music to summon up remembered or imagined homes. These opposing genuine and ersatz dialogues, along with BbGsC nostalgic musical ends, are explained below.

BbGsC MUSICS: *LAIKA* AND *XENITIA*
SONGS – 'IT'S ALL GREEK TO ME'

The term *Greek music* is used here as migrants use it, to describe all Greek or Cypriot musics. Some migrants understand the differences between genres. Nonetheless, they still choose to call them by the communally accepted term; it is all Greek to them. A number of genres listened to by migrants are involved, one way or another, in migrant apolitics. The clearest examples of the relationship between music, apolitics and placebo-nostalgia is found in the popular (*laika*) songs of Greece, particularly in the song sub-genre of *xenitia* (foreign lands), popular with older male members of the community. I also look at 'traditional' songs sung in Greek School, the institution that nurtures nostalgia from an early age.

For BbGsCs, *laika* is the most common genre and includes several other genres of Greek music[11] as well as Cypriot folk, thereby making it a prime example of identity blurring in migrant musical praxes. Many younger BbGsCs choose not to listen to Greek music at all, while older males, especially when in social situations, most often listen to old-*laika*, *demotica, rebetica* and *nishiotica* and, in more private moments, listen to *xenitia*: '"ξενιτιά" [*xenitia*] ... (xenos) ... means foreign ... refers to a foreign place ... a psychological state ... convey[ing] feelings of sadness ... denot[ing] the places where Greek[s] expatriate[d] ...' (Karra 2006, online). The words are very male-orientated, and their communal function accompanies music in the delineation of masculine nostalgia.[12] Songs of *xenitia* clearly both underline and generate personal and emotional notions; they are the most obvious examples of musical nostalgia amongst BbGsCs.

PLACEBOS AND APOLITICS OF *XENITIA*

Xenitia songs are key to older men's musical–apolitical praxes and prove to be a strong placebo-nostalgia facilitator.[13] These songs talk of not only nostalgia but also about how great it is to be Greek. Older male expatriates, being *model migrants* through their nostalgia and patriarchal social reality, 'have to do something about it as the men of the community' (Mallas 2012). They do this by getting involved in committees or through money offerings (usually both). This involvement is also understood by them to guard, Cerberus-like, their cultural continuation, thereby replying to fears of social degeneration. Such involvements are the conscious apolitics that migrants practice.

Crucially, the BbGsC priests, as symbolic embodiments of the churches,[14] consider the genre to be ethically sound for migrants to listen to (the priests are also frequent listeners to these songs). The churches not only understand the social needs of older male migrants, but also amplify them for financial and nationalistic benefit, creating opportunities for migrants to act out their need of nostalgia and patriarchal masculinity through migrant community hierarchies (e.g. committees or social gatherings where migrants can channel nostalgia through musical and culinary resources and behaviours understood as very masculine). The church inculcates these needs in younger migrants through cultural means (i.e. light-*laika* songs), announcing fears of social degeneration at every opportunity within and outside the church and attracting them through free meals (paid for by older male members) or financial aid.

These are only a micro-scale of the placebo-nostalgias that these migrants are prescribed. Older male migrants become, in a sense, shop-front dummies for the church's idea of Greekness, displaying ethically and ethnically sound models of migrancy for the youth, who may harbour fear and guilt for not being model migrants themselves, even as they hybridise their cultural heritage with British popular culture. The 'Cypriot' of their national mix is too often forgotten, as everything is also 'all Greek' to them. Placebo or not, the church's prescriptions successfully create a communal reality of the *all is Greek to me* kind.

GREEK SCHOOL SONGS AND THE JOINT NATIONAL CELEBRATION

Each parish's church and school operate as one in the construction of pastoral power and adult migrants' fragmented ethnic identity. Birmingham Greek schools function weekly on Sunday mornings before the liturgy, helping to instil in younger BbGsCs a need for a continued positionality and nostalgia towards their *homeland* and *motherland*. In Cyprus, secondary and high schools offer a cultural studies and musical education model more or less neutrally located between Greek and Cypriot culture. The two Birmingham schools adopt this same model, something that contributes to blurred identity in childhood and adulthood. In fact, many BbGsC students show no sociopolitical understanding of what this body of cultural resources might connote elsewhere.

The school holds four annual celebrations, and thus four repertoires are taught: 28 October, a Greek national celebration; Christmas; a combined marking of the Greek 25 March national day and the Greek-speaking Cypriot anniversary of 1 April, on which the next section focuses; and the end-of-school-year celebration. Through these four celebrations and from an early age, BbGsCs develop a fragmented identity platform, refined from naïve pictorial schoolbook abstractions about *homeland* and *motherland* into a nostalgic adulthood. How this identity-blurring process generates Greekness and manifests as ersatz nostalgia for the familiar (not for the source), and enables placebo-nostalgias to guide the apolitical praxes of migrants in adulthood, is illustrated by a field experience I had at the Apostle Andrew School during one of these celebrations.[15]

31 May 2013 was no ordinary Sunday for the migrants and children of the Apostle Andrew School. The event included singing, recitation and dancing, with the programme revealing more Greek (15) than Cypriot (3) songs, dances and poems. The mixture was designed to fit this joint occasion – as the community was observing (almost two months late) the combined marking of 25 March and 1 April national days – and the children marched into the church waving Greek and Cypriot flags, dressed in traditional mainland Cypriot and motherland Greek costumes.

The one Cypriot song performed that day, *1st April*, had Cypriotist-patriotic lyrics promoting Greekness and replicated the original, revealing how a rather simple melody has no need to be subsumed differently in a diasporic context. Featuring the lyrics, 'With the blood of heroes and in letters of gold – history recorded our sweet freedom', the song's melody and chord progression are 'borrowed' from the American Western ballad *Oh My Darling, Clementine*. It might surprise any Greek-speaking Cypriot that a momentous patriotic musical resource of their childhood is American, and not Greek at all; not to mention the fact that the song celebrates, for these Anglo-Cypriots, the beginning of the EOKA fight against the British. *1 April*, thus, fragments migrant identity further, even as it paradoxically acts as a unifying agent for the diasporic communal life there. Another example of identity blurriness (Greek/Cypriot) on the day was the fourth grade performance of a Greek (Cretan and Pontian) folk dance, *Susta*, and a Cypriot suite dance, the women's *Karchilamas*, as two parts of one dance. This blurring of cultural identity is something that has been developed as a unique way of subsuming a bicultural heritage, though many migrants still contend that everything is Greek to them!

Throughout the celebrations, I sat next to Nicola Christou, whose sons were performing. She emotionally testified, 'This brings back lots of memories. We did exactly the same routines when we were children as my two sons do today' – an attestation of nostalgia for childhood and an understanding of cultural heritage as all-Greek. Greek music for BbGsCs perhaps symbolises nostalgia with a crying quality that may echo the Homeric nostalgia of Odysseus' 'sobs and groans and anguish' (Fagles 1996, 157). In other words, it is an imagined nostalgia. Through listening to such songs, migrants shift 'from spatial to the temporal' homesickness, as attested to by Nicola, who never really lived in her home village of Mazotos. It is a 'memorandum home' (Malpas 2011, 88), impressionistically woven from the intermingling of intimate sounds and aromas during her Birmingham childhood years, leading to an ersatz nostalgia when, as an adult, she looks back on her childhood (the familiar), and not the actual musical traditions of her homeland. What

Birmingham-born migrants actually listen to or consume is largely irrelevant to this nostalgia, as they will be nostalgic about it anyway. Crucially, it is exactly this nurtured and ersatz nostalgia that enables intracommunal institutions to breed nostalgic 'monsters', dependent on the placebos they are prescribed.

CONCLUSION

During my ethnographic experience with BbGsCs, I witnessed how political discourse can evolve into apoliticality and, finally, depoliticisation; a process narrated in this chapter as moving from mainland macropolitics, to London-based mimetic politics, and finally, through acculturation, to institutionalised micropolitics manifesting as emotional and memory (musical) discourses. As oxymoronic as it might appear, and in spite of its nationalistic appellation, 'Greek' music in the BbGsC context proves to be a depoliticised platform. The music takes on apolitical meaning, involving religious and institutionalised micropolitical enactions, ultimately being neither nationalistic nor sectarian in its performance.

Birmingham migrants' conscious musical utterances are presented here as being divorced from native parallels and from the London mimetic paradigm, as they detach themselves with fragmented identity expressions and evolve as an ethnos into their new habitus of apolitics and micropolitical placebos. BbGsC (re)action to political discourse may be measured as a postmodern social outgrowing of nationalisms, ethnocentricisms and past-conflict references and dependence, where people move into contemporary cultural expressions, where macro- and micropolitics do not determine life and where people like Androniki and Zübeyde can once again live side by side. More broadly, as a utopia for some or a communally imagined reality for others, this chapter narrates and explains meta-narratively the twenty-first-century significance of cultural discourses that gain in momentum and in importance to other classic social-sciences-orientated discourses (politics, civil rights, etc.). BbGsC musical utterances prove to be a rejection of all meta-theories and an affirmation of key postmodernist tendencies.

NOTES

1. This chapter uses the term *praxis* in a Marxian way to denote the multifunctional extents and dimensions of human actions. *Migrant praxes*, therefore, means the dimensions that music inhabits within the community, not only as a listening habit, but also actively or passively (multifunctionally) as a social, political and psychological phenomenon. *Praxes*, therefore, include actions, expressions and gestures.

2. *Taksimi* here has no etymological relationship to the Arabic musical term *taqsim*, denoting a melodic musical improvisation prior to performance.

3. Tassos Isaac and Solomos Solomoû died at the hands of (mainland) Turkish TRNC officers during 'anti-Turkish invasion' protests at the UN Buffer Zone near Deryneia village.

4. The concept of blurred identity is researched and explained in greater detail in Poupazis (2013, 32–33).

5. Reading is always in the context of the reader's prior understandings, and thus mimesis-3 (the third stage of Ricoeur's *Threefold Mimesis*) refers to the world of the reader as well. For a more rigorous explanation of *Threefold Mimesis*, see Arto Laitinen's (2002) work on the self-interpretations and narrative identity of Paul Ricoeur.

6. The dearth of previous scholarship on LbGsCC cultural resources makes this chapter the first study in this field not only to counterpose musico-cultural perspectives from Greek-speaking Cypriot migrant subjects, but also to shift the public eye from London to Birmingham and to advance treatment of diasporic communities beyond historical and sociopolitical discourse as inherently plural and interactive.

7. My focus is on Birmingham and the community there, so any arguments here are drawn from and concern only them; they do not apply to any other Greek-speaking Cypriot diasporic communities, each of which has its own idiosyncratic habitus (*sensu* Bourdieu 1977, 1979). Bourdieu calculates *distinction* from the equation [(habitus) (capital)] + field = practise. With habitus, Bourdieu underpins 'generative structuralism' (1977: 22–30).

8. Foucault is talking about Catholicism here, but the point remains. Pastoral power is more reciprocal than other forms of power amongst BbGsCs.

9. Mr Costas Petrouis, Honorary Consul of the Republic of Cyprus in Birmingham, gave me this estimate on 14 November 2012. Apostle Andrew parish church's full title is the Cathedral of the Dominion of the Mother of God and St. Andrew the Apostle, and Apostle Luke's is the Orthodox Church of the Holy Trinity and St. Luke. The church of Apostle Andrew became a Cathedral by virtue of being the first Greek-Orthodox establishment in the Midlands. I use the names Apostle Andrew and Luke to describe the two parishes in the same way as migrants do.

10. For a more commodious and extensive analysis of placebo-nostalgia, see Poupazis (2014).

11. These genres are *rebetica*, folk *demotica* (from rural areas), folk *nishiotika* (from the islands) and other popular subgenres like dance music, rock and hip-hop.

12. This does not exclude the communal participation of females or younger males around these songs, however.

13. How *laika* and songs of *xenitia* act as nostalgic musical ends is explained in previous work (Poupazis 2013).

14. I utilise the testimonies of Father Kosmas Pavlidis, priest of Apostle Andrew Church, and Father Christos Stefanou, priest of Apostle Luke and St Trinity Church, men very much admired by migrant males, as being the closest voices to 'the church's'.

15. Similar observations and conclusions apply to Apostle Luke's school and to the broader community.

Chapter 12

Frame and Agency

The Public Performance of a Northwest Cameroonian Group in Ireland

Sheryl Lynch

A street parade is a messy, multi-sensorial affair. On this St. Patrick's Day in Dublin, I hear a confluence of Brazilian surdo, Latin-American reggaeton and Leo Delibes' Flower Duet from his opera Lakmé (1883). I manage to isolate the surdo, playing a syncopated samba rhythm, just as the Nowacire's parade participants march into view, placing their distinctive West African sound amidst the braid of disparate musicians. As they take their position directly in front of Parnell Square's Garden of Remembrance, I try to recognise the familiar faces of this group with whom I've been working, curious as to who may be behind the raffia and wooden engraved masks worn by the Juju dancers. Climbing on top of my friend's shoulders, I attempt to get a better view and to hear their tight North West percussion above Delibes's 'Flower Duet' blaring from a speaker belonging to the dance troupe behind them. Their North West colours emerge from the masses – vibrant orange, green, and red embroidery set against jet-black cotton fabric. There, in front of thousands of spectators on a blustery St. Patrick's Day in Ireland, are the members of the North West Association of Cameroonians in Ireland, Nowacire, for all to see and hear. (March 17, 2009)

The above reflection introduces the idea of 'diaspora space', which migrant parade participants inhabit. Avtar Brah asserts that it is a 'place between translocated and indigenous populations in a globalized world', which is marked by 'the entanglement of genealogies of dispersion with those of "staying put"' (Brah 1996, 181). Members of Nowacire, a migrant organisation and the subject of this chapter, exist and perform in this entangled intersection, using their music as a way of creating a space they wish to call home. The ethnographic vignette also evokes the *multisonance* that is the reality for many migrants in Ireland. Unlike Anderson's concept of 'unisonance', where

Figure 12.1 **Members of Nowacire gather for participation in St. Patrick's Day Parade, 17 March 2009**. Photo © Sheryl Lynch 2015.

music creates a powerful embodiment of solidarity (Anderson 1991, 145), the reality for diasporans[1] is quite different, constituted by multiple soundings across time and space.

The participation of a migrant group as represented by Nowacire in an Irish national holiday parade is significant for both performer and audience. It signals the state's efforts to include migrants into the fabric of 'Irishness' that it is willing to present to the public. The St. Patrick's Day parade is configured as a performance of ancient ritual for Irish people, a ritual that has been transformed and extended to accommodate a project of Irish patriotism and nationalism. The first St. Patrick's Parade was constructed by Irish immigrants in New York City in 1762 (Gladden Kelton 1985, 93), an American invention with specific political motivations for the Irish migrant population, created and perpetuated in a diaspora space. Nowadays, the parade is a source of pride and symbol of Irish identity for those living in Ireland and for the millions of Irish diasporans abroad. My analysis of the inclusion of this Cameroonian group in the parade highlights the steps certain Irish groups are taking towards integration, but it also sheds light on how far the state needs to go by problematising the ways that migrants are *presented* (as opposed to *represented*) publicly in Ireland.

The term 'The New Irish' refers to migrants who have settled in Ireland in the last twelve years, and it began to enter public discourse in 2007 (Redmond

2007, 17).[2] In 2014, Minister for Justice and Equality Frances Fitzgerald addressed over 4,000 'New Irish' at a citizenship ceremony in the Convention Centre in Dublin, welcoming 'the newest members of our national family of Irish citizens' (McCormack 2014). The new Irish – as distinct from the old, the established and, when the term is abused, as distinct from the 'real' Irish – are forging new identities as transitional communities. Northwest Cameroonian diasporans play a prominent role in Ireland's rapid transitional phase from a nation of predominantly white, Catholic outward migrants to one of Europe's most racially and religiously diverse countries.

After Northwest Cameroon became an Anglophone province, many Irish catholic nuns belonging to the Missionaries of the Sacred Heart arrived in Northwest Cameroon to teach catechism and English and to work in the clinics and hospitals of the area. These missionary experiences informed the biography of most of the North Westerners who now live in Ireland, as has their shared history of British oppression. Though many now live in a condition Chimamanda Ngozi Adichie calls 'choicelessness' (2013, 276), a lack of options for making a living and experiencing their adult life, I posit that Northwest Cameroonians also migrated to Ireland because, at the time (circa 2002) immigration laws were relatively open for West and Central African citizens in comparison with France, Germany, the United States and the United Kingdom. In addition, Ireland is an English-speaking country, making the transition easier for families. Finally, back in the early 2000s, the Republic of Ireland also had a reputation among North Westerners for being safer and friendlier than the United Kingdom.

This chapter, then, offers insight into a specific group of Cameroonians and how their musical performances are transformed in a mediated, migrant context. As such, this work contributes to the ongoing debate about the adoption of new, migrant-sensitive public and cultural policies in the Republic. Any examination of a public performance of music can tell a lot about what is valued by a particular migrant group and what it is they seek to maintain in their new home. As Martin Stokes observes, 'Music is in many migrant contexts a particularly important means of making a home, and imagining a future' (Stokes 2011, 31). This chapter also sheds light on the broader power dynamics of performing as a migrant in Ireland, in relation to cultural and immigration policies, integration funding and artistic autonomy. It explores the public frame and funding mechanisms, in particular, which work towards shifting a migrant music of the 'other' to an ethnic music of, and in, Ireland.

The chapter unfolds as follows. I introduce my fieldwork project with Ireland's Northwest Cameroonians, examining their efforts to construct a place for themselves in Irish society. I then unpack Irish and European policy around arts funding and migration. Returning to the St Patrick's Day event, I interrogate Nowacire's cultural and artistic agency in the parade context and conclude how that speaks to a politics of self-determination as well as integration.

PLACING

Based on five years of fieldwork with Nowacire, my research shows that musical performance is a particularly powerful medium in constructing public perceptions of, and by, a migrant group. Nowacire is an organisation that was set up in 2004 and currently has thirty-five active members, representing a community of about 120 men, women and children. It is intended for migrants from the Northwest, Anglophone region of Cameroon who are resident in Ireland but also accept members from the nearby West region who share their 'Grassfield' heritage. The people and culture of the West's Bangwa and the various clans of the Northwest region are commonly referred to as 'Grassfielders' in scholarship by historians, sociologists and anthropologists (Kaberry 1952; Argenti 1999, 2001, 2011; Chilver and Kaberry 1967). There is a rich shared culture among the many villages surrounding the urban centre of Bamenda. Traditional rituals based on an animistic religion, worshipping sylvestrian spirits, function alongside a Christian culture that established with the arrival of missionaries in 1913. Nowacire performs traditional music and dance from this region at public and private events in Ireland, and its mission statement is to 'bring together its members as a family in order to safeguard and promote the culture and tradition of the people of the North West Region of Cameroon who are resident in Ireland, in a very positive manner' (Nowacire 2015).

The establishment of organisations by immigrant groups is undoubtedly a mark of solidarity and the types of organisations tell ethnographers, policy makers and immigration authorities a lot about what is respected, needed or viewed as something that requires protection in the environment of a new home. Richard Kolm views the establishment of organisations that are exclusive to one ethnic group as a crucial event in the process of integration into a host society. It is this 'metamorphosis from an immigrant group to an ethnic group' (Kolm 1981, 6) which affords members a degree of visibility that is conducive to interaction with the dominant society. While visibility is undoubtedly powerful in itself, I would add that the *quality* of these public interactions is crucial in terms of how the group is understood. When Nowacire is presented publicly, there is always a hegemonic relationship determining the way in which the group's members can represent themselves. Performers are often presented by national/state organisations for the purpose of inclusion but despite the broader, inclusive intentions of the organisers, Nowacire is often presented in a tokenistic way that mitigates its artistic autonomy, thus denying its performances the power of representation and the potential of pedagogical interactions as a means of integration.

Ethnomusicologist Philip Bohlman suggests that 'diaspora situates music, musicians and musical culture in places distinguished by placelessness' (Bohlman 2001, 292). By highlighting issues of place and policy, I draw attention to the reality of placelessness experienced by some members of the Northwest Cameroonian diaspora in Ireland and highlight the multiple, ritualised attempts to re-imagine place through collective musical performance. Globalisation continues to complicate projects of place, and diasporic musical communities like the Northwest Cameroonian population of Ireland have become multi-sited in their practice, imagining and contestation of place. These ideas were expressed by Warren Azong, a mid-thirties' accountant from Northwest Cameroon, living in Ireland for over ten years now:

> I had to do the ironing on Sunday for the work week. I hate ironing, so I decided to put on a CD my friend had brought back to me from home. I felt like I was in Baba [a small village in the Upper Ngemba highlands, North West Cameroon]. I must have played it five times or something. It [music] brings close a faraway distance. It takes you back home. I mean that's where my heart is spiritually and everything else. On this album, they sing in my dialect, place names, the names of people I would have known since I was a kid ... All that was brought right here to my sitting room in rainy Navan. I was really feeling the home spirit.

When we talk, Warren regularly brings up the importance of place. It is something that is presented as imagined, as a memory and as a reality. He speaks of music's power to bring 'close a faraway distance'. Throughout my fieldwork, I have witnessed members of the community do this in a variety of ways: by listening to recordings from home, by watching DVDs of funerals in their hometown or by participation in life cycle rituals at events in Ireland. When a community is actively concerned with constructing its own place and its new place, a culture of contesting placelessness emerges. 'We have Another Home in View', sung at wakes to console through visions of the afterlife, is changed to the affirmation, 'We have another home indeed', to mark the context of migrancy, therefore upholding a musical tradition whilst maintaining its relevance for its performers' lived realities.

CONTESTING PLACELESSNESS

The reality of migration policy in Ireland has motivated Nowacire to adopt an agenda of civil information provision and cultural production/promotion.

It is noteworthy that the Cameroonian community from the Northwest has not set up religious organisations. Rather, members have individually joined churches of their choice, some Catholic, some Pentecostal, some long established locally. Organised, denominational religious practice has been left outside the remit of the work of Northwest societies in Ireland, allowing the focus to lie on secular issues such as employment, public profiles and representation, and moral support for a community facing the many challenges of settling in Ireland.

When studying cultural integration, one must merge research on integration *and* cultural policy. Frequent interaction between immigrants and member state citizens is a fundamental mechanism for integration. Shared forums, intercultural dialogue, education about immigrants and immigrant cultures and stimulating living conditions in urban environments enhance the interactions between immigrants and member state citizens (EU Commission 2005). Cultural dialogue, in particular, is important to Nowacire, a concept similarly valued by integration policy makers. 'Inter-cultural dialogue' is evident in number seven out of eleven EU-listed 'Common Basic Principles of Integration' (Lenihan 2008, 32). So, how do choices made by the Department of Justice and Foreign Affairs and the Department of Culture impact the bodies of Northwest Cameroonians in Ireland? How does cultural policy shape the format for public soundscapes that they engage in and help to create? A consideration of pre-recession and post-recession performances is needed, not solely in terms of the economic devastation that the crisis caused but also as a timeline for Ireland's immigration story. The Irish economic crisis (2008–2013) (Whelan 2013, 26)[3] has reduced the number of paid, public performances by Nowacire and increased the number of private performances for group members. The circumstances arising from the crisis are discussed in the following section.

THE PARTY'S OVER: OUTLINE OF PRE-RECESSION FUNDING REALITIES IN IRELAND

Between the years 1994 and 2008, Irish Arts Council funding rose by 400 per cent (Slaby 2011, 77). Ireland's cultural sector received huge grants from the European Union, resulting in the instantiation of Ireland's first Minister of Culture, Michael D. Higgins, in 1993–1997.[4] A plan of action commenced which saw the establishment of cultural centres nationwide, decentralising cultural institutions for the first time since the establishment of the state and expanding education and access programme funding. During this period, the composition of Ireland's citizenship transformed dramatically. Mark Maguire and Fiona Murphy deftly describe a shift from 'a mono-cultural emigrant nursery' to a rapidly growing diverse population (Maguire and Murphy 2012, 139). In 2002, the 'non-national' population of Ireland was 7 per cent and this grew to 10 per cent in just four years. The scale of change may be appreciated if we compare the United Kingdom's increase of 'non-nationals', which grew to less than 3 per cent over *thirty* years (Koehler et al. 2010, 13).

In 2008, Ireland's first Minister for Integration, Conor Lenihan, was appointed and he produced a report entitled *Migration Nation* (2008). The report outlined immigration law, citizenship, asylum processes and diversity management as areas weak in policy and in need of reform. Yet, it listed a methodology for integration without any data collected on Ireland's immigration situation at the time and suggested several solutions to integration problems which were not legally binding and which did not come to fruition. The subsequent minister, Mary White, introduced ministerial councils, whereby committees comprised of immigrants were given a forum to raise awareness of problems faced by immigrants in Ireland. Despite these reform plans, there is no shortage of criticism for Ireland's handling of integration, a critique most keenly expressed by The Migrant Integration Policy Index (MIPEX). MIPEX assesses governments' commitment to integration throughout Europe and has ranked Ireland lower than the United Kingdom, Italy and Spain, and on a par with racially conflicted Greece and Slovenia. Abel Ugba's work on migrant realities in Ireland places the responsibility on the state for its inadequate policies and lack of support for migrants here. He admits that Ireland historically did not participate in indentured labour drives but is just as responsible as the United Kingdom for mistreating new arrivals now. A key downfall is Ireland's immigration policies which 'dissuade the long-term presence of immigrant and minority ethnic groups' (Ugba 2009, 29). This makes parades featuring migrant performers seem tokenistic and indicative of domestic cultural tourism.

Another difficult facet of immigration life in Ireland, which directly affects North Westerners, is the Policy of Dispersal, part of the state's Direct Provision and Dispersal scheme (2000). The policy allocates the place of residence for refugees in Ireland in an effort to prevent the kind of ghettoisation that exists in the United Kingdom and France. In reality, this policy polices the bodies of men and women and prevents them from creating community, therefore limiting the opportunity to speak with or touch, let alone make music with, those that share their identity. The Direct Provision and Dispersal scheme has been referred to as 'a form of social dumping' (Fanning 2001, 11).

With regard to funding, there is now no official legislation binding the state to fund integration projects. However, there has been an effort to support diverse *workplaces* with the establishment of the Action strategy to support

Integrated Workplaces (Irish Human Rights and Equality Commission 2008). Funding for this strategy has been provided by the Office of the Minister for Integration and the Equality Authority. In terms of the everyday lives of North Westerners I work with, these policies succeed for those already on their feet; they serve the settled, economically useful migrant and do little to support the transition to obtaining that status.

Participants in my study regularly articulate a discourse of inclusion and a call for change at policy level. The level of awareness of a change in legislation and policy amongst my consultants was most evident when talking to a working mother in her twenties and a thirty-something father at the height of his finance career in Ireland. Both these individuals are highly involved in promoting and practising Northwest culture in Ireland. They engage with newcomers on a regular basis during their mentoring meetings with Nowacire. They do so because there is a clear absence of transition care for new migrants in Ireland. Northwest organisations step in and meet with young men and women who have arrived from Cameroon and end up marooned in hostels, often with basic English, waiting, waiting, waiting (Maguire and Murphy 2012, 4). Nowacire tries to circumvent the status limbo that many immigrants face by providing 'coaching' on the legal terminology that new migrants are expected to engage with when filling out registration forms in the Irish state. Nowacire spends a lot of time advising new arrivals on their education and employment options. This practical and ambitious approach characterises the monthly meetings of Nowacire. As Warren Azong states, 'We are a mentor group. We support new arrivals and get them on their feet so they can contribute to society here'. He often stresses the importance of supporting new migrants and assisting them in *contributing* (economically and socially) to Irish society.

Living in Ireland over ten years now, Warren's emphasis on contribution is certainly informed by critical 'welfare tourism' discourse prevalent in what is reported to be an increasingly racist contemporary Ireland (Immigration Council *Report on Racism* 2013; European Commission Against Racism and Intolerance, 19/02/2013: Fourth Report on Ireland). Accelerated immigration, which commenced in Ireland in the early 2000s, has called for rapid adaptation by both the Irish and the migrants who have arrived in a country used to saying *céad míle fáilte* (one hundred thousand welcomes) with the knowledge that they'll be saying *slán* (goodbye) to their visitors in the short term. Never before have those living in Ireland had to cohabit with this number of migrants making a new home on the island. During the Celtic Tiger years (2004–2007), when Ireland experienced the height of its economic boom, tensions between new migrants and the dominant society were managed. In the years from 2008 until the present (summer 2015), conflict and racism has increased as the majority of Irish people struggle financially, resulting in anger and frustration, which is often misdirected at minorities (Millward – Brown/Lansdowne 2012; NASC 2013, 4).[5]

FRAMING VOICES

In light of the present state of integration policy in Ireland presented above, public performance spaces of migrant groups have become increasingly politicised, and the ways in which performing migrants are 'framed' (i.e. with whom performers are juxtaposed, how much artistic autonomy they have, audience fees, clarity of view, clarity of sound, etc.) have become a far more sensitive issue. In framing Nowacire's performance in the St. Patrick's parade from my opening vignette, Veit Erlmann's distinction between 'representation' and 'presentation' is useful. In his study of World Music in the 1990s, Erlmann situates the world music artist (another 'other' in contradiction to one of unisonance) in a considerably powerless position; constrained by consumerism and pastiche, performance is no longer 'about representation but rather, *presentation*' (Erlmann 1996, 482). Presentation, in this instance, constitutes a 'rapid loss of referentiality' and artistic autonomy that is symptomatic of globalisation (Erlmann 1996, 482). Nowacire constantly negotiates between representation and presentation, something that is evident from the snapshots of interviews I have undertaken, which follow here. I include ethnographic interviews as much as possible in my work as a process of 'voicing'. This is a direct response to an appeal from a Cameroonian anthropologist (Nkwi 2010) and, in a separate publication, two Irish sociologists (Maguire and Murphy 2012) to put the human voice back into ethnography.[6] Mark Maguire and Fiona Murphy, authors of one of the first ethnographies on African migrants in Ireland, point out that 'all too often refugees, asylum seekers and other migrants have been presented in still images or as voiceless victims; too often their words have peppered journalism and official reports in disembodied and lifeless forms' (Maguire and Murphy 2012, 8).

BACK TO THE PARADE: MEDIATING EXPECTATIONS

When discussing the importance of participation in the parade with Warren Azong, the president of the association, he regularly comments on the significance the group places on public performance in Ireland. The masked dance of the Juju performed on St. Patrick's Day is an intricate choreographed medium that is layered with the animistic symbolism of traditional Northwest religion. This medium is extremely significant for North Westerners; it is both adored and feared, being performed with great respect and reverence. The male dancers are concealed with raffia and ornate wooden masks, transforming them into liminal figures that straddle this world and the afterlife and empowering them with the strength and knowledge of Northwest gods. Amidst the multisonance on that windy St. Patrick's Day, we hear a persistent ankle rattle rhythm, an audible contestation of placelessness. In order to sound out their place in the parade and to overcome the blending multisonance resulting from the aural enmeshment of Juju ankle rattle with operatic soprano, Nowacire increases their volume. In doing so, they claim placefulness.

Cultural knowledge pertaining to the Juju genre is passed from man to man and part of the aesthetics of the genre is the maintenance of mystery. Traditionally, joining a Juju group was a rite of passage, and only a select cohort was chosen by the Fon (chief) for initiation. Today, palatial Juju groups still exist in Cameroon, with the addition of secular, community-based troupes, which is where Warren learnt his skills. Below, he discusses the importance of performing this masked dance at the parade:

> We are proud that we have something that is valuable enough to put on a big stage. There is no bigger festival than St. Patrick's Day. The recruitment process to get a slot on O'Connell Street on St. Patrick's Day is ruthless. Not every group gets to have that platform. So, for us to be chosen ... I mean we did the parade four years in a row and they came back to us. So we have something that is really, really appreciated. That was beautiful. Again, the first year I deliberately didn't do the masquerade because I wanted to see observations, to see reactions. I mean it's amazing; the kids are looking at us and saying 'What the hell is this thing?' You know? And that is the buzz.

Warren then speaks about the relatively amateur status of Nowacire musicians and the struggle to find time and places to practice, as well as the exhaustion he experiences as the main motivator and teacher of the group:

> We would struggle to find two people who could join a real Juju band at home. This is something I have learned since primary school and I struggle because I'm trying to teach people to learn the drum. I'm teaching people the dance and I wanted to push this thing!

It is apparent that public performance, being 'in the frame', visible and audible, is at the forefront of the organisation's project. The reason behind this enthusiasm which is exhibited by the thirty-five active members from day one is twofold, constituting an internal and external target. It is external in that it is an effort to be seen, a feat of participation, a project of integration through performance. On the other hand, it is self-serving, performing an internal catharsis, an exhalation of pent-up cultural knowledge that has now been afforded a stage. Crucially, parade performances are, as Warren says, 'both' a project of performing an intimate ritual close to the hearts and spirits of North Westerners and an effort to engage in the dominant society and its cultural rituals. This external facet is just as complicated as the idea of an internal cultural performance where dancing is for each other, in the name of cultural maintenance. Reaching the external viewers and starting up a conversation is limited in a parade context as the performer is the giver, an interlocutor without a partner, dancing a soliloquy to a mute wall of spectators. That said, the visibility of the group is a powerful act of participation, a successful action in line with the organisation's mission statement, which is, to 'safeguard and promote' Northwest culture. The visibility and audibility of the community is powerful in transforming the landscape of the parade, of representing the diversity of civilian reality in Ireland today. However, the issue of representation, of who gets to represent whom and through what mediums, is inseparable from the discussion of Northwest culture in Ireland.

Muirne Bloomer, the artistic director of the 2009 St. Patrick's Day Parade, disclosed in an interview with me that the theme was based on a Persian story about a Bird King. A flock of birds embark on an epic journey in search of their king. They go through many stages such as rebellion, exhaustion and finally an epiphany that they are, in fact, their own kings and that this search for a leader was a formative test. Each performing group was assigned a theme representing the stages of this epic journey. The Cameroonian group was assigned 'knowledge'. Bloomer thought this apt due to the fact that the performers always wear masks when performing ritual genres such as Juju. The mask, according to Muirne, is an aesthetic symbol of hidden knowledge. The parade is a cultural entity unto itself, a unique creation that includes the symbols of cultural heritage such as Cameroon's Juju, without the context to explicate them. The masks represent knowledge of another kind entirely without the opportunity to impart the indispensable Juju knowledge that informs them.

Nowacire's Juju performers wear reddish brown, voluminous feathered costumes; expensive, time consuming and the product of revered work of royal tailors from 'back home'. In the Northwest, the royal feathered costume is called a *tangala*. The wearer is always a male, and he does not give his identity away even to other members of the group. The main solo singer of the group, Juliette Chi (also one of my primary collaborators), states that the masked individuals were called *Okodans*, originally from the village *Oku*. The *Okodans* traditionally dance at royal occasions. Their presence, therefore, was particularly appropriate at the 2009 parade because the Irish equivalent of a Fon or chief, President Mary McAleese, was observing the parade.

The general feedback from the parade seemed immensely positive, with interest of the public being maintained throughout the group's performance slot. The association was also recognised at an official level, winning the annual prize of the best participating group for 2009. However, in terms of representation, the parade format is not the ideal place to ingratiate dominant society with the complex musical culture of the Northwest. Musically, the event exudes 'placelessness' (Bohlman 2001, 292). Initially discussed by social geographer Edward Relph in 1976, 'insideness' (the degree of attachment and involvement a person has for a particular place) and 'outsideness' (the division between themselves and the place) (Relph 1976, 30) together constitute a fundamental dialectic in human life which is intensified in diasporic communities. Nowacire cultural practice is utilised to perform narratives on this continuum.

CONCLUSION

In the opening vignette, an aural blur of reggaeton, samba, Northwest percussion and an operatic aria were recounted. Most spectators at the parade were not aware of the ornithological concept of the parade or the Northwest role in the event as 'representing knowledge'. The group seemed happy to be involved in such a special occasion whilst being aware that they could not perform the way they would like. Warren Azong told me, 'We cannot do what we want to do. We are told what to do'. Juliette Chi said that 'the parade people mix everything up!' Any claim to authenticity in this context was discredited by the performers; the parade is a phenomenon unto itself and makes no assertions about representing a true portrait of the cultures involved in the event. But that was never the point.

Parades are inherently about spectacle; idiomatic snapshots of national ideals about culture. Returning to Veit Erlmann, it is a *presentation* of culture, rather than an opportunity to represent it. In the case of Ireland's newer multicultural facet of the St. Patrick's Day parade, the national event is an effort in integration which flirts with exoticism. However, it also stands as an example of a space where migrant issues may be negotiated and performed, leading to mutual understanding and real opportunities for a plurality of interaction with the minority groups presented.

NOTES

1. The etymology of the Greek diaspora derives from the composite verb *dia-* and *speírein*, meaning to be scattered, spread, dispersed or separated.

2. J. M. Redmond, 'The "New" Irish'. *The Irish Times*, 1 February 2007, 17. See in particular the comments section of Redmond's post. Claire McCormack article is evidence of the endurance of the term 'new Irish' in national media, 'New Irish Eyes are smiling as 4,000 become Citizens'. *The Irish Independent*, 5 July 2014. Accessed 18th April 2015, http://www.independent.ie/irish-news/news/new-irish-eyes-are-smiling-as-4000-become-citizens-30408260.html.

3. While the crisis is technically over, there remains a strict austerity policy implemented by the government that results in ongoing cuts to arts funding.

4. Higgins is president of Ireland since November 2011 and is a strong advocate for migrant rights.

5. See also the following report on racist graffiti outside the convention Centre while 4,000 new Irish received citizenship: Denise Lyons, 'Racist Graffiti Outside the Convention Centre Mars Citizenship Ceremonies for the New Irish Citizens'. *TheJournal.ie*, 4 July 2014. Accessed 22 April 2015, http://www.thejournal.ie/citizenship-ceremony-racism-1553655-Jul2014/. The graffiti says, 'Population Replacement Factory', alluding to the number of Irish who emigrated to find work since 2008 and facetiously suggesting that the new Irish are a government solution to the resulting brain drain.

6. Walter Gam Nkwi, from Kom, North West Cameroon has sought to position Kom folksong practitioners as powerful cultural repositories and transformers as he foregrounds what his North West participants have to say in his monograph, *Voicing the Voiceless* (Nkwi 2010).

Chapter 13

Politics of Public Representation

A Franco-German Museum Exhibition on Images of Immigrants

Yannik Porsché

This chapter[1] demonstrates how producers, visitors and journalists 'did politics' in a museum exhibition in Paris and Berlin. The exhibition focused on how foreigners (and immigrants in particular) were (and are) represented in the public spheres of both countries and presented recurring stereotypes and patterns of discrimination against immigrants. A selection of posters, films, acts of legislation etc. showed how immigrants throughout history, and especially in times of economic or political crises, served as scapegoats. The contemporary section of the exhibition showed how these representations continue, through, for example, the portrayal of Islam as a threat to European culture and security.

When producers and visitors negotiate public representations in museums, what is at stake is, on the one hand, how accurate the portrayals of the outside world are and on the other hand, because museums are seen as symbolically charged spaces, political representation is at stake in terms of exhibits serving as a proxy for someone, a collective or an institution (cf. Pitkin 1967, 8 f.; Spivak 1988, 275 ff.). A central question in museum work on migration is, thus, who can legitimately speak in the name of whom (Hampe 2005).

In the decision-making process of what to show, museum exhibitions often involve negotiation between several actors with different interests, including curators, museum directors, community members and politicians. In many cases, however, the finished exhibition constitutes an authoritarian portrayal that does not make visible the multiplicity of voices that were involved in the production process of the exhibition. Without acknowledging how exhibitions actively produce meaning and engage in practices of disciplining, they are frequently presented as supposedly neutral and objective mirrors of the world (cf. Bennett 1995). Moreover, museum exhibitions not only function as

179

'storages' of heritage but at times constitute spaces of contemporary political intervention.

Political discourse has been defined as a more (Schmitt 1996) or less (Arendt 2008) conflictual and public deliberation about common welfare that goes beyond the sum of private opinions as manifested in the voting of representatives. This increasingly pertains to the question of how informal actors (e.g. immigrant associations cooperating with the French museum of this case study) beyond governmental institutions frame a problem or a situation of conflict in their interactions (Hajer and Wagenaar 2003, 6, 12, 27).

From an ethnomethodological perspective on how people 'do politics' (cf. Clayman and Heritage 2002), I focus on practices of public interaction that participants – that is, museum staff, visitors and journalists – flag as politically contentious. From this perspective, I do not posit *a priori* whether the venue of the museums or the content of the exhibition is political or who counts as a political actor. Instead, I empirically analyse social everyday methods that do (or do not!) mark and order something or someone as a political issue or actor, respectively.

I also draw on post-structural work on the political[2] to analyse how antagonistic enemies and agonistic adversaries are dynamically constructed. In this view, actors like 'the public' or 'the immigrants' are not defined by their inherent and coherent interests but by relational articulations of 'difference' (what makes them distinct) and 'equivalence' (which opponents they have in common). Post-structuralist work also shows how political practices can have disruptive effects: sedimented institutional, social relations originating in political struggles, which can be reactivated when institutional rules and regularities are questioned, that is, politicised. At the same time, hegemonic strategies aim to naturalise and normalise social relations, that is, framing them as unpolitical (Laclau 2005, 117; Mouffe 1993; cf. Glynos and Howarth 2007, 144; Torfing 1999, 70).

Finally, a praxeological political ethnography underlines that political actors cannot be investigated independently from their concrete social, public, material and institutional resources and relational contexts (Hajer and Wagenaar 2003, 25 f.). Latour (2005) and Marres (2007) argue against exclusively focusing on procedural legitimation of political actors and on research that assumes that political issues objectively exist independently from the way in which they are engaged. Authors of Science and Technology Studies highlight that the issues that are debated, how these are publicly framed and the ways by which people and things are assembled through institutional, monetary ties, etc., all play an active role in creating political publics. Agoras such as museums merge knowledge construction with political opinion and issue formation, that is, politicisation. Finally, competing political positions in the public sphere – or representations of the public or immigrants – are the result of a collective work process that can be traced by ethnographically following the 'career' of their production (Scheffer 2014).

MICROSOCIOLOGICAL CONTEXTUALISATION ANALYSIS: AN ETHNOMETHODOLOGICAL, POST-STRUCTURAL AND ETHNOGRAPHIC METHODOLOGY

The microsociological contextualisation analysis used in this study draws on ethnomethodological, post-structural and ethnographic heuristics (Porsché forthcoming-a; 2015; 2014a; 2014b). Changing between these methodological registers enables us to identify different modes of how, and moments in which, participants are being political. First, ethnomethodological tools from conversation analysis (CA) 'dissect' single events of interaction to understand the complexity of ephemeral, multimodal and synchronous orchestrated practices of interaction, that is, the focus is on 'how' social practices are carried out in institutional contexts (Drew and Heritage 1992; Heritage and Clayman 2010).

Second, post-structural discourse analysis attends to similar markers of indexicality and polyphony, yet highlights the conditions of possibility of positioning practices in the broader discursive and institutional constellation. This work pays attention to power, that is, it is concerned with the question of 'when' practices are possible (Angermüller 2007). The understanding of power according to Foucault (2003a, 397; 2003b, 236–43) – as intertwined with knowledge, as a relational effect of discursive constellations and only existent in concrete micro practices – is compatible with attributions of (rights to and expectancies of) knowledge investigated in recent CA work (Heritage and Raymond 2005; Heritage 2012). In combination with a Foucauldian perspective, the interaction that is kept running by differences of knowledge appears as a political negotiation, which entails the possibility of resistance.

Third, multi-sited, analytical and 'bestranging' ethnography follows objects and plays with perspectives. The interest lies in (trans)sequential consequences of practices (Hirschauer and Amann 1997; Mohn 2002; Scheffer 2013; Scheffer 2010). The selective and focused human experiential perception is understood as a chance to include, for example, atmospheres and political commitment in the analysis. In addition to analysing recorded transcripts and publications, it appears useful to carry out observations, make ethnographic notes and collect documents.

At the heart of the contextualisation analysis is the question of how both social interactions and written text depend on and contribute to (re)producing the context. A focus on 'contextualisation cues' (Gumperz 1992; 1982, 131) ties together the three methodological strands in order to show how interactions (re)produce representations and power constellations. Looking at how exhibits are selected, how the exhibition is framed and from which positions and which representations are constructed, all shed light on who contributes to the 'politics of display'[3] and in what way.

POLITICS OF DISPLAY IN THE MUSEUM EXHIBITION

The following findings derive from a case study concerned with the production and reception of a Franco-German museum exhibition (Porsché forthcoming-b; 2014b; 2013; 2012). The exhibition was entitled '*À chacun ses étrangers? France – Allemagne 1871 à aujourd'hui / Fremde? Bilder von den Anderen in Deutschland und Frankreich seit 1871*'[4] and was first shown in Paris at the Cité Nationale de l'Histoire de l'Immigration (Cité, now called Musée de l'histoire de l'immigration) in cooperation with the Goethe Institute Paris, and six months later at the Deutsches Historisches Museum (DHM) and the Friedrichshain-Kreuzbergmuseum in Berlin.[5] Beginning with the foundation of the nation states (1871 as the *Reichsgründung* in Germany and first elections of the *Troisième République* in France), the exhibition guided visitors through a historical matrix comparing how immigrants were perceived and represented in the two respective countries. While historical phases constitute the central ordering principle in both versions of the exhibition, in the larger exhibition space in the DHM, parts of the room were more extensively dedicated to certain themes (anthropology, '*schwarze Schmach*',[6] anti-Semitism, the Algerian war, '*Gastarbeiter*',[7] and Islam). In the Cité, pieces of contemporary art accompanied the historical artefacts, most of which were shown in the DHM version.

POLITICAL MUSEUM VENUES

The institutions have very different (political) histories, something that frequently became relevant in the practices of producing and receiving the exhibition. In 1931, the French palace was part of a colonial exhibition before turning into a museum of colonial art and history and then – with much controversy – reopening as the museum and network of French immigration history in 2007 (Murphy 2007; Stevens 2008). The DHM was – also with much surrounding controversy – opened to the public as the German history museum in 1987. The main building previously served as an arsenal and then as a museum, which the Nazis used for propaganda and later became the German Democratic Republic history museum. The current permanent exhibition was opened to the public in 2006 (Heuser 1990; Maier 1992; Mälzer 2005; Ohliger 2002; Stölzl 1988).

The political relevance of the museum venue was pointed out most by visitors and museum staff in France. From the theoretical perspective chosen in the case study, the existence of a museum or its building only gains political relevance if it was made relevant, oriented to, or if it enabled or constrained further action.[8] The exhibition was one of the first projects organised by the newly founded institution, which is why journalists expected the exhibition to shed some light on the question of which political position the museum was taking. To some extent the decision to create a national museum on immigration in this colonial building was understood as a political statement. Instead of celebrating French superiority over, and exploitation of, its former colonies, the new museum's aim was to acknowledge and valorise immigrants' contributions to the French nation.

The political left initiated the concept of the museum project and its network, yet it was opened when Nicolas Sarkozy, from the political right, was president. This was understood by some – in the press, interviews or in the museum's guestbook – as an attempt to claim a traditionally left wing topic for the political right. Journalists, however, also articulated that Sarkozy did not inaugurate the Cité; it was his left-wing successor François Hollande, who did so in December 2014. Commentators, who did not view the museum's message as being in line with Sarkozy's depiction of immigration as a threat to French national identity, understood the former president's absence as a sign of his disapproval. At an occasion in which Sarkozy's minister for immigration visited the museum, protestors demonstrated against French immigration policies and a group of *sans papiers*, that is, immigrants without French documents of citizenship, also occupied rooms of the museum building to raise awareness of their situation. In the words of a member of staff of the Cité, the cultural and educational institution will always be tied up in political discussion – whether it chooses to or not:

> An institution like ours will always be obliged to justify its legitimacy in relation to the evolution of the politics of immigration. So ... it will always be considered as one of the tools of immigration politics. ... It is an institution that is in my opinion rather to be situated in the field of culture and education and [... the] task [of which is] to change the representations of immigration, of course its mission is to develop a country of immigration. But in this case we are considered [... as] the good conscience of governmental politics, which is in fact criticised for its excess ... of repression. (Interview, Cité staff)[9]

Hence, the museum both constituted a platform for political struggles and was seen as an ambiguous actor of politics. It was ambiguous because commentators disagreed about whether it spoke in the name of the government with an aim of depoliticising issues of exclusion and repression or, on the contrary, whether it spoke in the name of the government's critics.

PRESS REPORTS ON THE PRODUCTION
PROCESS OF THE EXHIBITION

The production process on the German side lends itself to a detailed analysis because of an allegation of political censorship. A text panel that introduced the present-day section of the exhibition was modified due to the disapproval of the Ministry of Culture (*Bundeskulturministerium*). The text 'While borders within Germany disappear, the European Union increasingly seals itself off from the outside. "Fortress Europe" is supposed to remain closed to refugees' was replaced with 'Since then through the Ministry for Migration and Refugees the state supports the integration of immigrants in Germany'.[10] A displeased member of the exhibition's German academic committee reported the modification to the media and the incident was then also discussed in the museum space. (See also Porsché 2015b on decisions of selections and material constraints in the production process, which were not publicly made into a political issue.)

The following media extract shows that it was important how processes and interactions in the institution were framed. In this example, a journalist recounts how a guide encouraged visitors to carefully compare the modified written label with the unaltered spoken text of the audio guide as she guided a tour through the exhibition. The same publishing house then published an article entitled 'The spoken word counts' (*Es gilt das gesprochene Wort*) in slightly different versions, in the *Tagesspiegel* (12.11.2009) and in the *Potsdamer Neueste Nachrichten* (12.11.2009). In essence, two different stories were presented. The coverage in one newspaper sounded more polemic than in the other (the differences are highlighted in the extract). Note that the focus was not on the content of the text panel, that is, the accuracy of representations of the public or the government in terms of how they deal with immigrants. Instead, debate in the press was concerned with how the panel had been modified and consequently with the issue of political censorship.[11]

DHM – Two versions of press coverage:

> The spoken word counts. Bone of contention migration: <u>Did the national cultural minister Bernd Neumann censor an exhibition in the German Historical Museum?</u>
>
> *Bone of contention migration.* The spoken word counts. <u>How the office of the national cultural minister Neumann exerts pressure on the German Historical Museum</u>

... Museum staff confirm to the Tagesspiegel that Neumann's apparatus exerted [massive] pressure, despite the fact that the official story is a different one. ... A historian who gives a tour through the exhibition, in any case encourages quietly [with a wink] to thoroughly compare the printed text to the spoken text. ... (Tagesspiegel, 12.11.2009/Potsdamer Neueste Nachrichten, 12.11.2009)[12]

In the heading of the two versions of the article, a shift of terms turns what in one version is a question of *whether* there was any censorship into a statement *that* censorship took place ('Did ... censor?' vs. 'How ... pressures'). In addition, the journalists describe the guide's conduct in different ways: according to one version, he only 'softly' suggests to compare the label with the audio guide and in the other, he did so 'with a wink'. In other words, in only one version did a supposedly ironic way of speaking find its way into the newspaper (Porsché 2012, 64). Depending on the publishing newspaper, different contextualisation cues also seem to make the news more interesting, entertaining or dramatic. In accordance with this explanation in the *Potsdamer Neueste Nachrichten*, the qualification was added that the ministry exerted 'massive' pressure on the museum staff to change the text. The political consequence of these two versions is that the version with the factual statement constitutes the attempt to close the debate in contrast to which a question encourages further speculation or discussion.

OPENING SPEECHES OF THE EXHIBITION

As if 'suggestions' from the Ministry of Culture to change a text panel a few days before the exhibition's opening were not enough, a representative of the ministry publicly criticised the exhibition on the day it opened. The following transcript is from a speech by the minister's spokesperson Ingeborg Berggreen-Merkel[13] and shows that in addition to the question of what was presented, removed or modified in the exhibition, she put herself in a position to influence processes of knowledge construction by framing what was shown.

DHM – Berggreen-Merkel's speech at the vernissage:

1. >Andererseits< was aber die Darstellung der Bundesrepublik angeht (.) so: (.) finde ich
   >However< with respect to the portrayal of the Federal Republic (.) we:ll (.) I find
2. ein wenig, dass in den Begleittexten zu den Dokumenten und Bildern (.) der Ausstellung
   a little that, in the accompanying texts to the documents and the images (.) of the exhibition

3. (.) der fremdenfeindliche Aspekt der Leistungen unseres Landes (.) bei der Integratio:n (.)
    (.) the xenophobic aspect of the achievements of our country (.) of integration:n (.)
4. ein wenig überlagert worden ist. Natürlich ist das Zusammenleben verschiedener Kulturen in
    has somewhat been dominated. Of course the living together of different cultures in
5. einem Staat (.) nicht immer einfach und sicherlich auch nicht immer konfliktfrei. Doch
    a state (.) is not always easy and surely also not always without conflict. Yet,
6. allgemein ist festzuhalten (.) Die Bundesrepublik Deutschland hat seit ihrer Gründung vor
    in general it is to be noted (.) The Federal Republic of Germany has since its foundation of
7. nunmehr sechzig Jahren (.) beachtliche Integrationsleistungen vollbracht.
    now sixty years (.) accomplished remarkable achievements of integration.
8. … Soweit meine Damen und Herren gestehen Sie mir (.) diese einigen kritischen
    … So far, ladies and gentlemen, please allow me (.) these few critical
9. Bemerkungen zum Begleittext der Ausstellung. Aber (.) das ist natürlich Sache (.) der
    comments to the text that is accompanying the exhibition. But (.) that is of course (.) up to the
10. Ausstellungs (.) macher, die hier (.) dieses verantworten.
    exhibition (.) organisers who here (.) are responsible for this.

The repeated mitigating contextualisation '(.) we:ll (.) I find a little …
has somewhat been dominated' (lines 1–2, 4) and the metapragmatic asking for permission (line 8) indicate that Berggreen-Merkel was aware of
the problematic nature of voicing criticism of the exhibition on the occasion of its opening. I argue that she was engaging in a competition with the
exhibition label about the objects' contextualisation. By directing her criticism at the accompanying text (and not the exhibits), Berggreen-Merkel
suggested that they allow for different readings, with the curators deemed
to have chosen one that does not correspond to reality. Instead, she frames
xenophobia and underlines the country's achievement of integration. She
shifts from her personal perception of the portrayal (line 1) to engaging in
an argument with a position that the curators are supposedly taking (lines
4–7). The problem of xenophobia (line 3) is, on the one hand, mitigated by
turning it into an issue of living together with occasional conflict (line 5).
Germany's achievement of integration is, on the other hand, stated as a fact
('it is to be noted', line 6). In the lines that are omitted in the extract, she
pre-emptively regrets a potential reading by the visitor that the majority of
the German population were xenophobic. This shows that even within the
monologue, she is speaking from, and commenting on, different positions.
In the last sentence of this extract, she assigns responsibility to the curators (lines 9/10). This can be read as a distancing of the ministry from the
exhibition. It also constitutes a hedging against a possible disapproval of
her questioning the curators' work and engaging in a definition of historical reality.

The issue of the text panel was subsequently also taken up in the opening
speech of the art director at the Kreuzbergmuseum's vernissage. Similar to

the DHM case, he suggested a possible misreading of the exhibition. In this speech, the art director made a politically engaged plea against 'Fortress Europe' which was well received by the audience. Arguably, the speaker and the applauding audience were publicly rearticulating a position that they imagined themselves sharing with others in collective political engagement (Zienkowski in review). In contrast to the DHM opening, this was not done with a general address to a generic national audience but rather by linking the supranational topic of Fortress Europe to the audience's presumed personal experiences, or knowledge, of the Berlin Wall. An invited DHM curator, who had prepared a formal written speech for the event and was going to follow this speaker, spontaneously changed his approach when he witnessed the casual atmosphere of the Kreuzbergmuseum's opening night. He took up the previous speaker's comment on Fortress Europe to position himself and the DHM exhibition in relation to the public debate carried out in the press about the modification of the text panel. He stated that the DHM exhibition was not meant to be critical of Europe. The aim was merely to point out the risk that mechanisms of exclusion continue on the European level.

These examples show, first, that once the production process of the exhibition was over, the positioning of political actors continued. Second, the struggle about how the exhibitions should be read continued. Here, different actors had different stages with different possibilities and constraints of contextualisation at their disposal. They could also draw on different grounds of legitimation,[14] where they competed about how to define the meaning of the exhibition and the question of how critical or political it was.

INSTITUTIONAL MUSEUM PERSPECTIVES

This section of the chapter will now compare how from the perspective of the different museums, people are *spoken about*, *spoken for* or *speak for themselves*. In other words, doing politics in the museum pertains to a combination of the questions of what is shown or written on a label; where this is done and who contributes to this decision-making process; and – last but not least – how interactions in the exhibition are carried out.

The different institutional approaches can be conceptualised with reference to a distinction by Lash and Lury (2007) between logics of 'representation' and logics of 'operationality' that are at work in culture industries. The DHM approach by and large adhered to a representative logic, that is, authentic objects, an interview or a text shown in the exhibition referred to a nation, the producers, a group of people or a phenomenon. The Kreuzbergmuseum, in contrast, serves as an example of operationality. In line with Lash and Lury

(2007) emphasising the movement and (de/re-)contextualisation of brand environments, the exhibition's artefacts and activities were moved from Paris to Berlin. The visitor was invited to 'use' the different exhibits and to connect them in a rhizomatic fashion in order to engage in new thoughts or discussion. Finally, the visitors were turned into authors by being allowed to add their own elements to the exhibition. As described in the logics of a 'global culture industry', some exhibits (such as a newspaper produced in the exhibition) were used outside of the architecturally circumscribed exhibition space.

The different cultural logics had consequences for the question of which publics were attracted by the exhibition and which publics were represented in the exhibition. Decisions of exhibition design centred on whether objects were presented with or without explanations (and whether these were additionally provided in English) as well as the scope and kind of advertising contributed to selecting the public (cf. Chaumier 2003). As a result, a higher proportion of museum visitors in the Kreuzbergmuseum were from the local neighbourhood (including immigrants who live in Kreuzberg) rather than international tourists. In contrast, the DHM is one of Berlin's major attractions for international tourists. The DHM followed a relatively traditional museum approach of representing and talking about the outside world. At least in its declared aim and in its exhibition design, the Kreuzbergmuseum is closer to the 'new museology' approach of a more democratic 'eco museum' in which people talk about their everyday lives. In comparison with the traditional DHM, the younger Cité institution can also be seen as an example of a 'new museology'. In an attempt to question museums' guises of objectivity and neutrality, the emphasis was less on authentic objects and more on discourse associated with them. In this approach, discourse was frequently tied to biographies of individual immigrants.

The institutional approach and the scope of public participation were also shaped by the interaction formats and publicity of the different cases. For example, the smaller exhibition element, which was shown on the ground floor of the Cité and later in the Kreuzbergmuseum, did not provoke much discussion in the Cité because guided tours were not organised. Moreover, in the Cité, this part of the exhibition was not given its own name or publicity. In contrast, regular guided tours in the well-advertised main exhibition shown on a different floor in the Cité and subsequently in the DHM encouraged discussions.

The different institutional perspectives become most visible when contrasting how immigrants were portrayed in the different museums. On the one hand, in the DHM, the idea was to represent immigrants at the end of the exhibition as individuals and in a positive light. Portraits by Angelika Kampfer showed people with headscarves and diverse ethnic backgrounds in Paris and Berlin who are 'well integrated' in terms of working in different kinds of jobs together with individuals who are less likely to have an immigrant background (see Figure 13.1). Headscarves were also presented on manikins in the DHM. Some visitors criticised the fact that immigrants and headscarves here were only displayed on the wall and in display cases. In fact, over the entire duration of my fieldwork in the DHM, I only saw a single visitor wearing a headscarf. In my ethnographic video recordings in the Kreuzbergmuseum exhibition, on the other hand, it was not an unusual sight

Figure 13.1 Portrait of women wearing headscarves. *Source*: Photo © Angelika Kampfer, DHM, 2009.

for visitors from a so called 'immigrant background' to be wearing headscarves. This can serve as an illustration of how (especially in the DHM) members of a majority society were talking about foreigners as *Others*. In contrast,
many staff and visitors in the Kreuzbergmuseum came from multicultural
backgrounds. A more personal connection was visible in this museum, for
instance, when a visitor told me that she knew one of the people in a photograph in the exhibition. She also talked about being born in Germany and
raised as a Christian by her German parents, before deciding to follow Islam
and to wear a headscarf.

By speaking *about* or *for* the people or immigrants, respectively, in the
DHM and Cité, the visitors were positioned at a distance to the portrayed
public (the modus of a representational democracy). In the Kreuzbergmuseum
format, in contrast, ideally people themselves participated in a public sphere
without referring to an abstract entity of the public (the modus of direct
democracy).

CONCLUSION

The findings presented in this chapter illustrate that the politics of display in these museums occurred on several levels and at several points
in time. Taking as a point of departure the practices that museum staff,
visitors and journalists marked as politically contentious and examining
the consequences of these practices by comparing institutional perspectives illustrated that first, where the museum exhibition was shown and
which political spokespeople or protestors visited the building was (especially in the French case) highly symbolic and frequently understood as a
political statement. Second, what was shown in an exhibition was political
with regard to whom or what exhibits represented and with respect to the
(reports on) selection processes that preceded their presentation. Third, how
political spokespeople and representatives of the museum framed what was
shown constituted a political activity in which they engaged in a competition about how to read the exhibitions. Finally, the chapter has shown that
who participated in which political negotiations of public representations
of immigrants depended very much on the perspective taken in and on the
institution.

NOTES

1. I would like to thank the editors and Jan Zienkowski for helpful comments on
a draft of this chapter.

2. 'Politics' and 'the political' are defined as making constitutive and subversive decisions in contingent situations, that is, making ontological statements in which several options exist, none of which is intrinsically, logically or structurally predetermined (Laclau 1990, 35; Rancière 2011). Sometimes 'politics' is used to denote competition of political parties within the state, whereas 'the political' refers to the structural ontology of politics or prior decisions that shape institutions of politics (Torfing 1999, 67).

3. Macdonald (1998, 3) calls 'politics of display' in museums the 'workings of power [... through t]he production, distribution and consumption of knowledge'.

4. Literally 'To Each Their Own Foreigners? France-Germany from 1871 until today / Foreigners? Images of the Others in Germany and France since 1871'.

5. Shown 16.12.2008–19.04.2009 in Paris and 15.10.2009–21.02.2010 in Berlin.

6. Black dishonour.

7. Guest workers.

8. See Porsché (2015b) on how the museum building is made politically relevant in guided tours conducted by museum staff.

9. The French original is: Une institution comme la nôtre va toujours être obligé de de justifier sa légitimité par rapport à l'évolution de la politique de l'immigration. Et donc ... elle va toujours va être considéré comme un des outils d'une politique d'immigration ... C'est une institution qui se situe à mon avis d'avantage dans le champ culturelle et de l'éducation et qui normalement ... son mission [... est de] changer les représentations d'immigration, bien évidemment ça va dans le sens de faire évoluer un pays d'immigration. Mais là, on est considéré comme ... la bonne conscience, d'une politique gouvernementale, qui est effectivement critiqué de son excès ... de répression.

10. The German original is: Während innerhalb Europas die Grenzen verschwinden, schottet sich die Gemeinschaft der EU zunehmend nach außen ab. Die 'Festung Europa' soll Flüchtlingen verschlossen bleiben [Das Bundesamt für Migration und Flüchtlinge fördert seitdem staatlicherseits die Integration von Zuwanderern in Deutschland].

11. For example, the *Frankfurter Allgemeine Zeitung* [13.11.2009] asked who was speaking through the label and argued that governmentally funded museums are legitimate mouthpieces of the government.

12. The German original is: Es gilt das gesprochene Wort. Zankapfel Migration: Hat Kulturstaatsminister Bernd Neumann eine Ausstellung im Deutschen Historischen Museum zensiert? [*Zankapfel Migration* Es gilt das gesprochene Wort. Wie die Behörde von Kulturstaatsminister Neumann Druck auf das Deutsche Historische Museum ausübt.] ... Gegenüber dem Tagesspiegel bestätigen Mitarbeiter des Museums, dass Neumanns Apparat [massiven] Druck ausgeübt habe, auch wenn die offizielle Darstellung anders lautet. ... Ein Historiker, der durch die Ausstellung führt, fordert jedenfalls leise [augenzwinkernd] dazu auf, den gedruckten Text gründlich mit dem gesprochenen Text zu vergleichen. ...

13. Transcription Notation – based on Gail Jefferson (2004)

underline	emphasis
(.)	micropause
>faster<	speaking faster than surrounding talk
Yea::h, I see::	extension of the preceding vowel sound

14. On the one hand, the curator could, for instance, claim to know what the intention of the exhibition was and what happened behind the closed doors of the institution. The journalist and the political spokesperson, on the other hand, were able to claim to be speaking for the general public or the ministry, respectively (Bußhoff 2000, 18).

Chapter 14

Welcoming Nations? Hospitality as a Proxy for National Identity

A Consideration of British and Scottish Contexts

Emma Hill

It is not unusual to encounter themes of hospitality in public discourse about immigration (Sayad 2004; Rosello 2001; Derrida 2000; Derrida and Dufour-mantelle 2000), nor is it unusual to encounter them in a UK context (Gibson 2007; Laachir 2007). In the recent political climate, matters of immigration have increasingly come to the fore (Phipps 2014, 180), featuring heavily in media focus upon the UK Independence Party's (UKIP) comparable success in the 2014 European parliamentary election (*BBC* 2014), as well as remaining of pivotal interest for the 2015 UK general election (Taylor 2015) and inevitably implicated in the ghost of election future for a possible 2017 EU Referendum (Phipps 2014, 180). Scotland's 2014 Referendum on independence from the rest of the United Kingdom also encouraged discussion about immigration, with the pro-independence campaign proposing policy that challenges current UK practice (cf. Scottish Government 2013b). Although immigration was not the focus of the major public debates of the independence campaign,[1] it remained (and continues to be) a thematic undercurrent of the movement, which expressed, at its core, ideas about border dynamics, belonging and identity (McDougall 2014; *BBC* 2014). UK-wide debates about immigration have similarly provoked broad conversations about British sovereignty and modern ('postcolonial') British identity and can be framed in terms of what kind of host-country the United Kingdom is perceived to be (and how it wishes to be perceived).[2] Amongst both these Scotland-focussed and broader UK discussions, and as will be demonstrated here, hospitality rhetoric is employed by both the political right and left to express arguments about immigration, so that whilst immigrants might be seen to be 'abusing the hospitality' of 'soft touch' Britain (Gibson 2007, 162), draconian Britain is seen simultaneously to be abusing its duty of hospitality towards its immigrants (Pirouet 2001, 4).

Yet, whilst in these public discussions hospitality rhetoric can be seen to address state-level issues – such as ethical and political approaches to immigration or the state-related practicalities of receiving immigration – the theme of hospitality can also be used to talk about issues much closer to home, such as access to welfare, education, housing or the labour market. Moreover, hospitality remains implicated in a more affective, everyday type of action as it is 'linked to the daily practices of ordinary citizens who offer hospitality' (Rosello 2001, 6). The hospitality metaphor, thus, provides a bridge between the practice of the state and the practice of the everyday, between the 'public' and the 'private', between scales of mass and micro moralities. In terms of immigration, the metaphor facilitates a complicated mix between the clinical decisions of the practical and the emotive decisions of the personal, so that statements such as that oft-repeated refrain of immigrants 'stealing our houses', 'stealing our jobs' (Slack and Hickley 2007; Brown 2012) or its (less-repeated) counter, 'building our economy, supporting our jobs' (Kirkup 2014a), become statements which comment more on the kinds of hospitality individuals, politicians or the state expect the United Kingdom to give. Of course, the heart of these statements rests beyond a discussion of the etiquette of hospitality and lies instead with opinions about the state, the nation and their identities; so that variously, the emasculated state is hoisted by its own petard of 'overly generous' hospitality or the 'humbled' state righteously receives the rewards of its inadequate hospitality.

In his preface to Abdelmalek Sayad's *Suffering of the Immigrant*, Bourdieu argues that a hospitality orientated approach to immigration 'regards the state as an expression of the nation, [which] justifies itself by claiming to base citizenship on … community, but also the false assimilationist "generosity" which … may conceal a chauvinism of the universal' (2007, xiv). In this chapter, I build on this statement to trace how, in the context of immigration in the United Kingdom, particular hospitality tropes, symbols and metaphors become 'system[s] of cultural signification' which are metonymic expressions of certain forms of national identities (Bhabha 2003, 1). I use a Derridean-based understanding of hospitality theory (Derrida 2000; Derrida and Dufourmantelle 2000) to analyse how these expressions of identity are set against and built at the expense of the immigrant Other. Finally, I argue that, to varying extents, hospitality is used as a proxy for expressing anxieties about national identity for the gain of political capital and at the expense of immigrants themselves.

To do this, I will look at two distinct usages of hospitality rhetoric in the context of immigration within the United Kingdom and will draw content from the 2010 to 2015 Conservative/Liberal Democrat Westminster government and the Scottish National Party (SNP) Holyrood Government in Scotland as of 2011. Specifically, I will compare the way in which two political leaders mobilise the theme by presenting a close reading of two speeches – one given by Prime Minister David Cameron in March 2013 and one given on his election in 2011 by former Scottish First Minister Alex Salmond. These two speeches mark significant political moments for their speakers and respective parties. Cameron's speech, given ostentatiously to respond to the lifting of transitional work restrictions on Bulgarians and Romanians, following these states' accession to the EU in 2007 (cf. Balch and Balabanova 2015), marks the development of an immigration-based battle between the Conservatives and UKIP for right-wing votes. Salmond's speech is his inaugural parliamentary speech as the first First Minister to lead a majority, single-party government in Holyrood. The theme of immigration, couched in terms of hospitality, allows him not only to set out an agenda for a vision of an independent Scotland but also to set out more immediate plans for Scotland's 'New Scots'. Amongst others, these two visions remain of relevance to Nicola Sturgeon's government today: post-Referendum, discussions about visions of an independent Scotland persist, whilst separately the 'New Scots' programme has reached implementation stage (Scottish Government 2013a). As such, although Salmond is no longer First Minister, his speech remains a keystone for current political developments in terms of both rhetoric and practice. John et al. (2013, 20) have noted that political speeches provide those in government an opportunity to set out a focussed, specific agenda from which policy, media and public reaction is directed. These two political speeches, thus, allow this chapter to look with momentary clarity at themes made more complex by their subsequent part in wider political, media and popular conversations. The two governments represent a relative polarity in opinion, with the Westminster government favouring a reduction in net migration and Holyrood arguing for an increase in migrants to Scotland (*Migration Watch UK* 2014; Scottish Government 2013b). Historically, the Westminster government has supported further restrictions both on entry to the United Kingdom and upon refugees and asylum seekers already resident,[3] whilst Holyrood has in the past used the extent of its devolved powers to improve conditions for immigrants (Cairney 2006, 430, 441; Piacentini 2012, 126–29; Sim and Bowes 2007, 743). The difference in these governments' respective approaches towards immigration provides a fruitful comparison of their use of the hospitality metaphor.

DERRIDA AND HOSPITALITY

Whilst the practice of hospitality has ancient roots (O'Gorman 2010), the study of hospitality theory is a relatively recent phenomenon. Still (2010, 1–2) suggests that its development is due to three major factors: increased migrant mobility and a concurrent increase in national hostility, a related trend in philosophical writing that is concerned with the effects of post-colonialism, and the rise of commercial hospitality. Derrida's writings on hospitality represent both his place in a wider postmodern trend[4] and his particular connection with the subject, which grew from a development (in the 'photographic' sense [Dufourmantelle 2000, 2]) of Emmanuel Levinas's ethics of hospitality. 'Hospitality' in Derrida's development draws on the everyday practices of domestic hospitality in order to talk about the relationship between the immigrant and the state, which was modelled as a relationship between the 'guest' (immigrant) and the 'host' (state) (Derrida 2000; Derrida and Dufourmantelle 2000).

This relationship between host and guest is modelled as a near paradox (Derrida and Dufourmantelle 2000, 25) in which the modern state is required by its own law to control and contain its hospitality[5] but to act on the principles of free and unlimited hospitality by universal absolute, which breaks with the "'pact" of hospitality ... so that I open up my home ... I *give place* to them, I let them come, I let them arrive and take place in the place I offer them, without asking of them either reciprocity ... or their names' (Derrida and Dufourmantelle 2000, 25). Derrida notes that this unconditional hospitality is an impossibility for the modern state (Laachir 2007, 178), for in its need for administrative rigour, the state argues that hospitality remains 'an obligation ... on the condition that the host, the *Wirt*, the one who receives, lodges or *gives asylum* remains the patron, the master of the household, on condition that he maintains authority *in his own home*' (Derrida 2000, 4; italics original). In other words, the state must only offer conditional hospitality[6] to the immigrant lest its sovereignty is threatened (Gibson 2007, 171).

Yet, even as these inhospitable activities of the state's technical apparatus proceed, the foundational power of the state is in its language of (in)hospitality. This language of host and guest enforces their binary relationship, so that the state and immigrant are understood as a form of Self and Other (Derrida and Dufourmantelle 2000, 25). Derrida comments that the Self/Other rendering of the host/guest relationship remains in tension because it at once frames the immigrant as a complete Other and unknowable to the Self, and as a quantifiable, nameable 'stranger' or 'foreigner' against which the administered Self (the state) can be defined (Derrida and Dufourmantelle 2000, 24–26). The state is, thus, able to both proclaim its identity against a generalised, totemic Other and confirm its identity by targeting real, specific peoples with specific policies. Meanwhile, the 'immigrant' is silenced, understood only in terms of what the state is not. 'Hospitality', Gibson argues, 'is a dead metaphor, invoked [by the state only] to "reflect on encounters with the stranger", so that the state "frequently imagines" its immigrants by "using this metaphor"' (2007, 159; Gibson quotes Rosello 2001, 2). In this way, the identity of the immigrant 'imagined' by the state both opposes and creates an 'imagined [national] identity' (Anderson 2006), identities that are each defined and redefined in accordance with the shifting needs of the sovereign state. In the following section, I analyse David Cameron's speech with regard to the mechanisms of the hospitality metaphor, before moving on to compare his use of the metaphor with that of Alex Salmond.

CAMERON, SALMOND AND THE HOSPITALITY METAPHOR

Cameron's Speech

The Conservative/Liberal Democrat coalition government, which has been in power in the United Kingdom since 2010, has (unsuccessfully) pursued a policy of reducing net migration (*MigrationWatch UK* 2014) by targeting the reduction of immigrants in a number of areas.[7] The coalition frequently argued that it has been compelled to take these measures to offset the increased number of immigrants who came to the United Kingdom under the previous New Labour government (Cameron: 'We are dealing with the mess we inherited from Labour', quoted in Brown 2013). In the difficult economic climate, it has also associated the 'stretched' resources of state welfare with its requirement for reduced immigration (Dominiczak 2013b). It frequently uses rhetoric which indicates that the hospitality of the United Kingdom is being exploited by migrant incomers which, it implies, endangers Britain's sovereignty. For the Conservative Party in particular, the links between immigration and the welfare state feed into the party's identity as a whole.

Whilst the following speech, given by Cameron at University Campus, Suffolk in July 2013, was ostentatiously intended to address the future arrival of migrants from Bulgaria and Romania at the end of the states' transitional periods, it also contained various layers of political motive, and its rhetoric and use of the hospitality metaphor anticipates the link between immigration and party identity. In it, Cameron uses the language of hospitality to evoke a particular form of British identity designed to appeal to a Conservative base. The following are excerpts from his speech:

> I believe that immigration has brought significant benefits to Britain ... from those who've come to our shores seeking a safe haven from persecution, to those who've come to make a better life for themselves and their families and, in the process, have enriched our society.

> This is our island story: open, diverse and welcoming, and I am immensely proud of it.

But while I've always believed in the benefits of migration and immigration, I've also always believed that immigration has to be properly controlled. Without proper controls, community confidence is sapped, resources are stretched. ...

Put simply, when it comes to illegal migrants, we should actually be rolling up that red carpet, and showing them the door. (Cameron 2013)

In these extracts, Cameron couches his commentary in terms of Britain's practice of hospitality. The 'island story' is one of Britain's welcome, providing a 'safe haven' that remains 'open' to those who wash up on its shores. And initially in this story, Britain gives hospitality freely to the abused, the hardworking and the family unit and reaps its rewards – the 'benefits' and 'enrichments' of immigration. But then, the story goes, this generous hospitality is abused by an unnamed guest that flouts the limits and 'control' of the state. Suddenly, Britain must protect itself from the 'sapping' and 'stretching' caused by these advantage-taking guests and must ('regrettably') limit its hospitality. Indeed, the story finishes, Britain has been so disadvantaged by 'illegal' migrants that it is compelled to a little inhospitality of its own and will take no nonsense by 'showing them the door'.

When Cameron invokes the imagined character of the immigrant, he simultaneously invokes the imagined character of Britain in opposition. He creates a multilayered narrative, creating instances of hospitality practice which signify both the character of the immigrant and the identity of the state. This narrative might be explained as follows: The 'story' begins with a statement of welcome, designed to start stirrings of British pride as it invokes laudable elements of national character, such as 'backing the underdog' or the national 'tradition' of giving inscrutable hospitality (Pirouet 2001, 1). However, even as this pride is stirred, it is scared into defensiveness: Gibson comments, 'The very openness to the Other, which Britain prides itself on, paradoxically raises anxiety over Britain's vulnerability to the Other. [... Such a welcome] places the nation and its identity at risk' (2007, 161). Having created an anxiety of the Other, Cameron's 'story' compounds the fear by creating a faceless figure which has destroyed communities and taken 'resources' (welfare). Set against the (implicitly) dishonest, ungrateful guest here, Britain appears a 'good egg' – although, the 'story' cautions, Britain has a tendency to be too emotional for its own good and leaves itself vulnerable to exploitation. Yet, even as Cameron's 'story' evokes vulnerability, it returns Britain to its former rational self by rallying that 'bulldog spirit' in the face of adversity and presenting it with controls on its hospitality (for if there's anything that's British, then it's self-control). Finally, Cameron presents his new, limited hospitality to his audience, which, as the very essence of 'firm but fair' play, is the antithesis of all those 'illegal' migrants it prevents from crossing its borders.

Cameron's 'story' uses hospitality both as a narrative frame and as a metaphor for his approach to immigration. The immigrant, constructed at once as vulnerable, hostile, exploitative and beneficial, both contrasts and creates Cameron's imagining of a particular type of British identity. This image of a tough, autonomous, yet vulnerable Britain is designed to appeal to those voters straying from the Conservative core – and particularly those tempted by UKIP. Meanwhile in theoretical terms, the figure of the immigrant remains rhetorically and structurally Othered through Cameron's myths of nationalistic identity, simultaneously empowering his administration. Though Cameron's model of the relationship between the host and guest can be readily mapped onto Derridean theory, the concurrent theme of British identity deflects attention from this philosophical opposition and ensures that the rhetoric remains discursively subtle. The combination of the hospitality theme with the theme of British identity encourages his listeners to focus on the threat of immigration to their own personal identity, so that a potentially dry immigration speech is given momentum by relateability. The combination of the 'technical' and the personal carries the speech and may, from a Conservative perspective and to a particular public, make it persuasive.

Salmond's Speech

The current Scottish Government, run by the economically central and socially left-leaning (SNP), is at political odds with Westminster over immigration. In contrast to the Westminster coalition, the SNP has been vocal in supporting an increase in immigration to Scotland as it sees it as a solution to Scotland's ageing population (Scottish Government 2013b, 425–26). However, the SNP argues that its immigration stance is based not only on pragmatism but also on reasons concerned with improving the integrity of the existing system (Scottish Government 2013b, 291). The Scottish government does not, however, have the power to develop its agenda into policy or law. The Scottish Parliament devolved from the centralised Westminster Parliament in 1999 and was given government status in 2007. As a devolved government, Holyrood has control of policy regarding Health, Housing, Education and Social Work, but immigration and citizenship policy remain (amongst other) reserved powers of the Westminster government (Cairney 2006, 431). In the meantime, Scotland remains comparatively new to the breadth of immigration experienced by other parts of the United Kingdom (Sim and Bowes 2007, 730), having experienced only isolated instances prior to the UK Dispersal scheme, which began in the early 2000s (Schuster 2000). When considering immigration in a Scottish context, attention should be paid to these additional factors, as well as to the political nuances connected to immigration: first because Scotland does not necessarily have the 'immigration tradition' of some of the other parts of the United Kingdom, second because the devolved arrangements mean that Holyrood cannot legally control who they host and third because these factors are directly relevant to the meanings and use of the hospitality metaphor.

Salmond's speech on his election as First Minister in 2011 was the first instance of a single party in Holyrood setting out its governmental agenda. Its themes continue to be of relevance and shape agenda in Nicola Sturgeon's SNP government today. It begins as follows:

> [The] voices of the past are joined in this chamber by the sound of 21st century Scotland.
>
> This land is their land, from the sparkling sands of the islands to the glittering granite of its cities. It belongs to all who choose to call it home.
>
> That includes new Scots who have escaped persecution or conflict in Africa or the Middle East.
>
> That is who belongs here but let us be clear also about what does not belong here.
>
> As the song tells us for Scotland to flourish then 'Let us be rid of those bigots and fools. Who will not let Scotland, live and let live'.
>
> Our new Scotland is built on the old custom of hospitality. (Salmond 2011)

Salmond's immigration narrative is dominated by themes of hospitality; however (and not unexpectedly), he presents a very different relationship between host and guest to that imagined by Cameron. Both speeches begin with a welcome; however, Salmond's welcome is one that implies that the guest will be welcomed on the terms of his own agency rather than by those terms imposed by the host. Scotland, he suggests, reciprocates the honour of being the guest's destination of choice by giving itself as 'home'. And, the story continues, for those who had less choice in their mobility ('those who have escaped persecution'), Scotland will equally provide a haven, as it will nurture those differences that might have forced them to flee. However, Salmond warns, a welcome will not be extended to everyone; those who might hamper this relationship, those who might curtail Scotland's hospitality, will not be given place in this Scottish welcome. For, he concludes, curtailing Scotland's hospitality would curtail a deep-rooted 'custom' of everyday hospitality, a custom that remains close to Scotland's heart.

Of course, just as Cameron's hospitality 'story' presents an imagining of British identity, Salmond's presents an imagining of Scottish identity. Salmond's reciprocal welcome imagines Scotland as a nation of humility and generosity which values people on the same terms regardless of background (cf. Mycock 2012, 55). Salmond's imagining of Scottishness places emphasis on people and on grassroots movements and states a resilience and resistance to those would deny the people's customs. Salmond does not explicitly name these deniers in his narrative, although the way in which he casts the Scottish people as simultaneously thwarted and resistive provides an indication of who this might be. The SNP has made no bones over its desire for Scotland to secede from the rest of the United Kingdom (Soule et al. 2012). In the past, it has been accused of focussing this desire in an 'ethnic nationalism', although in recent years it has supported a Scottish 'civic nationalism' (Mycock 2012, 55) and has argued for independence based on differences in values rather than ethnicity (Soule et al. 2012, 4–6). However, some commentators have identified in its identity rhetoric a tendency to associate acts of historical oppression against Scotland with the rest of the United Kingdom (rUK), and specifically the Anglo-British element of the UK government (Mycock 2012, 55–59), which, as it represents the largest population of the countries in the United Kingdom, has the capacity to be the dominant 'voice' in UK politics. As such, though the 'bigots and fools ... who will not let Scotland live and let live' in Salmond's speech readily refers to intolerance within Scotland itself, it could equally refer to and evoke the silent spectre of Anglo-British governance which has curtailed Scottish autonomy in the past and continues to do so through limited devolution.[8]

Within Salmond's hospitality story, this Anglo-British figure has particular traction as it allows a legitimised imagining of Scottish identity (Pittock 2008, 123) which supports Salmond's case for independence. The speech begins by very subtly reworking the historicised English/Scottish feud, so that the governing Anglo-British do not 'let Scotland live', whilst Scotland musters rebellion in the pastoral, archetypal Highland setting (for neither the 'sparkling sands' nor 'the glittering granite' are to be found in the Central Belt sandstone cities of Glasgow or Edinburgh) with which Scottish resistance is historically and mythically associated (Soule et al. 2012, 5–6). In the speech's hospitality frame, the figure of the Anglo-British is now cast as the Self – the host, the state – whilst Scotland is cast as the Other. This is a twist on both traditional understandings of Scottish identity, which imagine the Anglo-British as Other (Weber 2004, 1), and the established Derridean model of hospitality in which Salmond's Scotland – the nation that would so freely host its immigrants – is Othered in its own country by the invocation of the Anglo-British figure. However, Salmond's rhetoric argues that Scotland can now claim a 'horizontal comradeship' (Law 2012, 29) with its immigrants on the basis of a shared experience of external rule such as colonialism, oppression or discrimination (cf. Hussein and Miller 2006, 17). The rhetoric concludes, just as their immigrant brethren gained freedom by casting off their oppressors, the Scots too can be 'free' when they have done likewise. In Salmond's rhetoric, the old Scottish 'custom' of hospitality is something that has long been denied to Scotland. Salmond's 'new Scotland' will be apparent when Scotland again is made full Host in its home.

IMPLICATIONS OF HOSPITALITY RHETORIC

By presenting independence as the only way forward, Salmond confirms his original assertion that Scotland's old custom of hospitality will create its future. In doing so, he transforms his hospitality narrative into a multilayered, self-fulfilling discursive cycle, in which the shortcomings and oppression of Anglo-British governance legitimise 'new Scotland's' claim to this new form of hospitality. Whilst this particular creation of Scotland as a guest in its own home is undoubtedly politically motivated, Salmond's use of the language of hospitality is in itself compelling – it is both lyrical and earthy and gives the impression that he speaks of the people to the people; this combined with his employment of the hospitality metaphor gives immigration the potential to become an emotive hook in Scottish public discourse.[9]

Salmond's politicking of the hospitality metaphor does not come without precedent within the Scottish context. His protest that when it comes to

Figure 14.1 Discursive opposition between Anglo-British and Scottish imagined identities through the hospitality metaphor. *Source*: Author's Own.

immigration, Scotland is a guest in its own country, can be supported by the mixed successes of the Scottish government in opposing immigration measures imposed by Westminster – in which the majority of their victories have been on issues related to Holyrood's devolved powers (Piacentini 2012, 125–29; Scottish Affairs Committee 2011, 3–5), whilst the majority of losses relate to a failure to overturn policies related to reserved powers (for instance, the Scottish executive's failure to end dawn raids after pressure from the *Glasgow Girls* campaign[10]). Even so, the Scottish government has form in deploying the hospitality metaphor strategically. Previously, the Scottish government has combined and mobilised the imagined 'resistive and resilient' theme in tandem with the positioning as 'guest' to claim a common solidarity with those immigrants within Scotland targeted by the UK state (Ichijo 2009, 162). For the times that this resistance is successful, this combination has advantaged both migrant groups in Scotland and the Scottish government; for the unsuccessful campaigns, it may continue to empower its political creators by confirming their connection with the imagined national identity, although this does not come without its risks.[11]

Despite this politicking, immigration was treated with some responsibility by the SNP throughout its campaign for independence. Phipps (2014, 189) notes that the SNP's White Paper was a 'dry and paradoxically also exciting exercise in making distance and difference "proximate" and considering carefully how to legislate for and protect principals of hospitality as a state'. However, the 'No' vote of the Referendum ensures for now that Holyrood's rhetorical hospitable stance will not be put to the test of the practicalities of the immigration system – and the practice and rhetoric of state hospitality inevitably becomes much more complex when they become indelibly inscribed with the hierarchies and violences of border control and enforcement. One would hope that in any future for Scotland, solidarity of the 'guests' remains (although, one must then also ask, what vision for a relationship with the 'host'?).

Cameron's hospitality model does not demonstrate such solidarity. In my discussion of Cameron's hospitality rhetoric above, I argued that the figure of the immigrant acted as an oppositional sounding board from which particular myths of British identity were defined and legitimated. However, Cameron's rhetoric does not stop there; instead, it blurs the boundaries between the prerogative of his agenda-setting – what he says and persuades about the immigrant – and the responsibility of his policymaking and lawmaking – what he does to and because of the immigrant. Take, for instance, the following lines from his speech: 'I've always believed that immigration has to be properly controlled. Without proper controls, community confidence is sapped, resources are stretched'. Here, Cameron creates a silent, ambiguous immigrant figure, whose exploitative 'sapping and stretching' only serves to emphasise the generosity of the state. However, as this figure is imagined in the context of state action, this rendering of the immigrant subtly slips from the imaginary to reality. Now, the state's real-life actions (detention centres, dawn raids, welfare caps for immigrants, or 'Go Home' campaigns [*BBC* 2013]) can be brought to bear upon the immigrant and are justified by Cameron's rhetorical imagining of the figure. Moreover, such is the power of the host/guest hospitality binary, and because the state is defined in opposition to that which is related to the immigrant, even as the practical mechanisms of immigration perpetuate acts of inhospitality, the rhetoric confirms that 'Britain is a hospitable nation'. Under the umbrella of the hospitality theme, these mechanisms of inhospitality are closely related to Cameron's vision of British identity insofar as one legitimises the other and Britain can be seen as a nation of 'fair play' *because* it maintains detention centres and vice versa.

CONCLUSION

In both Cameron's and Salmond's speeches about immigration, hospitality and national or state identity are closely related. This is perhaps not surprising, for both use the binary of Self and Other to define and redefine their subjects of interest. However, as the far-reaching implications of the combination shown in this chapter demonstrate, this relationship goes beyond structural similarities; the themes are both complimentary and antagonistic. Similarly, just as Still comments of the hospitality theme, the theme of national identity also 'relates to crossing boundaries', including those between 'private and public, inside and outside, individual and collective, personal and political, emotional and rational, generous and economic' (Still 2010, 4). The combination of the two themes – and particularly the tension between the emotive and the administrative – makes for a charged and compelling rhetoric and perhaps goes some way to explain why immigration is so frequently a popular and fiercely fought topic.

It is perhaps for this reason that both Cameron and Salmond choose the theme of immigration to galvanise their respective political capital and appeal to publics concerned not only by borders but also by welfare, education and economy. Using the hospitality theme, thus, certainly has its advantages, for it allows people to talk about immigration in a way that addresses everyday concerns and facilitates a discussion that is far more accessible than conversations about the technicalities of immigration law. Yet, by mobilising hospitality as a proxy for national identity anxieties in order to gain political capital, both Cameron and Salmond move away from the two Derridean models of hospitality (conditional and unconditional hospitality). Instead, they blur the lines between opinionmaking and policymaking, so that their prerogative as heads of government – conditional hospitality or hospitality by law – is transformed into an imagined hospitality. Whilst hospitality by law cannot be said not to be self-interested, hospitality by opinion has self-interest right at its heart, for the purpose of hospitality by opinion is not to consider immigration only in terms of statutory law, but to consider immigration in terms of the power it will bring its speaker. In other words, it might be argued that when politicians view immigration through a hospitality lens, the gap between conditional and unconditional hospitality is widened by their deference to hospitality by opinion. Caught within a cycle of opinion, power and hostility, 'the immigrant', thus, faces increasingly uncertain times.

NOTES

1. It was overshadowed by issues surrounding the National Health Service, the currency union and the economy.

2. For instance, 'Poles are glad to call Britain home' (Sherwood 2014); 'Farage: parts of Britain are like a foreign land' (Sparrow 2014); 'Is Immigration good for Britain?' (Kirkup 2014b).

3. I refer here only to the Conservative/Liberal Democrat coalition, although scholars such as Gibson (2005) and Pirouet (2001) have noted that this is a trend in Labour and Conservative governments stretching back at least to the 1970s.

4. By 'postmodern', I refer, in the main, to the period after the Second World War. Though I also mean the term to loosely allude to Derrida's philosophy, his standing in the poststructural/postmodern traditions is frequently disputed, which is an argument beyond the scope of this chapter.

5. A conditional hospitality based on 'right, with law or justice as rights' (Derrida and Dufourmantelle 2000, 25).

6. A conditional hospitality that is restricted by the limitations of the law, the requirements of bureaucracy and the interests of the host and thus inherently contains acts of (bureaucratic, legal and political) inhospitality.

7. From the removal of the Post Study Work visa for international students in 2011 (*Immigration Matters* 2011), to the revamping of the UK Border Agency (now UK Visas and Immigration) in 2013 (Casciani 2013), to a number of more restrictive measures against asylum seekers (Home Office 2014), and to its objection to the arrival of nationals from new EU states, Bulgaria and Romania (Dominiczak 2013a).

8. A caveat: I do not mean to claim here, as has been popularly claimed in elements of the UK press, that the SNP or its leaders are 'anti-English'. My point here is that the (imagined) figure of Anglo-British governance provides a useful sounding board for an oppositional Scottish identity.

9. Scholarship shows mixed public predilection for this type of attitude, and immigration remains a contentious issue for the Scottish electorate (Lewis 2006).

10. The *Glasgow Girls* campaign was started in 2005 by a group of pupils (Amal Azzudin, Roza Salih, Ewelina Siwak, Jennifer McCarron, Toni-Lee Henderson and

Emma Clifford) from Drumchapel High (Glasgow) to protest the detention of a fellow pupil (Agnesa Murselaj) and her family. The campaign gained widespread public support and was successful in securing the release of the family (McLeish 2008). It continues to campaign on issues related to immigration and detention today.

11. As in the case of the fallout from the *Glasgow Girls* campaign, in which the failure of the (then) First Minister Jack McConnell to secure a protocol from Westminster to mitigate the effects of child detention by involving Scottish social services became a source of public outrage in Scotland (Cairney 2006, 441).

Chapter 15

'No nos vamos, nos echan'

Multimodal Framing of Spanish Youth Unemployment and Labour Migration in Social Media

Uta Helfrich and Ana Mancera Rueda

No nos vamos, nos echan ('We don't want to go, but they throw us out'). With this emblematic slogan, the Spanish movement Juventud Sin Futuro (JSF), 'Youth Without Future', has positioned itself in the ongoing discussion on youth unemployment and labour migration from Spain. JSF was founded in April 2011 in response to this precarious situation. Their website lists over 4,400 JSF *Chronicles of migrants*, in which young people indicate their name, age, education and final destination, and the reasons why they were forced to leave their country to make a living elsewhere. JSF is currently developing a very active campaign on social networks, spreading a large number of messages and videos, which have also impacted on traditional mass media. Thus, as a major actor in the discursive media construction of this phenomenon, JSF influences public opinion and attitudes towards (e)migration by defending and strengthening the self-image of migrants.

Our analysis focuses on discourse strategies employed by JSF and its followers on the movement's Facebook 'wall'. Drawing on the theoretical framework of Ziem (2008), Meier and Sommer (2012), and Fraas and Meier (2013), amongst others, we show how JSF reframes the concept of youth unemployment and labour migration in public media discourse.

YOUTH UNEMPLOYMENT, LABOUR MIGRATION AND THE SOCIAL MOVEMENT 'JSF'

During the last quarter of 2013, the youth unemployment rate in Spain amounted to 55.07 per cent,[1] one of the highest in Europe.[2] This has been a recurring issue of concern for every Spanish government of the last thirty-five years.[3] As far back as June 1979, the headlines of *El País*[4] read: *El paro español es un paro fundamentalmente joven* ('Young people are concerned by unemployment in Spain').

Currently, the Spanish labour market for young people is regarded as precarious and poorly paid, obliging many to leave their country in order to make a living elsewhere. According to recent data supplied by the Spanish National Institute for Statistics (INE, Instituto Nacional de Estadística de España), the number of Spanish people living abroad rose by 6.6 per cent in 2013[5] and now exceeds two million. Most of those who decide to emigrate in order to find a job are aged between twenty and thirty-four.[6] Ruiz-Gálvez (2013) argues:

> La temporalidad se ha establecido como forma contractual habitual muy por encima del promedio europeo. Más de una generación, con elevados niveles de cualificación, se está viendo afectada por el desempleo de larga duración [...] y por la incapacidad de lograr la independencia económica debido a la inestabilidad contractual y los bajos salarios. Una situación que ha profundizado la desigualdad y la pobreza (más del 32% de los jóvenes en 2012) además de obligar a casi 400.000 jóvenes a emigrar ante la falta de oportunidades (y no por el espíritu aventurero).[7]

This statement is a direct contradiction of the declaration of the Spanish Secretary of Immigration and Emigration, Marina del Corral, who in November 2012 implied that the phenomenon of youth emigration is due to the *impulso aventurero de la juventud* ('adventurous impulse of youth').[8] Slogans like the popular *No nos vamos, nos echan*, created by JSF as a 'crisis response mechanism' (de Rycker and Mohd Don 2013), also reject this interpretation. For instance, Marina Montoto, the JSF spokesperson,[9] explains one of the principal aims of this movement in these terms:

> ... romper un consenso asentado, según el cual la marcha de miles de jóvenes de este país está sólo determinada por sus decisiones y el espíritu aventurero. En cambio, lo que estamos haciendo es visibilizar en las redes y en el espacio público que esta decisión está mediada por unas condiciones sociales determinadas.[10]

JSF emerged in the spring of 2011 as a platform to unite various student associations in their protest against social cuts, imposed after the global financial crisis hit. The first political rallies took place in Madrid in October 2010, when trade unions protested against the work reforms proposed by the then socialist government under José Luis Rodríguez Zapatero. These protests also included calls for changes in higher education. On 31 March 2011, JSF made its first public appearance at a press conference and announced a big demonstration for April 7. On April 3, small groups of young people had gathered to paste JSF stickers on the windows of Banco Santander on the Universidad

Complutense campus in Madrid. The video of this symbolic action was rapidly spread on the Internet and received more than 10,000 clicks per day. Millions of messages were posted in social networks in order to call for participation in the demonstration scheduled for April 7, which proved to be a big success with 7,000 young people marching in the streets of Madrid, shouting *Sin casa, sin curro, sin pensión: ¡Sin miedo!* One of the banner headlines read: *Esto es solo el principio* ('This is only the beginning') and, indeed, it was. Since then, JSF has participated in numerous public actions,[11] for example, joining the appeal of the 15-M movement[12] through the platform of Democracia Real Ya and heading the Students' Subcommission of 15-M at Puerta del Sol. Starting in Madrid, JSF subsequently emerged in Barcelona and other Spanish cities, and in those centres worldwide where Spanish youth had emigrated to, with hundreds of young Spaniards regularly demonstrating against their forced exile due to the lack of work opportunities in Spain.

JSF AND SOCIAL MEDIA

As with other social movements, a big part of JSF's success lies in its capacity to mobilise people through social media. Thus, social media such as Facebook and Twitter become the predominant sources and brokers of information related with the protest. Information is generated by 'ordinary' citizens as well as by journalists, institutions and the media. As Devereux (2014, 299) argues,

> Citizen journalism and the use of new media and social media networks, in particular, have all been heralded within many mainstream media narratives as playing a key role in the push towards democracy. Although ... the actual degree to which new media and social media instigated these various forms of political activism has come to be hotly debated.

In this chapter, we limit ourselves to a corpus taken from Facebook in order to study some of the main multimodal discursive strategies used by JSF for drawing attention to the phenomenon of youth labour migration through this social network.

METHODS

Corpus

Displaying profiles of more than 1,200 million people, organisations, firms, etc., Facebook is currently the most popular social network worldwide, with only Google receiving more visits.[13] Data on Internet usage in Spain (Asociación para la Investigación de los Medios de Comunicación AIMC, December 2013)[14] suggests that typical Facebook users are aged between 18 and 44, female, with higher education or a university degree, have no children and logged in from home or from their work places. Since October 2009, Facebook has become the most important social network in Spain, far ahead of Twitter, Google+, LinkedIn, Instagram and Tuenti.

JSF's profile on Facebook (https://www.facebook.com/juventudsinfuturo) was established on 23 March 2011.[15] Ever since, JSF's Facebook 'wall'[16] has been storing thousands of messages and eighteen albums containing 2,443 photos and other contents. By March 2014, it had received 114,725 'likes'.[17] Our analysis focuses mainly on those messages posted by JSF itself on this platform and omits those posted on Twitter under the alias @juventudsin. Moreover, given the objectives of this study, which deals with discourse on youth labour migration, we will not consider those messages concerned with other current policies, for example, those of the conservative Rajoy government[18] against abortion, or educational reforms, etc. Our corpus consists of 500 messages posted between 24 March 2011 and 31 January 2014. We focus on the semiotic resources that occur in our data, the JSF Facebook wall, and show how they interact in framing this topic. Methodologically, we try to build a bridge between the so-called social-semiotic multimodal approach and the systemic functional approach distinguished by Jewitt (2009).[19]

ANALYSIS

Since human experience and its conceptualisation may be subject to change, frames are not necessarily stable entities, but, as social constructions, they are variable over time. This is certainly true for the concept under consideration.[20] Taking FrameNet[21] as a starting point, *labour migration* could be categorised within the frame DEPARTING, which is one[22] of the subframes of the more general 'parent' frame MOTION. The definition of the frame DEPARTING reads thus: 'A Theme moves away from a Source'.[23] The first part of the compound noun *labour migration* indicates the cause of departing. Among the lexical units which are classified within this frame, the list of verbs[24] given for Spanish – *alejarse* ('to escape'), *desertar* ('to desert'), *emigrar* ('to emigrate'), *exiliarse* ('to go into exile'), *largarse* ('to bunk/ to edge off'), *marcharse* ('to run away'), *retirarse* ('to back out'), *salir* ('to leave') – is most revealing with respect to the diversity of connotations cognitively coactivated in language processing.[25] Equally significant is the meaning potential derived from the subframe ESCAPING, which according to FrameNet seems cognitively closely related to that of DEPARTING.[26]

The concept of *labour migration* was originally part of economic terminology and is closely related to a particular sociohistorical phenomenon. It was first applied to Southern European emigrants who in the 1960s emigrated to America or other Northern European countries without any training to work as cheap, unqualified labourers.[27] This first wave of labour migration is often referred to in comments on the JSF Facebook profile:

(1)   Montse_Arenas (31-01-2014)
      50 años para atras,[28] *emigraban nuestros padres!! Ahora nos toca a nosotros.*
      ('50 years ago, our parents emigrated!! Now it's our turn')

The change in the scope of reference (*nosotros*) plays a crucial part in framing. In contrast to former migrant workers, today's young emigrants who have left in search of work mostly have a university education, which in the opinion of the general public, would almost guarantee a good job.[29] As a part of the conceptual frame, young people who try to make their living elsewhere are, therefore, confronted with implicit or explicit reproaches, like being 'deserters' for not taking up their responsibilities in their home country or being 'intruders' by virtue of taking away others' work in the new host country.

Whatever the platform, with its omnipresent slogan *No nos vamos, nos echan*[30] JSF provides a defiant legitimation against such accusations by asserting that leaving is not merely a 'lifestyle choice'. Simultaneously, the slogan contributes to framing the topic of labour migration, verbally, it focuses on the aspect of obligation, of being forced by others to do something that one under normal conditions would never do of one's own accord. The migrants' self-image – *we* – is put together as the exiled victim of circumstances that cannot be resisted (example (1) above: *nos toca a nosotros*, cf. also the frequent use of lexemes, *exilio, exiliar, exiliados*, etc.), whilst the active part in this is attributed to the unspecified 'other' (*nos echan*: verb with no specified subject; example (2) below: the uninflected infinitive form *bajar el desempleo expulsando*) bearing the blame for the economic situation. Labour migration and youth unemployment are, thus, presented as clearly interrelated, negative concepts, the first being the inevitable consequence of the second. There are repeated verbal statements to this effect on Facebook, either posted by users or by the movement itself; for example,

(2)   Juventud_SIN_Futuro (05-02-2014)
      Bajar el desempleo expulsando a los jóvenes al extranjero, a los mayores a casa y al resto a la economía sumergida. ...
      ('To reduce the unemployment rate by banishing young people to foreign countries, by sending older employees home, and the rest to the submerged economy')

Since labour migration is presently experienced as a direct consequence of youth unemployment, which, in turn, is not perceived as self-inflicted but as a negative consequence of the economic crisis, it accordingly receives a predominantly negative framing based on negative connotations such as 'insecure', 'instable', 'volatile', 'transitory', 'turbulent', 'precarious', etc.[31]

In our corpus, the construction of the concept of labour migration does not limit itself to the verbal level. Multimodal elements intervene and interact in framing, usually not only with an incremental effect, reinforcing the negative verbal message and migrants' image, but also with a complementary effect and adding new, positive facets to the concept, as will be explored later. JSF takes an active part in this (re)framing process by offering a platform for those affected directly or indirectly by labour migration, or indeed for anybody who is concerned by the issue. The label that appears on every platform run by the movement from 23 November 2013 to 2 May 2014 serves as an identity symbol for JSF. Whether it stands for itself or accompanies other messages,[32] this label presents labour migration as an involuntary journey that young people are forced to undertake: its pastiche design imitates an airline's luggage label (bar code, three-letter airport acronym, green stripes, etc.), but verbal elements like the slogan explained above, the movement's acronym and name in place of the airport and the phrase *300K JOVNS EXILIADOS* under the bar code effectively contribute to framing this journey into a negative one-way trip to nowhere (*Sin Futuro*).[33]

Similarly, the flight scheme is activated on another of its websites (see http://www.nonosvamosnosechan.net/)[34] by using well-known airport signs like *Departures*, *Arrivals*, *Baggage* and *Lift* as menu buttons and (re)conceptualising them by introducing verbal messages like *Nos echan del país*, *Exilio laboral*, *Vidas nómadas* in the sense of JSF's key concepts, in addition giving a new component to the frame, that of actively fighting against it, which is evoked by the last button *Organizarnos/Class fight*.

The same conceptual extension can be seen on Facebook, where the frame is again set by the luggage label in combination with an aerial photo of Plaza del Sol, the central square in Madrid where the 15-M protest movement was created and from which JSF originated. On JSF's website, we again find the luggage label as a recurrent element, this time together with the movement's name and, figuring as a kind of programmatic subtitle or motto, three hashtags in a row (*#sincasa#sincurro#sinmiedo*), which serve to strengthen the identity of all those affected by labour migration, since the illocutionary effect is that of an appeal: 'Although you may be without home, without work, nevertheless, be unafraid'.[35]

Similar mottos are frequently included in Facebook messages in the form of hashtags. On the technical level, hashtags are tagging tools, there to establish hypertextual links. On the social level, they serve to create an atmosphere of ambient awareness and affiliation, as described by Zappavigna (2011) with reference to Twitter. Hashtags have a unifying, strengthening potential inside the community, but may also reach users outside. Their semantic complexity gives them a real argumentative force in migrant workers' self-definition, their struggle for appreciation and calls for perseverance, as the following examples (3)–(5) show.

(3) Juventud_SIN_futuro (12-08-2013)
     Hoy, 12 agosto, es el día mundial de la juventud.
     Resumen local: paro, precariedad, exilio laboral, formación sólo para quien se la pueda pagar. Nada que celebrar gracias a las políticas del PPSOE y la Troika. L@s jóvenes seguimos #SinCasa,#SinCurroy #SinFuturo
     Pero que lo tengan muy claro: seguimos también #SinMiedo, y vamos a seguir defendiendo nuestros derechos.[36]

(4) Londres_NoNosVamosNosEchan (14-03-2013)
     #NoNosVamosNosEchan es una iniciativa que denuncia la situación de exilio forzoso de la juventud precaria. Queremos organizar una respuesta a la situación que nos obliga a la juventud a elegir entre paro, precariedad o exilio.[37]

(5) Juventud_SIN_futuro (14-03-2013)
     Como ya sabéis, estamos avanzado en la fase tres de nuestra campaña #NoNosVamos. Hemos creado grupos de facebook en las ciudades donde más solicitudes hemos recibido, y estamos trabajando para intentar agrupar a todas aquellas. ...[38]

The framing of the topic is reinforced by several types of inserted texts and (audio-) visual resources. The selection of an avatar that accompanies the name or alias of a person is equally significant in framing the topic in terms of cultural and/or world knowledge, either by taking up frames put up earlier in the discussion by others or by activating other frames. Thus, the flight or journey frame proposed by JSF, which uses the luggage label as an avatar, is taken up by Daniel_Giovanni's avatar (a photo of an escalator) or by Carolina_ Ruiz's presentation of a photo of an airport façade. Another frame frequently evoked through avatars is the revolutionary one. For example, user José_Carlos, by choosing the image of hands of a protesting crowd and the number *15* scribbled in chalk as an avatar, positions the topic of labour migration within the Spanish protest movement 15-M. Similarly, Francisco_Jose_Isla_ Calderon selects the well-known portrait of Che Guevara, while the image of a powerful comic strip hero used by the alias Otilio_Delacapa_Caida sets the fight against labour migration in a more general protest context.

Enrrique_Maroto's avatar provides another, slightly different example. In his Facebook message, which is a call to join in a siege of the Spanish Congress of Deputies, he employs several tools together to multiply the intended effect – the choice of capital letters (shouting in net typography) in order to present the appeal, the hyperlink (https://www.facebook.com/ events/143019945857320/) to the announcement of the appeal on Facebook and, finally, the poster itself, with the roaring lion of the 25A movement that announces the siege (*Asedia el Congreso*). Contradictory to this is the joyful typography[39] on the poster linking this event to the Spanish *movida*[40] and the avatar (the *Spanish* way, revolution as part of *evolution*). These two elements seem to be a playful take on the 'normal' revolution frame and evoke the very different qualities of a big, peaceful party. However, the verbal message on the poster is clear enough: *No vamos a seguir jugando con sus reglas. Nuestra paciencia se ha agotado.* (We won't play any more by their rules. Our patience is exhausted.)

Facebook messages are often accompanied by a combination of inserted texts, (audio-)visual resources and hyperlinks. This may serve to draw attention on a related forthcoming event and mobilise people for this or for other activities beyond the virtual world and, of course, to stimulate discussion about the topic and share the experience of labour migration. Instances of this can also be seen when JSF (26-02-2013) presents the calls of two co-campaigners, www.nonosvamosnosechan.net and Grupo_Apoyo_Izquierda_Plural, for real and virtual participation through hypertextual links to their platforms and interactive tools such as the like, share or comment buttons.[41] The photo there is an example of the virtual gallery of www.nonosvamosnosechan.net and shows a young male posing like a kidnap victim, but the text of his handwritten panel, *Pablo. 24 años. ¿Te exilias o 'k ase'? Me quedo luchando*[42] *#NoNosVamosNosEchan*, positions the message within the revolutionary frame and works as an appeal not to give in but to engage in the fight against labour migration.

The integration of multimodal elements tends to underlie a process of recontextualisation. In a highly political context like labour migration, the insertion of a multimodal element has more than mere documentary value. Its selection makes a definite statement of the uploader's position; for example, Piroclast_del_Monte (12-08-2013), who draws attention to a newspaper interview with the sociologist Zygmunt Bauman, an expert in the subject of the concept of *liquid work*,[43] by quoting in addition the relevant hyperlink (http:// politica.elpais.com/.../act.../1318808156_278372.html) as well as the title and subtitle of the article *El 15-M es emocional, le falta pensamiento Zygmunt Bauman advierte del peligro de que la indignación termine evaporándose* ('the 15-M movement is highly emotional, it lacks thought: Zygmunt Bauman warns of the danger that indignation ends up by fizzling out'). In order to stimulate further discussion on the subject of labour migration, JSF posts a shared hyperlink adding a diagram on income development (19-06-2013), which is, in turn, reinforced by David_López_Arias (19-06-2013), who inserts a hyperlink to a pdf document with official data on the labour market provided by the Spanish Institute for Statistics INE (http://www.ine.es/daco/daco42/salarial/prinre10.pdf) in order to authenticate his argument.

Reference to information distributed by other media constitutes a constant. Media content has the effect of an argument based on authority and reinforces assumptions made by the members of the JSF movement – see, for example, JSF's message (31-12-2013) which contains the hyperlink to a press release published by the newspaper *Público* asserting that the real unemployment rate exceeds the official data supplied by the Spanish and Portuguese governments. References to press news obey a general, recurrent pattern: normally, the photo of the digital edition of the newspaper is inserted as an eye-catcher, followed by the hyperlinked headline through which users can proceed directly to the web page of the medium in question. What is more interesting is that the piece of reproduced news is always preceded by a short summary or a phrase integrating and framing it within the group's ideology. In other words, apart from its ideational function as a reference, it also serves as an argument and thus fulfils an exceedingly interpersonal function. Symptomatically, the concluding paragraph of the preceding text in JSF's message (31-12-2013) (*'Condenarnos a esta forma de vida es la apuesta política del 1%, de la Trokia y toda la maquinaría neoliberal. Pero entre tod@s podemos hacer que el 2014 sea por el contrario el año en el que digamos basta, nos organicemos y peleemos junt@s. Somos el 99% y vamos a pelear por una vida que merezca la pena ser vivida'*[44]) seeks to incite the followers of JSF's profile on Facebook to combine in the 'fight' (*pelear*) for their rights.

The material depicted is, therefore, not necessarily just reproduced as it was found, but rearranged to fit into the frame of argumentation. This is a regular scheme followed by all users, for example, Guitarero_Rock_Andres (12-08-2013), who posts a screenshot from a YouTube video showing a demonstration put down by the police and the hyperlink to the music video (la polla-nuestraalegrejuventud http://www.youtube.com/watchßv=z6Rtn3o7xvw) in order to fortify his argumentation of history repeating itself. For example, JSF posts a shared link (31-01-2014)[45] that refers to the journey frame, consisting of multiple elements, that is, the photo of an airport check-in counter, the beginning of the corresponding Spanish article with its dual, Spanish and English headers (*Lo que cabe en una maleta*, 'What fits in a suitcase'), which was first posted on the website of Colectivo-Provisional. People who follow the hyperlink to read further discover that what is reproduced here as a photo originally came from a three-minute video produced by ColectivoProvisional.[46]

Sometimes, we also find reproductions of newspaper cartoons that fit with JSF's message – to make public the precarious situation of Spanish young people as a result of the economic crisis. This is the intention of a cartoon by Forges, a well-known Spanish caricaturist, in *El País*. On Facebook, the cartoon is preceded by a short provocative message by JSF (24-07-2013), *A los que llenan y reciben sobres les sobra la universidad y les sobran universitari@s en este país. Que se vayan ellos*, apparently without any explicit addressee. However, those readers who are up-to-date with Spanish news would easily draw the implicit reference to PP politicians.[47]

Another function of inserting multimodal elements such as news or information from other media is that of testifying to the success of a call for action broadcasted by JSF to the members of this movement. There is an example of this (JSF 19-05-2011), where the front page of The *Washington Post*, one of the most prestigious newspapers in the world, is reproduced as a means to confirm the high turnout in one of the reunions that took place in the Puerta del Sol owing to 15-M. Although the photo and headline of the original article seem somewhat contradictory, the (less prominent) newspaper headline's negative connotation, *A spring of frustration in Spain*, is outweighed by the framing title *Spanish Revolution*[48] chosen by JSF for its message and the eye-catching photo up front, with its warm and inviting atmosphere, which combine to turn it into a positive concept.

Obviously, the framing of a topic through multimodal elements within the social networks is a frequently used instrument of (implicit or explicit) propaganda. The Facebook profile of JSF includes numerous hyperlinks to interviews given by group members or prominent members of associated movements such as Marea Granate[49] (e.g. JSF 23-12-2013), with yet another allusion to the journey frame.

Whilst all the examples seen so far serve an incremental function in framing the topic, the integration of hyperlinks to other media content can, however, also have a gradual conflicting function, acting as a criticism of the inserted information. This is the case with JSF (10-10-2011), where the hyperlink refers the user to the documentary 'Documentos TV' broadcasted on Radio Televisión Española, in which young people are referred to as the *generación perdida* ('lost generation'). Doubt has already been cast on this term in the initial message, concluding with an appeal to demonstrate against this unwelcome public image and hence to become the *protagonista de [su] propia historia* ('protagonist of one's own narrative').

Here and in other examples, JSF uses multimodal elements seeking to construct a positive self-image through its Facebook profile, thus delegitimising the actions or discourse of members of the so-called *exo-group* (van Dijk 1997) who represent the contrary ideology. Here, the exogroup consists of speculators, bankers and big businessmen, the Spanish president, members of his government, representatives of the governing party and politicians (Spanish and European) in general. By rearranging faces and texts, multimodal resources style them as objects of derision, for example, in JSF (16-10-2012) where President Rajoy is presented in the fashion of a remodelled movie poster, an intertextual reference to the Coen brothers' film *No Country for Old Men*. The last word of the Spanish film title, *No es país para viejos*, is replaced by its antonym *jóvenes*, in the process accusing Rajoy of chasing young people out of the country. The third-person plural (*encarecen* 'they make more expensive', *retrasan* 'they set back', *retiran* 'they cut', *quitan* 'they take away') is an allusion to the government, which is held responsible for implementing these measures. The subtitle of this would-be film, *Se acabaron las Chuches*, is a direct quotation from a statement made by Rajoy himself to underline the necessity of his austerity politics, and, in addition, in this photomontage, Rajoy's face replaces the face of the actor Javier Bardem, who in the film is the incarnation of the bloody psychopath with a predilection for violence and philosophy. Another example of this is JSF (25-10-2013) posting a picture of the president together with the Spanish Secretary of State for Employment and Social Security, Fátima Báñez, joined in silent prayer that God may help to distract the public from realising that their unemployment policy has proved a complete failure.

By delegitimising the exogroup in this (ironic) way, JSF strengthens the image of the exiled, its own image and that of its followers. The network provides other interactive tools such as the like-button or comments which add to this effect and contribute to framing the topic; the message referred to above (25-10-2013) for instance, was shared 2,581 times and 'liked' 1,004 times. In addition to the opportunity for expressing publicly one's preference for a certain message, photo, video, initiative or comment posted by others, the like-button allows the user to receive the most recent posts of this profile on the wall. For example, the photo in JSF (25-10-2013) received more than 20 comments and even led to a discussion between users. Whilst some commentators verbally vent their anger on politicians and their followers of whatever political party,[50] others combine their verbal comments with a lamentation on the dilemma of labour migration facing the young.[51] There are other users still, who like JSF itself argue through multimodal framing; for example, Juan_Jiménez_Martínez (26-11-2013), who posts a hyperlink to a YouTube video showing the homecoming of a young woman migrant as proof of how a 'bad trip' may come to a good end.

CONCLUSION

In this chapter, we have analysed multimodal framing of the public image of Spanish youth labour migration in social media. Our analysis was based on a corpus of messages posted on the Facebook wall of the movement called JSF. Following the theoretical framework of Ziem (2008), Meier and Sommer (2012) and Fraas and Meier (2013), amongst others, we have shown how JSF uses additional means in the framing of the topic of youth unemployment and labour migration in public media discourse. JSF plays an active part in the discursive media construction of this phenomenon; by using the social networks, JSF not only defends and strengthens migrants' self-image, but also influences public opinions and attitudes towards emigration.

The JSF concept of labour migration in this corpus is predominantly shaped by two evoked subframes, the (involuntary) journey frame and the revolution frame. Our analysis confirms that so-called 'visual framing' (Fraas and Meier 2013) is the most potent means of multimodal framing. The intersemiosis between verbal and, particularly, non-verbal multimodal elements referring to these frames develops an argumentative value of its own: contrary to the conceptual frame identified by FrameNet, DEPARTING for work reasons here no longer equals ESCAPING, but by integrating the idea of STANDING UP and TAKING PEACEFUL ACTION TOGETHER against something that is felt to be unjust acquires a more positive, active connotation. When referring to the endogroup, the argumentative effect of multimodal framing is additive and incremental (reinforcing the verbal message and migrants' image) or complementary (adding new, positive facets to the concept of labour migration), whereas a conflicting or contradictory effect is achieved by making reference to the exogroup (delegitimising the exogroup's actions and image as negative). Multimodal framing, thus, plays an important role in the movement's mobilisation activities.

Social movements such as JSF have a strong interest in this kind of 'strategic' framing (Johnston and Noakes 2005) since (competing) frames are used everywhere in political and social issues, and who wins these debates depends on which frame dominates (Lakoff 2004). Recently, much of this discursive framing has taken place in a social media context, where multimodal elements constitute an important device, one that is frequently employed by users in framing. Their function is by no means merely informative or documentary. The multimodal setting up and connecting of frames virtually 'opens' new discursive 'rooms', which develops their own coherence and argumentative force in remodelling existing concepts. Since multimodal elements operate on the implicit, unconscious level, they often pass unnoticed and the more they do so, the more powerful they are in framing and reframing a topic in public discourse.

NOTES

1. According to the latest EPA survey on the workforce, 'Encuesta de Población Activa Cuarto Trimestre de 2013', http://www.ine.es/daco/daco42/daco4211/epa0413.pdf. Rev.: 21-02-2014.

2. With the average European rate being less than half of this figure at 22.5 per cent.

3. Solutions that have been put forward by the first reform of the *Estatuto de los Trabajadores* (1984) or the so-called *Estrategia para el Emprendimiento y el Empleo Juvenil* (2013) consist of temporary work, 'flexible' contracts for young people, etc. Cf. also 'Cada vez más precarios contra el paro', *El País*, 24-02-2013. http://economia.elpais.com/economia/2013/02/23/actualidad/1361649213_622949.html. Rev.: 21-02-2014.

4. This newspaper belongs to the PRISA group, a Spanish media and communication company with a centre-left ideology and a worldwide activity in 22 European and American countries. In Spain, PRISA is the leader in media (press, radio broadcasting and television) and in the book market. According to recent data on media usage and diffusion provided by the Spanish Association for Media Research (May 2014), *El País* is the paper with the highest daily circulation in Spain, with 1,685,000 readers per day.

5. Cf. INE, 'Estadística del Padrón de Españoles Residentes en el Extranjero. Datos a 1-1-2014', http://www.ine.es/jaxi/menu.do?type=pcaxis&path=/t20/p85001/a2014/&file=pcaxis. Rev.: 21-03-2014.

6. The number of young emigrants listed was 366,313, the real number presumably being higher. It is estimated that thousands of young people are leaving Spain every week.

7. 'More than anywhere in Europe, temporary contracts have become the norm in Spain. More than one generation, with high qualification, is being affected by long term unemployment ... and by the impossibility to reach economic independence due to contractual instability and low wages. This situation has deepened inequality and poverty (more than 32 per cent of young people in 2012), and is forcing almost 400,000 young people to emigrate because of the absence of opportunities (and not because of their adventurous spirit)'. Cf. blog posting '¿Qué les queda a los jóvenes?' *Público*, 20-02-3013). http://blogs.publico.es/econonuestra/2013/02/20/que-les-queda-a-los-jovenes/. Rev.: 21-02-2014.

8. Cf. Newspaper article 'Juventud Sin Futuro: "El exilio de los jóvenes es un problema político"', *Público*, 03-04-2013. http://www.publico.es/actualidad/453096/juventud-sin-futuro-el-exilio-de-los-jovenes-es-un-problema-politico. Rev.: 21-02-2013.

9. According to its members, this movement has no 'leaders'. All decisions are made unanimously in committees with clearly defined aims.

10. 'To break with the general consensus according to which the escape of thousands of young people from this country is caused only by their own free will and adventurous spirit. Quite the contrary is true. Therefore, we are visualising through social media and in the public space that their decision to leave is caused by this very

special social situation'. https://www.youtube.com/watch?v=cLrOZ71f664&feature= youtu.be. Rev.: 21-3-2014. In a symbolic act, Marina Montoto appeared in this press conference with an empty chair as a symbol for all the young people who left their country in order to find a job elsewhere.

11. For instance, in events like the inauguration of the Foro Social in Madrid on 6 May 2010, the 'encierro de trabajo' as an action against the implementation of the project *Estrategia Universidad 2015* in the Philosophical Faculty of Universidad Complutense de Madrid during the week of 9–13 May 2010, or the performance in front of a branch of the bank on 11 May 2010 where a group of young people symbolically liberated democracy from the market. Cf. *Juventud Sin Futuro* (2011), a programme written by the movement's leading members; an account of all these actions can be found in the section 'Cronología de Juventud Sin Futuro'.

12. The name of the so-called '15-M movement' refers to the demonstration which took place in Madrid on 15 May 2011, where more than 40 persons pitched their tents in the central place of Puerta del Sol, in order to protest against the two-party system and for a more participative democracy. In particular, protest was directed against banks and the policies of the two leading Spanish political parties, that is, the labour party Partido Socialista Obrero Español and the right-wing party Partido Popular. From there, the movement expanded to other Spanish towns and to other countries.

13. According to Facebook's own data, cf. http://www.Facebook.com/advertising/? campaign_id=402047449186&placement=pf&extra_1=0. Rev.: 20-02-2014.

14. Cf. http://download.aimc.es/aimc/J5d8yq/macro2013ppt.pdf. Rev.: 27-02-2014.

15. Albeit, the 'official date of birth' indicated on Facebook is 7 April 2011.

16. The so-called 'wall' is the central element through which Facebook users may get in touch: 'A Facebook wall is the area on a profile or page where friends and "fans" can post their thoughts, views, or criticisms for everyone to see. Walls have three viewing settings: user + others, just the user, and just others. These settings can be changed by clicking the "filters" option at the top of the wall. Most walls automatically display the "user + others" option, showing posts, links, tagged material, and other information posted by both the page's operator and their friends or fans. Walls also incorporate the news feed, displaying updates made by the user such as statuses, links, pictures, and other recent activity'. Cf. http://whatis.techtarget.com/definition/ Facebook-wall. Rev.: 06-03-2014.

17. See JSF profile on Facebook. https://es-es.facebook.com/juventudsinfuturo. Rev.: 09-03-2014.

18. Has been in power since 21 December 2011.

19. Cognitive theory holds that frames are mental structures which conceptualise human experience and organise our thought. In a media setting, the production and reception of cognitive structures and schemata are activated and (re)contextualised depending on processes of social (inter)action. This more or less conscious process of activation and (re)contextualisation is called framing.

Depending on the medium, the multiple modes involved in framing on different levels may vary and may comprise colour, gesture, movement, gaze, voice and music. The repertoire of 'meaning-making resources' (Jewitt 2014) relevant for framing in computer-mediated communication (CMC) is even more complex.

As Bucher (2007, 2010, 2013), Meier and Sommer (2012), Fraas and Meier (2013), Stöckl (2014) and others point out, the range of multimodal elements that take part in the construction of meaning and that may add to framing a topic in CMC includes inserted textual and (audio-)visual resources (e.g. avatars, inserted pictures, photos, cartoons, maps, diagrams, audios or videos), hypertextual devices like hyperlinks or hashtags and interactive devices such as the like/dislike button and comments. The choice and combination of multimodal elements by a particular (discourse) actor in a particular CMC discourse constitutes a multimodal 'supertext'. Stöckl (2012) distinguishes between a number of coherence effects produced by the intermodal interaction of these elements: additive, reinforcing, complementary, hierarchical, divergent or (semantically) conflicting.

All of the above has to be taken into account in the following multimodal analysis of the discursive construction of youth labour migration in Spanish social media discourse.

20. Cf., for instance, zur Nieden (2013), who analyses the cyclical dynamics of the concept of the right of migration with reference to Spain and Argentina.

21. Cf. http://gemini.uab.es/PublicFrameReport/frames/displayReport.php?frame=Departing. Rev.: 21-02-2014.

22. Twenty 'child' frames in total (e.g. REMOVING, CHANGE_DIRECTION, SELF_MOTION, FLUIDIC_MOTION, etc.).

23. In the case we are dealing with here, the *theme* is the persons and the *source* is Spain. Note that 'the Source may be expressed or it may be understood from context, but its existence is always implied by the motion predicate itself'. Cf. http://gemini.uab.es/PublicFrameReport/frames/displayReport.php?frame=Departing. Rev.: 21-02-2014.

24. 'All the verbs in this frame express some change of location, away from one place and to another'. Cf. http://gemini.uab.es/PublicFrameReport/frames/displayReport.php?frame=Departing. Rev.: 21-02-2014.

25. Cf. below.

26. FrameGrapher visualises the relations between frames as a graph with 'parent' frames pointing to 'child' frames. Cf. http://gemini.uab.es/FrameGrapher/grapher.php. Rev.: 21-02-2014.

27. Cf. Wengeler's study (2003) of the topoi of the German discourse on migration, which covers the same, first wave of labour migration from 1960 to 1985.

28. All quotations from the corpus are reproduced in their original orthography and grammar.

29. Interestingly enough, the example given in Spanish FrameNet for the non-core value of 'Duration of the departing event' uses the verb *emigrar* and refers to the phenomenon of youth migration: *Durante los últimos treinta años, HAN EMIGRADO muchos jóvenes de nuestro país.* Cf. http://gemini.uab.es/PublicFrameReport/frames/displayReport.php?frame=Departing. Rev.: 21-02-2014.

30. The slogan is also used as a multimodal element (e.g. hashtag; see below).

31. In a similar way, the sociologist Zygmunt Bauman in his book *Liquid Modernity* (2002) used this concept to describe the negative effects of globalisation on identity construction. Bauman also comments on the closely associated concept of *liquid*

work, another technical term that used to have a positive connotation until recently, when in connection with the global economic crisis, this term made its appearance in public discourse. Indeed, the change of register from specialists' to common language involved a considerable shift in the conceptual framing of labour migration.

32. That is, it is also used as an avatar by JSF in their tweets or facebook messages (see below).

33. Furthermore, *sin* in the movement's name as well as in its alias on Facebook is written in capital letters to attract attention.

34. This platform serves as a photo gallery and archive of photos, chronicles, etc. related to the topic of labour migration.

35. This argument is consistently renewed by JSF, for example, explicitly on Facebook.

36. 'Today August, 12th, is world youth day. Local balance: unemployment, precarity, labour migration, formation only for those who can pay. Nothing to celebrate thanks to the politics of the PPSOE and the Troika. We young people continue #WithoutHome #WithoutWork and #WithoutFuture. But you can take for granted that we also continue #WithoutFear, and we are going to keep on defending our rights'.

37. '#NoNosVamosNosEchan is an initiative that denounces the situation of forced exile of the precarious youth. We want to organise our response to this situation which forces us young people to choose between unemployment, precarity, or exile'.

38. 'As you all know, we are advancing in phase three of our campaign #NoNosVamos. We have created facebook groups in those cities where we have received the most requests, and we are working on bringing them all together'.

39. As commented before, typography is one of semiotic sources that add to meaning, cf. Payrató (2012): 'La tipografía nos abre para empezar múltiples posibilidades, y solo hay que pensar en los distintos tipos de letra que nos ofrece cualquier procesador de textos actual'.

40. This term designates the atmosphere of change that 'moved' the country in the 1980s after decades of Franco's dictatorship.

41. The number of times the invitation is followed is counted and presented numerically (1,358 likes and 1,470 shares by 13-02-2014), and thus becomes another means of positive framing, which might incite others to participate, too (cf. below).

42. 'Pablo. Aged 24. Are you emigrating or what are you going to do? I'm staying to fight'.

43. Cf. footnote 28.

44. 'To condemn us to this kind of life is the political bet of only 1 per cent, of the Trokia and of this whole neoliberal apparatus. But nevertheless, we all can work together in 2014 and say "basta", organize ourselves, and fight. We are 99 per cent and we are going to fight for a life that is worth living'.

45. 'Me da rabia no tener elección y saber que te tienes que ir, y que lo más probable es que no puedas volver'.

'La gente siempre te dice: Qué buena oportunidad! Qué bien! Tu pones buena cara pero ... que te echen, y no tener más remedio, no tener elección ... es bastante duro'. #NoNosVamosNosEchan ('It makes me angry not to have a choice but to know that you have to leave, and that the most probable thing is that you won't be able to return' (...) 'People always keep saying to you: What a good opportunity! Great! And you grin and bear it, but ... that it is quite hard to accept that throw you out, and that you have no remedy, no choice'. #NoNosVamosNosEchan)

46. Cf. http://vimeo.com/85259432. Rev.: 21-02-2014.

47. The reference is to the ex-treasurer of the Partido Popular, Luis Bárcenas, who revealed that he had been distributing envelopes containing money to party leaders.

48. The term used by JSF is how the movement is known at the international level.

49. The alias *MareaGranate* ('ruby flood') is a pun on the exodus of people with a ruby-coloured Spanish passport.

50. Cf. the comment by Alhambra_Ría:

Alhambra_Ría (25-10-2013)
Pero quien ha votado a esta gente!!! (But who voted for them!!!)

which, in turn, received answers like the following, displaying bold *face-threatening acts* (Brown and Levinson 1978) against politicians and followers of any political party:

Ana_Isabel_Sobrado Pérez (25-10-2013)
Algunos desalmados sin conciencia los han votado. (The cruel and unscrupulous voted for them.)

Juanjo_Casafranca (25-10-2013)
y mucha gente engañada porque estuvieron cuatro años haciendo ver que ellos tenían el dinero guardado para cuando ganaran y asi joder al zp y a los sociatas ... mintieron.
(and many of those who feel cheated because for four years they pretended that they were saving the money for after the election, and therefore fuck you, Zapatero and your damn socialists. They were lying.)

Ignacio_Martinez_Zabala (25-10-2013)
putos ladrones, a la cárcel debieran ir ('Fucking thieves, they should be sent to prison')

Fanny_González (25-10-2013)
Pero a ver ahora quien vota por estos panda de chorizos. ... ('But who then votes for such a gang of thieves and fraudsters')

51. Cf. Miguel AngelCampons Rentero (25-10-2013)
hijos de putaaaa, y que los jovenes tengamos k seguir emigrando ('Fuck, and we Young people have to keep on emigrating').

Chapter 16

Conclusion

Opportunities for Resistance Through Discourse

Amanda Haynes, Eoin Devereux, James Carr,
Martin J. Power and Aileen Dillane

THE DISCURSIVELY CONSTRUCTED MIGRANT OTHER

The majority of the chapters in this volume rehearse a depressing tale of how state, media and other discourses serve to racialise, criminalise and stigmatise migrants. While the cases examined refer to specific local contexts, the discourses and practices which are unveiled share significant similarities across time and space. Chapters by Bruno on the Italian Landings; by Carr on the experiences of Muslims in Ireland and by Reed on 'honour killings', for example, convincingly evidence how dominant discourses function to 'other' migrants. The mainstream media routinely circulate content which presents the migrant and migration in a predominantly negative light (see chapters by Marron et al. on the Roma Children Case in Ireland and Lähdesmäki and Saresma on 'Islam Night' in Finland). In a populist media setting, the framing of stories about migrants within a criminality, security or contaminant frame seems to have been exacerbated in recent years – a development that we feel has been aided and abetted by the shrinkage in media ownership and the renewed focus on the marketisation of (populist) news. Similarly, within mainstream political discourse, we encounter a range of discursive positions which problematise migrants or, at best, offer too narrow a range of explanations (see chapters by Burroughs, Hill, Power et al.) concerning migration. Aside from the predictable anti-immigrant sentiments expressed by political parties on the far right such as the Finns Party or UKIP, many of the chapters in this collection point to the failure of those in the political centre to adequately explain the complexities and positive benefits of migration. Often, of course, what *isn't* said is just as important as what *is* said, as Marron et al.'s chapter reminds us all too starkly.

action/inaction

DISCOURSE AS POLITICALLY GENERATIVE

Marron et al. exemplify that discourses concerning migration matter, in that they can influence not only public attitudes and beliefs, but also the actions (or inactions) of powerful agents of the state in responding to migration and migrants. In regard to physically and socially distant outgroups (Baston and Ahmed 2009), it is not their (or indeed our) shared reality that shape policy responses, but how the dimensions and understandings of that reality are communicated and explained to the public and their political representatives. Discourses are generative – they act 'upon the world and its inhabitants'; as a practice that 'defines problems to be addressed; [and] ... delimits the parameters within which that constructed problem can be acted upon'. For Fekete (2015a), dominant media and political discourses create and cultivate a fear of and hostility towards people seeking safety and security in Europe; presenting 'migrants ... as toxic waste, a dangerous mob, human flotsam, an unstoppable flood and a terrorist threat' (Fekete 2015a). These discourses fuel racism among the general public while distracting from the structural reasons as to why people have made the effort to seek a new life in the West (Fekete 2015a). What then are the prospects for disrupting these discourses and popularising a new way of thinking about migration?

PROSPECTS FOR RESISTANCE

At the time of writing in September 2015, the plight of Syrian refugees dominates the media. Images of men, women and children throwing themselves in desperation at the borders of Fortress Europe enter our homes nightly. Meanwhile, political and public discourses persist which describe migrants as a threat to our lifestyle and as criminal (Fekete 2015a; Waller 2014); Hungarian Prime Minister Viktor Orbán has spoken of an alleged incompatibility of Muslim people fleeing Syria with European values; while some journalists present migrants as 'cockroaches' (Fekete 2015a; see also Bruno in this volume).

Yet, volunteers stand waiting in Germany, Turkey and France to welcome refugees fleeing the Syrian conflict. Football supporters in Germany hold aloft banners proclaiming their support for those seeking refuge, with the text 'Refugees Welcome' accompanied in some cases by an image of a man, woman and child visibly fleeing. Inspired by their fellow supporters on the continent, various fan groups across Europe unfurled banners with the same 'refugees welcome' message,[1] with social media playing no small part in distributing these images (Gibson 2015; Kelly 2015). In London and Dublin, the public rally to lobby for their respective states to welcome additional families. School children are gathering donations of tents and clothing for those trying to make their way to safety. Across Europe, politicians are announcing plans to accommodate thousands of newcomers – multiples of international minimum requirements. In this present moment, discourses that prioritise individual safety over state security and border control have gained sufficient ground in the West to alter the political response to Syrian refugees in an unprecedented fashion.

Positive public and political responses to the migration of Syrian refugees have been made possible by a temporary victory in shaping public and political discourse surrounding the particular category of migrant. As the ultimate outgroup, everything is stacked against the migrant eliciting empathy (Batson and Ahmed 2009), but for a while at least, anti-immigration scaremongering has been drowned out by public acceptance of the validity of a humanitarian response to people fleeing Syria. Contrast Germany's Willkommenskultur-backed pledge to resettle 35,000 Syrian refugees (UNHCR 2015) with the nationalist-fuelled policies of criminalisation, securitisation and outright aggression pursued by Hungary and the generative power of discourse becomes overwhelmingly apparent.

For much of the West, this shift in our frameworks of understanding was not without its price; it was paid for in blood – the public spectacle of the deaths of hundreds if not thousands of migrants, culminating in the global dissemination of the image of a single toddler drowned on the edges of perceived sanctuary. Even so, interactions between empathy and race in events like Hurricane Katrina (Sommers et al. 2006) cause us to question whether even these images would have been as effective had Syrian refugees not looked so much like 'us', had Aylan not so closely resembled one of Europe's privileged children. Moreover, it is questionable whether a discourse of empathy would have achieved such volume had the perception of a shared threat in ISIS not primed political actors to align with refugees' interests. Arguably, the discursive battle to construct Syrian refugees as legitimate and deserving is currently swinging in their favour, because the politics of the conflict in which they are enmeshed has served to momentarily (and arguably grudgingly) align centre-right and left, *in spite* of any shift in the discourse regarding migration generally.

The confluence of events which was required to produce this response, we argue, means that this popularisation of a humanitarian approach to refugees is limited and passing.[2] What we may carry forward from this experience, however, is the understanding that the numbers of those who can be swayed are large enough to change policy. That is an important realisation. Migration is an inherently political act and issue, being about seeking, granting and denying access to resources, opportunity and privilege. Our understandings of migration are, hence, heavily influenced by our own politics – our own approaches to ownership and redistribution. The fundamental value systems and beliefs on which they rest are not so easy to shape and influence.

However, what the Syrian conflict demonstrates is that between the poles of active left- and right-wing actors, there is a very significant (possibly apathetic or inactive) middle mass – and they can be swayed and mobilised. Here we argue is the site and the reason for resistance.

How then to interrupt the dominant discourse regarding migration? By what means can subjugated knowledge (Foucault 1980a) of migrant experiences and alternative futures (Ohlin Wright 2010) be disseminated and revealed to the movable middle?

MIGRANT AGENCY

Some of the chapters in this volume demonstrate how migrants can engage in resisting hegemonic discourses. These range from low-level 'Produser' (Ritzer et al. 2012) cultural production – the creation and dissemination of stickers which counter the hegemonic and taken-for-granted assumptions concerning migrants, for example, to more organised street protests, such as the 2006 'Day Without An Immigrant', as documented by De Genova.

Identity work by migrants is further evidence of agency. Several of the chapters in this book examine how positive and hybrid identities may be forged by migrants. Hanafin shows how this hybridisation works amongst the second-generation Irish in Britain who return 'home' to Ireland. Three of this book's chapters put cultural practices in the form of music, dance and parades to the fore. All represent significant contexts in which identities and relationships can be built and sustained. Morad shows how Salsa helps to consolidate group identity amongst Latino migrants and creates the possibility of more positive relationships with the host society in Israel. Poupazis examines the complex relationship between music, religion and politics in terms of how Cyprus is remembered by Greek-speaking Cypriots in Birmingham. Lynch's account of the 'diaspora space' occupied by migrant Cameroonians in Ireland during a St. Patrick's Day Parade in Dublin serves to remind us of the participatory possibilities afforded to migrants through cultural activities and practices. Cultural events such as parades are opportunities to bring about integration and break down cultural barriers. Care, however, has to be taken to ensure that such activities do not serve to further exoticise or stereotype migrants.

ONLINE ACTIVISM

For both migrant and host country activists, the role of the Internet as a platform for resistance has developed since the 1990s (Kahn and Kellner

[handwritten marginalia: outdated, simple analysis of activist potential]

2004). The Internet can serve as a virtual public sphere allowing individuals and groups to campaign, to become empowered, and to raise their otherwise suppressed voices with minimal resource requirements (Fenton 2008). While we do need to exercise caution over the sometimes extravagant claims made concerning the power of Citizen Journalism (see Devereux 2014, 257–72), the advent of social media does allow possibilities to challenge hegemonic discourses. Helfrich and Mancera Rueda (in this volume) show how the Spanish JSF movement has successfully used Facebook as a means of challenging dominant discourses concerning young migrants. The chapter documents how the contents of a social media setting can be used to reframe a discourse and to influence, in turn, the ways in which Spanish youth unemployment and migration is explained within the mainstream media. In essence, they demonstrate how online social networks provide a means to carve 'out a space beyond the stereotype' (Morey and Yaqin 2011, 206).

During the current Syrian crisis, social media platforms have served as a means to co-ordinate offline movements in support of refugees. In their own right, however, they have served as an important means to signal support for those seeking refuge and to subvert dehumanising constructions of the 'migrant Other'. The mobilisation of social media platforms, in particular, Facebook and Twitter, to make such discursive interventions affirms the argument that 'new media developments in technoculture make possible a reconfiguring of politics and culture and a refocusing of politics in everyday life' (Kahn and Kellner 2004, 93).

Fenton (2008, 232) cautions that while technological advancements can be understood as the 'next site of hope' for political, discursive resistance, concerns remain that it is too chaotic and fragmented to generate coherent political action. The erratic manifestation of web-based activism as 'phases of visibility and ... of relative invisibility' (Fenton 2008, 234; see also Open Society Foundations 2015) leads to questions regarding how long-term actors can harness or at least capitalise on these peaks and troughs of popular (in)action and sustain resistance. Moreover, social media is not just a tool for resistance, but also another site of struggle – malign actors also utilise social media to promulgate hate and hostility towards others, raising questions of how these sites can be policed and the hate-filled discourses they disseminate stopped at source (Kahn and Kellner 2004; Marron et al. in this volume; also Stormfront 2015). At a more macro level, the question of power and ownership has to be front and centre in the debate on social media as a site of resistance. In the aftermath of September 11, the Internet and communications therein have become the focus of powerful tools of governmental surveillance; the 'digital panopticon' (Kahn and Kellner 2004, 89). The question of how counter-discourses emerge in this securitised context raises potentially numerous fields for inquiry, not in the least the limits of resistance and the place of 'hackitvists' and 'technoactivists' (Kahn and Kellner 2004, 90–91 resp.). As Lorde (cited in Waller 2014, 255) argues, 'The master's tools will never dismantle the master's house'. Relatedly, it is also important to remember inequalities of access, be they economically or politically derived and the manner in which they restrict resistance from below (Fenton 2008).

ALTERNATIVE FRAMEWORKS OF UNDERSTANDING

Arguably, even more challenging than the question of *how* to disseminate alternative framings of migration, is the question of which alternative frameworks of understanding will effectively disrupt dominant discourses, which as this volume demonstrates, construct the migrant other as abject (Tyler 2013) and undeserving.

One tactic is to focus on disassembling the 'myths' (Lens 2002, 141) of migration, via evidence-based interventions. The editors of this volume hold that those who are privileged enough to be engaged full-time in the generation of knowledge have a moral obligation to engage with such strategies – to intervene where they possess the evidence necessary to counter the misinformation which is the fuel of scaremongering, and the critical thinking skills to question erroneous assumptions which feed a politics of fear. Yet, we acknowledge that this reactive approach, in isolation, provides limited potential for sustainable change. The danger in merely confining oneself to countering anti-immigration discourses is that they remain in possession of that generative space. Furthermore, Hajer and Versteeg (2009) and Power, Haynes and Devereux (2013) note that the rebuttal of negative framings may, in fact, serve to reinforce, rather than undermine, their perceived salience. Accordingly, providing alternative frameworks of understanding may be more effective in redirecting debate.

If we seek to draw from the experience of the Syrian conflict, the question arises as to whether strategies that rely upon empathy, not for humanity, but for the specificity of a particular migrant experience are either an ethical or a sustainable basis for resistance to dominant anti-immigrant discourses. Even if we can bring ourselves to accept the necessity of legitimising each new claim to compassion with the recounting of personal tragedy, will we not see a replication of the 'compassion fatigue' of the 1990s (Moeller 1999)?

The editors of this volume understand migration as a human right and assert the value of disseminating this framework of understanding. Applying the discourse of universal human rights to the act of migration and migrant integration provides a robust defence against discourses, which seek to exclude migrants on the basis of the stigmatisation of their particular fundamental characteristics. However, we acknowledge arguments that a human rights discourse has limitations, particularly with regard to refugees and stateless persons (Marshall 2009; Douzinas 2007; Lentin 2010). Universal human rights may be accorded by international bodies, but they must be enforced by nation states, who themselves are often the source of transgressions. Thus, while international human rights are important to the protection of outgroups who lack citizenship or kinship (Estévez 2012), individual states may resist enforcing rights, which may destabilise the existing hegemony.

Alternative discourses that emphasise the positive contribution which migrants (can) make to their host society have some utility in addressing the moveable middle. However, as valid as they may be, the individual who fundamentally understands life as a zero-sum gain, in which our gain must be to his or her disadvantage, will only view migrant creativity, industry and talent as a threat (see Semyonov et al. 2008; Coenders et al. 2005).

Each approach has its own advantages and limitations. A fundamental myth, whose disassembling may create space for some of these alternative discourses to gain ground, is that of border control (see Nicholas de Genova in this volume). It may be that the only sustainable mode of resistance to the dominant anti-immigrant discourse to emerge from the current Syrian crisis is the understanding that migration is inevitable. Whether forced out or drawn in, millions of human beings will continue to do whatever is necessary to obtain a better life for themselves and for their families. Perhaps, our ubiquitous exposure to footage and images of Syrian families dying to enter the West has at least provided an appreciation that neither sea, nor razor wire, nor land mines will stop migration. If we struggle to sustain either a charity-based or a rights-based approach to migration, perhaps the starting point for a more constructive bi-partisan conversation begins with the common consensus that migration – significant, long-term migration – is inevitable. The discursive battleground shifts, then, from our borders to our streets, schools and homes, and to the question of how we will all live together.

NOTES

1. This is in stark contrast to the actions of the fans of some Polish football clubs such as Ruch Chorzów, Radomiak Radom, Polonia Bytom, Lechia Gdansk, Legia Warszawa and Lech Poznan who displayed banners stating they were against the 'Islamization of Poland' and chanted anti-refugee songs (see http://www.ultras-tifo.net/news/3757-refugees-welcome-or-not.html). Moreover, Lech Poznan fans boycotted their game in the Europa League on 17 September 2015, in protest at the decision of European football's governing body, UEFA, to donate €1 from every ticket sold to

a fund to assist migrants and refugees (see http://www.ultras-tifo.net/news/3760-lech-poznan-supporters-boycott-europa-league-match.html).

2. Even as we write the silence of most Western European nations with regard to Hungarian state violence towards Syrian refugees and Austria's decision to limit refugee border-crossings signals, the fragility of the humanitarian framework of understanding (Aljazeera 2015).

Bibliography

Abu-Lughod, Lila. 2011. 'The Seductions of the "Honor Crime"'. *Differences: A Journal of Feminist Cultural Studies* 22(1): 17–63.

Acuña, Rodolfo. 1996. *Anything But Mexican: Chicanos in Contemporary. Los Angeles*. New York: Verso.

Adichie, Chimamanda Ngozie. 2013. *Americanah*. New York: Alfred A. Knoff.

Agamben, Giorgio. 2006/2009. *Che cos'è un dispositivo?* English Translation 'What is an Apparatus?' In *What is an Apparatus? And Other Essays*, translated by David Kishik and Stefan Pedatella. Stanford: Stanford University Press.

AHA. 2013. 'Foundation Homepage'. Accessed November 22. http://theahafoundation.org.

Ahern, Dermot. 2004. *Dáil/Written Answers 593, cols. 642*, November 24.

Ahern, Dermot. 2005. *Dáil Debates 609, cols. 1702*, November 10.

Ahern, Dermot. 2009. *Dáil/Written Answers 679, cols. 192*, March 31.

Ahern, Dermot. 2009. *Dáil/Written Answers 693, cols. 391*, November 3.

Ahern, Dermot. 2009. *Dáil/Written Answers 696-698, cols. 924*, December 2.

Ahmed, Sara. 2004. *The Cultural Politics of Emotion*. Edinburgh: The Edinburgh University Press.

Akan, Murat. 2009. 'Laïcité and Multiculturalism: The Stasi Report in Context'. *The British Journal of Sociology* 60(2): 237–56.

Aljazeera. 2015. 'Austria Imposes Border Controls over Influx of Refugees'. Accessed September 18. http://www.aljazeera.com/news/2015/09/hungary-declares-state-emergency-refugee-influx-150915081707010.html.

Allen, Bernard. 2006. *Joint Committee on European Affairs*, February 1.

Allen, Chris and Jorgen Nielsen. 2002. 'Summary Report on Islamophobia in the EU after 11 September 2001'. Accessed 23 August 2015. http://fra.europa.eu/fraWebsite/attachments/Synthesis-report_en.pdf.

Allen, Chris. 2010. *Islamophobia*. Farnham: Ashgate Publishing.

Alsultany, Evelyn. 2012. *Arabs and Muslims in the Media: Race and Representation after 9/11*. New York: New York University Press.

Ameli, Saied R., Merali Arzu and Ehsan Shahghasemi. 2012. *France and the Hated Society: Muslim experiences*. Wembley: Islamic Human Rights Commission.

Anderson, Benedict. 1991. *Imagined Communities*. Revised edition. London and New York: Verso.

Anderson, Benedict. 2006. *Imagined Communities: Reflections on the Origins and Spread of Nationalism*. London: Verso.

Andersson, Ruben. 2012. 'A Game of Risk: Boat Migration and the Business of Bordering Europe'. *Anthropology Today* 28(6): 7–11.

Andersson, Ruben. 2014a. 'Hunter and Prey: Patrolling Clandestine Migration in the Euro-African Borderlands'. *Anthropological Quarterly* 87(1): 119–49.

Andersson, Ruben. 2014b. *Illegality, Inc.: Clandestine Migration and the Business of Bordering Europe*. Berkeley: University of California Press.

Angermüller, Johannes. 2007. *Nach dem Strukturalismus. Theoriediskurs und intellektuelles Feld in Frankreich*. Bielefeld: transcript Verlag.

Anthias, Floya. 1992. *Ethnicity, Class, Gender and Migration: Greek Cypriots in Britain*. Aldershot: Brookfield, Avebury.

Appadurai, Arjun. 1996. *Modernity at Large: Cultural Dimensions in Globalization*. Minneapolis, Minn: University of Minnesota Press.

Arendt, Hannah. 1951/1968. *The Origins of Totalitarianism*. New York: Harvest/ Harcourt.

Arendt, Hannah. 2008/1967. *Vita Activa, oder vom tätigen Leben*. München: Piper.

Argenti, Nicholas. 1999. *Is this How I Looked When I First Got Here? Pottery and Practice in the Cameroon Grassfields*. London: British Museum Press.

Argenti, Nicholas. 2001. 'Kesum-Body and the Politics of the Gods: The Politics of Children's Masking and Second-World Realities in Oku (Cameroon)'. *Journal of the Royal Anthropological Institute* 7(1): 67–94.

Argenti, Nicholas. 2005. 'Dancing in the Borderlands: The Forbidden Masquerades of Oku Youth and Women (Cameroon)'. In *Makers and Breakers: Children and Youth in Postcolonial Africa*, edited by Alcinda Honwana and Filip de Boeck, 121–49. Oxford: James Currey Publishers.

Argenti, Nicholas. 2011. 'Things of the Ground: Children's Medicine, Motherhood and Memory in the Cameroon Grassfields'. *Africa* 81(2): 269–94.

Article 18. 1922. '*Constitution of the Irish Free State*'. Accessed 27 January 2015. www.irishstatutebook.ie/1922/en/act/pub/0001/print.html.

Awad, Ibrahim. 2009. *International Migration Programme – The Global Economic Crisis and Migrant Workers: Impact and Response*. Geneva: International Labour Office.

Azong, Warren. 2014. Interview with Sheryl Lynch, July 20.

Azov, Adi. 2002. Interview with Moshe Morad, August 18.

Baily, John. 2005. 'So Near, So Far: Kabul's Music in Exile'. *Ethnomusicology Forum* 14(2): 213–33.

Baker, Paul. 2010. 'Representations of Islam in British Broadsheet and Tabloid Newspapers 1999–2005'. *Journal of Language and Politics* 9(2): 310–38.

Balch, Alex and Ekaterina Balabanova. 2015. 'Ethics, Politics and Migration: Public Debates on the Free Movement of Romanians and Bulgarians in the UK, 2006–2013." *Politics* 2: 1–17.

Bale, Tim. 2008. 'Politics Matters: A Conclusion'. *Journal of European Public Policy* 15(3): 453–64.

Barrett, Alan. 2009. 'What Do Migrants Do in a Recession?' Paper presented at the ESRI Policy Conference – *The Labour Market in Recession*, Economic and Social Research Institute, Dublin, April 30.

Barrett, Alan and Yvonne McCarthy. 2008. 'Are Ireland's Immigrants Integrating into its Labour Market?' *International Migration Review* 42(3): 597–619.

Basel Mission Archives. 2015. Accessed April 22. http://www.bmarchives.org/items/show/100203764.

Batson, C. Daniel and Nadia Ahmad. 2009. 'Using Empathy to Improve Intergroup Attitudes and Relations'. *Social Issues and Policy Review* 3: 141.

Bauder, Harald. 2008a. 'Media Discourse and the New German Immigration Law'. *Journal of Ethnic and Migration Studies* 34(1): 95–112.

Bauder, Harald. 2008b. 'Neoliberalism and the Economic Utility of Immigration: Media Perspectives of Germany's Immigration Law'. *Antipode* 40(1): 55–78.

Bauder, Harald. 2008c. 'Immigration Debate in Canada: How Newspapers Reported, 1996–2004'. *International Migration and Integration* 9: 289–310.

Bauder, Harald. 2013. 'Why We Should Use the Term Illegalized Immigrant'. *RCIS Research Brief No. 2013/1*, Accessed 1 October 2013. http://www.ryerson.ca/content/dam/rcis/documents/RCIS_RB_Bauder_No_2013_1.pdf.

Bauder, Harald and Jan Semmelroggen. 2009. Immigration and Imagination of Nationhood in the German Parliament'. *Nationalism and Ethnic Politics* 15(1): 1–26.

Bauman, Zygmunt. 2002. *Liquid Modernity*. Oxford: Blackwell.

BBC. 2013. 'Home Office "Go Home" Campaign Probed by ASA'. *BBC News*. Accessed 5 June 2014. http://www.bbc.co.uk/news/uk-england-23632096.

BBC. 2014. 'UK European Election Results'. *BBC News*. Accessed 30 January 2015. http://www.bbc.co.uk/news/events/vote2014/eu-uk-results.

BBC. 2015. 'Newsnight'. First broadcast September 4, by BBC Two.

Bennett, Tony. 1995. *The Birth of the Museum: History, Theory, Politics*. London: Routledge.

Benson, Rodney. 2009. 'What Makes News More Multiperspectival? A Field Analysis'. *Poetics* 37(5): 402–18.

Berger, Jonah and Katherine Milkman. 2012. 'What Makes Online Content Viral?' *Journal of Marketing Research* 49(2): 192–205.

Berger, Peter L. and Thomas Luckmann. 1996. *The Social Construction of Reality*. New York: Doubleday & Co.

Berlant, Lauren. 2008. *The Female Complaint. The Unfinished Business of Sentimentality in American Culture*. Durham: Duke University Press.

Bertrand, Gilles. 2004. 'Cypriots in Britain: Diaspora(s) Committed to Peace?' *Turkish Studies* 5(2): 93–110.

Bhabha, Homi K. 2013. 'Introduction: Narrating the Nation'. In *Nation and Narration*, edited by Homi K. Bhabha, 1–7. London: Routledge.

Binotto, Marco. 2004. 'La cronaca'. In *Fuoriluogo. L'immigrazione e i media italiani*, edited by Marco Binotto and Valentina Martino, 45–81. Cosenza: Rai-Pellegrini.

Binotto, Marco. 2012. 'La «signora in nero»: non c'è immigrazione senza cronaca'. In *Gigantografie in nero. Ricerca su sicurezza, immigrazione e asilo nei media italiani*, edited by Marco Binotto, Marco Bruno and Valeria Lai V., 15–30. Raleigh NC: Lulu Press.

Binotto, Marco. 2015. 'Tracciare confini. Metafore, frame e spazi nella definizione del nemico'. In *Tracciare confini. L'immigrazione e i media italiani*, edited by Marco Binotto, Marco Bruno and Valeria Lai. Milano: FrancoAngeli.

Binotto, Marco, Marco Bruno, and Valeria Lai, eds. 2012. *Gigantografie in nero. Ricerca su sicurezza, immigrazione e asilo nei media italiani*. Raleigh NC: Lulu Pres.

Binotto, Marco and Valentina Martino, eds. 2004. *Fuoriluogo. L'immigrazione e i media italiani*. Cosenza: Rai-Pellegrini.

Blåfelt, Antti. 2004. 'Eläköön perusjamppa'. *Helsingin Sanomat*, June 10.

Bohlman, Philip. 2001. 'Diaspora'. In *The New Grove Dictionary of Music and Musicians*, 2nd edition by Sadie Stanley, 292–95. London: Macmillan.

Boomgaarden, Hajo G. and Rens Vliegenthart. 2009. 'How News Content Influences Anti-immigration Attitudes: Germany, 1993–2005'. *European Journal of Political Research* 48(4): 516–42.

Borland, Katherine. 2009. 'Embracing Difference: Salsa Fever in New Jersey'. *Journal of American Folklore Society* 122(486): 466–92.

Bos, Linda and Kees Brants. 'Populist Rhetoric in Politics and Media: A Longitudinal Study of the Netherlands'. *European Journal of Communication* 29(6): 703–19.

Bourdieu, Pierre. 1977. *Outline of a Theory of Practice*. 1st ed. Cambridge: Cambridge University Press.

Bourdieu, Pierre. 1979. La distinction: critique sociale du jugement. Paris: Les Éditions de Minuit.

Bourdieu, Pierre. 1980. *Questions de sociologie*. Paris: Minuit.

Bourdieu, Pierre. 1992. *Les règles de l'art. Genèse et structure du champ littéraire*. Paris: Seuil.

Bourdieu, Pierre. 2007. Preface to *The Suffering of the* Immigrant, by Abdelmalek Sayad, translated by David Macey, xi–xiv. Cambridge: Polity.

Boym, Svetlana. 2001. *The Future of Nostalgia*. London: Basic Books.

Brah, Avtar. 1996. *Cartographies of Diaspora: Contesting Identities*. London: Routledge.

Bredeloup, Sylvie. 2012. 'Sahara Transit: Times, Spaces, People'. *Population, Space and Place* 18(4): 457–67.

Brooker, Charlie. 2011. 'The News Coverage of the Norway Massacre Killings was Fact-free Conjecture'. *The Guardian, July 24.* Accessed 30 November 2014. http://www.guardian.co.uk/commentisfree/2011/jul/24/charlie-brooker-norway-mass-killings?INTCMP=SRCH.

Brown, Martyn. 2012. 'Immigrants Do Take British Jobs'. *Daily Express.* Accessed June 5, 2014. http://www.express.co.uk/news/uk/294891/Immigrants-do-take-British-jobs.

Brown, Martyn. 2013. 'David Cameron Joins Shed Raid for Illegal Immigrants'. *Daily Express.* Accessed 5 June 2014. http://www.express.co.uk/news/uk/449461/David-Cameron-joins-sheds-raid-for-illegal-immigrants.

Browne, Peter. 2004. 'Céilí House'. *Fleadh Programme*. Accessed 14 January 2015. http://comhaltas.ie/music/treoir/detail/ceili_house/.

Bruno, Marco. 2004. 'L'ennesimo sbarco di clandestini'. In *Fuoriluogo. L'immigrazione e i media italiani*, edited by Marco Binotto and Valentina Martino, 95–107. Cosenza: Rai-Pellegrini.

Bruno, Marco. 2014a. 'Lampedusa/Italia. La costruzione giornalistica dell'«emergenza» e la politica televisiva dei numeri'. *Comunicazionepuntodoc* 9: 53–73.

Bruno, Marco. 2014b. *Cornici di realtà. Il frame nell'analisi dell'informazione*. Milano: Guerini e Associati.

Bryant, Rebecca and Yiannis Papadakis. 2012. 'Introduction: Modalities of Time, History, and Memory in Ethnonational Conflicts'. In *Cyprus and the Politics of Memory: History, Community and Conflict*, edited by Yiannis Papadakis and Bryant Rebecca, 1–26. London: IB Tauris & Co Ltd.

Bubot Niyar (Paper Dolls). Directed by Tomer Heymann. 2006. Tel Aviv: Claudius Films, L.M. Media, Film Sales Company, and The Heymann Brothers Films.

Bucher, Hans-Jürgen. 2007. 'Textdesign und Multimodalität. Zur Semantik und Pragmatik medialer Gestaltungsformen'. In *Textdesign und Textwirkung in der massenmedialen Kommunikation*, edited by Jürgen Spitzmüller, 49–77. Konstanz: UVK Verlagsgesellschaft.

Bucher, Hans-Jürgen. 2010. 'Multimodalität – eine Universalie des Medienwandels: Problemstellungen und Theorien der Multimodalitätsforschung'. In *Neue Medien neue Formate. Ausdifferenzierung und Konvergenz in der Medienkommunikation*, edited by Hans-Jürgen Bucher, Thomas Gloning and Kathrin Lehnen, 41–79. Frankfurt/New York: Campus.

Bucher, Hans-Jürgen. 2013. 'Online-Diskurse als multimodale Netzwerk-Kommunikation. Plädoyer für eine Paradigmenerweiterung'. In *Online-Diskurse. Theorien und Methoden transmedialer Online-Diskursforschung*, edited by Claudia Fraas, Stefan Meier and Christian Pentzold, 57–101. Cologne: von Halem.

Buckley, Marella. 1997. 'The Irish among the British and the Women among the Irish'. In *Location and Dislocation in Contemporary Irish Society*, edited by Jim McLoughlin, 94–132. Cork: Cork University Press.

Burawoy, Michael. 1976. 'The Functions and Reproduction of Migrant Labour: Comparative Material from Southern Africa and the United States'. *American Journal of Sociology* 81(5): 1050–87.

Burroughs, Elaine. 2015. 'The Discourse of Controlling Illegal Immigration in Irish Parliamentary Texts'. *Journal of Language and Politics* 14(4): 479–500.

Burroughs, Elaine and Zoe O'Reilly. 2013. 'Discursive Representations of Asylum Seekers and Illegal Immigrants in Ireland'. *Journal of Arts and Humanities* 7(2): 59–70.

Bußhoff, Heinrich. 2000. *Politische Repräsentation. Repräsentativität als Bedingung und Norm von Politik*. Baden-Baden: Nomos-Verl.-Ges.

Bussolini, Jeffrey. 2010. 'What is a Dispositive?' *Foucault Studies* 10: 85–107.

Cadogan, Marian. 2008. 'Fixity and Whiteness in the Ethnicity Question of Irish Census 2006'. *Translocations* 3(1): 50–68.

Cahn, Claude. 2003. 'Racial Preference, Racial Exclusion: Administrative Efforts to Enforce the Separation of Roma and Non-Roma in Europe through Migration Controls'. *European Journal of Migration and Law* 5(4): 479–90.

Cairney, Paul. 2006. 'Venue Shift Following Devolution: When Reserved Meets Devolved in Scotland'. *Regional and Federal Studies* 16: 429–445.

Calvanese, Ernesto. 2011. *Media e immigrazione tra stereotipi e pregiudizi. La rappresentazione dello straniero nel racconto giornalistico.* Milano: FrancoAngeli.

Cameron, David. 2013. 'Speech on Immigration and Welfare Reform'. Presented at University Campus Suffolk, June 25. Accessed 27 May 2014. https://www.gov.uk/government/speeches/david-camerons-immigration-speech.

Cangelosi, Danielle. 2011. 'A Question of Honor: Police Say Iraqi Immigrant Father Targeted Daughter in Honor Killing'. *Fox News*, August 5. Accessed 18 January 2013. http://www.foxnews.com/us/2011/08/05/question-honor-iraqi-immigrant-father-targets-daughter-in-honor-killing/

Caritas-Migrantes. different editions., 2007–2011. *Dossier statistico immigrazione.* Roma: Idos.

Carr, James. 2016. *Experiences of Islamophobia Living with Racism in the Neoliberal Era.* London: Routledge.

Carr, James and Amanda Haynes. 2013. 'A Clash of Racialisations: The Policing of "Race" and of Anti-Muslim Racism in Ireland'. *Critical Sociology.* Accessed 15 September 2015. doi: 0896920513492805.

Casciani, Dominic. 2013. 'UK Border Agency "Not Good Enough" and Being Scrapped'. *BBC News.* Accessed 5 June 2014. http://www.bbc.co.uk/news/uk-politics-21941395.

Cassia, Paul Sant. 2000. 'Exoticizing Discoveries and Extraordinary Experiences: "Traditional" Music, Modernity, and Nostalgia in Malta and Other Mediterranean Societies'. *Ethnomusicology* 44(2): 281–301.

Central Bureau of Statistics. 2004. *The Statistical Abstract of Israel – Annual Report 2003.* [in Hebrew]. Jerusalem: The Government of Israel.

Central Statistics Office. 2006. '*Census Figures from 2006*'. Accessed 14 July 2010. http://www.cso.ie/census/Census2006Results.htm.

Central Statistics Office. 2009. *Population and Migration Estimates April 2009.* Cork: Central Statistics Office.

Central Statistics Office. 2010. *Live Register Additional Tables – June 2010.* Cork: Central Statistics Office.

Central Statistics Office. 2011. 'Population Usually Resident and Present in the State by Age Group, Sex, Birthplace and CensusYear'. *Census 2011 Table CD614.* Cork: Central Statistics Office.

Central Statistics Office. 2012. 'Census 2011: This is Ireland (Part 1)'. Accessed 23 August 2015. http://www.cso.ie/en/census/census2011reports/census2011thisisirelandpart1/.

Cesari, Jocelyn. 2004. *L'Islam à l'épreuve de l'Occident.* Paris: La Découverte.

Chaumier, Serge. 2003. 'Quelle exposition, quel média, et pour quel public?' *Média-Morphoses* (9): 58–62.

Chavez, Leo R. 1998/1992. *Shadowed Lives – Undocumented Immigrants in American Society.* Orlando, Florida: Harcourt Brace College Publishers.

Chesler, Phyllis. 2010. 'The Other Side of Jihad – Honor Killings'. *Fox News*, June 11. Accessed 18 January 2013. http://www.foxnews.com/opinion/2010/06/11/phyllis-chesler-honourhonour-killings-families-jihadists-west/.

Chesler, Phyllis. 2011. 'Honor Killings in Buffalo and Arizona? Two Trials Prove This is Happening Here'. *Fox News*, January 24. Accessed 18 January 2013. http://www.foxnews.com/opinion/2011/01/24/honor-killings-buffalo-arizona-trials-prove-happening/.

Chi, Juliette. 2012. Interview with Sheryl Lynch, June 4.

Chilver, Elizabeth M. and Phyllis M. Kaberry. 1967. 'The Kingdom of Kom in West Cameroon'. In *West African Kingdoms in the Nineteenth Century*, edited by Daryll Forde and Phyllis M. Kaberry, 123–51. London: International African Institute; Oxford University Press.

Christophorou, Chrostophoros, Sanem Şahin and Synthia Pavlou. 2010. *Media Narratives, Politics and the Cyprus Problem. Peace Research Institute Oslo Report 01-2010*. Oslo: PRIO.

Christou, Nicola. 2013. Interview with Michalis Poupazis, May 31.

Cikara, Mina, Emile G. Bruneau and Rebecca Saxe. 2011. 'Us and Them: Inter-Group Failures of Empathy'. *Current Directions in Psychological Science* 20(3): 149–53.

Cisneros, J. David. 2008. 'Contaminated Communities: The Metaphor of "Immigrant as Pollutant" in Media Representations of Immigration'. *Rhetoric and Public Affairs* 11(4): 569–602.

Clayman, Steven and John Heritage. 2002. *The News Interview: Journalists and Public Figures on the Air*. Cambridge: Cambridge University Press.

Clough Marinaro, Isabella and Nando Sigona. 2011. 'Introduction. Anti-Gypsyism and the Politics of Exclusion: Roma and Sinti in Contemporary Italy'. *Journal of Modern Italian Studies* 16(5): 583–89.

Coenders, Marcel, Marcel Lubbers and Peer Scheepers. 2005. *Majority Populations' Attitudes towards Migrants and Minorities*. Vienna: European Monitoring Centre on Racism and Xenophobia.

Cohen, Stanley. 2002. *Folk Devils and Moral Panics*. New York: Routledge.

Cohen, Stanley and Jock Young, eds. 1981. *The Manufacture of News. Social Problems, Deviance and the Mass Media. Revised edition*. London: Constable-Sage.

Cole, Juan. 2011. 'Islamophobia and American Foreign Policy: A Comparison between Europe and the United States'. In *Islamophobia: The Challenge of Pluralism in the 21st Century*, edited by John L. Esposito and Ibrahim Kalin, 127–43. Oxford and New York: Oxford University Press.

Collett, Elizabeth and Frank Laczo. 2006. Introduction to Managing Migration in Ireland: A Social and Economic Analysis, by National Economic and Social Council and the International Organisation for Migration, 1–8. Dublin: National Economic and Social Council (NESC).

Connaughton, Paul. 2007. *Dáil Debates 641, cols. 159*, November 7.

Considine, Mairead and Fiona Dukelow. 2010. *Irish Social Policy: A Critical Introduction*. Dublin: Gill and MacMillan.

Constandinides, Pamela. 1977. 'The Greek Cypriots: Factors in the Maintenance of Ethnic Identity'. In *Between Two Cultures: Migrants and Minorities in Britain*, edited by James Watson, 269–300. Oxford: Wiley-Blackwell.

Constandinides, Susie. 1993. 'The Cypriot Community in the United Kingdom: Two Family Case Studies'. *British Journal of Guidance & Counselling* 21(1): 46–55.

Cowen, Brian. 2007. *Dáil Debates 640, cols. 502*, October 24.

Cowen, Brian. 2009. *Dáil Debates 679, cols. 281*, April 1.

Crawford, Seymour. 2003. *Dáil Debates 565, cols. 375*, April 10.

Cuffe, Ciaran. 2011. Interview with Elaine Burroughs, October 11.

Cvajner, Martina and Giuseppe Sciortino. 2010. 'Theorizing Irregular Migration. The Control of Spatial Mobility in Differentiated Societies'. *European Journal of Social Theory* 13(3): 389–404.

Cyprus Statistical Service. 2011. 'Census'. Accessed 6 May 2012. http://www. mof.gov.cy/mof/cystat/statistics.nsf/census-2011_cystat_en/census-2011_cystat_en?OpenDocument.

D'Angelo, Paul and Jim A. Kuypers, eds. 2010. *Doing News Framing Analysis. Empirical and Theoretical Perspectives*. New York-London: Routledge.

Dahl, Julia. 2012. '"Honor-Killing" Under Growing Scrutiny in the U.S.' *CBS News*, April 4. Accessed 18 January 2013. http://www.cbsnews.com/2102-504083_162-57409395.html.

Dal Lago, Alessandro, ed. 1998. *Lo straniero e il nemico. Materiali per l'etnografia contemporanea*. Genova-Milano: Costa & Nolan.

Daynes, Sarah. 2005. 'The Musical Construction of the Diaspora: The Case of Reggae and Rastafari'. In *Music, Space and Place: Popular Music and Cultural Identity*, edited by S. Whiteley, A. Bennett and Stan Hawkins, 25–41. Aldershot: Ashgate Publishing Limited.

De Genova, Nicholas. 2002. 'Migrant "Illegality" and Deportability in Everyday Life'. *Annual Review of Anthropology* 31: 419–47.

De Genova, Nicholas. 2005. *Working the Boundaries: Race, Space, and 'Illegality' in Mexican Chicago*. Durham, NC: Duke University Press.

De Genova, Nicholas. 2007. 'The Production of Culprits: From Deportability to Detainability in the Aftermath of "Homeland Security."' *Citizenship Studies* 11(5): 421–48.

De Genova, Nicholas. 2010a. 'The Management of "Quality": Class Decomposition and Racial Formation in a Chicago Factory'. *Dialectical Anthropology* 34(2): 249–72.

De Genova, Nicholas. 2010b. 'The Queer Politics of Migration: Reflections on "Illegality" and Incorrigibility'. *Studies in Social Justice* 4(2): 101–26.

De Genova, Nicholas. 2012. 'Border, Scene and Obscene'. In *A Companion to Border Studies*, edited by Thomas Wilson and Hastings Donnan, 492–504. Oxford: Wiley-Blackwell.

De Genova, Nicholas. 2013. 'Spectacles of Migrant "Illegality": The Scene of Exclusion, the Obscene of Inclusion'. *Ethnic and Racial Studies* 36(7): 1180–198.

De Genova, Nicholas. 2013a. 'Spectacles of Migrant "Illegality": The Scene of Exclusion, the Obscene of Inclusion'. *Ethnic and Racial Studies* 36(7): 1180–98.

De Genova, Nicholas. 2013b. '"We Are of the Connections": Migration, Methodological Nationalism, and "Militant Research"'. *Postcolonial Studies* 16(3): 250–58.

Department of Justice and Foreign Affairs. 2014. 'Office for the Promotion of Migrant Integration'. Accessed December 24. www.integration.ie.

Derrida, Jacques. 2000. 'Hospitality'. *Angelaki: Journal of the Theoretical Humanities* 5: 3–18.

Derrida, Jacques and Anne Dufourmantelle. 2000. *Of Hospitality: Anne Dufourmantelle Invites Jacques Derrida to Respond*, translated by Rachel Bowlby. Stanford, CA: Stanford University Press.

Devereux, Eoin. 2014. *Understanding the Media*, 3rd edition, London: Sage Publications.

Dominiczak, Peter. 2013a. 'Tory Activists Call on David Cameron Not to Open Borders to Romanians and Bulgarians'. *The Telegraph*. Accessed 5 June 2014. http://www.telegraph.co.uk/news/uknews/immigration/10542018/Tory-activists-call-on-David-Cameron-not-to-open-borders-to-Romanians-and-Bulgarians.html.

Dominiczak, Peter. 2013b. 'We Will Block Benefits to New EU Migrants, Says Cameron'. *The Telegraph*. 5 June 2014. http://www.telegraph.co.uk/news/uknews/immigration/10524285/We-will-block-benefits-to-new-EU-migrants-says-Cameron.html.

Dorell, Oren. 2009. '"Honor Killings" in USA Raise Concern'. *USA Today*, 30 November 2009. Accessed 18 January 2013. http://usatoday30.usatoday.com/news/nation/2009-11-29-honor-killings-in-the-US_N.html.

Douzinas, Costas. 2000. *The End of Human Rights: Critical Legal Thought at the Turn of the Century*. Oxford: Hart.

Downes, Lawrence. 2013. 'Borderline Insanity at the Fence in Nogales'. *New York Times*, 7 December. Accessed 19 April 2015. http://www.nytimes.com/2013/12/08/opinion/sunday/borderline-insanity-at-the-fence-in-nogales.html?pagewanted=1&nl=todaysheadlines&emc=edit_th_20131208.

Drew, Paul and John Heritage, eds. 1992. *Talk at Work: Interaction in Institutional Settings*. Cambridge: Cambridge University Press.

Dunn, Kevin M., Natasha Klocker and Tanya Salabay. 2007. 'Contemporary Racism and Islamophobia in Australia: Racialising Religion'. *Ethnicities* 7(4): 564–89.

Dunn, Timothy J. 2009. *Blockading the Border and Human Rights: The El Paso Operation that Remade Immigration Enforcement*. Austin: University of Texas Press.

Durand, Jorge and Douglas S. Massey. 2004. *Crossing the Border: Research from the Mexican Migration Project*. New York: Russell Sage Foundation.

Durkan, Bernard. 2008. *Dáil Debates 647, cols. 337*, February 14.

Durkan, Bernard. 2011. Interview with Elaine Burroughs, September 22.

Economic & Social Research Institute. 2010. *The Irish Economy*. Accessed 26 July 2010. http://www.esri.ie/irish_economy/.

Ehrkamp, Patricia. 2010. 'The Limits of Multicultural Tolerance? Liberal Democracy and Media Portrayals of Muslim Migrant Women in Germany'. *Space and Polity* 14(1): 13–32.

Electronic Intifada, Accessed 24 December 2013. http://electronicintifada.net/content/tel-aviv-suicide-bombing-and-illegal-foreign-workers/4320.

Embassy of Finland. 2015. 'Ethnic Groups and Minorities in Finland'. Accessed January 14. http://www.finland.org/public/default.aspx?nodeid=46121&contentlan=2&culture=en-US.

ENAR Ireland. 2014. 'Debunking Myths and Revealing Truths about the Roma'. Accessed 14 May 2015. http://cms.horus.be/files/99935/MediaArchive/publications/roma%20final%20pdf.pdf.

ENAR Ireland. 2015. 'iReport.ie Quarterly Reports'. Accessed May 15. https://www.ireport.ie/about-ireport-ie/.

ENAR Ireland. 2015a. 'Reports of Racism in Ireland: 2nd Quarterly Report of iReport.ie. October-November-December 2013'. Accessed 30 August 2015. http://enarireland.org/wp-content/uploads/2014/03/iReport-QR23.pdf.

English, Damien. 2007. *Dáil Debates 641, cols. 149*, November 7.

Entman, Robert. M. 1993. 'Framing Toward Clarification of a Fractured Paradigm'. *Journal of Communication* 43(4): 51–58.

Eriksen, Thomas Hylland. 1995. 'Politics and Power'. In *Small Places Large Issues*, edited by Thomas Hylland Eriksen, 157–75. London: Pluto Press.

Erjavec, Karmen. 2003. 'Media Construction of Identity through Moral Panics: Discourses of Immigration in Slovenia'. *Journal of Ethnic and Migration Studies* 29(1): 83–101.

Erlmann, Veit. 1996. 'The Aesthetics of the Global Imagination: Reflections on World Music in the 1990s'. *Public Culture* 8: 467–87.

Esposito, John L. and Sheila B. Lalwani. 2010. 'Honor Killings: Is Violence Against Women a Universal Problem, Not an Islamic Issue?' *The Huffington Post*, September 4. Accessed 24 February 2014. http://www.huffingtonpost.com/john-l-esposito/violence-against-women-a_b_705797.html.

Esses, Victoria M., John F. Dovidio, Lynne M. Jackson and Tamara L. Armstrong. 2001. 'The Immigration Dilemma: The Role of Perceived Group Competition, Ethnic Prejudice, and National Identity'. *Journal of Social Issues* 57(3): 389–412.

Estévez, Ariadna. 2012. *Human Rights, Migration, and Social Conflict: Toward a Decolonized Global*. London: Palgrave Macmillan.

European Commission. 2004. *Study on the Links Between Legal and Illegal Migration*. Brussels: European Commission.

European Commission Against Racism and Intolerance. 2013. '*European Commission Against Racism and Intolerance, 19/02/2013: Fourth Report on Ireland*'. Accessed 22 December 2014. http://www.coe.int/t/DGHL/MONITORING/ECRI/Library/PressReleases/127-19_02_2013_Ireland_en.asp.

European Monitoring Centre on Racism and Xenophobia. 2006. 'Muslims in the European Union: Discrimination and Islamophobia'. Accessed 23 August 2015. http://fra.europa.eu/fraWebsite/attachments/Manifestations_EN.pdf.

European Union Agency for Fundamental Rights. 2009. 'EU-MIDIS Data in Focus Report: The Roma'. Accessed 30 August 2015. http://ec.europa.eu/justice/discrimination/files/roma_midis_survey_en.pdf.

European Union Agency for Fundamental Rights. 2012. 'Ireland: FRANET National Focal Point Social Thematic Study. The situation of Roma 2012'. Accessed 19 April 2015. http://fra.europa.eu/sites/default/files/situation-of-roma-2012-ie.pdf.

Facchini, Giovanni, Anna Maria Mayda, Luigi Guiso and Christian Schultz. 2008. 'From Individual Attitudes towards Migrants to Migration Policy Outcomes: Theory and Evidence'. *Economic Policy* 23(56): 651–713.

Fagles Robert, trans. 1996. *Homer*. Westminster: Penguin Books.

Faloppa, Federico. 2011. *Razzisti a parole (per tacer dei fatti)*. Roma-Bari: Laterza.

Fan, Rui, Jichang Zhao, Yan Chen and Ke Xu. 2013. 'Anger is More Influential than Joy: Sentiment Correlation in Weibo'. Accessed 14 January 2015. http://arxiv.org/abs/1309.2402.

Fanning, Bryan. 2001. *On No Man's Land: Asylum Seekers in Ireland and the Limits of Social Citizenship*. Dublin: University College Dublin Press.

Fanning, Bryan. 2002. *Racism and Social Change in the Republic of Ireland*. Manchester: Manchester University Press.

FÁS. 2007. *Irish Labour Market Review 2006: A FÁS Review of Irish Labour Market Trends and Policies*. Dublin: FÁS.

FÁS. 2009. *Irish Labour Market Review 2008*. Dublin: FÁS.

Feed, Lisa and Jonathan Leach. 2012. 'Was Noor the Victim of an Honor Killing?' *CBS News*, September 1. Accessed 18 January 2013. http://www.cbsnews.com/8301-18559_162-57408082/was-noor-almaleki-the-victim-of-an-honor-killing/.

Fekete, Liz. 2009. *A Suitable Enemy: Racism, Migration and Islamophobia in Europe*. London and New York: Pluto Press.

Fekete, Liz. 2015. 'Where Monoculturalism Leads'. *Institute of Race Relations*. Accessed January 14. http://www.irr.org.uk/news/where-monoculturalism-leads/.

Fekete, Liz. 2015a. 'When Solidarity Fails'. Institute of Race Relations, Comment 27 August 2015. Accessed September 2. http://www.irr.org.uk/news/when-solidarity-fails/

Fenton, Natalie. 2008. 'Mediating Hope: New Media, Politics and Resistance'. *International Journal of Cultural Studies* 11(2): 230–48.

Fianna Fáil Minister. 2011. Interview with Elaine Burroughs, September 15.

Finnpanel. 2013. 'Results from the TV Audience Measurement'. Accessed 14 January 2015. http://www.finnpanel.fi/en/tulokset/tv/kk/ohjkan/2013/10/yle2.html.

Flecker, Jörg, ed. 2007. *Changing Working Life and the Appeal of the Extreme Right*. Aldershot: Ashgate.

Flynn, Kieran. 2006. 'Understanding Islam in Ireland'. *Islam and Christian-Muslim Relations* 17(2): 223–38.

Foucault, Michel. 1971. *L'ordre du discours: leçon inaugurale au Collège de France prononcée le 2 décembre 1970*. Paris: Gallimard.

Foucault, Michel. 1972. *Archaeology of Knowledge*. 1st edition. New York: Harper & Row.

Foucault, Michel. 1977/1994. *Dits et écrits, vol. III: 1976–1979*. Paris: Gallimard.

Foucault, Michel. 1980. 'The History of Sexuality'. In *Power/Knowledge: Selected Interviews and Other Writings, 1972–1977*, edited by Colin Gordon, 183–194. New York: Pantheon Books.

Foucault, Michel. 1982. 'The Subject and Power'. *Critical Inquiry* 8(4): 777–95.

Foucault, Michel. 1980a. 'Two Lectures'. In *Power/Knowledge: Selected Interviews and Other Writings, 1972–1977*, edited by Colin Gordon, 78–109. New York: Pantheon Books.

Foucault, Michel. 1991. 'Governmentality'. In *The Foucault effect. Studies in governmentality*, edited by Graham Burchell, Colin Gordon, and Peter Miller, 87–104. Hertfordshire: Harvester Wheatsheaf.

Foucault, Michel. 2003a/1977. 'Das Spiel des Michel Foucault'. In *Schriften in vier Bänden. Dits et Ecrits. Band III 1976–1979*, edited by Michel Foucault, 391–429. Frankfurt/Main: Suhrkamp.

Foucault, Michel. 2003b/1977. 'Vorlesung vom 14. Januar 1976'. In *Schriften in vier Bänden. Dits et Ecrits. Band III 1976–1979*, edited by Michel Foucault, 231–50. Frankfurt/Main: Suhrkamp.

Foucault, Michel and Gilles Deleuze. 1977. 'Intellectuals and Power'. In *Language, Counter-memory, Practice*, edited by Donald F. Bouchard, 205–17. New York: Ithaca, Cornell University Press.

Fox, Jon E., Laura Moroşanu and Eszter Szilassy. 2012. 'The Racialization of the New European Migration to the UK'. *Sociology*. Accessed 15 September 2015. doi:0038038511425558.

Fraas, Claudia and Stefan Meier. 2013. 'Multimodale Stil – und Frameanalyse. Methodentriangulation zur medienadäquaten Untersuchung von Online-Diskursen'. In *Angewandte Diskurslinguistik. Felder, Probleme, Perspektiven*, edited by Kersten Sven Roth and Carmen Spiegel, 135–61. Berlin: Akademie-Verlag.

FrameNet. 2014. 'FrameNet project'. Accessed February 24. https://framenet2.icsi.berkeley.edu.

Frost, Diane. 2008. 'Islamophobia: Examining Causal Links Between the Media and "Race Hate" from "Below"'. *International Journal of Sociology and Social Policy* 28(11): 564–78.

Gale, Peter. 2004. 'The Refugee Crisis and Fear. Populist Politics and Media Discourse'. *Journal of Sociology* 40(4): 321–40.

Gamson, William A. 1992. *Talking Politics*. Cambridge: Cambridge University Press.

Gamson, William A. 2001. Foreword to *Framing Public Life: Perspectives on Media and Our Understanding of the Social World*, edited by Stephen D. Reese, Oscar H. Jr. Gandy and August E. Grant, IX–XI. Mahwah, NJ: Lawrence Erlbaum Associates.

Gamson, William A. and Andre Modigliani. 1989. 'Media Discourse and Public Opinion on Nuclear Power: A Constructionist Approach'. *The American Journal of Sociology* 95(1): 1–37.

Garner, Steve. 2007. 'Ireland and Immigration: Explaining the Absence of the Far Right'. *Patterns of Prejudice* 41(2): 109–10.

Garner, Steve. 2009. 'Ireland: From Racism Without "Race" to Racism Without Racists'. *Radical History Review* 104: 41–56.

Geertz, Clifford. 1998. 'Deep Hanging Out'. *The New York Book Review* 45(16): 69.

George, Vic and Geoffrey Millerson. 1967. 'The Cypriot Community in London'. *Race & Class* 8(3): 277–92.

Gibbons, Norah. 2010. *Roscommon Child Care Case: Report of the Inquiry Team to the Health Service*. Dublin: Health Service Executive.

Gibson, Owen. 2015. 'English Football Supporters' Groups To Show "Refugees Welcome" Banners'. The Guardian, September 3. Accessed September 4. http://www.theguardian.com/football/2015/sep/03/english-football-supporters-groups-refugees-welcome-banners.

Gibson, Sarah. 2007. 'Abusing Our Hospitality: Inhospitableness and the Politics of Deterrence'. In *Mobilizing Hospitality: The Ethics of Social Relations in a Mobile World*, edited by Jennie Germann Molz and Sarah Gibson, 159–76. Lancaster: Lancaster University.

Gill, Aisha. 2006. 'Patriarchal Violence in the Name of "Honour"'. *International Journal of Criminal Justice Sciences* 1(1): 1–12.

Gilmartin, Mary. 2013. 'British Migrants and Irish Anxieties'. *Social Identities* 19(5): 637–52.

Gilmore, Ruth Wilson. 2007. *Golden Gulag: Prisons, Surplus, Crisis, and Opposition in Globalizing California*. Berkeley: University of California Press.

Githens-Mazer, Jonathon and Robert Lambert. 2010. *Islamophobia and Anti-Muslim Hate Crime: A London Case Study*. Accessed 20 July 2014. http://centres.exeter.ac.uk/emrc/publications/Islamophobia_and_Anti-Muslim_Hate_Crime.pdf.

Gladden Kelton, Jane. 1985. 'New York City St. Patrick's Day Parade: Invention of Contention and Consensus'. *The Drama Review: TDR* 29(3): 93–105.

Glynos, Jason and David Howarth. 2007. *Logics of Critical Explanation in Social and Political Theory*. London: Routledge.

Godfrey, Luke. 2012. 'Foucault's Interpretation of Modernity'. Accessed 14 May 2013. http://www.e-ir.info/2012/10/26/foucaults-interpretation-of-modernity/.

Goldberg, David T. 2001. *The Racial State*. New York: Wiley-Blackwell.

Gordon, Colin. 1991. 'Governmental Rationality: An Introduction'. In *The Foucault Effect. Studies in Governmentality*, edited by Graham Burchell, Colin Gordon and Peter Miller, 1–51. Hertfordshire: Harvester Wheatsheaf.

Government of Ireland. 1991. 'Section 12 of the Child Care Act'. Accessed 14 May 2015. http://www.irishstatutebook.ie/eli/1991/act/17/section/12/enacted/en/html.

Grewal, Inderpal. 2013. 'Outsourcing Patriarchy'. *International Feminist Journal of Politics* 15(1): 1–19.

Grue, Jan. 2009. 'Critical Discourse Analysis, Topoi and Mystification: Disability Policy Documents from a Norwegian NGO'. *Discourse Studies* 11(3): 305–28.

Gumperz, John J. 1982. *Discourse Strategies*. Cambridge: Cambridge University Press.

Gumperz, John J. 1992. 'Contextualisation & Understanding'. In *Rethinking Context: Language as an Interaction Phenomenon*, edited by Alessandro Duranti and Charles Goodwin, 229–52. Cambridge: Cambridge University Press.

Gusfield, Joseph R. 1967. 'Moral Passage: The Symbolic Process in Public Designations of Deviance'. *Social Problems* 15: 175–88.

Guy, Will, André Liebich and Elena Marushiakova. 2010. 'Improving the Tools for the Social Inclusion and Non-discrimination of Roma in the EU'. Accessed: 30 August 2015. http://ec.europa.eu/justice/discrimination/files/improving_tools_roma_inclusion_summary_en.pdf.

Hainmueller, Jens and Danie J. Hopkins. 2014. 'Political Attitudes Toward Immigration'. *Annual Review of Political Science* 17: 225–49.

Hajer, Maarten and Wytske Versteeg. 2009. *Political Rhetoric in the Netherlands: Reframing Crises in the Media*. Washington, DC: Migration Policy Institute.

Hajer, Maarten A. and Hendrik Wagenar, eds. 2003. *Deliberative Policy Analysis. Understanding Governance in the Network Society*. Cambridge: Cambridge University Press.

Hall, Stuart. 1996. 'Introduction: Who Needs "Identity"?' In *Questions of Cultural Identity*, edited by Stuart Hall and Paul du Gay, 1–17. London: Sage.

Hall, Stuart. 1997. 'The Work of Representation'. In *Representation: Cultural Representations and Signifying Practices*, edited by Stuart Hall, 13–74. London: Sage.

Hall, Stuart. 2006. 'The Whites of Their Eyes'. In *The Discourse Reader*, edited by Adam Jaworski and Nikolas Coupland, 2nd edition, 396–406. New York: Routledge.

Hall, Stuart, Chas Critcher, Tony Jefferson, John Clarke and Brian Roberts. 1978. *Policing the Crisis. Mugging, the State, and Law and Order*. London: Macmillan.

Hampe, Henrike, ed. 2005. *Migration und Museum. Neue Ansätze in der Museumpraxis*. Münster: Lit Verlag.

Hands, Joss. 2011. *@ is for Activism. Dissent, Resistance and Rebellion in a Digital Culture*. New York: PlutoPress.

Hardt, Michael. 2007. 'Foreword: What Affects are Good For'. In *The Affective Turn. Theorizing the Social*, edited by Patricia Ticineto Clough and Jean Halley, ix–xiii. Durham: Duke University Press.

Hassan, Mehdi. 2015. 'As a Muslim, I'm Fed Up With the Hypocrisy of the Free Speech Fundamentalists'. *Huffington Post*, January 13. Accessed January 14. http://www.huffingtonpost.co.uk/mehdi-hasan/charlie-hebdo-free-speech_b_6462584. html?ncid=tweetlnkukhpmg00000008.

Haynes, Amanda. 2007. 'Mass Media Re-Presentations of the Social World: Ethnicity and Race'. In *Media Studies: Key Issues and Debates*, edited by Eoin Devereux, 162–90. London: Sage.

Haynes, Amanda, Eoin Devereux and Michael Breen. 2006. *Fear, Framing, and Foreigners. The Othering of Immigrants in the Irish Print Media*. Accessed 16 December 2014. http://hdl.handle.net/10395/1350.

Haynes, Amanda, Eoin Devereux and Michael Breen. 2009. 'In the Know? Media, Migration and Public Beliefs in the Republic of Ireland'. *Translocations*, 5(1): 1–22.

Haynes, Amanda, Martin J. Power and Eoin Devereux. 2010. *How Irish Politicians Construct Transnational EU Migrants*. Limerick: Doras Luimní.

Helle, Anna. 2013. 'Työ, talous ja tunteet Kari Hotakaisen Ihmisen osassa [Work, economy, and emotions in Kari Hotakainen's novel The lot of man]'. *Kulttuurintutkimus* 30(3): 3–14.

Helfrich, Uta. in press. 'Mobilität und Mobilisierung – Social Media als Protest- und Aktionsraum'. In *Mobilität & Sprache – Mobility & Language*, edited by Marietta Calderón and Bernadette Hofinger. Frankfurt/Main: Lang.

Hellman, Heikki. 1999. *From Companions to Competitors: The Changing Broadcasting Markets and Television Programming in Finland*. Tampere: University of Tampere.

Hennessey, Michelle. 2013. 'Roma Child Incidents Result of "Pure, Raw, Naked, Poisonous Racism."' The Journal.ie, October 24. Accessed 14 May 2015. http://www.thejournal.ie/roma-children-racism-1145782-Oct2013/.

Heritage, John. 2012. 'Epistemics in Action: Action Formation and Territories of Knowledge'. *Research on Language and Social Interaction* 45(1): 1–29.

Heritage, John and Steven Clayman. 2010. *Talk in Action: Interactions, Identities, and Institutions*. Chichester: Wiley-Blackwell.

Heritage, John and Geoffrey Raymond. 2005. 'The Terms of Agreement: Indexing Epistemic Authority and Subordination in Talk-in-Interaction'. *Social Psychology Quarterly* 68(1): 15–38.

Heuser, Beatrice. 1990. 'Museums, Identity and Warring Historians on History in Germany'. *The Historical Journal* 33: 417–40.

Heyman, Josiah. 2004. 'Ports of Entry as Nodes in the World System'. *Identities* 11(3): 303–27.

Hickman, Mary J. 1998. 'Reconstructing Deconstructing "Race": British Political Discourses about the Irish in Britain'. *Ethnic and Racial Studies* 21(2): 288–307.

Hickman, Mary J. 2000. '"Binary Opposites" or "Unique Neighbours"? The Irish in Multi-Ethnic Britain'. *Political Quarterly* 71(1): 50–58.

Hickman, Mary J., Sarah Morgan, Bronwen Walter and Joseph Bradley. 2005. 'The Limitations of Whiteness and the Boundaries of Englishness: Second-Generation Irish Identifications and Positionings in Multiethnic Britain'. *Ethnicities* 5(2): 160–82.

Hickman, Mary J., Lyn Thomas, Sara Silvestri and Henri Nickels. 2011. '"Suspect Communities"? Counter-terrorism Policy, the Press, and the Impact on Irish and Muslim communities in Britain'. London Metropolitan University. Accessed 15 May 2015. http://www.statewatch.org/news/2011/jul/uk-london-met-suspect-communities-findings.pdf.

Hirschauer, Stefan and Klaus Amann. 1997. 'Die Befremdung der eigenen Kultur. Ein Programm'. In *Die Befremdung der eigenen Kultur: zur ethnographischen Herausforderung soziologischer Empirie*, edited by Stefan Hirschauer and Klaus Amann, 7–52. Frankfurt/Main: Suhrkamp.

Hoctor, Máire. 2004. *Dáil Debate 579, cols. 579*, February 4.

Hoggett, Paul, Hen Wilkinson and Pheobe Beelell. 2013. 'Fairness and the Politics of Resentment'. *Journal of Social Policy* 42(3): 567–85.

Holland, Catherine. 2011. 'Muslim Expert: "I Hope this Barbarian Gets the Full Force of Our Law"'. *AZ Family*. January 24. Accessed 19 February 2013. http://www.azfamily.com/news/soto/Muslim-expert-I-hope-this-barbarian-gets-the-full-force-of-our-law-114478114.html.

Holland, Kitty. 2014. '*Waterford Anti-Roma Protests Criticised as "Cowardly and Racist"'*. The Irish Times, October 27. Accessed 30 August 2015. http://www.irishtimes.com/news/social-affairs/waterford-anti-roma-protests-criticised-as-cowardly-and-racist-1.1978572.

Holloway, John. 1994. 'Global Capital and the National State'. *Capital and Class* 52: 23–49.

Home Office. 2014. *Immigration Bill becomes Law*. London: Home Office and UKBA.

Hosford, Paul. 2014. 'Intimidation of Roma people in Waterford "Effectively a Lynch Mob" – Minister'. The Journal.ie, October 28. Accessed 30 August 2015. http://www.thejournal.ie/roma-protest-waterford-gerry-adams-1749416-Oct2014/.

House of Commons and Scottish Affairs Committee. 2011. *UK Border Agency and Glasgow City Council: Third Report of Session 2010–11*. London: House of Commons and Scottish Affairs Committee.

Human Rights First. 2009. *Violence Against Roma: Hate Crime Survey*. Accessed 30 August 2015. https://www.humanrightsfirst.org/wp-content/uploads/pdf/FD-080609-factsheet-violence-against-roma.pdf.

Hussain, Mustafa. 2000. 'Islam, Media, and Minorities in Denmark'. *Current Sociology* 48(4): 95–116.

Hussein, Asifa M. and William L. Miller. 2006. *Multicultural Nationalism: Islamophobia, Anglophobia and Devolution*. Oxford: Oxford University Press.

Ichijo, Atsuko. 2009. 'Sovereignty and Nationalism in the Twenty-first Century: The Scottish Case'. *Ethnopolitics* 8: 155–172.

Idos-Unar. 2014. *Dossier Statistico Immigrazione 2014 – Rapporto UNAR*. Roma: Edizioni Idos.

Ieracitano, Francesca and Camilla Rumi. 2014. 'La rappresentazione mediale dell'emergenza: il caso degli sbarchi a Lampedusa'. *Sociologia* 48(1): 85–93.

Illouz, Eva. 2007. *Cold Intimacies. The Making of Emotional Capitalism*. Cambridge: Polity Press.

Immigrant Council of Ireland. 2013. 'Immigration Council *Report on Racism* 2013'. Accessed March 6, http://www.immigrantcouncil.ie/media/pressreleases/643-racism-report-requires-urgent-action-complacency-not-an-option.

Immigration Matters. 2011. 'Tier 1 Post-Study Work Visa to be Abolished'. Accessed 5 June 2014. www.immigrationmatters.co.uk.

Inspired by Muhammed. 2015. Public perceptions of Islam, Muslims and the Prophet Muhammed. Accessed 10 June 2015. http://www.inspiredbymuhammad.com/yougov.php.

Irish Human Rights and Equality Commission. 2008. '*Integrated Workplace Policy 2008*'. Accessed 21 April 2015. http://www.equality.ie/Files/Integrated%20Workplaces.pdf.

Istat (Istituto Italiano di Statistica). 2014. '*Migrazioni internazionali e interne della popolazione residente Anno 2013*. Report 9'. Accessed 18 January 2015. www.istat.it.

Iyengar, Shanto. 1991. 'Framing Responsibility for Political Issues: The Case of Poverty'. *Political Behaviour* 12(1): 19–40.

Iyengar, Shanto. 1991. *Is Anyone Responsible? How Television Frames Political Issues*. Chicago: University of Chicago Press.

Iyengar, Shanto. 2005. 'Speaking of Values: The Framing of American Politics'. *The Forum* 3(3): 1–8.

Jefferson, Gail. 2004. 'Glossary of Transcript Symbols with an Introduction'. In *Conversation Analysis: Studies from the First Generation*, edited by Gene H. Lerner, 13–31. Amsterdam/Philadelphia: John Benjamins.

Jenkins, Richard. 1994. 'Rethinking Ethnicity: Identity, Categorization and Power'. *Ethnic and Racial Studies* 17(2): 197–223.

Jewitt, Carey, ed. 2014. *The Routledge Handbook of Multimodal Analysis*. London/New York: Routledge.

John, Peter, Anthony Bertelli, Will Jennings and Shaun Bevan. 2013. *Policy Agendas in British Politics*. Palgrave Basingstoke: Macmillan.

Johnston, Hank and John A. Noakes, eds. 2005. *Frames of Protest. Social Movements and the Framing Perspective*. Lanham: Rowman & Littlefield.

Juventud Sin Futuro. 2011. *Juventud sin futuro*. Barcelona: Icaria Editorial.

Kaberry, Phyllis M. 1952. *Women of the Grassfields*. London: H.M.S.O.

Kahn, Richard and Douglas Kellner. 2004. 'New Media and Internet Activism: From the "Battle of Seattle" to Blogging'. *New Media and Society* 6(1): 87–95.

Kapchan, Deborah. 2006. 'Performing Home and Anti-home in Austin's Salsa Culture'. *American Ethnologist* 33(3): 361–77.

Karra, Maria. 2006. 'Greek Cultural Keywords: Language Reflecting Culture Through Vocabulary'. 2012. http://www.proz.com/translation- articles/articles/637/.

Karyotis, Georgios. 2012. 'Securitization of Migration in Greece: Process, Motives, and Implications'. *International Political Sociology* 6(4): 390–408.

Kearney, Michael. 2004. 'The Classifying and Value-Filtering Missions of Borders'. *Anthropological Theory* 4(2): 131–56.

Kehoe, Paul. 2004. *Dáil Debates 591, cols. 769*, November 2.

Kemp, Adriana, Rebecca Raijman, Julia Resnik and Silvina Schammah-Gesser. 2000. '"Making it" in Israel? Non-Jewish Latino Undocumented Migrant Workers in the Holy Land'. *Estudios Interdisciplinarions De America Latina Y El Caribe* 11(2): 113–36.

Kelly, Daniel. 2015. '"Refugees Welcome" – One League of Ireland Club Opens their doors'. Newstalk, September 3. Accessed September 21. https://www.newstalk.com/reader/47.302/54469/0/.

Kenny, Enda. 2006. *Dáil Debates 621, cols. 726*, June 13.

Kenny, Enda. 2008. Dáil Debates 666, *cols. 9*, November 5.

Keren, Michael. 2006. *Blogosphere. The New Political Arena*. Lanham: Lexington Books.

Khosravi, Shahram. 2010. *'Illegal' Traveller: An Auto-Ethnography of Borders*. Basingstoke, UK: Palgrave Macmillan.

Khosravinik, Majid. 2009. 'The Representation of Refugees, Asylum Seekers and Immigrants in British Newspapers during the Balkan Conflict (1999) and the British General Election (2005)'. *Discourse & Society* 20(4): 477–98.

Kiely, Richard, Frank Bechhofer, Robert Stewart and David McCrone. 2001. 'The Markers and Rules of Scottish National Identity'. *The Sociological Review* 49(1): 33–55.

King-O'Riain, Rebecca. 2007. 'Counting on the "Celtic Tiger": Adding Ethnic Census Categories in the Republic of Ireland'. *Ethnicities* 7(4): 516–42.

Kirkup, James. 2014a. 'Immigration has a Positive Impact, Says Office for Budget Responsibility Head'. *The Telegraph*. Accessed June 5. http://www.telegraph.co.uk/news/uknews/immigration/10570839/Immigration-has-a-positive-impact-says-Office-for-Budget-Responsibility-head.html.

Kirkup, James. 2014b. 'EU Elections 2014: Is Immigration Good for Britain?' *The Telegraph*. Accessed May 28. http://www.telegraph.co.uk/news/worldnews/europe/eu/10822956/EU-elections-2014-Is-immigration-good-for-Britain.html.

Kitt, Michael. 2009. *Dáil Debates 686, cols. 336*, June 30.

Koehler, Jobst, Frank Laczko, Christine Aghazarm and Julia Schad. 2010. *Migration and the Economic Crisis in the European Union: Implications for Policy*. Brussels: IOM Press.

Koğacıoğlu, Dicle. 2004. 'The Tradition Effect: Framing Honor Crimes in Turkey'. *Differences: A Journal of Feminist Cultural Studies* 15(2): 119–51.

Kolm, Richard. 1981. *The Change of Cultural Identity: An Analysis of Factors Conditioning the Cultural Integration of Immigrants (American ethnic groups)*. North Stratford, New Hampshire: Ayer Co Publishers.

Korteweg, Anne C. and Gökçe Yurdakul. 2009. 'Islam, Gender, and Immigrant Integration: Boundary Drawing in Discourses on Honour Killing in the Netherlands and Germany'. *Ethnic and Racial Studies* 32(2): 218–38.

Korteweg, Anne C. and Gökçe Yurdakul. 2010. Religion, Culture and the Politicization of Honour-Related Violence: A *Critical Analysis of Media and Policy Debates in Western Europe and North America*. Geneva: United Nations Research Institute for Social Development.

Krippendorf, Klaus. 2004. *Content Analysis: An Introduction to Its Methodology*, 2nd edition. Thousand Oaks: Sage.

Laachir, Karima. 2007. 'Hospitality and the Limitations of the National'. In *Mobilizing Hospitality: The Ethics of Social Relations in a Mobile World*, edited by Jennie Germann Molz and Sarah Gibson, 177–92. Lancaster: Lancaster University.

Labi, Nadya. 2011. 'An American Honor Killing: One Victim's Story'. *TIME Magazine*, February 25. Accessed 18 January 2013. http://www.time.com/time/nation/article/0,8599,2055445,00.html.

Laclau, Ernesto. 1990. *New Reflections on the Revolution of our Time*. London: Verso.

Laclau, Ernesto. 2005. *On Populist Reason*. London: Verso.

Lähdesmäki, Tuuli. 2013. 'Cultural Activism as a Counter-discourse to the European Capital of Culture Programme: The Case of Turku 2011'. *European Journal of Cultural Studies* 16(5): 598–619.

Lähdesmäki, Tuuli and Tuija Saresma. 2014a. 'The Intersections of Sexuality and Religion in the Anti-interculturalist Rhetoric in Finnish Internet Discussion on Muslim Homosexuals in Amsterdam'. In *Building Barriers and Bridges. Interculturalism in the 21st Century*, edited by Gabriele Strohschen and Jonathan Gourlay, 35–47. Oxford: Inter-Disciplinary Press.

Lähdesmäki, Tuuli and Tuija Saresma. 2014b. 'Re-framing Gender Equality in Finnish Online Discussion on Immigration'. *NORA – Nordic Journal of Feminist and Gender Research* 22(4): 299–313.

Laitinen, Arto. 2002. 'Charles Taylor and Paul Ricoeur on Self-interpretations and Narrative Identity'. In *Narrative Research: Voices of Teachers and Philosophers*, edited by Rauno Huttunen, Hannu L. T. Heikkinen and Leena Syrjala. 57–76. Finland: SoPhi Academic Press.

Lakoff, George. 2004. *Don't Think of an Elephant! Know Your Values and Frame the Debate – The Essential Guide for Progressives*. London: Chelsea Green Publishing.

Latour, Bruno. 2005. 'From Realpolitik to Dingpolitik or How to Make Things Public'. In *Making Things Public – Atmospheres of Democracy*, edited by Bruno Latour and Peter Weibel, 4–31. Cambridge, MA: The MIT Press.

Law, Alex. 2012. 'Between Autonomy and Independence: State and Nation in Devolved Scotland'. In *Social Justice and Social Policy in Scotland*, edited by Gerry Mooney and Gill Scott, 25–42. Bristol: Policy Press.

Leach, Jonathan. 2012. 'A Reporter's Journey: Revealing the Honor Violence Epidemic'. *CBS News*, April 5. Accessed 18 January 2013. http://www.cbsnews.com/8301-504083_162-57409993-504083/a-reporters-journey-revealing-the-honor-violence-epidemic/.

Lecadet, Clara. 2013. 'From Migrant Destitution to Self-Organization into Transitory National Communities: The Revival of Citizenship in Post-Deportation Experience in Mali'. In *The Social, Political and Historical Contours of Deportation*, edited by Bridget Anderson, Matthew Gibney and Emanuela Paoletti, 143–58. New York & London: Springer.

Lee, John J. 1989. *Ireland: 1912–1985: Politics and Society*. Cambridge: Cambridge University Press.

Lenihan, Brian. 2008. *Dáil Debates 648, cols. 57*, February 21.

Lenihan, Conor. 2008. 'Migration Nation: Statement on Integration Strategy and Diversity Management'. Accessed 22 April 2015. http://www.integration.ie/website/omi/omiwebv6.nsf/page/AXBN-7SQDF91044205-en/$File/Migration%20Nation.pdf.

Lens, Vicki. 2002. 'Public Voices and Public Policy: Changing the Societal Discourse on "Welfare"'. *Journal of Sociology and Social Welfare* 29(1): 137–54.

Lentin, Ronit. 2002. 'Antiracist Responses to the Racialisation of Irishness: Disavowed Multiculturalism and its Discontents'. In *Racism and Anti-Racism in Ireland*, edited by Ronit Lentin and Robbie McVeigh, 243–56. Belfast: Beyond the Pale Publications.

Lentin, Ronit. 2010. 'Human Rights, Violence and Anti-racism'. Accessed 17 September 2015. http://www.ronitlentin.net/2010/10/17/human-rights-migrants-and-anti-racism/.

Lentin, Ronit and Robbie McVeigh. 2006. *After Optimism? Ireland, Racism and Globalization*. Dublin: Metro Eireann.

Leshem, Elazar (El'āzār Lešem) and Judith T. Shuval, eds. 1998. *Immigration to Israel: Sociological Perspectives*. Piscataway, NJ: Transaction Publishers.

Levush, Rith. 2015. 'Guest Worker Programs: Israel'. *Library of Congress website*, Accessed 31 August 2015. http://www.loc.gov/law/help/guestworker/israel.php.

Lewis, Justin, Mason Paul and Kerry Moore. 2011. 'Images of Islam in the UK: The Representation of British Muslims in the National Press 2000–8'. In *Pointing the Finger: Islam and Muslims in the British Media*, edited by Julian Petley and Robin Richardson, 40–66. Oxford: Oneworld.

Lewis, Miranda. 2006. *Warm Welcome? Understanding Public Attitudes to Asylum Seekers in Scotland*. London: Institute for Public Policy Research.

Liddle, Joanna and Shirin Rai. 1998. 'Feminism, Imperialism and Orientalism: The Challenge of the "Indian woman"'. *Women's History Review* 7(4): 495–520.

Liljeström, Marianne and Susanna Paasonen, eds. 2010. *Working with Affect in Feminist Readings: Disturbing Differences*. London: Routledge.

Lomax, Alan. 1959. 'Folk Song Style'. *American Anthropologist* 61: 927–54.

Luukka, Teemu. 2014. 'Yle on jäänyt kauas tavoitteistaan [Yle has not reached its goals]'. *Helsingin Sanomat*, May 27.

Luukka, Teemu and Juha Roppola. 2014. 'Kokoomus repii kaulaa – perussuomalaisten kannatus alhaisimmillaan kahteen vuoteen [The National Coalition Party rushes on ahead – the support of the Finns Party lowest in two years]'. *Helsingin Sanomat*, August 18.

Lyons, Denise. 2014. 'Racist Graffiti Outside the Convention Centre Mars Citizenship Ceremonies for the New Irish Citizens'. *TheJournal.ie* July 4. Accessed 22 April 2015. http://www.thejournal.ie/citizenship-ceremony-racism-1553655-Jul2014/.

Maas, Utz. 1984. *As the Spirit of Community Found in Language: Language in National Socialism*. Opladen: Westdeutscher Verlag.

Mac Éinri, Piaris and Allen White. 2008. 'Immigration into the Republic of Ireland: a Bibliography of Recent Research'. *Irish Geography* 41(2): 151–79.

Macdonald, Sharon, ed. 1998. *The Politics of Display: Museums, Science, Culture*. London: Routledge.

Maguire, Mark and Fiona Murphy. 2012. *Integration in Ireland: The Everyday Lives of African Migrants*. Manchester: Manchester University Press.

Mahdon, Yehiel. 2002. Interview with Moshe Morad, August 18.

Maier, Charles S. 1992/1988. *Die Gegenwart der Vergangenheit. Geschichte und die nationale Identität der Deutschen*. Frankfurt/Main: Campus Verlag.

Mailman, Stanley and Stephen Yale-Loehr. 2005. 'Immigration Reform: Restrictionists Win in the House'. *New York Law Journal*, December 28.

Mäkinen, Katariina. 2013. 'Rajoja ja säröjä. Talous maahanmuuttovastaisessa keskustelussa. [Borders and ruptures. Economy in anti-immigration-minded discussion]'. *Poliittinen talous* 1(1). Accessed 13 January 2015. http://www.poliittinentalous.fi/ojs/index.php/poltal/article/view/2.

Mallas, Eftihios. 2012. Interviews with Michalis Poupazis, November 15 and 19.

Malpas, Jeff. 2011. 'Philosophy's Nostalgia'. In *Philosophy's Moods: The Affective Grounds of Thinking*, edited by Hagi Kenaan, 87–104. Berlin: Springer Science & Business Media.

Mälzer, Moritz. 2005. 'Ausstellungsstück Nation. Die Debatte um die Gründung des Deutschen Historischen Museums in Berlin'. In *Gesprächskreis Geschichte*, edited by Dieter Dowe, 1–144. Bonn: Friedrich-Ebert-Stiftung.

Mancera Rueda, Ana and Uta Helfrich. 2014. 'La crisis en 140 caracteres: el discurso propagandístico en la red social Twitter'. *Cultura, Lenguaje y Representación* 12: 59–86. http://dx.doi.org/10.6035/clr. 2014.12.4.

Maneri, Marcello. 1998. 'Lo straniero consensuale. La devianza degli immigrati come circolarità di pratiche e di discorsi'. In *Lo straniero e il nemico. Materiali per l'etnografia contemporanea*, edited by Alessandro Dal Lago, 236–72. Genova-Milano: Costa&Nolan, 1998.

Maneri, Marcello. 2011. 'Media Discourse on Immigration. The Translation of Control Practices into the Language We Live By'. In *Racial criminalization of migrants in 21st Century*, edited by Salvatore Palidda, 77–93. London: Ashgate.

Mani, Lata. 1988. *Contentious Traditions: The Debate on Sati in Colonial India.* Berkeley: University of California Press.

Markas, Jay Joseph. 2011. 'I Beg Your Pardon, Rem Koolhaas'. Accessed 18 June 2013. http://bigapplepreserves.blogspot.co.uk/2011_05_01_archive.html.

Marres, Noortje. 2007. 'The issues Deserve More Credit: Pragmatist Contributions to the Study of Public Involvement in Controversy'. *Social Studies of Science* 37(5): 759–80.

Marshall, Nicole. 2009. '*Revisiting Human Rights Discourse: The Challenge of Environmental Refugees to International Moral and Legal Norms*'. APSA 2009 Toronto Meeting Paper. Accessed 4 August 2015. http://ssrn.com/abstract=1451624.

Marx, Karl. 1867/1976. *Capital: A Critique of Political Economy*, Volume One. New York: Penguin Books.

Massey, Douglas S. 2005. 'Backfire at the Border: Why Enforcement without Legalization Cannot Stop Illegal Immigration'. *Trade Policy Analysis* 29. Washington, DC: Center for Trade Policy Studies, Cato Institute.

Matsuoka, Atsuka and John Sorenson. 2001. *Ghosts and Shadows: Construction of Identity and Community in an African Diaspora*. Toronto: University of Toronto Press.

McClintock, Anne. 1995. *Imperial Leather: Race, gender, and Sexuality in the Colonial Contest*. New York: Routledge.

McClure, Brigid. 2014. '"Endless Possibilities" Embodied Experiences and Connections in Social Salsa Dancing'. *PhoenEX*, 9(2): 112–35.

McCombs, Maxwell E. and Donald L. Shaw. 1972. 'The Agenda-Setting Function of Mass Media'. *Public Opinion Quarterly* 36(2): 176–87.

McCormack, Claire. 2014. 'New Irish Eyes are Smiling as 4,000 Become Citizens'. *The Irish Independent*, July 5. Accessed 18 April 2015. http://www.independent.ie/irish-news/news/new-irish-eyes-are-smiling-as-4000-become-citizens-30408260.html.

McDougall, Blair. 2014. 'Independence Essay'. *The Scotsman*. Accessed May 28. http://www.scotsman.com/news/independence-essay-blair-mcdougall-on-the-union-1-3424487.

McDowell, Michael. 2003. *Dáil/Written Answers 569, cols. 556*, March 12.

McElgunn, Joanne. 2011. 'Al-Qaeda's Irish Terror Cell: Jihad Fanatics Hiding Out amongst Us'. *The Irish Sun*, May 5.

McGinley, Dinny. 2004. *Dáil Debates 593, cols. 499*, November 204.

McGrath, Finian. 2005. *Joint Committee on Justice, Equality, Defense and Women's Rights*, December 14.

McGrath, Finian. 2011. Interview with Elaine Burroughs, October10.

McLaren, Lauren. 2001. 'Immigration and the New Politics of Inclusion and Exclusion in the European Union: The Effect of Elites and the EU on Individual-level Opinions Regarding European and Non-European Immigrants'. *European Journal of Political Research* 39: 81–108.

McLaren, Lauren and Mark Johnson. 2004. 'Understanding the Rising Tide of Anti-Immigrant Sentiment'. In *British Social Attitudes: The 21st Report*, edited by Alison Park, John Curtice, Katarina Thomson, Catherine Bromley and Miranda Phillips, 169–201. London: Sage.

McLeish, Jean. 2008. 'Their Fight to End Dawn Raids'. *TES Connect.* Accessed 5 June 2014. https://www.tes.co.uk/article.aspx?storycode=2313937.

Meer, Naser, ed. 2013. *Racialization and Religion. Race, Culture and Difference in the Study of Antisemitism and Islamophobia.* London: Routledge.

Meetoo, Veena and Heidi Mirza. 2007. 'There is Nothing Honourable about Honour Killings: Gender, Violence and the Limits of Multiculturalism'. *Women's Studies International Forum* 30(3): 187–200.

Meier, Stefan and Vivien Sommer. 2012. 'Multimodalität im Netzdiskurs. Methodisch-methodologische Betrachtungen zur diskursiven Praxis im Internet'. In *Entwicklungen im Web 2.0,* edited by Torsten Siever and Peter Schlobinski, 97–115. Frankfurt: Lang.

Mezzadra, Sandro. 2001. *Diritto di fuga: Migrazioni, cittadinanza, globalizzazione.* Verona, Italy: Ombre corte.

Mezzadra, Sandro. 2004. 'The Right to Escape'. *Ephemera* 4(3): 267–75.

Mickelsson, Rauli. 2011. 'Suomalaisten nationalistipopulistien ideologiat [Ideologies of the Finnish nationalist-populists]'. In *Populismi. Kriittinen arvio* [Populism. A Critical View], edited by Matti Wiberg, 147–74. Helsinki: Edita.

Migration Observatory. 2013. *Bordering on Confusion: International Migration and Implications for Scottish Independence.* Oxford: University of Oxford.

Migration Watch UK. 2014. 'What is the Problem?' Accessed June 5. www.migrationwatchuk.org/what-is-the-problem.

Miles, Robert and Malcolm Brown. 2003. *Racism.* 2nd edition. London and New York: Routledge.

Millward – Brown / Lansdowne. 2012. *Public Attitudes Towards Immigration Survey.* Dublin: Commissioned by The One Foundation.

Miskovic, Maja. 2009. 'Roma Education in Europe: In Support of the Discourse of race'. *Pedagogy, Culture & Society* 17(2): 201–20.

Mitropoulos, Angela. 2006. 'Autonomy, Recognition, Movement'. *The Commoner* 11: 5–14.

Modood, Tariq. 2012. 'Is There a Crisis of Secularism in Western Europe'. *Sociology of Religion* 73(2): 130–49.

Moeller, Susan. 1999. *Compassion Fatigue: How the media sell disease, famine, war and death.* New York: Routledge.

Mohanty, Chandra Talpade. 1991. 'Under Western Eyes'. In *Third World Women and the Politics of Feminism,* edited by Chandra Talpade Mohanty, Anna Russo and Lourdes M. Torres, 51–80. Indianapolis: University of Indiana Press.

Mohn, Bina Elisabeth. 2002. *Filming Culture. Spielarten des Dokumentierens nach der Repräsentationskrise.* Stuttgart: Lucius & Lucius.

Montini, E. J. 2009. 'Subtracting "Honor" from "Honor Killing"'. *The Arizona Republic*, October 29. Accessed 25 February 2013. www.azcentral.com/members/Blog/EJMontini/66193.

Morad, Moshe. 2011. 'Music of the Underdog: Sociological and Musical Similarities between Muzika Mizrahit and Salsa'. In *Returning to Babel: Jewish Latin American Experiences, Representations, and Identity,* edited by Amalia Ran and Jean Axelrad Cahan, 121–42. Leiden: Brill Press.

Morey, Peter and Amina Yaqin. 2011. *Framing Muslims: Stereotyping and Representation after 9/11*. Cambridge, Massachusetts and England: Harvard University Press.

Mouffe, Chantal. 1993. *The Return of the Political*. London: Verso.

Mouffe, Chantal. 1995. 'The End of Politics and the Rise of the Radical Right'. *Dissent* 42(4): 498–502.

Mouffe, Chantal. 2005. *On the Political*. London: Routledge.

Moulier Boutang, Yann. 1998. *De l'esclavage au salariat. Economie historique du salariat bridé*. Paris: Presses Universitaires de France.

Moulier Boutang, Yann. 2001. 'Between the Hatred of All Walls and the Walls of Hate: The Minoritarian Diagonal of Mobility'. In *'Race' Panic and the Memory of Migration*, edited by Meaghan Morris and Brett de Bary, 105–30. Aberdeen and Hong Kong: Hong Kong University Press.

Moulier-Boutang, Yann and Stany Grelet. 2001. 'The Art of Flight: An Interview with Yann Moulier-Boutang'. *Rethinking Marxism* 13(3/4): 227–35.

Mountz, Alison. 2010. *Seeking Asylum. Human Smuggling and Bureaucracy at the Border*. London: University of Minnesota Press.

Murphy, Maureen. 2007. *Un palais pour une cité. Du musée des Colonies à la Cité nationale de l'histoire de l'immigration*. Paris: Réunion des musées nationaux.

Musarò, Pierluigi and Paola Parmiggiani, eds. 2014. *Media e migrazioni. Etica, estetica e politica del discorso umanitario*. Milano: FrancoAngeli.

Mycock, Andrew. 2012. 'SNP, Identity and Citizenship: Reimagining State and Nation'. *National Identities* 14: 53–69.

Myers, Amanda Lee. 2011. 'Iraqi Immigrant to be Tried for Daughter's Death'. *NBC News*, January 2. Accessed 18 January 2013. http://www.msnbc.msn.com/id/40878687/ns/us_news-crime_and_courts/t/iraqi-immigrant-be-tried-daughters-death/#.UPmIsB2rmYY.

Myrmidoni, Androniki. 2013. Interview with Michalis Poupazis, May 8.

NASC. (2013) *In from the Margins: Roma in Ireland. Addressing the structural discrimination of the Roma community in Ireland*. Accessed 19 April 2015. http://www.nascireland.org/wp-content/uploads/2013/05/NASC-ROMA-REPORT.pdf.

NASC: The Irish Immigrant Support Centre. 2013. 'Submission to Joint Oireachteas Committee on Justice, Equality and Defence on Integration, Multiculturalism and Combating Racism'. Accessed 22 April 2015. http://www.nascireland.org/wp-content/uploads/2013/10/Nasc-Justice-Committee-Integration-Submission.pdf.

Nascimbene, Bruno. 2012. 'Condanna senza appello della "politica dei respingimenti"? La sentenza della Corte europea dei diritti dell'uomo Hirsi e altri c. Italia'. *Documenti IAI - Istituto Affari Internazionali*, 12(2): Accessed 8 September 2014. http://www.iai.it/pdf/DocIAI/iai1202.pdf.

National Consultative Committee on Racism and Interculturalism. 2007. '*The Muslim Community in Ireland: Challenging So of Myths [sic] and Misinformation*'. Accessed 27 September 2013. http://www.nccri.ie/pdf/ChallengingMyths-Muslims.pdf.

Naughten, Denis. 2009. *Dáil Debates 682, cols. 648*, May 14.

Naughten, Denis. 2009. *Select Committee on Justice, Equality, Defense and Women's Rights*, October 9.

Naughten, Denis. 2009. *Select Committee on Justice, Equality, Defense and Women's Rights*, May 7.

Naughten, Denis. 2011. Interview with Elaine Burroughs, September 22.

Navarro, Laura. 2010. 'Islamophobia and Sexism: Muslim Women in the Western Mass Media'. *Human Architecture: Journal of the Sociology of Self-Knowledge* 8(2): 95–114.

Nevins, Joseph. 2002/2010. *Operation Gatekeeper and Beyond: The War On 'Illegals' and the Remaking of the USA-Mexico Boundary*, 2nd Edition. New York: Routledge.

Nezer, Orly. 2001. *An Analysis of the Appeals to Mesilah – The Characteristics of the Persons Approaching Mesilah, between January and June 2001* [in Hebrew]. Tel Aviv: Mesilah, The Centre for Assistance and Information for the Foreign Community in Tel Aviv.

Nezer, Orly and Edna Alter. 2002. *An Analysis of the Appeals to Mesilah: The Characteristics of the Persons Approaching Mesilah, between July and December 2001* [in Hebrew]. Tel Aviv: Mesilah, The Centre for Assistance and Information for the Foreign Community in Tel Aviv.

Ní Laoire, Caitríona. 2002. 'Discourses of Nation among Migrants from Northern Ireland: Irishness, Britishness and the Spaces in-Between'. *Scottish Geographical Journal* 118(3): 183–99.

Ní Laoire, Caitríona. 2008a. 'Complicating Host-Newcomer Dualisms: Irish Return Migrants as Home-Comers or Newcomers?' *Translocations: Migration and Social Change* 4(1): 35–50.

Ní Laoire, Caitríona. 2008b. '"Settling Back"? A Biographical and Life-Course Perspective on Ireland's Recent Return Migration'. *Irish Geography* 41(2): 195–210.

Niessen, Jan, Thomas Huddleston and Laura Citron. 2007. *Migrant Integration Policy Index*. Brussels: British Council and Migration Policy Group.

Nikunen, Kaarina and Karina Horsti. 2013. 'The Ethics of Hospitality in Changing Journalism: A Response to the Rise of the Anti-immigrant Movement in Finnish Media Publicity'. *European Journal of Cultural Studies* 16(4): 489–504.

Nkwi, Walter Gam. 2010. *Voicing the Voiceless*. Bamenda, Cameroon: Langaa RPCIG.

Nomani, Asra Q. 2009. 'Honor Killing On Main Street'. *The Daily Beast*, November 4. Accessed on 24 February 2013. http://www.thedailybeast.com/articles/2009/11/05/honor-killing-on-main-street.html.

Norris, Pippa, Montague Kern and Marion R. Just. 2003. *Framing Terrorism: The News Media, the Government and the Public*. New York-London: Routledge.

Nowacire official website. 2015. Accessed 22nd April. www.nowacire.org.

Ó Murchú, Labhras. 2009. *Seanad Debates 194, cols. 288*, March 3.

O'Caoláin, Caoimhghín. 2011. Interview with Elaine Burroughs, October 10.

O'Doherty, Kieran and Amanda Lecouteur. '«Asylum seekers», «boat people» and «illegal immigrants»: Social Categorisation in the Media'. *Australian Journal of Psychology* 59(1): 1–12.

O'Donoghue, John. 2004. *Dáil Debates 583, cols. 1258*, April 21.

O'Donoghue, Siobhán. 2010. 'Recognising and Responding to Racism Experienced by Migrant Workers'. Irish Left Review. Accessed 6 July 2010. http://www.irishleftreview.org/2010/07/05/recognising-responding-racism-experienced-migrant-workers/?utm_source=feedburner&utm_medium=email&utm_campaign=Feed%3A+irishleftreview%2Ffeed+%28Irish+Left+Review%29.

O'Flynn, Noel. 2003. *Dáil Debates 565, cols. 354*, April 10.

O'Gorman, Kevin. 2010. *The Origins of Hospitality and Tourism*. Oxford: Goodfellow.

O'Mahoney, John. 2007. *Dáil Debates 641, cols. 162*, November 7.

Oakley, Robin. 1970. 'Cypriots in Britain'. *Race Today* 2: 99–102.

Oakley, Robin. 1979. *Family Kinship and Patronage: The Cypriot Migration to Britain – Minority Families in Britain*. Macmillan: London.

Office of the Press Ombudsman. 2014. 'European Network Against Racism Ireland and the Irish Independent'. Accessed 15 May 2015. http://www.presscouncil.ie/decided-by-press-ombudsman/european-network-against-racism-ireland-and-the-irish-independent.2356.html.

Official Statistics of Finland (OSF). 2014. 'Population Structure'. Accessed November 4. http://stat.fi/til/vaerak/tau_en.html.

Ohliger, Rainer. 2002. 'Thesen für ein Migrationsmuseum'. In *Das historische Erbe der Einwanderer sichern. Die Bundesrepublik Deutschland braucht ein Migrationsmuseum. Dokumentation zur Fachtagung Brühl 4–6. Oktober.* 28–43.

Okely, Judith. 2014. 'Recycled (mis)representations: Gypsies, Travellers or Roma Treated as Objects, Rarely Subjects'. *People, Place and Policy* 8(1): 65–85.

Olin Wright, Erik. 2010. *Envisioning Real Utopias*. London: Verso.

Open Society Foundations. 2015. 'From the Front Lines in Ferguson: A Conversation about Policing, Race, and Justice'. Podcast. Accessed August 4. https://www.opensocietyfoundations.org/podcasts.

Osservatorio di Pavia – Demos Pi. 2014. '"La Grande Incertezza". Rapporto sulla sicurezza e l'insicurezza sociale in Italia e in Europa. Significati, immagine e realtà. Percezione, rappresentazione sociale e mediatica della sicurezza'. Accessed 8 September 2014. http://www.osservatorio.it/download/rapporto_Osservatorio_Europeo_Sicurezza_febbraio_2014.pdf.

Palidda, Salvatore, ed. 2011a. *Racial Criminalization of Migrants in 21st Century*. London: Ashgate.

Palidda, Salvatore. 2011b. 'A Review of the Principal European Countries'. In *Racial Criminalization of Migrants in 21st Century*, edited by Salvatore Palidda, 23–30. London: Ashgate.

Pan, Zhongdang and Gerald M. Kosicki. 1993. 'Framing Analysis: An Approach to News Discourse'. *Political Communication* 10(1): 55–76.

Papapavlou, Andreas and Pavlos Pavlou. 2002. 'The Interplay of Language Use and Language Maintenance and the Cultural Identity of Greek Cypriots in the UK'. *International Journal of Applied Linguistics* 11(1): 92–113.

Payrató, Lluís. 2012. 'Local/global, teoría/praxis, textual/multimodal... La lingüística aplicada como mediación y análisis crítico'. In *La lingüística aplicada en la era de la globalización,* edited by Àngels Llanes Baró, Lirian Astrid Ciro, Lídia Gallego Balsà and Rosa M. Mateu Serra, 35–47. Lleida: Edicions de la Universitat de Lleida.

Pernaa, Ville, Niko Hatakka, Mari K. Niemi, Ville Pitkänen, Erkka Railo and Matti Välimäki. 2012. 'Median vaaliagenda ja jytky [Election agenda of media and the "big bang"]'. In *Jytky. Eduskuntavaalien 2011 mediajulkisuus* [The Big Bang and the Media Publicity of the Parliamentary Election 2011], edited by Ville Pernaa and Eerkka Railo, 396–410. Turku: Kirja-Aurora.

Pesta, Abigail. 2010. 'An American Honor Killing'. *Marie Claire*, July 8. Accessed 18 January 2013. http://www.marieclaire.com/world-reports/news/honourhonour-killings-in-america.

Pesta, Abigail. 2011. 'An American Honor Killing: Justice is Served'. *The Huffington Post*, February 24. Accessed 24 February 2013. http://www.huffingtonpost.com/abigail-pesta/an-american-honor-killing_b_827448.html.

Petrouis, Costas. 2012. Interview with Michalis Poupazis, November 14.

Phipps, Alison. 2014. '*Scotland's Future*, Hospitality and Social Healing'. *Hospitality and Society* 2: 179–192.

Piacentini, Teresa. 2012. 'Solidarity and Struggle: An Ethnography of the Associational Lives of African Asylum Seekers and Refugees in Glasgow'. PhD diss., University of Glasgow.

Pickering, Sharon. 2001. 'Common Sense and Original Deviancy: News Discourses and Asylum Seekers in Australia'. *Journal of Refugee Studies* 14(2): 169–86.

Pieridou-Skoutella, Avra. 2007. 'The Construction of National Musical Identities by Greek Cypriot Primary School Children – Implications for the Cyprus Music Education System'. *British Journal of Music Education* 24(3): 251–66.

Pirouet, Louise. 2001. *Whatever Happened to Asylum in Britain? A Tale of Two Walls*. New York: Berghahn.

Pitkin, Hannah F. 1967. *The Concept of Representation*. Berkeley: University of California Press.

Pittock, Murray. 2008. *The Road to Independence? Scotland since the Sixties*. London: Reaktion.

Pitts Jr., Leonard J. 2009. '"Honor" Killings Shows Lack of Faith in Culture's Mores'. *The Arizona Daily Star*, November 9. Accessed 11 February 2013. http://azstarnet.com/news/opinion/honor-killing-shows-lack-of-faith-in-culture-s-mores/article_e06be998-2dcc-559c-a0af-d6fccdaec331.html.

Pole, Antoinette. 2010. *Blogging the Political. Politics and Participation in a Networked Society*. New York & London: Routledge.

Porsché, Yannik. 2012. 'Public Representations of Immigrants in Museums. Towards a Microsociological Contextualisation Analysis'. *COLLeGIUM – Studies Across Disciplines in the Humanities and Social Sciences. Language, Space and Power: Urban Entanglements* 13: 45–72.

Porsché, Yannik. 2013. 'Multimodale Marker in Museen'. In *Was machen Marker? Logik, Materialität und Politik von Differenzierungsprozessen*, edited by Eva Bonn, Christian Knöppler and Miguel Souza, 113–151. Bielefeld: Transcript.

Porsché, Yannik. 2014a. 'Der "Bologna Prozess" als Wissensterritorium. Eine Kontextualisierungsanalyse'. In *Diskursforschung. Ein interdisziplinäres Handbuch. Vol. 2.*, edited by Martin Nonhoff, Eva Herschinger, Johannes

Angermuller, Felicitas Macgilchrist, Martin Reisigl, Juliette Wedl, Daniel Wrana and Alexander Ziem, 379–403. Bielefeld: Transcript.

Porsché, Yannik. 2014b. '*Re-presenting Foreigners – Representing the Public. A Microsociological Contextualisation Analysis of Franco-German Knowledge Construction in Museums*'. PhD diss., Johannes Gutenberg University of Mainz/ University of Burgondy.

Porsché, Yannik. 2015a. 'Kontextualisierung am Schnittpunkt von Museumsraum und Öffentlichkeit. Ethnomethodologische, poststrukturale und ethnographische Analyseheuristiken'. In *Methoden einer Soziologie der Praxis*, edited by Franka Schäfer, Anna Daniel and Frank Hillebrandt, 239–65. Bielefeld: Transcript.

Porsché, Yannik. 2015b. 'On the Move: Temporalities in a Franco-German Museum Exhibition on Representations of Immigrants'. In *Ethno-Architecture and the Politics of Migration*, edited by Mirjana Lozanovska, 199–214. London: Routledge.

Porsché, Yannik. forthcoming-a. 'Contextualising Culture – From Transcultural Theory to the Empirical Analysis of Participants' Practices'. In *Downscaling Culture: Revisiting Intercultural Communication*, edited by Jaspal Singh, Argyro Kantara and Dorottya Cserzö. Newcastle: Cambridge Scholars.

Porsché, Yannik. forthcoming-b. 'Discursive Knowledge Construction or "There is Only One Thing Worse Than Being Talked About and That is not Being Talked About"'. In *Wissen transnational. Funktionen – Praktiken – Repräsentationen*, edited by Peter Haslinger, Alexandra Schweiger and Justyna A. Turkowska. Marburg: Herder Institut.

Poupazis, Michalis. 2013. *Nostalgia and Traditional Music in the Greek-Cypriot Diaspora: An Ethnomusicological Study of the Greek-Cypriot Community in Birmingham*. Accessed 16 October 2014. https://www.academia.edu/6723245/ Nostalgia_and_Traditional_Music_in_the_Greek-Cypriot_Diaspora_An_Ethno-musicological_Study_of_the_Greek-Cypriot_Community_in_Birmingham.

Poupazis, Michalis. 2014. '"Placebo Nostalgia": The Greek-Cypriot Diaspora in Birmingham, Its Churches, and Limits to Who Can Belong'. In *Sense of Belonging: in a Diverse Britain*, edited by Eddie Halpin, Alan Hunter, Karim Murji, Alpaslan özerdem, Richard Race, Simon Robinson and Mustafar Demire, 79–106. London: Dialogue Society.

Power, Martin J., Amanda Haynes and Eoin Devereux. 2012. 'From the Mouths of Janus: Political Constructions of Transnational EU Migrants in Ireland'. *Irish Communications Review* 13(1): 3–18.

Power, Peter. 2008. *Dáil Debates 648, cols. 22*, February 21.

Poynting, Scott and Greg Noble. 2004. '*Living with Racism: The Experience and Reporting by Arab and Muslim Australians of Discrimination, Abuse and Violence since 11 September 2001*. Report to the Human Rights and Equal Opportunity Commission'. Accessed 23 August 2015. http://www.stepone.org.au/media/1712/ living%20with%20racism.pdf.

Preston, Julia. 2013. 'Amid Steady Deportation, Fear and Worry Multiply Among Immigrants'. *New York Times*, 22 December. Accessed 12 December 2014. http://

www.nytimes.com/2013/12/23/us/fears-multiply-amid-a-surge-in-deportation.htm l?nl=todaysheadlines&emc=edit_th_20131223&_r=0.

Primetime Investigates. '*Slave Labour Ireland*'. RTE1. 1 December 2008, 21:30.

Pugh, Michael. 2004. 'Drowning not Waving: Boat People and Humanitarianism at Sea'. *Journal of Refugee Studies* 17(1): 50–69.

Pujante, David and Esperanza Morales-Lopez. 2008. 'A Political Action Against Popular Opinion: Aznar's Final Speech Before the Spanish Parliament Justifying the War in Iraq'. *Journal of Language and Politics* 7(1): 71–98.

Pupcenoks, Juris and Ruan McCabe. 2013. 'The Rise of the Fringe: Right Wing Populists, Islamists and Politics in the UK'. *Journal of Muslim Minority Affairs* 33(2): 171–84.

Quassoli, Fabio. (2013) '"Clandestino": Institutional Discourses and Practices for the Control and Exclusion of Migrants in Contemporary Italy'. *Journal of Language and Politics* 12(2): 203–25.

Quinn, Emma. 2003. *European Migration Network Annual Report on Statistics on Migration, Asylum and Return: Ireland*. Ireland: European Migration Network.

Quinn, Emma. 2005. *Migration and Asylum in Ireland: Summary of Legislation, Case Law and Policy Measures and Directory of Organizations, Researchers and Research 2005*. Ireland: European Migration Network.

Quinn, Emma. 2010. *Country Profile: Ireland, Focus Migration Country Profile No. 19*. Hamburg: Hamburg Institute of International Economics (HWWI) in cooperation with The German Federal Agency for Civic Education and Network Migration in Europe.

Quinn, Emma and Gerard Hughes. 2004. *The Impact of Immigration on Europe's Societies: Ireland*. Dublin: European Migration Network.

Quinn, Emma and Gillian Kingston. 2012. *Practical Measures for Reducing Irregular Migration: Ireland*. Ireland: European Migration Network.

Ramadan, Tariq. 2015. 'The Paris Attackers hijacked Islam but There is No War Between Islam and the West'. *The Guardian*, January 9. Accessed 14 January 2015. http://www.theguardian.com/commentisfree/2015/jan/09/paris-hijackers-hijacked-islam-no-war-between-islam-west.

Rancière, Jacques. 2011. *Moments politiques. Interventionen 1977–2009*. Zürich: diaphenes.

Rattansi, Ali. 2007. *Racism: A Very Short Introduction*. Oxford: Oxford University Press.

Reception and Integration Agency (RIA). 2011. 'Reception and Integration Agency (RIA) Annual Report 2011'. Accessed 24 December 2014. http://www.ria.gov.ie/en/RIA/RIA%20Annual%20Report%20(A3)2011.pdf/Files/RIA%20Annual%20Report%20(A3)2011.pdf.

Reception and Integration Agency (RIA). 2013. 'Reception and Integration Agency (RIA) Annual Report 2013'. Accessed 24 December 2014. http://www.ria.gov.ie/en/RIA/RIA%20Annual%20Report%20(A4)2013.pdf/Files/RIA%20Annual%20Report%20(A4)2013.pdf.

Redmond, John M. 2007. 'The "New" Irish'. *The Irish Times*, February 1.

Reegan. 2010. Interview with Shery Lynch, June 25.

Reese, Stephen. D. 2001. 'Framing Public Life: A Bridging Model for Media Research'. In *Framing Public Life: Perspectives on Media and our Understanding of the Social World*, edited by Stephen D. Reese, Oscar H. Gandy Jr. and August E. Grant, 7–32. London: Routledge.

Reese, Stephen D., Oscar H. Jr. Gandy and August E. Grant, eds. 2001. *Framing Public Life: Perspectives on Media and Our Understanding of the Social World*. Mahwah, NJ: Lawrence Erlbaum Associates.

Reimers, Eva. 2007. 'Representations of an Honor Killing'. *Feminist Media Studies* 7(3): 239–55.

Relph, Edward. 1976. *Place and Placelessness*. Pion Publishers: London.

Richardson, Jo. 2014. 'Roma in the News: An Examination of Media and Political Discourse and What Needs to Change'. *People, Place and Policy* 8(1): 51–64.

Ricoeur, Paul. 1984. *Time and narrative. Vol. 2*. Chicago: University of Chicago Press.

Ricolfi, Luca. 1997. *La ricerca qualitativa*. Roma: Nuova Italia Scientifica.

Ritivoi, Andreea Deciu. 2002. *Yesterday's Self: Nostalgia and the Immigrant Identity*. Maryland, US: Rowman & Littlefield.

Roediger, David R. and Elizabeth D. Esch. 2012. *The Production of Difference: Race and the Management of Labour in USA History*. New York: Oxford University Press.

Rojo, Luisa M. and Teun van Dijk. 1997. '"There was a Problem and it was Solved." Legitimating the Expulsion of Illegal Immigrants in Spanish Parliamentary Discourse'. *Discourse and Society* 8(4): 523–67.

Rosello, Mireille. 2001. *Postcolonial Hospitality: The Immigrant as Guest*. Stanford, CA: Stanford University Press.

Rubin, Paul. 2010. '"Honor Thy Father:" The Inside Story of the Young Muslim Woman "Honor-Killed" by Her Father Because He Believed She'd Become Too Americanized'. *Phoenix New Times,* April 1. Accessed 25 February 2013. http://www.phoenixnewtimes.com/2010-04-01/news/honourhonour-thy-father-the-inside-story-of-the-young-muslim-woman-honourhonour-killed-by-her-father-because-he-believed-she-d-become-too-americanized/.

Ryan, James. 2004. 'Inadmissible Departures: Why Did the Emigrant Experience Feature so Infrequently in the Fiction of the Mid-Twentieth Century?' In *The Lost Decade: Ireland in the 1950s*, edited by Dermot Keogh, Finbarr O'Shea and Carmel Quinlan, 226–37. Cork: Mercier Press.

Said, Edward. 1997. *Covering Islam: How the Media and the Experts Determine How We See the Rest of the World*, Vintage Edition. London: Vintage Books.

Sakaranaho, Tuula. 2006. *Religious Freedom, Multiculturalism, Islam: Cross-reading Finland and Ireland*. Leiden & Boston: Brill.

Salmela, Mikko. 2014. 'Emotional Roots of Right-wing Political Populism'. Paper presented at the Cultural and Rhetorical Aspect of Political Populism conference, University of Jyväskylä, Finland, October 24–25.

Salmond, Alex. 2011. '*Election of First Minister*'. Presented at Scottish Parliament on 18 May 2014. Accessed 27 May 2014. http://www.scotland.gov.uk/News/Speeches/Speeches/First-Minister/electionfm2011.

Salter, Mark B. and Genevieve Piché. 2011. 'The Securitization of the US–Canada Border in American Political Discourse'. *Canadian Journal of Political Science* 44(4): 929–51.

Saltzman, Sammy Rose. 2009. 'Police Charge Iraqi Father Who Allegedly Ran Over "Westernized" Daughter'. *CBS News*, November 2. Accessed 18 January 2013. http://www.cbsnews.com/8301-504083_162-5494860-504083.html.

Saresma, Tuija. 2012. 'Miesten tasa-arvo ja kaunapuhe blogikeskustelussa [Equality of men and resentment speech in blog comments]'. In *Sukupuoli nyt! Purkamisia ja neuvotteluja* [Gender now! Dismantlings and negotiations], edited by Hannele Harjunen and Tuija Saresma, 13–34. Jyväskylä: Kampus Kustannus.

Saresma, Tuija. 2014a. 'Sukupuolipopulismi ja maskulinistinen standpoint-empirismi [Gender populism and masculinist standpoint-empiricism]'. *Sukupuolentutkimus – Genusforskning* 27(2): 46–51.

Saresma, Tuija. 2014b. 'Maskulinistiblogi feministidystopiana ja kolonialistisena pastoraalina [The masculinist blog as feminist dystopia and colonialist pastorale]'. In *Maisemassa. Sukupuoli ja kansallisuus suomalaisuuden kuvastoissa* [In the Landscape: Gender and Nationality in the Imageries of Finnishness], edited by Tuija Saresma and Saara Jäntti, 249–84. Jyväskylä: University of Jyväskylä.

Saresma, Tuija. forthcoming. 'Kauna tunnerakenteena Timo Hännikäisen esseekoelmassa *Ilman: Esseitä seksuaalisesta syrjäytymisestä* [Resentment as structure of feeling in the essay collection *Without: Essays on sexual displacement* by Timo Hännikäinen]'. In *Kirjallisuus ja tunteet* [Literature and Emotions], edited by Anna Helle and Anna Hollsten. Helsinki: The Finnish Literature Society.

Sayad, Abdelmalek. 2004. *The Suffering of the Immigrant*. West Sussex: Wiley.

Schabner, Dean and Sarah Netter. 2011. 'Muslim Man Guilty of "Honor-Killing" in Daughter's Death'. *ABC News*, February 22. Accessed 18 January 2013. http://abcnews.go.com/US/muslim-man-guilty-honor-killing-daughters-death/story?id=12975396.

Schain, Martin. 2008. 'Why Political Parties Matter'. *Journal of European Public Policy* 15(3): 465–70.

Scharbrodt, Oliver. 2012. 'Muslim Immigration to the Republic of Ireland: Trajectories and Dynamics Since World War II'. *Éire-Ireland: A Journal of Irish Studies* 47(1&2): 221–43.

Scharbrodt, Oliver and Tuula Sakaranaho. 2011. 'Islam and Muslims in the Republic of Ireland: An Introduction to the Special Issue'. *Journal of Muslim Minority Affairs* 31(4): 469–85.

Scheffer, Thomas. 2010. *Adversarial Case-Making. An Ethnography of the English Crown Court*. Amsterdam: Brill.

Scheffer, Thomas. 2013. 'Die trans-sequentielle Analyse – und ihre formativen Objekte'. In *Grenzobjekte. Soziale Welten und ihre Übergänge*, edited by Reinhard Hörster, Stefan Köngeter and Burkhard Müller, 89–114. Wiesbaden: Springer.

Scheffer, Thomas. 2014. 'Das Bohren der Bretter – Zur trans-sequentiellen Analyse des Politikbetriebs'. In *Formationen des Politischen. Anthropologie politischer Felder*, edited by Jens Adam and Asta Vonderau, 333–61. Bielefeld: Transcript.

Scherer, Matthew. 2007. 'Micropolitics Quote'. In *Encyclopedia of Governance*, edited by Mark Bevir, 563. London: Sage.

Schmitt, Carl. 1996/1932. *Der Begriff des Politischen*. Berlin: Duncker & Humblot.

Schuster, Liza. 2000. 'A Comparative Analysis of the Asylum Policy of Seven European Governments'. *Journal of Refugee Studies* 13: 118–132.

Scott, John and Gordon Marshall. 2005. *Oxford Dictionary of Sociology*. Oxford: Oxford University Press.

Scott, Mike R. 1999. *WordSmith Tools*. Oxford: Oxford University Press.

Scottish Government. 2013. *New Scots: Integrating New Scots in Scotland's Community 2014–2017*. Edinburgh: Scottish Government.

Scottish Government. 2013. *Scotland's Future: Your Guide to an Independent Scotland*. Edinburgh: Scottish Government.

Scully, Marc. 2010. 'Discourses of Authenticity and National Identity among the Irish Diaspora in England'. PhD diss., The Open University.

Scully, Marc. 2012. 'The Tyranny of Transnational Discourse: "authenticity" and Irish Diasporic Identity in Ireland and England'. *Nations and Nationalism* 18(2): 191–209.

Sein, Rita Sorina. 2014. *Racial Discrimination, Deprivation, Segregation and Marginalisation as a Reinforcement of the Practice of Child Marriage*. European Roma Rights Centre Report. Accessed 30 August 2015. http://www.errc.org/cms/upload/file/gender-fellowship-report-sorina.pdf.

Semyonov, Moshe, Rebeca Raijman and Anastasia Gorodzeisky. 2008. 'Foreigners' Impact on European Societies: Public Views and Perceptions in a Cross-national Comparative Perspective'. *International Journal of Comparative Sociology* 49(5): 5–29.

Seroussi, Edwin. 2003. '*Yam tikhoniyut*: Transformations of the Mediterranean in Israeli Music'. In *Mediterranean Mosaic: Popular Music and Global Sounds*, edited by Goffredo Plastino, 179–98. New York and London: Routledge.

Shear, Michael D. 2014. 'Obama, Daring Congress, Acts to Overhaul Immigration'. *New York Times*, 20 November. Accessed 14 December 2014. http://www.nytimes.com/2014/11/21/us/obama-immigration-speech.html?emc=edit_th_20141121&nl=todaysheadlines&nlid=44765954.

Sherwood, Harriet. 2014. 'Ten Years on and Poles are Glad to Call Britain Home'. *The Guardian*. Accessed May 28. http://www.theguardian.com/uk-news/2014/apr/26/polish-immigration-britain-cities-elections.

Sim, Douglas and Alison Bowes. 2007. 'Asylum Seekers in Scotland: The Accommodation of Diversity'. *Social Policy and Administration* 41: 729–49.

Singh, Jaggi. 2003. 'The Tel Aviv Suicide Bombing and Illegal Foreign Workers'. *The Electronic Intifada*, Accessed 24 December 2013. http://electronicintifada.net/content/tel-aviv-suicide-bombing-and-illegal-foreign-workers/4320.

Slaby, Alexandra. 2011. 'Whither Cultural Policy in Post Celtic Tiger Ireland (2008–2013)'. *The Canadian Journal of Irish Studies* 37(1/2): 76–97.

Slack, James and Matthew Hickley. 2007. '10,000 Council Houses Given to Immigrants in a Year'. *Daily Mail Online*. Accessed 5 June 2014. http://www.dailymail.co.uk/news/article-484632/10-000-council-houses-given-immigrants-year.html.

Smith, Helena. 2013. 'At least 10 "Promising" Leads on Roma Camp Girl: Blonde, Blue-eyed Maria (4) Discovered by Greek Police in Raid on Roma settlement' The Irish Times, October 23rd. Accessed 15 September 2015. http://www.irishtimes.com/news/world/europe/at-least-10-promising-leads-on-roma-camp-girl-1.1567437.

Smith, Julie. 2008. 'Towards Consensus? Centre-right Parties and Immigration Policy in the UK and Ireland'. *Journal of European Public Policy* 15(3): 415–31.

Sommers, S., E. Apfelbaum, K. Dukes, N. Toosi and E. Wang. 2006. 'Race and Media Coverage of Hurricane Katrina: Analysis, Implications, and Future Research Questions'. *Analyses of Social Issues & Public Policy* 6(1): 39–55.

Soule, Daniel P. J., Murray S. Leith and Martin Steven. 2012. 'Scottish Devolution and National Identity'. *National Identities* 14: 1–10.

Southern Poverty Law Centre. 2015. 'Extremist Files, Robert Spencer'. Accessed 16 April 2015. http://www.splcenter.org/get%20informed/intelligence%20files/profiles/Robert%20Spencer.

Spanish FrameNet. 2014. 'Spanish FrameNet (SFN)'. Accessed February 24. http://sfn.uab.es.

Sparrow, Andrew. 2014. 'Farage: Parts of Britain are "Like a Foreign Land"'. *The Guardian.* Accessed May 28. http://www.theguardian.com/politics/2014/feb/28/nigel-farage-ukip-immigration-speech.

Spivak, Gayatri Chakravorty. 1988. 'Can the Subaltern Speak?' In *Marxism and the Interpretation of Culture*, edited by Cary Nelson and Lawrence Grossberg, 271–313. London: Macmillan.

Spivak, Gayatri Chakravorty. 1994. 'Can the Subaltern Speak?' In *Colonial Discourse and Post-Colonial Theory Reader*, edited by Patrick Williams and Laura Chrisman, 66–111. Herfordshire: Harvester Wheatsheaf.

Stafford, Kathryn. 2011. 'Father Claims Alleged "Honour Killing" was an accident' *The Peoria Times*, January 27. Accessed 21 February 2013. http://www.peoriatimes.com/news/headlines/article_71180a54-2a25-11e0-94d4-001cc4c03286.html.

Stangor, Charles and Chris Crandall, eds. 1961. *Stereotyping and Prejudice, Frontiers of Social Psychology series*, 22. New York: Psychology Press.

Stephen, Lynn. 2008. '*Los Nuevos Desaparecidos*: Immigration, Militarization, Death, and Disappearance on Mexico's Borders'. In *Security Disarmed: Critical Perspectives on Gender, Race, and Militarization*, edited by Barbara Sutton, Sandra Morgen and Julie Novkov, 122–58. New Brunswick, NJ: Rutgers University Press.

Stevens, Mary. 2008. '*Re-membering the Nation: The Project for the Cité nationale de l'histoire de l'immigration*'. PhD diss., University College London.

Still, Judith. 2010. Introduction to *Derrida and Hospitality: Theory and Practice*. Edinburgh: University of Edinburgh Press.

Stöckl, Hartmut. 2012. 'Werbekommunikation semiotisch'. In *Handbuch Werbekommunikation. Sprachwissenschaftliche und interdisziplinäre Zugänge*, edited by Nina Janich, 243–62. Tübingen: UTB Francke.

Stöckl, Hartmut. 2014. 'Semiotic Paradigms and Multimodality'. In *The Routledge Handbook of Multimodal Analysis*, edited by Carey Jewitt, 274–86. London/New York: Routledge.

Stokes, Martin. 2011. 'Migrant/migrating Music in the Mediterranean'. In *Migrating Music*, edited by Jason Toynbee and Byron Dueck, 28–37. London: Routledge.

Stölzl, Christoph, ed. 1988. *Deutsches Historisches Museum. Ideen, Kontroversen, Perspektiven*. Berlin: Propyläen.

Stormfront. 2015. 'Homepage'. Accessed September 22. https://www.stormfront.org/forum/.

Tang, Terry. 2011. 'Iraqi Father Guilty in "Honor Killing"'. *The Arizona Daily Star*, February 23. Accessed 21 February 2013. http://azstarnet.com/news/state-and-regional/iraqi-father-guilty-in-honor-killing/article_10b903c5-1fe5-5a6f-a6b5-12eebfdd520f.html.

Taylor, Matthew. 2015. 'Surge in Migrant Voters Could Swing Vote in Key UK Constituencies'. *The Guardian*. Accessed 30 January 2015. http://www.theguardian.com/politics/2015/jan/29/surge-in-voters-born-overseas.

Taylor, Steven J. and Robert Bogdan. 1984. *Introduction to Qualitative Research Methods: The Search for Meanings*. New York: John Wiley & Sons.

Teerling, Janine and Russell King. 2011. '*Cyprus as a Multi Cyprus as a Multi-Diasporic Space*'. *Working Paper No. 67*. Sussex Centre for Migration Research, University of Sussex. Accessed 6 August 2014. http://www.academia.edu/download/30915449/mwp67.pdf.

Terman, Rochelle L. 2010. 'To Specify or Single Out: Should We Use the Term "Honor Killing"?' *The Muslim World Journal of Human Rights* 7(1): 1–39.

The Irish Times. 2009. 'Launch of Festival of World Culture'. *The Irish Times*, July 20.

Thévenot, Laurent. 2011. 'Power and Oppression From the Perspective of the Sociological Engagements: A Comparison with Bourdieu´s and Dewey´s Critical Approaches to Practical Activities'. *Irish Journal of Sociology* 19(1): 35–67.

Thompson, Ginger and Sarah Cohen. 2014. 'More Deportations Follow Minor Crimes, Records Show'. *New York* Times, 6 April. Accessed November 14. http://www.nytimes.com/2014/04/07/us/more-deportations-follow-minor-crimes-data-shows.html.

Titley, Gavan. 2015. 'All Aboard the Migration Nation'. In *Ireland Under Austerity: Neoliberal Crisis, Neoliberal Solutions*, edited by Colin Coulter and Angela Nagle, 192–218. Manchester: Manchester University Press.

Torfing, Jacob. 1999. *New Theories of Discourse. Laclau, Mouffe and Zizek*. Oxford: Blackwell.

Tosi Cambini, Sabrina. 2011. 'The Social Dangerousness of the Defendant is "At One with Her Own Condition of Being Nomadic": Roma and Sinti in Italian Courts of Law 1, 2'. *Journal of Modern Italian Studies* 16(5): 652–66.

Tracey, Marshall. 2000. 'Racism and Immigration in Ireland: A comparative analysis'. MPhil diss., Trinity College Dublin, Ireland.

Triandafyllidou, Anna. 2000. 'The Political Discourse on Immigration in Southern Europe: A Critical Analysis'. *Journal of Community and Applied Social Psychology* 10: 373–89.

TTI – Transatlantic Trends. 2011. 'Immigration. 2011. Key Findings'. Accessed 24 July 2014. http://trends.gmfus.org/immigration/key-findings/.

TTI – Transatlantic Trends. 2014. '*Transatlantic Trends: Mobility, Migration, and Integration. Key Findings from 2014 and Selected Highlights from Transatlantic Trends and Transatlantic Trends: Immigration 2008–13*'. Accessed December 4. http://trends.gmfus.org/immigration-2014/.

Tuchman, Gaye. 1972. 'Objectivity as a Strategic Ritual: An Examination of Newsmen's Notions of Objectivity'. *American Journal of Sociology* 77(4): 660–79.

Turner, Jonathan. 2007. 'Self, Emotions, and Extreme Violence: Extending Symbolic Interactionist Theorizing'. *Symbolic Interaction* 30(4): 501–30.

Tyler, Imogen. 2013. *Revolting Subjects: Social Abjection and Resistance in Neoliberal Britain*. London: Zed Books.

Ugba, Abel. 2009. *Shades of Belonging: African Pentecostals in Twenty-first century Ireland*. Trenton, New Jersey: Africa World Press Inc.

United Nations High Commissioner for Refugees (UNHCR). 2015. 'Resettlement and Other Forms of Admission for Syrian Refugees'. Accessed September 18. http://www.unhcr.org/52b2febafc5.pdf.

Van Der Valk, Ineke. 2003. "Right-wing parliamentary discourse on immigration in France." *Discourse and Society* 14(3): 309–48.

van Dijk, Teun A. 1991. *Racism and the Press*. New York: Routledge.

van Dijk, Teun. A. 1993. 'Denying Racism: Elite Discourse and Racism'. In *Racism and Migration in Western Europe*, edited by J. Solomos and J. Wrench, 179–93. Oxford: Berg.

van Dijk, Teun. 1997. *Discourse as Social Interaction*. London: Sage Publications.

van Dijk, Teun A. 1997. 'Political Discourse and Racism: Describing Others in Western Parliaments'. In *The Language of Politics of Exclusion*, edited by Stephen H. Riggins, 3–64. London: Sage.

van Dijk, Teun A. 1998. *News as Discourse*. Hillsdale: Lawrence Erlbaum Associates.

van Dijk, Teun A. 2000. 'New(s) Racism: A Discourse Analytical Approach'. In *Ethnic Minorities and the Media*, edited by Simon Cottle, 33–49. Milton Keynes, UK: Open University Press.

van Dijk, Teun A. 2000a. 'Theoretical Background'. In *Racism at the Top. Parliamentary Discourses on Ethnic Issues in Six European States*, edited by Ruth Wodak and Teun A. van Dijk, 13–30. Austrian Federal Ministry of Education, Science and Culture.

van Dijk, Teun A. 2000b. 'Parliamentary Debates'. In *Racism at the Top. Parliamentary Discourses on Ethnic Issues in Six European States*, edited by Ruth Wodak, and Teun A. van Dijk, 45–78. Austrian Federal Ministry of Education, Science and Culture.

van Dijk, Teun A. 2003. 'Critical Discourse Analysis'. In *The Handbook of Discourse Analysis*, edited by Deborah Schiffrin, Deborah Tannen and Heidi E. Hamilton, 2nd edition, 352–371. Malden, MA: Blackwell Publishing.

van Dijk, Teun A. 2009. 'Critical Discourse Studies: A Sociocognitive Approach'. In *Methods of Critical Discourse Analysis*, edited by Ruth Wodak and Michael Meyer, 62–86. London: Sage.

Van Gorp, Baldwin. 2005. 'Where is the Frame? Victims and Intruders in the Belgian Press Coverage of the Asylum Issue'. *European Journal of Communication* 20(4): 484–507.

van Nieuwkerk, Karin. 2004. 'Veils and Wooden Clogs Don't Go Together'. *Ethnos* 69(2): 229–46.

Vliegenthart, Rens and Conny Roggeband. 2007. 'Framing Immigration and Integration. Relationships Between Press and Parliament in the Netherlands'. *International Communication Gazette* 69(3): 295–319.

Vollmer, Bastian A. 2011. 'Policy Discourses on Irregular Migration in the EU-Number Games and Political Games'. *European Journal of Migration and Law* 13(3): 317–39.

Walgrave, Stefan and Knut De Swert. 2004. 'The Making of the (issues of the) Vlaams Blok'. *Political Communication* 21(4): 479–500.

Waller, Maugerite. 2014. 'Immigrant Protest and the Courts of Women'. *In Immigrant Protest: Politics, Aesthetics and Everyday Dissent*, edited by Katarzyna Marciniak and Imogen Tyler, 243–67. Albany: State of New York University Press.

Walter, Bronwen. 2008. 'Voices in Other Ears: "Accents" and Identities of the First- and Second-Generation Irish in England'. In *Neo-Colonial Mentalities in Contemporary Europe?: Language and Discourse in the Construction of Identities*, edited by Guido Rings and Anne Ife, 174–82. Cambridge: Cambridge Scholars Publishing.

Walter, Bronwen. 2013. 'Transnational Networks across Generations: Childhood Visits to Ireland by the Second Generation in England'. In *Migrations: Ireland in a Global World*, edited by Mary Gilmartin and Alan White, 17–35. Manchester: Manchester University Press.

Waxer, Lise. 1961. *Situating Salsa: Global Markets and Local Meanings in Latin Popular Music*. London: Routledge.

Weber, Victoria. 2004. 'Scottish, English, British, European Identities: A Literature Review'. *Youth and European Identity*. Accessed 27 May 2014. http://www.sociology.ed.ac.uk/youth/research_papers1.html.

Weinberg, Abraham A. 1961. *Migration and Belonging – A Study of Mental Health and Personal Adjustment in Israel*. The Hague: Martinus Nijhoff.

Wengeler, Martin. 2003. *Topos und Diskurs. Begründung einer argumentationsanalytischen Methode und ihrer Anwendung auf den Migrationsdiskurs (1960–1985)*. Tübingen: Niemeyer.

Werbner, Pnina. 2005. 'Honor, Shame and the Politics of Sexual Embodiment among South Asian Muslims in Britain and Beyond: An Analysis of Debates in the Public Sphere'. *HAGAR: Studies in Culture, Polity & Identities* 6(1): 25–47.

Westlind, Dennis. 1996. *The Politics of Popular Identity: Understanding Recent Populist Movements in Sweden and the United States*. Lund Political Studies 89. Lund: Lund University Press, 1996.

Whelan, Karl. 2013. 'Ireland's Economic Crisis: The Good, the Bad, and the Ugly'. *Paper Presented at Bank of Greece Conference on the Euro Crisis, Athens*, May 24. Accessed 18 January 2015. http://www.karlwhelan.com/Papers/Whelan-IrelandPaper-June2013.pdf.

White, Mary. 2009. *Dáil Debates 675, cols. 401*, February 18.

Wodak, Ruth. 1996. *Disorders of Discourse*. London: Longman.

Wodak, Ruth. 2014. 'Old Wine in New Bottles? Analysing Right-wing Populist Discourse'. Keynote Paper presented at the Cultural and Rhetorical Aspect of Political Populism conference, University of Jyväskylä, Finland, October 24–25.

Wodak, Ruth, Rudolf De Cillia, Martin Reisigl and Karin Liebhart. 2009. *The Discursive Construction of National Identity.* Edinburgh: Edinburgh University Press.

Wodak, Ruth and Michael Meyer. 2009. 'Critical Discourse Analysis: History, Agenda, Theory and Methodology'. In *Methods of Critical Discourse Analysis*, edited by Ruth Wodak and Michael Meyer, 2nd edition, 1–33. London: Sage.

Wodak, Ruth and Teun A. van Dijk. 2000. *Racism at the Top: Parliamentary Discourses on Ethnic Issues in Six European States.* Klagenfurt: Drava Verlag.

Yle. 2014a. 'Toimintaperiaatteet [The Operational Principles]'. Accessed December 17. http://yle.fi/yleisradio/toimintaperiaatteet.

Yle. 2014b. 'This is Yle'. Accessed 15 January 2015. http://yle.fi/yleisradio/about-yle/this-is-yle.

Younge, Gary. 2015. 'Charlie Hebdo: The Danger of Polarised Debate'. *The Guardian*, January 11. Accessed 14 January 2015. http://www.theguardian.com/commentisfree/2015/jan/11/charie-hebdo-danger-polarised-debate-paris-attacks.

Zhang, Yan and Barbara M. Wildemuth. 2009. 'Qualitative Analysis of Content'. In *Applications of Social Research Methods to Questions in Information and Library Science*, edited by Barbara M. Wildemuth, 308–319. Westport: Libraries Unlimited.

Ziem, Alexander. 2008. *Frames und sprachliches Wissen. Kognitive Aspekte der semantischen Kompetenz.* Berlin/New York: de Gruyter.

Zienkowski, Jan. 2015. 'Marking a Sense of Self and Politics in Interviews on Political Engagement: Interpretive Logics and the Metapragmatics of Identity'. *Journal of Language and Politics.* (in review).

Zur Nieden, Birgit. 2013. *Konjunkturen der Migration. Spanisch-argentinische Diskurse und Politiken um das Recht auf Migration.* Berlin: Verlag Walter Frey.

Index

List of Contributors

Michael Breen is Full Professor and Dean of Arts at Mary Immaculate College, University of Limerick, Ireland. He completed his M.S. and PhD at Syracuse University. Professor Breen is the chair of the European Social Survey and also of the European Values Study, and a director of both the Centre for Culture, Technology and Values and the Irish Centre for Catholic Studies, located in Mary Immaculate College. He is a past Irish Research Council for the Humanities and Social Sciences Research Fellow.

Marco Bruno is Assistant Professor of Sociology of Culture and Communication in the Department of Communication and Social Research at Sapienza University of Rome, Italy. His research focuses on journalism, mass media and cultural diversity (with particular reference to Islam and migratory processes), communication and political phenomena. Among his publications are *L'islam immaginato. Rappresentazioni e stereotipi nei media italiani* (2008) and *Cornici di realtà. Il framing e l'analisi dell'informazione* (2014).

James Carr works as a teaching fellow in the Department of Sociology, University of Limerick, Ireland. His research interests include contemporary racisms, in particular anti-Muslim racism, with research published in *Critical Sociology* and a monograph entitled *Experiences of Islamophobia: living with racism in the neoliberal era* (Routledge, 2015). James continues to engage in fieldwork with diverse Muslim communities across the Republic of Ireland researching experiences of, and responses, to anti-Muslim racism.

Elaine Burroughs researches migration in the Irish and European contexts. She is the author of the book *Political and Media Discourses of Illegal*

Immigration in Ireland (2015). She has also published a number of articles in peer-reviewed journals. Elaine is currently undertaking research in University College Dublin, Ireland. She also teaches in the National University of Ireland, Maynooth, and is the editorial assistant for the international journal *Social and Cultural Geography*.

Nicholas De Genova is Reader in Urban Geography and a Director of the Cities Research Group at King's College London, UK. He is the author of *Working the Boundaries: Race, Space, and 'Illegality' in Mexican Chicago* (2005), co-author of *Latino Crossings: Mexicans, Puerto Ricans, and the Politics of Race and Citizenship* (2003), editor of *Racial Transformations: Latinos and Asians Remaking the United States* (2006), and co-editor of *The Deportation Regime: Sovereignty, Space, and the Freedom of Movement* (2010).

Eoin Devereux is Associate Professor in Sociology at the University of Limerick, Ireland, and Adjunct Professor in Contemporary Culture at the University of Jyvasklya, Finland. He is the author of the academic best-seller *Understanding the Media*, 3rd edition (2014) and is a co-editor with Aileen Dillane and Martin J. Power of *Morrissey: Fandom, Representations and Identities* (2011) and *David Bowie: Critical Perspectives* (2015).

Aileen Dillane is an ethnomusicologist based in the Irish World Academy of Music and Dance at the University of Limerick, Ireland. She is a founding member and co-director of the 'LimerickSoundscapes' project. Her other research interests include traditional, vernacular and popular musics of Ireland, the United States and Australia; songs of social protest; and music and the utopian impulse. Aileen co-directs the *Popular Music and Popular Culture*, and *Power, Discourse and Society* research clusters, and the *Ralahine Centre for Utopian Studies* at the University of Limerick.

Sara Hannafin is a PhD candidate at the National University of Ireland, Galway, where she is researching the return migration of the second-generation Irish from Britain, research which was initially motivated by her own experience as a second-generation-returned migrant. Her interest lies in the way in which (some) places become meaningful and significant to people, how this shapes identities and motivates behaviour for individual and, where second-generation returnees are placed in discourses about immigrants and returnees in general.

Amanda Haynes is Senior Lecturer in Sociology at the University of Limerick, Ireland. Amanda's research interests focus on the analysis of discursive constructions as processes of exclusion and strategies for inclusion and their relationship to hostility and discrimination, particularly on the basis of racialisation, gender ethnicity, migrant status and social class. Her current research and writing projects centre on hate crime; political constructions of migrants and gendered and racialised hostility. Her research has been funded by the European Union, the Irish Research Council and the Irish Council for Civil Liberties.

Uta Helfrich is Full Professor of Romance Linguistics at Göttingen University, Germany. Her research interests focus on language variation and change, the semantics, syntax and pragmatics of discourse in general, and on political and media linguistics in particular, covering both traditional and 'new' media communication (CMC). Recent publications on CMC include 'La crisis en 140 caracteres: el discurso propagandístico en la red social Twitter'. In: *Cultura, Lenguaje y Representación* 12 (2014), 59–86.

Emma Hill is currently undertaking research for her PhD in the Department of Languages and Intercultural Studies at Heriot-Watt University, Edinburgh, UK. Her research is focused on the ways in which migrant peoples have themselves heard in both the public and private spheres, particularly with reference to the Somali population in Glasgow. More generally, her interests include topics concerning migration, identity, memory, place and text. She is a member of the Intercultural Research Centre at Heriot-Watt University and *Transformations in European Society* Doctoral Training programme in partnership with Ludwig-Maximillian Universität.

Ann Marie Joyce is a PhD candidate in Sociology at the University of Limerick, Ireland. Funded by the Irish Research Council, her PhD research critically engages the contemporary discursive framing around anti-prostitution and anti-trafficking campaigning in Ireland. Ann Marie is the chairperson of the Sibéal Feminist & Gender Studies Network for Postgraduate and Early Career Researchers. Her research interests are in feminist theory, sexuality and gender studies, and in migration.

Tuuli Lähdesmäki (PhD, DSocSci) is an academy research fellow and an adjunct professor/docent working at the Department of Art and Culture Studies, University of Jyväskylä, Finland. Lähdesmäki's major research interests include identity and heritage politics and discursive meaning-making processes in contemporary culture. Her current research projects EUCHE (the Academy of Finland) and EUROHERIT (the European Research Council) explore the construction of a European cultural heritage and identity.

Sheryl Lynch is an ethnomusicologist with a focus on migration and gender. She was awarded the prestigious Irish Research Council Scholarship for her research on Ireland's Cameroonian community, and she completed her PhD at University College Dublin in the autumn of 2015. In addition to lecturing at Dublin City University, she shares her research at conferences and seminars throughout Ireland, the United Kingdom and Europe. Her work has appeared in *The Musicology Review*, *Spéis* and the multidisciplinary volume *Death in Dublin*.

Ana Mancera Rueda is Associate Professor at University of Sevilla, Spain. Her areas of interest include the study of descriptive Spanish syntax, with special attention to colloquial speech, the relations between orality and writing and the language of mass media, and (im)politeness phenomena and analysis of political discourse in social networks. Recent publications on CMC include *El español coloquial en las redes sociales* (2014).

Aileen Marron is a PhD candidate at the Department of Sociology, University of Limerick. The title of her PhD is 'Irish Print Media Coverage of the Public Sector at a time of Economic Crisis: An Analysis of Discursive and Organisational Practices'. This research is funded by the Irish Research Council. Her research interests include framing theory, political economy of the media, media representations and social inequality.

Moshe Morad is an ethnomusicologist and radio broadcaster in Israel. His experience in the music industry includes having been global marketing director at EMI Music and head of the Hemisphere label. Morad's main research interest involves music and identity among minorities. He completed his PhD at SOAS, University of London, in 2013. His book *Fiesta de diez pesos: Music and Gay Identity in Special Period Cuba* was published in January 2015 and received an Honorable Mention for the Alan Merriam Prize that year.

Yannik Porsché is Researcher in the Sociology Department at Goethe University Frankfurt/Main, Germany. His PhD at the University of Mainz and at the Université de Bourgogne in Dijon dealt with museum exhibitions about public representations of immigrants in France and Germany. He is currently working on social, cultural and organisational forms of knowledge generation and circulation in the crime prevention work of the police.

Michalis Poupazis is a PhD student and a sessional lecturer in ethnomusicology at University College Cork, Ireland. His doctoral work explores the cultural world of Greek- and Turkish-speaking Cypriot migrants in Birmingham, aiming to make available findings from the diaspora as a resource for improving inter-communal relations in Cyprus. Michalis is a committee member and the newsletter editor for both ICTM Ireland and IASPM UK and Ireland.

Martin J. Power is Lecturer in Sociology, with a specific focus on the sociology of urban regeneration, at the University of Limerick, Ireland. He has published widely on the persistence of class inequality in Irish society and on media representations of stigmatised housing estates in Ireland. His publications include the co-authored 'Scapegoating during a time of crisis: A critique of post-celtic Tiger Ireland' in *Sociology*, 48:5 (2014).

Autumn M. Reed received her PhD from the University of Maryland, Baltimore County, USA. Her research examines the critical and often taken-for-granted relationships in discourse, knowledge and power. Her current project employs critical discourse analysis to understand how US news representations of the 2009 'honour killing' of Noor Almaleki are a site for discursive construction of boundaries between the Muslim, Middle Eastern and South Asian minority community and majority members of the US nation.

Tuija Saresma (PhD, MsocSci) is Adjunct Professor/Docent of Contemporary Culture and Senior Researcher at the research project Populism as Movement and Rhetoric (funded by the Academy of Finland) at the Department of Art and Culture Studies, University of Jyväskylä, Finland. Saresma is PI of the research projects 'Idealisation of home, nation, and everyday life in the Finnish blogosphere' (Finnish Cultural Foundation) and 'Arts of Belonging' (Kone foundation).